Kant's Moral Metaphysics

Kant's Moral Metaphysics

God, Freedom, and Immortality

Edited by
Benjamin J. Bruxvoort Lipscomb
and James Krueger

De Gruyter

ISBN 978-3-11-048159-4
e-ISBN 978-3-11-022004-9

Library of Congress Cataloging-in-Publication Data

Kant's moral metaphysics : God, freedom, and immortality /
edited by Benjamin J. Bruxvoort Lipscomb and James Krueger.
    p. cm.
  Includes bibliographical references and index.
  ISBN 978-3-11-022003-2 (hardcover : alk. paper) 1. Kant,
Immanuel, 1724-1804. 2. Ethics. 3. Philosophical theology. I.
Lipscomb, Benjamin J. Bruxvoort. II. Krueger, James.
  B2799.E8K43 2010
  193--dc22
                                              2010011702

Bibliographic Information published by the Deutsche Nationalbibliothek

The Deutsche Nationalbibliothek lists this publication in the Deutsche
Nationalbibliographie; detailed bibliographic data are available in the Internet
at http://dnb.d-nb.de

Printing and binding: Hubert & Co. GmbH & Co. KG, Göttingen
∞ Printed on acid-free paper

Printed in Germany

www.degruyter.com

Table of Contents

Note on Texts vii

Introduction 1

Section I. Moral Motivation, Moral Metaphysics

1. Karl Ameriks
   Reality, Reason, and Religion in the Development
   of Kant's Ethics 23

2. Benjamin Lipscomb
   Moral Imperfection and Moral Phenomenology in Kant 49

Section II. Interpreting Freedom

3. Patrick Frierson
   Two Standpoints and the Problem of Moral Anthropology 83

4. Jeanine Grenberg
   In Search of the Phenomenal Face of Freedom 111

Section III. The Highest Good

5. David Sussman
   Something to Love: Kant and the Faith of Reason 133

6. James Krueger
   Duties, Ends and the Divine Corporation 149

Section IV. Epistemology and the Supersensible

7. Andrew Chignell
   Real Repugnance and Belief about Things-in-Themselves:
   a Problem and Kant's Three Solutions 177

8. Patrick Kain
   Practical Cognition, Intuition, and the Fact of Reason 211

Section V. Epistemology and Religion

9. Lee Hardy
Kant's Reidianism: The Role of Common Sense in
Kant's Epistemology of Religious Belief 233

10. Eric Watkins
Kant on the Hiddenness of God 255

11. Rachel Zuckert
Kant's Account of Practical Fanaticism 291

References 319

Index 333

Note on Texts

As is customary, citations to Kant's works refer to the volume and page number of *Kant's gesammelte Schriften*, Akademie Ausgabe, Berlin: Walter de Gruyter, 1902-. Citations to the *Critique of Pure Reason* include the usual reference to the first ("A") or second ("B") editions. Except as noted in the text, all translations are from the *Cambridge Edition of the Works of Immanuel Kant* (series editors Paul Guyer and Allen Wood, New York, Cambridge University Press, 1996-). Any modifications to translations are noted in the text.

Two essays in this volume have been published elsewhere, in part or in whole. Chapter 10, "Kant on the Hiddenness of God," appeared in *Kantian Review* 14:1 (2009) pp. 81-122. Parts of Chapter 7 appeared in "Are Supersensibles Really Possible? Kant on the Evidential Role of Symbolization," in V. Rhoden, T. Terra, G. Almeida (Eds.), *Recht und Frieden in der Philosophie Kants*, Berlin, DeGruyter, 2008, and parts appeared in "Real Repugnance and Knowledge of Things-in-Themselves: A Problem from Locke in Kant and Hegel," in F. Rush, K. Ameriks, J. Stolzenberg (Eds.), *Internationales Jahrbuch des Deutschen Idealismus*, 7, Berlin, DeGruyter, 2010. The authors and the editors are grateful to the publishers for permitting the material to reappear here.

Introduction

James Krueger and Benjamin Lipscomb

Toward a Synoptic Vision: reading Kant metaphysically, reading him whole

In the interpretation of any past philosopher, contemporary philosophical interests shape how the interpretive task is conceived. The problems that interpreters bring to a text and the philosophical "common
sense" of the age affect how interpretive questions are raised and addressed. There is no reason to view this in an exclusively negative light,
as a simple conflict between distorted whiggish history and honest historical scholarship. Shifting approaches can bring to light important
dimensions of a thinker's work that have not been recognized. Moreover, the dialectic between scholarship that attempts to uncover the
original context in which a thinker wrote and scholarship that looks to
past figures for useful perspectives on questions of present interest can
be a fruitful spur to deeper understanding.

One can see this dialectic at work in the history of Kant scholarship.
In the introduction to his *Interpreting Kant's* Critiques, Karl Ameriks
identifies three "waves" of interpretation (Ameriks 2003, pp. 1-3). The
first, he asserts, was characterized by historically grounded, "extensive
synoptic treatments" such as those offered by Hermann Cohen, H. J.
Paton, and Norman Kemp Smith.[1] A second wave of interpreters turned
their attention to issues of then-current interest in the wider philosophical community, focusing on narrower segments of Kant's work and
often leaving behind questions of historical context. Ameriks holds up
the works of, e.g., P. F. Strawson and Jonathan Bennett as exemplifying
this approach.[2] Finally, a third, more recent wave of interpreters has
attempted both to engage with current philosophical debates and to
remain sensitive to the historical context of Kant's writings.[3] Ameriks

---

1   See Cohen 1978, 1987 and 2001; Paton 1936 and 1947; Smith 1923.
2   See Strawson 1966, Bennett 1966 and 1974.
3   For examples of this latest wave, see: Allison 1983, 1990, 2001; Guyer 1979, 1987,
     2000a; Prauss 1983.

sees much to praise in this latest wave, yet notes something it typically abandons, namely the vision of the whole Kantian corpus characteristic of the first wave. Very few contemporary scholars are in a position to offer such a vision. Requiring both knowledge of current philosophical debates and a historically sensitive understanding of the primary sources, the third wave has had the effect of discouraging general accounts of the Kantian project.

One way to return to a more synoptic vision is for groups of scholars with overlapping concerns and overlapping convictions to work in concert. If few are in a position, all by themselves, to construct a comprehensive view of Kant's thought, collaboration, bringing together the differing expertise of mutually sympathetic scholars, can help. This volume aspires to make such a contribution. It takes up a particular set of issues, in and around Kant's practical philosophy, but in such a way as to highlight connections across Kantian texts. Indeed, the volume as a whole embodies an argument, an argument for the necessity of treating issues in one area of Kant's mature corpus in the full context of his Critical project—daunting though this can be. While each essay focuses on an aspect of Kant's practical philosophy, the whole attempts to show how discussion of Kant's practical philosophy clarifies, and is clarified by, the full range of Critical texts.

What are the overlapping concerns and overlapping convictions of the scholars represented here? Briefly, they are reengaging the controversial metaphysical claims associated with Kant's Critical philosophy. Thus the argument of this volume has a second aspect, connected to the first: it is our contention that when one reads Kant more holistically, one has a harder time ignoring his metaphysical commitments, and that when one reengages with Kant's metaphysical commitments, one picks up clues as to how he can be read more holistically.

This way of reading Kant is both old and new. The second wave of Kant interpreters, characterized above, was notable both for its narrow foci and for its attempts to make Kantian claims palatable to an age in which metaphysical commitments (other than those of scientific naturalism) were viewed with deep suspicion. In these respects, the second wave broke with the interpretive tendencies of earlier Kant scholars, in and before what Ameriks identifies as the first wave.[4] Unlike some aspects of second-wave scholarship, the anti-metaphysical trend—and even, to some extent, the focused topicality—has carried over into more recent scholarship. As Fredrick Beiser observes, in the *Cambridge Companion to Kant and Modern Philosophy*, "Since the 1960s there has been a movement afoot in the Anglophone world to purge Kant's

---

4   On this history, see Zuckert 2004.

philosophy of all metaphysics, to make Kant scrubbed and sanitary for a more positivistic age" (Beiser 2006, p. 589). New attempts at holistic and metaphysically substantive readings of Kant, such as this volume offers and recommends, must respond to this anti-metaphysical trend, even as they attempt to recapture the synoptic character of first-wave scholarship. But what form does the trend take, in connection with Kant's practical thought?

Realism and Constructivism: the place of metaphysics in Kant's moral philosophy

A number of recent writers, including several contributors to this volume, have challenged metaphysically "anodyne" interpretations of Kant.[5] Such work, however, has remained largely focused on the interpretation of Kant's theoretical philosophy.[6] In our view, it is particularly important to examine Kant's practical philosophy in light of his theoretical philosophy. This has been a minority position in Kant studies over the past generation, for reasons plainly dependent upon the overall anti-metaphysical mood. Many recent interpreters have suggested that the core claims of Kant's practical philosophy can be separated from the substantive metaphysical commitments that Kant endorsed in other domains of his Critical philosophy. This school of interpretation, associated with the late John Rawls and his students, sees Kant's practical philosophy as essentially anti-realist. Moral norms are not based on realities independent of the agent, but are, rather, constructed by each rational agent. This interpretation of Kant's views is attractive for two sets of reasons, one arising from general philosophical trends, and the other pertaining more directly to the interpretation of Kantian texts. This reading is attractive, first, because it renders Kant's theory more consistent with contemporary naturalism by eliminating now disfavored Kantian doctrines such as the noumenal-phenomenal distinction or the existence of God.[7] At the same time, this reading is attractive because of doubts concerning Kant's arguments for the "prac-

---

5   See e.g. Guyer 1987, Langton 1998, and Watkins 2005. "Anodyne" is Paul Guyer's term.

6   Two exceptions to this generalization are Daniel Guevara and contributor Patrick Kain. See Guevara 2000 and Kain 2004, 2006.

7   See Rawls 1977 and Korsgaard 1996b. For explicit interactions with Kant by these authors, see Rawls 2000 and Korsgaard 1996a. Other scholars with a similar view of Kant include Onora O'Neill, Andrews Reath, and J. B. Schneewind. See O'Neill 1989, Reath 2006, and Schneewind 1998.

tical postulates"—the existence of God, libertarian freedom, and the immortality of the soul.

This "constructivist" reading of Kant sees in Kant's practical philosophy an argument that our status as rational agents implies a proper procedure for practical deliberation. As Rawls observes, "Constructivism sees the substantive principles that express the order of moral values as constructed by a procedure the form and structure of which is taken from the conceptions and principles implicit in our practical reasoning" (Rawls 2000, p. 241). We do not seek to evaluate the goodness of ends, say, by directly investigating the ends themselves. The goodness is not to be found in them, whether in their nature or in their relationship to other things in the world. Rather, as Christine Korsgaard observes,

> the Kantian approach frees us from assessing the rationality of choice by means of the apparently ontological task of assessing the thing chosen.... Instead, it is the reasoning that goes into the choices itself—the procedure of full justification—that determines the rationality of the choice and so certifies the goodness of the object. (Korsgaard 1996a, p. 261)

Such readings also serve to give Kant an important place in a popular understanding of the history of moral philosophy, an understanding on which that history involves a gradual disentangling of moral beliefs from particular metaphysical commitments. It is not just that Kant turns from ontological to procedural justifications for moral claims; he is the crucial figure that shows us how to extricate ethics from ontology. Morality has traditionally been understood to be tied to metaphysical beliefs: notably, in the freedom of human persons (to choose right or wrong courses of action), in a God (or gods) who serve as judge(s) of moral character, and in an afterlife as the locus of a final judgment on individual behavior. The ability to offer moral views that do not require reference to any such metaphysical commitments is regarded, by constructivist interpreters and others, as a form of philosophical progress. Kant is given an important place in their narratives despite the fact that Kant himself asserts that some such beliefs are necessary (necessary, at least, from the practical point of view).

Constructivist interpretive approaches, not surprisingly, have led to an emphasis on some Kantian claims at the expense of others. Some of these latter claims, as already indicated, were of manifest importance to Kant himself. This by itself would be some reason to look again at Kant's arguments. But we maintain, further, that these claims and Kant's defenses of them are of greater philosophical interest than has generally been acknowledged. The arguments assembled in this collection are, in cumulative effect, an argument for this further conclusion. While the contributors to this volume differ about the ultimate plausibility of various of Kant's metaphysical commitments, they are unified by the belief that there is more to be said, both for and about these commitments, than has commonly been allowed.

Feeling and Reality

The opening pair of essays take up, in different ways, one of these understudied topics in Kant's practical philosophy: the character and source of moral feeling. Ameriks's point of departure is some recent historiography (particularly in German) of the development of Kant's practical philosophy, while Benjamin Lipscomb's reflections begin with Kant's pessimism about our moral nature. Despite this difference, the two find their way to a common set of questions: what is moral feeling, according to Kant? How does it arise? And what are the implications of this feeling, the conditions of its possibility? In this way, both are engaged with the twin tasks of this volume: reading Kant with an eye toward now-untimely metaphysical commitments, and reading him holistically.

Respect's unique status as a feeling not grounded in sensibility is highlighted in the first section of Kant's *Groundwork of the Metaphysics of Morals*. In an important note, Kant anticipates objections to this idea, writing "It could be objected that I only seek refuge, behind the word *respect*, in an obscure feeling, instead of distinctly resolving the question by means of a concept of reason" (4:401n). Kant attempts to respond to this concern, asserting that "though respect is a feeling, it is not one *received* by means of influence; it is, instead, a feeling *self-wrought* by means of a rational concept and therefore specifically different from all feelings of the first kind, which can be reduced to inclination and fear" (*Ibid.*). Such passages, however, only serve to highlight the difficult tightrope that must be walked. Respect is essential to understanding moral motivation for Kant, and yet its status is far from clear, straddling the realms of inclination and pure reason.

On constructivist readings, this problem is transformed from one with metaphysical roots to a simple epistemic distinction. Rawls has relatively little to say about respect in his lectures on Kant, and when he does, he characterizes it as a psychological disposition to act according to the dictates of pure practical reason. He writes, "Kant believes that we have certain moral dispositions—moral feeling and conscience, love of one's neighbor and respect for oneself—that are natural dispositions of the mind to be affected by concepts of duty. No one has a duty to acquire these natural dispositions, as they are antecedent dispositions

on the side of feeling." Nonetheless, "our awareness of these dispositions is not of empirical origin, but is known to us only from a knowledge of the moral law and its effect on our sensibility" (Rawls 2000,
189). In this way, the dual nature of moral feeling is resolved into an
epistemic distinction. The disposition is itself a natural, psychological
one, and as such not significantly different from other psychological
dispositions we might possess. The difference is that knowledge of the
moral law, not some sensible experience, leads to our *awareness* of this
moral disposition. Ameriks's and Lipscomb's interpretations present a
more metaphysically laden view, on which reason must both "determine the will immediately" (5:71) and yet "become the incentive" to
moral behavior, become the moral feeling of respect.

How this can be—how the law of reason can be (in us) identical
with a feeling—is, as Ameriks and Lipscomb recognize, the great interpretive question in this domain of Kant's thought. Kant himself thought
of it as among the great questions in practical philosophy, referring to it
in lectures as the "philosophers' stone." Like other questions raised in
this volume, though, it has sometimes been ignored. Ameriks contends
that this is in part because it seems to attribute to Kant a series of metaphysical extravagances. "Genuine Kantian respect," he writes, "requires
nothing less than a non-empirical cause (free will), a non-empirical
object (pure law), and a mysterious…non-empirical kind of 'self-
imposition'. This can all sound too remarkable to be true."

Again, Ameriks takes as his point of departure recent historiography of the development of Kant's thought. In particular, he takes up an
argument by Kant's biographer, Manfred Kuehn, that Kant's pre-
Critical lectures on ethics "stress psychological aspects of ordinary
human motivation" in contrast to the allegedly incredible accounts of
moral motivation (incredible both metaphysically and psychologically)
of the Critical period, and particularly of the *Critique of Practical Reason*. In Kuehn's view, Kant became increasingly and wrongly insistent
upon a sensually abstracted, "pure" conception of ethics, a conception
that drove him to downplay what Kant called "practical anthropology"
and eventually to posit an extraordinary, *sui generis* feeling-that-isn't-a-
feeling, respect. Ameriks argues, in contrast to Kuehn, that the true
story of the development of Kant's thought is one of deep, enduring
commitment to both the a priori ("pure") grounds of ethics and to the
serious study of "psychological aspects of ordinary human motivation."
The Critical development in Kant's practical philosophy was not an
increasingly stern abstraction from the empirical but a dawning realiza-

tion that his theoretical innovation, transcendental idealism, enabled him to better articulate and defend his dual commitments.[9]

In his contribution, Lipscomb explores at length the dynamics of the a priori feeling, *Achtung*, which he speaks of, similarly, as a "bridge between the noumenal self and its phenomenal experience." Lipscomb's point of departure, again, is Kant's conception of human moral imperfection. Lipscomb defends an overall interpretive approach to Kant's practical philosophy on which Kant's conception of human moral imperfection is a "skeleton key" opening the whole. Tracing this conception through the *Groundwork* and second *Critique* into *Religion within the Boundaries of Mere Reason*, Lipscomb shows how Kant develops a characteristic moral phenomenology in response to his conception of our moral nature, a phenomenology that once identified can be seen at work across Kant's ethical writings.

Lipscomb, like Ameriks, defends an interpretation of Kant's practical philosophy as metaphysically realist. But while Ameriks stresses that Kant is a transcendental idealist about space and time, not about value, Lipscomb highlights the realist implications of the phenomenology of respect. It is a feeling, he remarks, that posits an object of awe over-against the agent. And although the agent participates in the reality, reason, that respect takes as its object, in the experience of respect, it is nonetheless construed as other.

The Empirical and the Intelligible

Both Lipscomb and Ameriks set their analyses of Kant on moral motivation in the context of his transcendental idealism and the distinction it posits between phenomena and noumena, i.e., appearances and things-in-themselves. And both Ameriks and Lipscomb construe moral feeling as the empirical manifestation or counterpart of our noumenal selves. But this very way of putting it—that moral feeling is a manifestation of our noumenal selves, that the self one experiences in time is the empirical counterpart of a noumenal self—is controversial. It is in fact one of the central loci of controversy between metaphysically anodyne interpretations of Kant and the interpretations of Kant preferred by many contributors to this collection. Should we, in interpreting Kant, mark a metaphysical distinction, or merely an epistemic one, between a world existing "in itself" and the spatiotemporally arranged, conceptually schematized appearances that constitute our experience?

---

9   Ameriks's view in this regard is similar to that defended in Guevara 2000.

Many contemporary scholars—notably, again, John Rawls and his students—prefer to speak instead of "two standpoints" on reality. Kant repeatedly insists that it is only through morality, only through the exercise of practical reason, that we have any grounds for positive beliefs about noumena.[8] Two-standpoint theorists set aside the question of whether the standpoint of practical reason—the standpoint we occupy when we deliberate or evaluate action in terms of reasons—reveals to us how things are in themselves, in a way that the standpoint of theoretical or scientific reason does not. It is a different standpoint, occupied with a different activity, and that activity has its own constitutive rules (or, in Kantian language, "conditions of possibility"). As Korsgaard suggests of these two standpoints, each has

> its own territory…. From the explanatory standpoint of theoretical reason, nothing is easier to understand than that a human being might evade duty when it is in conflict with her heart's desire. From the normative standpoint of practical reason her sacrifice of her freedom for some mere object of inclination is completely unintelligible. These two standpoints give us two very different views of the world. (Korsgaard 1996a, p. 173)

The advantages of this view, particularly in terms of metaphysical simplicity, are not hard to identify. As Korsgaard observes, this view means that "Kant's theory of freedom of the will" requires no "extravagant ontological claims." So understood, she contends, we do not have to believe that human beings are "radically different sorts of creatures than the mundane rational animals we suppose ourselves to be" (Korsgaard 1996a, p. 183).

The question of whether to interpret Kant as committed to two worlds or merely to two standpoints is particularly acute with respect to the metaphysics of agency. Is Kant committed to the view that we are, in ourselves, free? Or does Kant regard this question as inappropriate, and maintain merely that we must regard ourselves as free from one of two standpoints? If we adopt the former, more metaphysical interpretation, how are we to understand the relation between the noumenal and the phenomenal, and especially between our noumenal and phenomenal selves? Each of the second pair of essays, by Jeanine Grenberg and Patrick Frierson, takes up these issues.

In Jeanine Grenberg's essay, she focuses on the last problem mentioned above, the problem of how to understand the relation between our noumenal and phenomenal selves. Taking for granted a two-world characterization of Kant's transcendental idealism, she asks, "can we really say that a sensibly affected agent operating in the phenomenal

---

8   A theme taken up by several essays, later in the volume—most conspicuously, by Andrew Chignell.

world, yet guided by an apparently other-worldly intelligible act," is a truly *unified* agent?

Working mainly from the *Critique of Pure Reason* (indeed, mainly from the Third Antinomy), but taking care to relate what she finds there to Kant's practical works, Grenberg tries to identify a solution, in Kant's own doctrine, to the problem of relating our "intelligible character" to our "empirical character." She contends that there is such a solution: an analogue of what Kant calls "schematization." Schematization, recall, is the process Kant posits to explain how non-sensible concepts of the understanding are related to sensible intuitions. Now, schematization in the strict sense—the harmonization of concepts and intuitions, enabling empirical cognition—cannot directly address the problem of how empirical character and intelligible character relate. But, Grenberg argues, we can see Kant gesturing toward an analogous process of "harmonizing" the empirical and the intelligible. Her suggestion is that this takes place, just as in schematization proper, through a "determination of time." In the practical case, the determination of time has to do with the temporal experience of being obligated.

Frierson's concerns lie one step back from Grenberg's. His essay explores a series of problems for two-standpoint interpretations of Kant's theory of freedom, problems highlighted by, among others, Dana Nelkin and by Eric Watkins. Though these problems can be variously expressed, they are fundamentally two: the "theory-in-deliberation" problem and the "grounding" problem.

The first is the problem of how a construal of ourselves as unfree (from the theoretical standpoint) should relate to our construal of ourselves as free (from the practical standpoint), especially in moments of deliberation. It seems perfectly appropriate—even necessary—to acknowledge in deliberation claims generated from the theoretical standpoint. How then can we avoid a contradiction within the practical standpoint, both acknowledging the claim that we are unfree and excluding it by claiming (on practical grounds) that we are free? Frierson holds that, with the aid of a distinction between first-order and second-order claims, two-standpoint theorists can successfully address this first problem.

After disposing also of the grounding problem—the problem of how, on a two-standpoint interpretation, one can account for the asymmetries in Kant's discussions of noumena and phenomena—Frierson suggests that there is a third problem, similar in structure to the theory-in-deliberation problem, that poses a greater threat to two-standpoint interpretations: "the problem of anthropology." Briefly, the problem of anthropology is how to make use from the practical standpoint of a set of claims with obvious practical significance: anthropological claims.

These are claims about the influences that operate causally on human decision-making. Especially as a parent or educator, but even as a citizen or friend, one should not ignore such claims and the truths they represent. But, again, how can one bring together in deliberation both the claim that we are subject to causal manipulation and the claim that we are radically free. At the end of his essay, Frierson suggests how a two-standpoint theorist might begin to respond.

Frierson is cautiously optimistic about the prospects of this response, though it is not clear to him how it should be worked out in detail. His is the first of several essays in the volume that engage critically but deeply with metaphysically robust interpretations of Kant. His essay, like David Sussman's and Rachel Zuckert's, manifests a characteristic of the contributors we noted in passing earlier: what brings them together is not a set of shared metaphysical commitments, but the conviction that "there is much more to be said, both for and about these commitments, than has commonly been allowed."

What We May Hope

Human freedom is but one of three "practical postulates" that Kant believes we must accept from a practical point of view. The latter two are the existence of God and the immortality of the soul. Kantian arguments for these postulates are premised on the claim that morality directs us to strive toward the "highest good," a condition in which happiness is allocated to persons in proportion to their virtue. Many recent Kant scholars have rejected this premise and thus the arguments that follow from it. As Lewis White Beck famously wrote in his commentary on the second *Critique*, the highest good "is not important to Kant's philosophy for any practical consequences it might have, for it has none" (Beck 1960, p. 245). If this claim is right, then Kant's justification for the practical postulates is, of course, undermined.

It is worth distinguishing, however, at least two stages in the critical response to the highest good in the English-speaking world over the past sixty or so years. The first, corresponding with the emergence of the positivistic recasting of Kant's thought, is essentially dismissive of any important role for the notion, except, perhaps, as a device for attempting to secure the unity of practical and theoretical reason (*Ibid.*).

On this view, there is no need to provide a general end for moral conduct. In every case where human beings must choose and act, an end is provided by the faculty of desire, given the immediate context of action. As Jeffrie Murphy writes, "the whole procedure of looking for a

material content to fill out Kant's formalism is, for the most part, spurious—spurious because this content is already quite obviously given in
the context of common moral experience" (Murphy 1965, p. 102). This
means there is no need for something like the highest good within
Kant's moral philosophy. There is no further practical need for an overarching, final moral purpose. If it plays any role at all, it is purely architectonic. As such, the argument goes, the doctrine of the highest good
cannot ground belief in the existence of God or in the immortality of
the soul. These postulates can be dismissed as unnecessary additions to
an already complete moral view.

Something like this interpretation has enjoyed broad support until
the last couple of decades. In that time period, there has been a shift in
the general understanding of Kant's arguments concerning the highest
good. This more recent view rejects the essentially dismissive reading,
yet contends that, properly understood, Kant's arguments do not require
reference to any religious foundation for support. Instead, a purely
secular version of the highest good is defended, one which only necessitates belief in the possibility of a moral community: a kingdom of
ends possible through human action. As Rawls argues, what is required
of us is that we believe, on some rational basis, that such a realm of
ends is possible. What is required, then, is not "the postulates of God
and of immortality" but rather "certain beliefs about our nature and the
social world.... We can believe that a realm of ends is possible in the
world only if the order of nature and social necessities are not un-
friendly to that ideal." This means

> we must believe, for example, that the course of human history is progres-
> sively improving, and not becoming steadily worse, or that it does not fluctu-
> ate in perpetuity from bad to good and from good to bad. For in this case, we
> will view the spectacle of human history as a farce that arouses loathing of our
> species. (Rawls 2000, pp. 319-20)

Thus, the possibility of a kingdom of ends plays an important role for
Kant, but that role is not understood to necessitate any form of religious
belief.

David Sussman's contribution to this volume adds a dimension to
this interpretation by articulating a different understanding of why we
have to take the highest good as an end. This understanding, drawing
largely on Kant's discussions in the *Religion*, focuses on the need to
find something to love in morality (and in humanity) and, Sussman
contends, supports an interesting form of faith (setting aside the question of the object of that faith). In this way, he shifts attention away
from the discussions of the highest good in the second *Critique*, and
highlights the importance of Kant's understanding of the relationship
between faith and love as articulated in the *Religion*.

Sussman argues that in order to be a virtuous person, I must "generally understand morality as something that enriches my life, as something that I normally accept gladly." This does not mean that one can never do one's duty reluctantly, or with a grumbling, grudging demeanor. Rather, what it means is that this cannot be our general attitude toward our moral convictions if we are to develop the right sort of character. Sussman illustrates with the example of caring for one's children. While one might not respond with joy to a late-night diaper change, the general disposition to regard one's obligations toward one's children with love and even relish is necessary if one is to live up to those obligations. In this way, Sussman asks what is necessary for the right sort of moral character, rather than what is necessary for moral action in any particular case, in order to locate an important role for something like the highest good. This can provide the basis for regarding one's dispositions in the right light, even in the face of a world that does not always cooperate in our attempts to achieve happiness through observing our duty.

By contrast, James Krueger's contribution directly and critically examines political, secular readings of the highest good. He argues that while the historical task may be part of what the highest good bids us to pursue, hope in the completion of this task is insufficient. He suggests that the problem the highest good is meant to solve is deeper than our moral or political failings; it is beyond the unassisted power of human beings to solve. While humans can and must contribute to the solution, ultimately some power whose scope outstretches the human is necessary to shape the world so as to make the highest good possible, and secure the intelligibility of moral action across all possible circumstances.

Thus, Krueger disputes Rawls's contention that hope in political progress is sufficient to motivate and justify moral commitment. He argues that no matter what political arrangements exist, or how committed human beings are to moral action, tragedy threatens. As Kant suggests, the problem that must be solved by reference to some final end is that the natural order takes no account of moral character. This blindness of the natural order, combined with the inability of human beings to be certain whether any action is ever, truly, performed from duty, means that there is a gap between what natural laws necessitate, and what moral considerations demand of us. Closing that gap, he argues, is beyond human power and yet this is what we may, and must, hope.

Reason's Needs

While these understandings of the highest good assert that it plays a more than merely architectonic role, it certainly does play such a role. Understanding how reason is a unity, and how the highest good and the practical postulates express or contribute to this unity is a crucial task for any synoptic vision of Kant's philosophy. Kant repeatedly asserts, throughout his Critical corpus, the legitimacy of "assent from a need of pure reason" (5:142), where the need is demonstrated by reason in its practical use but the assent takes the form of a belief. Any comprehensive understanding of Kant's metaphysical views must speak to the epistemology undergirding his metaphysical claims. It must be able to say, in particular, what kind of belief is grounded in practical reason: what its warrant is, how it relates to other beliefs, and so on. The fourth section of this volume is focused on these (general) epistemological issues.

In one of the most famous passages in the first *Critique*, Kant asserts that he "had to deny knowledge in order to make room for faith [*Glaube*]" (Bxxx). This faith (or belief), however, is not acceptance absent any possible evidence. Kant believes that arguments can be given in support of a number of beliefs (that human beings are free, that God exists, that human souls are immortal), the objects of which lie beyond the scope of theoretical reason. These arguments do not give us theoretical knowledge. However, the practical use of reason in some sense supports belief in each of these propositions. Moreover, as Patrick Kain points out in his essay, at least with respect to moral obligation and human freedom, Kant refers to such beliefs as constituting practical cognition (*Erkenntnis*) or even practical knowledge (*Wissen*). What, then, is the epistemic status of these propositions, these *practical* cognitions? Are there degrees of warrant for beliefs held from a practical point of view? What is the relationship between beliefs we are compelled to accept from a practical point of view, and those that count as theoretical knowledge?

On the one hand, we can see Kant as saying that reason in its practical use can support beliefs that are unsupported by reason in its theoretical use. We can thus talk about the supremacy of practical reason. Yet at the same time, the arguments of the first *Critique* do not set limits only for theoretical reason. They set limits for practical reason as well. It is clear, for example, that if theoretical reason were to establish the impossibility of God's existence, or the impossibility of human freedom, then reason, in its practical use, could not support those beliefs. *Knowledge* (or should we say, "theoretical knowledge"?) must be

denied in order to make room for a different kind of belief (even practical knowledge?). In other words, we need to know (in some sense) that
the theoretical use of reasons does not rule out what the practical use of
reason prompts us to believe. Thus, the supremacy of practical reason
does not mean that the practical use of reason *trumps* the theoretical.
Rather, it means that practical reason shines into places *where theoretical reason gives no light*.

Unsurprisingly, such claims met with great skepticism in the mid-
twentieth century, during the second wave of interpretation Ameriks
describes. Not only did Kant defend metaphysical beliefs widely regarded as dubious, he argued for such beliefs on practical grounds despite the failure of theoretical reason to ground such beliefs and despite
the impossibility of connecting such beliefs with sensible experience.
On the other hand, Kant's repeated admonitions that we need to be
wary of disputes concerning "empty" ideas suited the positivist perspective. His limitation of (theoretical) knowledge to objects of possible experience, ruling out such knowledge of "things-in-themselves"
suggested a deep skepticism toward metaphysical speculation, a skepticism mid-century interpreters shared.

All this leaves something of a puzzle. On the one hand, Kant's
theoretical writings, notwithstanding the metaphysical overtones of his
talk of a "supersensible world," seem to limit the scope of human reason, and to support a generally dismissive attitude toward metaphysical
speculation. On the other hand, Kant says striking things about things-
in-themselves from a practical point of view, going so far as to claim:

> Freedom is real, for this idea reveals itself through the moral law. But among
> all the ideas of speculative reason freedom is … the only one the possibility of
> which we know [*wissen*] *a priori*, though without having insight into it, be-
> cause it is the condition of the moral law, which we do know [*wissen*]. (5:4)

Now, of course, knowledge of the possibility of freedom is not the
same as knowledge of freedom, and Kant is clear that we "have no insight" into freedom. But we know the moral law and that grounds a
form of belief that appears to go beyond what theoretical reason establishes. Since Kant had already argued, in the first *Critique,* that we cannot prove we are *not* free, the possibility invoked here would seem to
be something further. Such a reading is only strengthened by Kant's
insistence that the possibility of freedom is the only thing we know in
the sense indicated. If the impossibility of an argument for the impossibility of freedom was all that was meant by the possibility of freedom,
there would be nothing unique about this. Kant argues similarly for the
impossibility of proving the existence or non-existence of God.

How, then, do we reconcile Kant's claims about the limits of theoretical reason with such "knowledge" or "belief" from a practical point

of view? How do we understand the epistemic status of such beliefs? What differentiates "knowledge" of the possibility of freedom from the kind of belief that is justified with respect to the existence of God and immortality of the soul? These questions have not received the attention that they deserve.

Two essays in this volume, by Andrew Chignell and Patrick Kain, address this shortcoming. Chignell directly confronts one of the central challenges in understanding Kant's account of practically grounded belief. As noted, Kant is clear about the need for ideas to have positive content, for them to be something more than empty "thought–entities" (A771/B799). In other words, ideas must have content if they are to figure in beliefs. Since belief in God, the immortality of the soul, or human freedom cannot be grounded in any possible experience, the standard source of content, sensible intuition, is unavailable in these cases. Thus, Kant must either provide a different etiology of the content of such beliefs, or confront a positivistic challenge that would undermine his claims concerning them. If such beliefs do not have content, what is the sense in saying we must assent to them? What could belief in empty propositions amount to?

Chignell argues that this problem runs deeper than just a concern about empty beliefs. He argues that even after a belief is shown to have positive content, there is a question of whether or not that content is "harmonious" or "repugnant." As he puts it, the content of some beliefs "may be such that they can be thought, entertained, analyzed, and shown to be logically consistent, but still be such that no corresponding object even *could* obtain in reality." Such a belief would not be empty, but it would not represent a real (as against merely logical) possibility. He surveys three possible solutions to this problem, each latent in Kant's works. The first appeals to the very needs of reason that generate, for example, belief in God, as themselves supplying positive content. A second appeals to a form of practical cognition, witnessed, for example, in Kant's discussion of "the fact of reason" in the second *Critique*. There, we are said to know the reality of the moral law even though that knowledge is not provided by sensible experience. The content of that knowledge—reason's becoming practical and determining the will—might itself count as a demonstration of the real possibility of the object in question. A final, unexpected solution can be found in Kant's discussions of symbolization, particularly in his aesthetic theory in the *Critique of the Power of Judgment*. Symbolization, Chignell argues, provides a kind of fragmentary insight, an indication that "the content of the idea is really harmonious rather than really repugnant, and goes at least some way toward attaching genuine intuitional content to the marks included in the ideas."

Patrick Kain takes up a related set of issues. Kant claims that our knowledge of the possibility of freedom is grounded in our knowledge of the moral law. This, Kant claims, we know as a "fact of reason." Here, Kant introduces a grounding for belief, a "fact," that is strikingly different from any other "fact" he discusses. How does the fact of reason ground our practical "knowledge" of freedom?

On Kain's view, the fact of reason helps explain why Kant distinguishes practical knowledge of the possibility of freedom from practical belief in God and the immortality of the soul. The "given-ness" of the fact of reason marks a similarity between it and intuition, allowing it to play a similar role in practical cognition to that played by intuition in theoretical cognition. Since belief in God, or in the immortality of the soul, is not grounded in this fact of reason as belief in one's freedom is, we can distinguish at least two kinds of practical cognition: one that results in "knowledge," the other resulting in "belief" falling short of knowledge.

If one accepts the general possibility of practical cognition, other lines of inquiry suggest themselves. In particular, many of the arguments Kant offers concerning religious belief take on greater interest. Claims about the grounds of such belief, or even about divine attributes, which might have appeared as simple violations of Kant's dicta concerning the impossibility of knowledge of supersensibles, can be embedded in a coherent framework. The contributions of Lee Hardy and Eric Watkins are examples of such new ventures in Kantian religious epistemology.

Hardy suggests that Kant's general epistemology begins with belief-forming dispositions that ground a broad "common-sense" foundation for our knowledge. What the Critical philosophy provides, on this reconstruction, is a philosophical response to considerations that might undermine common-sense beliefs. That defense, however, presupposes the rationality of the dispositions that ground common-sense beliefs. Hardy contends this same pattern holds in Kant's arguments concerning religious belief. In this way, Kant's arguments are not meant to establish, from the ground up, the rationality of belief in God. Rather, the aim is to defend our native disposition to belief against skeptical arguments. Understood in this way, Hardy contends, Kant's religious epistemology is surprisingly congenial to, e.g., the Scottish common-sense tradition and to contemporary anti-foundationalists who often take the Scottish tradition as their inspiration and Kant as a target.[9]

---

9   Ameriks too presents "a commonsense Kant," on partly overlapping grounds, in Ameriks 2005.

Watkins asks a different question, one that arises within the Judeo-Christian philosophical tradition. If, as that tradition suggests, it is crucial that we believe in God, it is unclear why God does not make his existence so obvious to human beings that they cannot help believing. What reason could there be for an omnipotent God to remain hidden if salvation crucially depends on belief in God? Kant took up this question in a number of places, and offered both practical and theoretical arguments to explain why God does not reveal himself more directly. The practical arguments maintain that negative consequences would follow for human virtue (or human freedom) if we were more directly cognizant of God's existence. The theoretical arguments maintain that, due to the nature of human cognitive capacities, God is incapable of revealing himself to us: not because of some limitation in him, but because of limitations in us.

Watkins finds the practical arguments unconvincing, but argues that the theoretical arguments are worthy of greater scrutiny. He identifies four different theoretical arguments in Kant's writings. One focuses on God not being an object given in space and time. The second considers God's being unconditioned. The third turns on divine perfection, while the fourth relates to divine infinitude. Of these arguments, he contends that the third and fourth are the most convincing, and that they don't depend on controversial aspects of Kant's broader understanding of cognition.

Conclusion

Again, this volume has two principal aims. One is to adopt (and thereby encourage) a more-than-usually comprehensive view of the Kantian corpus, resisting the urge to too-rigidly separate, in particular, Kant's theoretical and practical projects. A second, connected aim is to exhibit the philosophical interest of Kant's metaphysical commitments, particularly as they relate to practical matters. Not only does such an approach reveal connections across Kantian texts, it also forces one to consider arguments that have been neglected within recent Kant scholarship. In this introduction, we have tried to highlight how the several topics that our contributors address *all* work toward *both* aims.

We said at the outset, though, that the challenge of Kant scholarship today is, in part, to respond sensitively both to current debates and to Kant's Enlightenment context. What the first ten essays do not do, for the most part, is situate Kant's writings within Enlightenment discussions of controversial metaphysical commitments (especially religious commitments). Rachel Zuckert accomplishes this in her essay, taking up Kant's understanding of fanaticism. She argues that while Kant can be grouped with other Enlightenment thinkers who warn against the dangers of fanaticism in political life, and while Kant certainly seeks to set religion within the boundaries of mere reason, there are also important and interesting ways in which his understanding of fanaticism differs from the understandings of his contemporaries.

In approaching Kant's discussions of fanaticism, she argues, it is important to distinguish theoretical or epistemological error from practical or moral error. Unlike other Enlightenment thinkers, such as John Locke, Kant does not regard fanaticism simply as a lapse of theoretical reason. Kant is committed, moreover, to the view that practical reason supports beliefs, the objects of which are beyond the scope of theoretical reason. Kant's account turns, then, not on whether one embraces ideas of the supersensible, but on whether one claims sensible experience of their objects.

Zuckert's reconstruction of Kant on fanaticism suggests a perpetual dialectic between Kant's account of fanaticism and the practical arguments for religious belief discussed elsewhere in this volume. In particular, there seems to be a danger inherent in practical reason's ability to ground beliefs in supersensibles. The danger is that of falling into fanaticism. A fully rounded understanding of the relationship between the epistemology of practically grounded belief, offered elsewhere in this volume, and fanaticism as Zuckert characterizes it, is a task suggested but not carried out within this volume.

There are many others. If we accept that, ultimately, a two-standpoints interpretation is more defensible, as Frierson and many contemporary writers argue, what then are we to make of the metaphysically rich understanding of moral motivation offered by Ameriks and Lipscomb? If we accept that Kant offers a robust "practical" epistemology, as Chignell and Kain urge, can Kant's practical worries associated with belief in the supersensible (as highlighted by Zuckert) be assuaged? How do Chignell and Kain's epistemological arguments affect our understanding of the highest good, which they do not address, but which is supposed to ground our belief in at least two of the practical postulates? Several of our contributors appeal to Kant's doctrine of schematization to assist us in theorizing practically grounded belief. How far can the analogy with schematization be developed, and what are its full implications for a comprehensive Kantian epistemology? This list of questions can, of course, be extended. Our hope is that this collection will prove provocative in precisely this way.

Thus, while this volume can be taken as an argument for reading Kant more holistically and for more closely examining his metaphysical commitments, it has been no part of our intention to assemble a tightly unified account, either of Kant's Critical project or even simply of the metaphysical beliefs to which his practical philosophy commits him. Rather, our intent, particularly in this introduction, has been to highlight the range of unexplored and underexplored questions and the richly interesting, sometimes conflicting answers that arise when one accepts our more general argument and its inherent challenge. Our hope is that we and our colleagues, by highlighting these questions and answers, can contribute to the ongoing dialectic between contemporary philosophical concern and careful historical reconstruction, and can assist others in working toward a more synoptic understanding.

Any volume of this sort emerges out of the hard work of many people. In particular, we wish to acknowledge the support of the Council for Christian Colleges and Universities, whose Initiatives Grant program funded some of the preparations for this volume. We are particularly grateful to program officer Harold Heie, who offered helpful advice and encouragement throughout the grant period. The grant we received enabled us to stage a summer workshop where many of the papers collected here were first read and discussed. Thanks to all participants in that workshop: Karl Ameriks, Andrew Chignell, Patrick Frierson, Lee Hardy, John Hare, Patrick Kain, Houston Smit, Angela Smith, and Rachel Zuckert. We also thank the Notre Dame Center for Ethics and Culture, its director, David Solomon, and his assistant, Tracy Westlake, for seeing to many, many workshop details. Our grant also supported a second gathering, this time a conference at Houghton College, co-sponsored by the eastern region of the Society of Christian Philosophers. Jeanine Grenberg, David Sussman, and Eric Watkins first signed on to the project as invitees to that event. We thank all the participants in that conference for their insights, and thank especially the members of the Society's eastern region, who tolerated an abnormally large number of Kant scholars joining them for their annual meeting. We owe thanks to Gertrud Grünkorn, Monika Pfleghar and Kerstin Haensch of Walter de Gruyter for walking us through the publication process, and to Daniel Metzger for assistance with the index. Finally, Benjamin Lipscomb wishes to acknowledge the patience of Susan his wife, and Josephine, Ernest, and Ralph, his children, during a lot of long days at the office. His in-laws Ralph and Elaine Bruxvoort merit special thanks for helping keep the household running, right at the end of the editing process.

Section I

Moral Motivation, Moral Metaphysics

.

CHAPTER 1

Reality, Reason, and Religion in the Development of Kant's Ethics

Karl Ameriks

Kant scholars need, from the very start, to keep in mind at least three different kinds of developments: first and foremost, developments in Kant's own thought, second, changes in our own philosophical and interpretive views in general, and, third, developments in historical research on Kant's own texts and work as a teacher. My point of departure here is one recent development of the third kind—a newly edited text of Kant's early ethics lectures—but I will also touch on some more general issues. My central question is an old and still very unsettled one: what, if anything, are the key marks of the so-called "Critical" breakthrough in Kant's ethical thought—and what light can a new historical exploration of this issue shed on the links between Kant's concerns with "the three r's": reality, reason, and religion? My answer to this question will proceed from taking very seriously Kant's opening remark from his lecture announcement of 1765, which promises to "always consider philosophically and historically what actually happens before [indicating] what ought to happen...and [concentrate on] human nature that remains always the same, and upon its particular place in creation" (Kuehn 1995, p. 391, n. 30).[1]

With regard to the development of Kant's own views, matters are especially complex in the area of practical philosophy. I take the major dividing line between Kant's pre-Critical and Critical positions in general to be the emergence of two basic doctrines, doctrines that are defined theoretically rather than practically. First, there is the metaphysical doctrine of the transcendental ideality of space and time, which is presented already in the *Inaugural Dissertation* of 1770, and, second, there is what can be called the "global" idealism thesis, which is presented originally in the 1781 *Critique of Pure Reason* and can be said to

---

[1] See "M. Immanuel Kant's Announcement of the Programme of his Lectures for the Winter Semester 1765-6" (2:311).

define the Critical period proper. The global thesis builds on the claim
that spatio-temporality is ideal, but it goes significantly further than this
claim, insisting that all our determinate theoretical knowledge is about
what is only transcendentally ideal precisely because this knowledge is
restricted to what is spatio-temporal. What is most significant here is
that these claims apparently need not affect the most fundamental features of Kant's ethics, because basic normative concepts, such as
"good" and "right," can remain what they are irrespective of how space
and time are classified metaphysically. Nonetheless, there are very influential philosophers, such as John Rawls, who have claimed that the
doctrine of transcendental idealism is in some sense central to Kant's
ethics and not only his theoretical philosophy.[2] Were this claim true, it
would be natural to expect that Kant's ethics could not take on anything
like its proper form until the Critical period.

For Kantians who are not dedicated Rawlsians, it is not easy to be
persuaded by claims about the direct ethical relevance of transcendental
idealism, at least in the standard terms in which I have just defined it.
Nonetheless, without going so far as to follow Rawls's own specific
reasons, one could still hold that prior to the path-breaking publication
of the first *Critique*, or at least before some time in the later 1770s,
there are significant differences in Kant's ethical views.[3] Notice, however, that even if the general notion of some key division in the development of Kant's ethical thought is granted, many quite different explanations of it are still possible. On the one hand, there are many
interpreters who would say that the striking feature of Kant's early
thought is that it had an all-too-"metaphysical," "realist," and "rationalist" notion of practical philosophy, and that, irrespective of what one
says about the exact details of transcendental idealism, the Critical period brings with it a new constructivist notion of ethics, one that contrasts deeply with metaphysical and moral realist orientations.[4] On the
other hand, other interpreters—such as Manfred Kuehn, whose views
will be my main concern here—have suggested that there are strands in
Kant's early period that are significantly more appealing than either a
constructivist or metaphysical approach to his philosophy. For such
interpreters, these strands at least temporarily connect Kant with an
ethics that is "realist" in a promising but basically non-metaphysical
sense insofar as they reveal an appreciation for anthropological considerations concerning motivation.

---

2   See Rawls 1980.
3   See e.g., Allison 1990; Schneewind 1998; Kuehn 2004.
4   See work by Schneewind and other 'Rawlsians,' especially Korsgaard 1996b.

The general idea behind this relatively empirical approach can be made understandable by simply considering some titles. The fact that Kant's first two *Critiques* are called the *Critique of Pure Reason* and the *Critique of Practical Reason* is much more surprising than it might at first seem.[5] It suggests at first that the author of the Critical system might not have been thinking far enough ahead when he rushed these books to press, since his titles, with their quite different qualifications of the term "reason," left him with an awkward and never correctible asymmetry.[6] Amazingly, none of Kant's books is entitled "Critique of Theoretical (or Speculative) Reason," although it is precisely that kind of reason which would appear to be the major object of Kant's criticism. If he had only given his first *Critique* that title, he would have had what he always lacked, a fully matching partner for his second *Critique*. And yet: precisely by instead introducing the crucial word "pure" in his 1781 title (and not breaking philosophy down explicitly into its theoretical and practical branches), Kant revealed from the start what is most at stake in his Critical philosophy. For, surely, the main overall aim of that philosophy is to scrutinize—and in part attack and in part vindicate—the pure contentions of "reason" in the broadest sense.[7]

No matter what his books might have been called, however, Kant's Critical work—precisely insofar as it concerns purity—does involve contrasting treatments of the two main branches of philosophy. Theoretical philosophy (and theory in general) is scolded insofar as it tries to stay "too pure," that is, to make determinate claims from concepts alone, while not heeding the bounds set by sensibility in general and our forms of space and time in particular. Practical philosophy (and praxis in general), however, is scolded insofar as it makes the opposite mistake, the error of not recognizing that there are, supposedly, entirely pure practical principles that can be legitimated by categorical moral reason apart from considerations of sensibility. Put rather crudely, but in terms that Kant himself suggests, the general Critical lesson seems to be that theoretical reason can and should "get dirty," that is, restrict its determinate a priori claims to the domain of our sensibility, whereas practical reason can and should "stay clean," that is, insist on a priori

---

5   The title of Kant's third *Critique* (*Kritik der Urteilskraft*) is more controversial. It may well have been mistranslated in English for more than two centuries and probably should be called, as Paul Guyer has proposed for the Cambridge edition, *Critique of the Power of Judgment* rather than *Critique of Judgment*.

6   See Beck 1960.

7   This point was obscured, with unfortunate consequences, by the tendency of Kant's first follower, Karl Reinhold, to refer to Kant's book just as the "Critique of Reason." See Reinhold 2005.

claims that are not limited to the domain of sensibility.[8] And yet: there are also important counterbalancing points that are missing in this simple characterization. First, no matter how critical it is, the *Critique of Pure Reason* also relies on some entirely pure capacities of theoretical reason, exhibited in the basic forms of judgment, the pure categories, and the power of reflection in general. Second, and even more relevant for present purposes, the Kantian defense of pure practical reason is regularly accompanied by a positive account of features that are not entirely pure. It is no wonder, then, that a spate of books has appeared recently with titles such as *Kant's Impure Ethics*.[9] Their main aim, presumably, is not to embarrass Kant but to defend him, and to show how Kant offers a variety of broadly empirical considerations that help to fill out his ethics so that it is not as vulnerable as it may seem to the common objection of being too pure, too unrealistically detached from the circumstances of human practical life.

This point leads back to the second of the three kinds of development relevant to contemporary interpretation, namely, developments having to do with our own fundamental philosophical perspectives. Inevitably, each era pays special attention to certain ways of approaching ethics that seem most fruitful to it. In times like our own, when there is a conflicting mix of attitudes (both metaphysical and anti-metaphysical), it is not surprising to find a sharp clash of views on what is central and valuable in Kant, especially in relation to his constant concern with religion.

There are many quite different reactions to what I will call "Kant's religion." What I mean by that phrase is not any particular book, doctrine, or personal attitude but the undeniable fact of the many detailed and patient discussions of religious and theological themes throughout his work. Typical twentieth-century philosophers such as John Rawls, for example, who worked in a broadly positivist environment, dutifully acknowledged the presence of these considerations but treated them as an unfortunate curiosity, something that can be excised, leaving the core Critical doctrines undisturbed.[10] More recent commentators, such as Frederick Beiser, are now willing to argue that, at least for the purpose of being historically accurate and properly understanding what

---

8   See Kuehn 2004, p. xvi, on "*gesäubert*" in the *Groundwork of the Metaphysics of Morals* (4:388-9).
9   Louden 2000. See Frierson 2003, for an insightful discussion of Louden and similar authors (e.g., Allen Wood, G. Felicitas Munzel, and Jeanine Grenberg).
10   See Rawls 2000. The secular tendency of these lectures is followed closely in the work of many of his influential students. Rawls' own unease on this topic can be better understood now that further evidence has been published concerning his turn away from an early intense involvement with religion. See Rawls 2009.

Kant meant to "get at" in his practical philosophy, not only metaphysics as such but specifically Christian ideas should be given a central role after all.[11] There is a third group of scholars, such as John Hare,[12] whose work has gone even further by taking Kant's religion very seriously from a philosophical position sympathetic to Christianity, even while presenting this Kantian position in an analytic manner meant to be relevant for a broad secular audience.

Each of these three kinds of approach is certainly worth considering in detail, but my main concern is with a fourth kind of interpretation. This is the broadly empiricist and generally non-religious approach to Kant, and his early ethics in particular, which is proposed, on both historical and systematic grounds, in some of Manfred Kuehn's recent work. In his standard-setting biography of Kant, as well as in several other places, Kuehn has revealed many striking ways in which Kant should be understood as offering views that parallel anti-pietist views within Germany as well as radical enlightenment views held by empiricists such as Hume.[13] Kuehn's perspective is thus an important potential corrective to readers who may move too quickly in trying to bring Kant into positive contact with Christianity.

These four scholarly approaches to the significance of Kant's religion for Critical ethics can be contrasted in the following, very rough terms. The Beiser Approach takes Kant's religion to be highly relevant historically (i.e., interpretively) without presuming that it is attractive philosophically. The Rawls Approach largely abstracts from historical considerations and quickly dismisses the philosophical significance of Kant's religion, whereas the Hare Approach (initially) largely abstracts from historical considerations raised in recent German scholarship and argues in support of the philosophical significance of Kant's religion. The Kuehn Approach strikes me as especially significant because it alone backs up a rejection of the philosophical significance of Kant's religion with detailed historical-developmental considerations. Given this situation, I propose to explore a fifth option, a double-track, positive approach concerned with working out a historically as well as philosophically oriented apology for Kant's religion, that is, a defense that is prepared to meet Kuehn-style considerations on their own ground by looking at the early development of Kant's ethics.

An ideal occasion for a confrontation of these views—and an exploration of a broadly empiricist approach—has been provided by a

---

11 See Beiser 2006, and cf. Firestone and Palmquist 2006.
12 See Hare 1996 and 2001, and also work by authors such as Robert M. Adams, C. Stephen Evans, A. W. Moore, David Sussman, and the late Philip Quinn.
13 See Kuehn 2001.

recent publication that illustrates the third kind of development mentioned earlier, namely, a development within contemporary historical
work concerning primary sources. (New publications by Kant himself
are of course no longer to be found, but other new items, including
relevant correspondence and fragments in his hand, continue to crop
up.) In 1991 the Marburg Kant Archive issued a newly edited and significantly improved version of the famous 1764-5 private "Notes" that
Kant inserted in his copy of the *Observations on the Beautiful and the
Sublime* (1764).[14] The 1980s and 1990s also saw the discovery, publication, and translation of thousands of pages of notes by attendees of
Kant's lectures on ethics as well as on metaphysics, logic, and anthropology. Some of these items led to significant corrections of previously
available material, and in general their publication revealed a remarkable underlying continuity in Kant's thought from the very first notes
taken by Herder at the lectures of 1762.[15]

More recently, in 2004 a newly edited version of notes on Kant's
1773-4 or (perhaps most likely) 1774-5 ethics lectures was published
by de Gruyter in a volume that stands outside the Academy edition.[16] It
is edited by Werner Stark, a longtime editor of Kant material at the
Marburg Kant Archive and a leading historical scholar involved with
the latest and most carefully edited Academy volumes. Stark's edition
is based on the Kaehler version of Kant's ethics lectures. This 2004
volume finally gives a properly edited version of material that was, in
part, edited by Paul Menzer in 1924 and found its way into the Academy edition, vol. 27, edited hastily by Gerhard Lehmann in 1974-9. The
material in Menzer's edition was the basis for a very familiar English
version, in a volume called *Lectures on Ethics*, edited in 1930 by Louis
Infield, and of the best-known part (the "Moral Collins") of the material
from Academy volumes 27 and 29 that was itself the basis for a 1997
Cambridge edition of four sets (one from each decade of his teaching)
of student notes from Kant's lectures on ethics.[17] In Stark's edition,
unlike all the others, there are extensive, up-to-date historical notes to
the text, and Stark provides a historical Postscript that explains the full

---

14 See Kant 1991. Cited hereafter (in my translation) as Rischmüller, with ms. page number. This important set of "notes" (*Bemerkungen*, which have also sometimes been called "remarks") will soon be receiving a complete English translation in the Cambridge
edition of Kant's works, and selections from it are already translated as "Notes on the
Observations on the Beautiful and the Sublime."
15 These seminal lecture notes still await a definitive edition. My appreciation for them
has been influenced by the ongoing research of Steven Naragon. See also Zammito
2002, and Shell 2009.
16 Kant 2004.
17 This English edition is a welcome replacement for the long out of date Kant 1930,
although a handy, up-to-date student edition is lacking in English.

background of the Kaehler notes and argues for their pre-eminent reliability.[18] Kuehn adds a forceful philosophical Introduction to the volume, which argues for the special systematic value of their pre-1780s perspective. The main focus of my argument concerns the provocative proposals of this Introduction and its suggestion that Kant would have done better if he had held to the positions sketched in the Kaehler lectures, which are supposedly more empiricist, that is, less "pure," and yet "realist" in a practical but non-metaphysical sense (Kuehn 2004, p. ix).

Five Key Issues: respect, interest, desire, happiness, and religion

Kuehn's views are especially relevant because he appreciates that from the beginning Kant tended to approach ethics from a general philosophical perspective that gives primacy to fundamental metaphysical considerations rather than detailed factual or normative arguments.[19] This is evident already in the early lectures (in part because they are forced to take up the long list of traditional issues addressed in the texts by Baumgarten that provided the basis for Kant's teaching in those years[20]), even though on the whole they are still somewhat more concrete than Kant's two best-known books on ethics, the *Groundwork* and the second *Critique*, which explicitly dwell on foundational issues. The key question is whether Kant's increasing abstractness in these Critical publications was merely a matter of expository form or whether it involved, as Kuehn contends, substantive (wrong) turns.

    Rather than arguing, in total contrast to Kuehn, that Kant was or should have been entirely "pure" throughout his treatment of basic ethical notions, I will present a complex mixed position, namely, that, from the early 1760s on, Kant was, at the base level of his theory, an ethical purist (never seriously tempted by empiricism), and yet he *always* supplemented his purism to some degree, and for the most part in a fitting way, when, at a *secondary* level, he incorporated broadly anthropological considerations and modified his views on various epistemological issues.

---

18   The issues here concern, for example, some passages that are left out in the Collins version of the lectures, which is the one that was selected for the Cambridge edition.

19   See Kuehn 2004, p. vii.

20   Kant 2004, pp. 415-28, includes a very helpful appendix with a concordance of Kant's lectures and Baumgarten's ethics.

Kuehn's discussion covers five key issues that any Kantian ethicist must confront: the relations of pure practical reason to the specific phenomena that Kant calls (1) "respect," (2) "interest," (3) "the faculty of desire," (4) the "necessary end of happiness," and (5) the "postulate" of some sort of belief in God as necessary for human beings to maintain proper moral motivation. These issues are all very important and interrelated, although I will concentrate on the first three.

Respect

We are now so familiar with Kant's distinctive philosophical use of the term "respect" (*Achtung*) that it may be very difficult for some of us even to imagine that it involved a significant innovation, in German as well as English. The Critical philosophy's use of the term surprised and perplexed a sympathetic contemporary reader, Friedrich Schiller. It is thus understandable that Dieter Henrich would regard Kant as the first "to use it in its current sense."[21] Kuehn notes, however, that this remark is misleading, insofar as our current dictionaries have not yet caught up with theory. For the main "current sense" of the term is not the Kantian philosophical one, which, above all, designates respect for a pure, normative, and formal law (Kuehn 2004, p. xii). Instead, even in German, as in English, the term ordinarily designates an attitude directed toward something empirical, such as persons[22] or institutions, or, in the paradigm Prussian case, a combination of these, as in respect for an officer (a use that Kuehn notes is found already in Lessing and Herder). The emphasis on law is not the only striking aspect of Kant's account, according to which respect ultimately involves at least three special features all at once: (1) a non-empirically rooted source, that is, a will whose causality is "absolutely free"; (2) a more than "merely intellectual" approval of the pure moral law; and (3) a rational submission to this law as something that is experienced not as a wholly external force but instead as something "imposed on ourselves as necessary in itself."[23]

In addition to all the obvious difficulties that this threefold claim directly raises, there is also a general methodological problem because, as Kuehn points out, Kant's procedure here reveals that he is by no means

---

21 See Kuehn 2004, p. xii, n. 8, which refers to Dieter Henrich's early work. See especially Henrich 1994 and 2009.

22 Cf. Darwall 2004.

23 See 4:401n. This famous note discusses many more key features of respect than can be treated here. See Ameriks 2003, Part II, and Ameriks 2006, ch. 4.

merely "analyzing a given unclear concept" but is insisting on a substantive and heretofore unrecognized systematic meaning (Kuehn 2004, p. xiii). This fact can seem to count against a general interpretive proposal on which Kuehn and I are in agreement, namely that, contrary to what has often been thought, Kant, in his starting points, places great reliance on common sense.[24] The interpretive problem here is that, if Kant's special notion of respect is not simply an odd and arbitrary speculative invention—as Kuehn sometimes suggests—but is ultimately rooted—as Kant insists—in commonsense feelings accessible to any ordinary person, then it can be difficult to see how this notion could have all the remarkable non-empirical implications that Kant attaches to it.

Kuehn and others properly stress that Kant's claims about pure respect are remarkable.[25] Merely empirical feelings of respect for particular persons are easy enough to explain psychologically, but, as was just noted, an instance of genuine Kantian respect requires nothing less than a non-empirical cause (free will), a non-empirical object (pure law), and a mysterious—and therefore easily misunderstood—non-empirical kind of "self-imposition." This can all sound too remarkable to be true. Nonetheless, I believe that each of these remarkable peculiarities can be defended by a patient Kantian apologist. Note that at the start of Kant's Critical theoretical philosophy a very similar issue arises concerning the relation of its non-empirical claims to common sense. In the first *Critique*, Kant insists on beginning with judgments that are in one sense as basic as "sound common sense"—for example, that we share a common space and time and mathematics —and yet these judgments are eventually claimed to have revolutionary, non-empirical implications.[26] Consider basic geometric or arithmetic judgments. Contrary to well-known skeptical positions of his era, Kant does not take the objective validity of such judgments to be an issue; for him they go "without saying," as givens of common sense, in a broad sense. However, just as with the now relatively "familiar" idea of respect for moral law, we may forget that Kant's ultimate philosophical interpretation of the nature of mathematical judgments—as opposed to their mere evident validity—is not by any means taken to be already a part of, and vindicated by, the

---

24   See Ameriks 2005 and Kuehn 1987. Kant's famous reference in the "Notes" to the impact upon him of Rousseau's democratic ideas is often cited (2:216-7), but it has been overlooked that, right before this reference, Kant makes a strong general point about common sense: "One must teach youth to honor common sense [*den gemeinen Verstand*] for moral as well as logical reasons" (Rischmüller, p. 35).

25   Cf. Siep, 2009.

26   Cf. Bird 1998, and see Ameriks 2006, Introduction.

commonsense attitude on its own.[27] It requires instead a series of higher-level claims on Kant's part, for it is his distinctive breakthrough to insist (for better or worse) that only careful philosophical reflection reveals that the nature of such mathematical judgments ultimately has to be classified, all at once, as certain, synthetic, and a priori.

Kant can hardly have meant these points to be trivialities of common sense, for he prides himself on being the first person clearly to explain and emphasize them.[28] And it is only once he has established his second-level philosophical point, about the nature of our mathematical judgment as synthetic a priori, that he can and does go on to argue, at a third level, that such judgments also require a non-empirical source (pure intuiting), a non-empirical object (the pure intuited), and a non-empirical kind of "self-determination" (as forms constitutive of our own pure sensibility).[29] The methodological analogy with moral respect should be clear enough by now. Kant is not assuming that by mere common sense we already know that respect demands all the non-empirical elements he eventually asserts.[30] Rather, Kant holds that, first, there are concrete and valid moral claims already made and acknowledged at the commonsense level, and, second, philosophical reflection (and not mere common sense) reveals that the proper understanding of these claims involves the specific notion of respect for a "categorical imperative"—the practical correlate of the synthetic a priori in mathematics—and, third, the explanation of how all this is possible eventually requires the introduction of further non-empirical elements definitive of the moral will's efficient ground, formal object, and ultimate nature. Hence, in both theoretical and practical philosophy, Kant's transcendental argumentation involves a process of coming to appreciate an *actual* base-level experience that is *argued*, first, to involve an *implicit* commitment to at least some substantive necessities

27 Similarly, already in the "Notes" (Rischmüller, p. 21), Kant says that simple moral acts need at first to come from basic "feeling" rather than an intellectual grasp of the concept of their underlying rule: "Early on, a simple person has a feeling for what is right...if one instructs him from the first by rules, then he will never have a feeling for [the concept of] right."

28 See Kuehn 1995, on how it took Kant himself a long time to appreciate this point.

29 These forms are similar to—but also unlike—the moral law, for although the form of that law is also constitutive of a faculty of our own, namely reason, this faculty is not restricted, whereas sensibility is.

30 The Kaehler lectures (Kant 2004, p. 58) call moral action "from [*aus*] intellectual inclination" an *Unding* (i.e., an absurdity). It is important to consider whether the "from" here is to be understood simply phenomenologically, which would give sense to the charge of absurdity (because it would be odd for Kant to say that the intellect itself has inclinations)—or simply causally, which does not seem totally absurd, because it would be odd to think that the intellect cannot play some role in generating "inclinations," that is, feelings of some sort, as in Kant's ultimate theory of the feeling of moral respect.

and, then, a number of further metaphysical preconditions of these necessities. That the judgments are substantive and necessary may be something that Kant believes ordinary persons could never coherently deny, but his main goal is to show how it is that, as higher-level theorists, we must explicitly affirm that these pure features (not yet understood in ordinary life) are really there, and that they can at least be defended as such against the attacks of other schools of philosophy.

Of course, even if this interpretive point about Kant's method is granted, and even if one does not immediately insist on the position of a moral skeptic or anti-realist, one can still wonder whether any of the remarkable claims about the non-empirical features of respect that turn out to be central in Kant's ultimate theory are at all plausible, especially once we consider what human nature is actually like. From Kuehn's perspective, the Critical Kant is unnecessarily going far beyond the more sober empirical considerations in his earlier lectures, which do not yet spell out the full Critical account of pure respect and instead stress psychological aspects of ordinary human motivation. I believe, however, that the orthodox Kantian has an adequate reply, one that works especially well within the framework of Kant's overall system. Non-empirical sources, objects, and self-determinations need not be as mysterious or gratuitous as many interpreters assume. By the time of these lectures Kant had, after all, already developed on non-practical grounds a metaphysics of transcendental idealism that leaves room in principle for all of these kinds of items. Moreover, even apart from a consideration of that metaphysics, something very like each of these items can be found even now in respectable thinking carried out without any attachment to Kant's system: in mainline libertarian views of the sources of human action, in non-relativist notions of the object of morality, and in rationalist and even theological theories of the determination of value as internal to the nature of a fully rational being.

The third of these notions, the idea of moral law as in some sense self-legislated, is perhaps the one that has caused the most perplexity. Mature Kantian respect seems thereby inextricably bound up with a radical notion of moral autonomy. The idea that the will as such imposes a law upon itself can seem to be both the luring heart of the Kantian position and the sign of a mad, egocentric leap into an abyss—for, as Kierkegaard and Anscombe insist, how can something count as a law truly ruling over one, if one has simply imposed it on oneself?[31]

---

31   The history of this notion is complicated, because its major source is surely Rousseau's thought that to be free is to follow a law that one has imposed on oneself, and Rousseau of course spoke primarily in social and political terms. It is therefore understandable that J. B. Schneewind, Charles Larmore, and others have followed Rawls in stressing a

The proper orthodox answer is that Kantian "auto-nomy" is not simple imposition, and it can be understood in terms that are neither private and arbitrary nor even "merely" social or constructivist.[32] Kant himself always spelled it out as a way of rejecting *very specific* forms of heteronomy according to which lawgiving by another is equated with imposition by a completely external or ultimately contingent force—such as our given physical and psychological nature, or strictly positive civil or canon law—that has no inescapable moral weight.[33] The familiar anti-Kantian worry arises largely from a common but unfounded presumption that Kantian autonomy must itself be some kind of merely contingent process of constituting rules by fiat or a constructive procedure that still remains strictly individual or, at most, merely human. We need not presume that this is Kant's intent, however, for he insists that the "will" that matters here is precisely the will as such (*Wille*), not the mere operation of any particular individual's will (*Willkür*), that this is precisely the "rational" will (since *Wille* is practical reason), not any arbitrary form of volition, and that it therefore wills a "law"(*nomos*) that is not at all contingent—not even in the general sense in which the universal Kantian structures of space and time, or even of human sociality and legality, are transcendentally contingent insofar as they, unlike the absolutely necessary moral law, rest on forms of sensibility.

All this implies that truly Kantian autonomy is the last thing that Kierkegaard and Anscombe should reject as being too subjective, for it should be understood as the kind of law that we must think of as structuring the actions of a proper divine being.[34] This is so, not because the divine will follows the human will, but rather because one's proper conception of the human will must follow one's conception of a fully proper rational will—which for Kant is something that we must conceptualize in terms of a divine will, whether or not we affirm that such a will is actual.

Moreover, this absolutist position is a theme that can be recognized throughout Kant's entire public career. It can be found constantly in the late lectures on metaphysics, on ethics, and on religion, as well as in the very first "writings" that are generally taken to reflect Kant's distinctive moral standpoint, the "Notes" of 1764/5. In one striking passage, Kant already makes the main relevant point, even if he does not yet use terms such as "law", "respect", or "self-legislation": "The highest ground for

---

constructivist reading of Kant. See, however, Krasnoff 1999; and Ameriks 2006, ch. 11, "On Two Non-Realist Interpretations of Kant's Ethics."

32   See Hare 2001, and Kain 2004, 2005, and 2006.
33   See O'Neill 2004.
34   Cf. Adams 1999.

creating is because something is good . . . [God] is also pleased with all that is good, and most with that which leads to the highest good. The first is good as ground, the second as a consequence" (Rischmüller, p. 28).[35] Kant's main point here and in similar early statements is that a fully rational being does what is proper because it is proper, that is, fully rational; not that something becomes proper simply because a powerful or intelligent being wills it to be so.[36] The "good as ground" is that value which good items have as such, in their very nature, and the "good as consequence" is the secondary value that such items can have once they are actualized in this contingent world and become part of an appropriately satisfying end state. This most basic axiological idea holds to the end of Kant's work, irrespective of whether one goes on to consider items such as human willing, rightness, or respect. No "Copernican Turn" toward a transcendental idealism of *value* as such ever takes place—even though, of course, the metaphysical implications of the theoretical doctrine of transcendental idealism (and various ancillary empirical considerations) play a crucial role in helping to explain how human agents can originate their actions, conceptualize their concrete objects, and appreciate the full motivation and structure of their attachment to them.

Interest

There is an obvious objection to this interpretation: that quotations like this from Kant's early work might express a fundamentally pre-Critical, because heteronomous attitude.[37] There is evidence that at least until around 1770, Kant often understood practical philosophy in terms of an orientation toward something called "ontological perfection," and this would seem to express precisely the kind of basing of moral interest on an "object" outside of us that he later directly criticized when espousing autonomy in works such as the *Groundwork* and second *Critique*.

So it may well seem—but when one looks closely at such texts, it always turns out that Kant's later objection to this "perfectionist" kind of objectivity is limited, and by no means needs to be understood as an espousal of autonomous subjectivity requiring a rejection of moral or value objectivity as such. His main arguments against traditional per-

---

35   Cf. the following remarks from "Moral Herder": "Supposing the arbitrium of God to be known to me, where is the necessity that I should do it, if I have not already derived the obligation from the nature of the case?" (27:9). Cf. 27: 4, on acts that are good "for their own sake."

36   Cf. the similar rejection of "theological morality" in the second *Critique*, 5:32.

37   See Kuehn 1995, p. 377, and cf. *Inaugural Dissertation*, 2:396.

fectionism, when he comes explicitly to reject it, are based entirely on a
specific presumption that the traditional theorist's interest in such perfection is too vague or else must be conceived as resting wholly on an
empirically "given" end, that is, an object chosen simply because we
anticipate a contingent pleasure from it, distinct from the act of willing
itself.[38] Putting aside the separate issue of whether to accept Kant's
"specific presumption" about other theorists, nothing in his work counts
against understanding Kant himself as continuing to hold that the fundamental concern of proper action is the valuable as such, as opposed to
its incidental effects—and that this can be regarded as something
"completely objective" until specific reasons are given for saying otherwise.[39] Moreover, Kant never expresses an objection to saying that
we should be morally oriented toward something that can be called an
"end" or "purpose," as well as an "object," as long as that end concerns
what is *necessarily* valuable, and valuable in a way that is intrinsic to
the willed action as such.[40]

Kant goes on, to be sure, to make additional specific presumptions
that this kind of necessary value is grounded in what he calls "form,"
not "matter," that is, in the form of a will oriented toward that which is
lawful as such, is consistently willable in universal terms, and expresses
a respect for persons as rational wills and "ends in themselves." Here
again, particular questions about such specific presumptions should not
obscure the structure of Kant's key claim, which is not that we should
respect what is necessarily valuable because it can be willed lawfully,
but is rather that we should respect what can always be willed lawfully
because it (supposedly) is obviously not merely contingently valuable—and, in particular, not dependent on psychological presumptions
about pleasure, which he thinks would preclude necessary moral objectivity.[41]

---

38 In places such as the second *Critique* (5:40f.) Kant obviously has the school of Christian Wolff in mind. It does not seem that Kant himself (at least after 1762) was ever
drawn to this kind of perfectionism. See "Moral Herder" (27:16): "moral perfection…
according to the taste of the philosophy of Wolff which continually based perfection on
the relation between cause and effect, and thus treated it as a means to ends grounded in
desire and aversion."

39 See again "Moral Herder" (27:9).

40 This general point has also been stressed in a variety of ways by other interpreters, e.g.
Allen Wood and Barbara Herman.

41 Similarly, against popular mid-twentieth-century interpretations, it is crucial to note that
for Kant the categorical status of morality, and the meaning of "ought" in this context,
is not determined fundamentally by mere independence from one's individual desires
(social codes could be "categorical" in this way); rather, it is because certain items are
necessarily, rather than hypothetically, valuable that they are correlative with categorical imperatives, and so independence from the contingency of particular given desires is
simply one condition and a common sign of that status.

For some time, several German Kant scholars have argued (as Kuehn himself notes) that already in fragments from as early as the 1760s there are traces of Kant's coming to believe that this kind of necessary moral objectivity can be correlated with the notion of consistent rational willing as such, that is, with maxims that can be consistently universalized by a plurality of rational agents.[42] Without deciding how well these early fragments implicitly express, or closely approximate, the published Critical formulae of the categorical imperative, it still can be allowed that they indicate a strongly objective orientation, and that throughout his career, Kant never seriously entertained a standard for the content of morality based on something entirely empirical and contingent. But then, one may well ask, why has this point not been clearly recognized by all interpreters, and why is it that Kant himself admittedly began to speak regularly and explicitly in terms of the categorical imperative only in the Critical period?

Clarifying some distinctive features of Kant's theory of the faculties may help to explain these interpretive mysteries. One issue complicating matters during Kant's pre-Critical period is the fact that, from early on, Kant was struck by the broadly "sensory" aspects of human moral experience that Hutcheson especially impressed upon him, namely, that a merely intellectual appreciation does not by itself explain or fully characterize our practical attachment to a value, our qualitative sense of it, and our decisive motivation to actualize it. The mere acknowledgment of the truth of a moral principle is not the same thing as the feeling involved in being committed to it, vividly appreciating it, and actually willing it. Until Kant had developed his mature theory of pure respect, which provides an objective place for moral feeling as ever-present but consequent upon rational moral perception and the proper orientation of a free will, his options in discussing our moral sensibility were limited. In the meantime, he wrote vaguely about "moral feeling" as in some way a possible "basis" for moral orientation, which can leave the impression that he might have been seriously entertaining an ultimately empiricist theory.[43]

In fact, though, even these early considerations are consistent with a model according to which the role of sense is, at most, simply to provide a distinctive and *vivid kind of access* to the moral law, and thus also an enhanced motivation during the course of our experience of genuine "moral insight"—something that cannot be accounted for by

---

42 See Henrich 1966, and Schmucker 1961. Cf. Kuehn 1995, p. 383, and Kuehn 2004, p. xxx, n. 39; also see Kant, "Reflexionen," 19: 113, 116f., 122.

43 See the discussion, at Kuehn 1995, p. 384, of Kant's view of morality in the *Inaugural Dissertation* (1770) as "essentially based on ideas in the Platonic sense."

either strictly intellectual or arbitrary volitional factors.[44] Feeling properly "gripped" by value is not the same kind of experience as merely
"knowing" it or blindly "opting" for it, or even both of these together.
Despite these broadly "phenomenological" concessions to sense, however, there is no reason to suppose that Kant ever thought that what is
valuable as such is simply a reflection of what different people happen
to feel. Just as later with mathematical intuition, it surely could have
seemed natural for him to suppose even then that we may have some
faculties that are substantive and disclose necessity even if they are not
entirely conceptual. His key Critical move, I believe, was finding a
way—through the doctrine of the categorical imperative—to bring rational conditions *more explicitly* back into his account of moral experience without sacrificing an appreciation for the phenomenology of feeling.

A remaining interpretive mystery is why Kant made this move only
at the relatively late time that he did. My hypothesis is that until Kant
could find some metaphysical way to avoid being restricted by determinism, he saw no clear solution to the problem of the "foundation" of
morality. He had to fear that action based on either sense (or arbitrary
will) or intellect alone, or even some kind of "clear" combination of
them—such as Mendelssohn and the Wolffians proposed—would still
leave morality itself questionable because it threatened to take away
any chance for us to exercise agency in a way that is both genuinely
responsible and objective.[45] Hence, it is no wonder that for a while (i.e.,
until 1770), Kant expressed himself as very unclear about what he regarded as the epistemic "basis" of moral principles—although he did
always hold that, whatever that basis is, if it is to concern (as it must) a
genuine "principle," it would have to be consistent with the broadly
intellectual demand of being truly objective.[46]

Faced with the same problem of accounting for the key shift in
Kant's views in the 1770s, Kuehn has a different hypothesis. He takes
Kant's Critical turn to be basically a matter of denying a general "con-
tinuity thesis" about sense and reason (i.e., the thesis that one faculty is

---

44 Note that already in "Moral Herder" (27:4), Kant insists that this "feeling" must have a
    "universal" and "unequivocal" status, and thus is unlike any typical empirical feeling.
    In general, when Kant allows talk of feeling or sentiment as a basis of morality, he has
    in mind Rousseau's sharp contrast between "natural" (in the sense of original and uni-
    versal) and artificial sentiments.

45 Hence, when Kant has this mature theory in place in the 1780s, he uses it directly to
    attack compatibilism, e.g., in his 1783 "Review of Johann Heinrich Schulz's 'Attempt
    at an Introduction to a Doctrine of Morals for all Human Beings regardless of Different
    Religions, Including an Appendix of Capital Punishment'" (8:10-4).

46 On this point there is no difference between, e.g., Kant's *Inaugural Dissertation* (1770),
    § 7, and the second *Critique* (1788).

simply a less clear version of the other), in practical as well as theoretical philosophy. This is an intriguing hypothesis that is obviously relevant to both main branches of Kant's philosophy. In practical philosophy in particular, it reminds us that Kant can be understood as having found a common ground for rejecting both his empiricist and rationalist predecessors, for they, unlike the Critical philosophy, can be understood as merely proposing to "clarify," in different ways, principles that are already given in sense.[47] So far, so good—but problems arise when Kuehn goes on to combine his hypothesis with the further (and much more controversial) statement that "morality *became* objective" for Kant at this time (Kuehn 1995, p. 374, my emphasis). Against this claim, it can be argued that Kant's major shift had to do instead with finding a better way to conceive the metaphysical and psychological details of a moral orientation that was *already assumed* to be objective.

A significant difficulty with Kuehn's account is that it downplays the fact that, by the 1770s, Kant had a new and very significant reason for taking practical philosophy beyond our "mere understanding"—no matter how, in light of the continuity thesis, this faculty is conceived, that is, in either a slightly more intellectual or a slightly more sensory manner. That extra reason is that, after his 1770 commitment to transcendental idealism, Kant could much more easily highlight not only the general discontinuity of sense and intellect but also the distinctive volitional character of practical life and its even more fundamental "discontinuity" with the other faculties. Kuehn touches on these matters, but only indirectly, when he says that at this time morality, supposedly, became objective for Kant just as "space (and time) became subjective," that is, transcendentally ideal (Kuehn 1995, p. 374).[48] On the interpretation I have been proposing, however, instead of speaking of morality as ever "becoming" objective for Kant, one should say simply that, with the doctrine of the transcendental ideality of space and time, Kant finally found a new and essential way (supposedly) for morality to *remain* objective—and not be hostage to the external determinations of a given "nature," that is, something which is either merely empirical or dogmatic and quasi-theological.

In particular, with—and only with—the doctrine of the transcendental ideality of spatio-temporal nature, Kant was finally in a position to allow the transcendental freedom and uncaused causality that, since

---

47   See the helpful discussion of Kant and Mendelssohn at Kuehn 1995, p. 380.
48   Kuehn is citing Kant, "Reflexionen," 6353 (18:679).

the early 1760s, he had believed essential to a moral will.[49] Although the doctrine of transcendental idealism does not assert that moral talk about "oughts" can be grounded in a strict proof of our absolute freedom, it does allow us to say something crucial in defense of what Kant takes to be the most important actual feature of ourselves. Once accepted, this doctrine (and, Kant believes, only this doctrine) makes it rationally permissible for us to hold the basic belief that we are absolutely free agents, and that the mere regularities of natural laws need not, for all we can know, count against taking the "oughts" of morality to be genuine categorical imperatives. We no longer need to worry that our actions, and especially our moral volitions, have to be conceived as mere effects of nature (even of a nature that might somehow arrange for us always to attain the pleasures of getting what we want).[50] In other words, only after discovering transcendental idealism could Kant defend the phenomenon of a pure interest in morality in a way that allows us to hold to what he called its crucial sublimity, involving, all at once, its strong objectivity, freedom, and "heavenly origin" (Kuehn 1995, p. 384)[51]

The Faculty of Desire

To understand Kant's position fully, it is essential to move beyond the mere twofold contrast of sense and reason, and to realize that Kant always works with a threefold account of the faculties. In addition to sensibility and understanding (broadly conceived so as to include "reason"), Kant holds that there is an irreducible faculty of will. Because of the tradition that he inherited, he calls this the "faculty of desire" (*Begehrungsvermögen*). Unlike the typical English understanding of "desire," however, Kant's term leaves open the question of whether this distinctively practical faculty is determined by sense, or whether it might work in a pure practical way not originally influenced by sense.[52]

Kant understands sense, reason, and will (using all these terms again in a broad sense) as, in turn, increasingly complex basic faculties that need to be kept distinct although they are closely related to each other in a number of different ways. "Sense" and "reason" can each be

---

49 These points are the ones cited at R 6353, and they correspond to what is already in "Moral Herder" (27:4): "but morally free actions have a goodness which is assessed, not by the effect, but by the (free) intent."

50 This is true, for example, even if these effects are perceived not merely by sense but intellectually as "perfectly" suited to satisfy our talents. See 5:39f.

51 Kuehn is citing "Reflexionen," 6618 (19:111).

52 Kant defines it simply as a faculty of being a cause through representations. See 5:9n.

understood, for example, either as terms for ways of experiencing something or as shorthand for particular kinds of content that are objects of experience. Hence there are, from the start, at least four different ways that sense and reason might relate to each other morally. One could believe that sensory feeling, as an experiential activity, is what discloses either sensory or rational contents as morally overriding. Or, one could hold that it is intellectual activity that discloses either sensory or rational contents as most important. This is why, for example, Kant can discuss even intellectual perfectionist theories as still oriented toward sensory expectations.[53] One might "feel" that an intellectual life will be most satisfying, or one might instead move through use of the intellect to believe that certain sensory satisfactions would be most satisfying. (Moreover, sensing and reasoning activities can each occur not only as crucial ways of coming to believe that something is valuable but also as incidental background causes and effects of such beliefs.)

Without getting into the complexities of Kant's mature theory and the crucial third faculty of will that he is especially concerned with, it should be clear that Kant can allow a very significant role to sense (broadly speaking) throughout practical life, even for agents who are oriented primarily by the relatively objective and intellectual attitude advocated by the Stoics and Wolff.[54] That is, Kant too can allow that various intense sensory features may be constantly present in the experiences that lead us to, issue from, and define a large part of the "perfections" enjoyed even in such a moral life. The important point is that all these sensory factors are conceived as at least implicitly "incorporated" in and filtered through an intellectual component, and it is only this filtering that Kant regards as able to guarantee the kind of *necessary* objectivity that he takes to be crucial, and that mere "subjective" forces such as education or moral feeling alone cannot provide.

In general, Kant treats reason as a higher faculty that can build on but also must go beyond mere sense. Recall that in the first *Critique*, one of Kant's main points is that even if, because of the pure sensible forms of space and time, there are elements of cognition that are strictly speaking not intellectual, still nothing from sensibility can amount to a proper cognitive act without the judgment of the intellect. The relationship of these faculties is therefore not entirely symmetric because intellectual activities, such as the cognitions of a pure intellect unlike ours, could take place without any sensing at all. Kant holds a similarly asymmetric and broadly rationalist view in the practical sphere. With-

---

53 See e.g., 5:41.
54 See e.g., 5:40f.

out some formative intellectual activity, the givens of sense do not even amount to practical principles that can be discussed, evaluated, and acted upon. Moreover, given what Kant holds throughout his philosophy about the intelligibility of a completely pure notion of moral law and its relation to a possible divine being, it is clear that he also believes that in principle there is a way that a being could be properly practical without any sensory experiences or contents. This is simply to acknowledge Kant's oft-repeated point that the moral law, as the fundamental practical principle, must be formulated in general, rational terms—e.g., the principle of respecting rational beings as such—that do not *necessarily* involve any sensible conditions and hence a constraining imperatival form.

Despite this general primacy of reason over sense in Kant's theoretical and practical philosophy, it is also true that when he focuses on the human situation, he stresses that human beings, unlike pure intellects, always require sensory as well as rational contents for practical as well as theoretical life. To understand Kant's position here on the complex nature of human practical life, it might help to recall that, despite his criticisms, Kant follows his predecessor Baumgarten in three crucial respects.[55] First, they both discuss our moral life entirely under the heading of pure obligation; second, they call the moral imperatives that humans need to follow "necessitating,"[56] which means not only that they are necessarily proper (unlike contingent human laws) but also that they involve an element of constraint (because human beings have a sensory faculty that does not of itself line up with morality); and third, they hold that the feature of sensory happiness is not absolutely fundamental to moral life as such but should be considered in relation to what human beings (precisely as creatures "of need") may need to expect from more powerful forces, such as a divine being. There are, of course, various specific ways in which Baumgarten, in his account of our knowledge of divine beneficence, is much more "dogmatically" teleological and theological than Kant. Despite these differences, though, the points of similarity are enough to explain Kant's constant choice of Baumgarten's texts for his ethics lectures.

Kant's theory of the will inherits all these complexities. Kant does not understand the will as a free-floating and whimsical capacity for choice or as an inevitable putting-into-action of what has been disclosed by either sense or intellect. For him, will is practical reason, which is to say that it always incorporates practical principles. And yet, will goes beyond mere intellect by always involving, as the very word

---

55   See Schwaiger 2009.
56   See e.g., Kant 2004, p. 29.

for it in Kant's faculty theory indicates, some element of "desire," something conative and not simply cognitive. This element of "desire" is understood very generally, and need not involve either a mere feeling of pleasure, or a principle oriented toward this feeling. For, without a basis in any antecedent feeling, the will can on its own decide to actualize what is lawful, and this in turn can generate the peculiar, non-empirically originated, pure moral feeling that Kant eventually calls "respect".

This point is relevant to properly understanding why Kant says that pure moral reason's thought of duty can determine us "immediately" as a "sufficient" incentive for the will.[57] In saying this, he means that the will is in this case not dependent on, or "mediated by," a *prior* desire; this, however, still allows Kant to hold that, even when our will is moral, it in fact always operates in us alongside a desire in the sense of at least some feeling immediately consequent upon choice. The role of respect as pure moral feeling is precisely to provide an appropriate qualitative factor, between the proper orientation of the will in itself, and its eventual upshot in action, so that Kant can say that his theory, despite its purism, is consistent with the phenomenological fact of the constant presence of feeling in all human action, even of the most noble kind.[58]

Retrospect: reason and sense in a realistic morality

In general, Kant's mature theory exhibits the structure of a realistic rationalism that acknowledges a constant but secondary and supplementary role for sense in all four of its basic aspects: in its account of the *possibility*, *content*, *motivation*, and *authority* of pure moral reason. The role of sense with respect to the issue of possibility has already been reviewed. For Kant, a proper human action requires not only the ultimate and non-empirical feature of an agent's uncaused causing but also the penultimate and phenomenological feature of a pure moral feeling that is caused by the proper orientation of a free will in a sensible being and that in turn precedes the appropriate empirical effort and action of the agent.

With respect to content, sense again plays an ineliminable but secondary role in Kant's theory of human morality. Kant does not deny

---

57 See e.g., 5:71.

58 This point can meet the worry that Kant's later notion of the categorical imperative and its role in motivation somehow is incompatible with the empirical or "phenomenological" remarks of the ethics lectures. See Kuehn 2004, p. 34, and cf. Ameriks 2006, ch. 4.

that a human being, as sensible, must always have some particular, sensible ends as well as the general end of happiness. His theory of moral law and obligation simply requires that our constant interest in happiness should never take precedence over respect for law as such. Kant even stresses that as long as agents restrict themselves to an interest in happiness proportional to what is deserved, they ought to pursue such happiness under the heading of the highest good. And since, according to Kant, the conditions of the realization of this good require us to posit the assistance of a being that has the traditional powers of a divine person, reason itself brings us to postulate such a being. However one may assess the validity of Kant's argument, it clearly is one more instance of Kant's search for a realistic morality that satisfies reason and sense together but respects the ultimacy of reason.

Thirdly, with respect to motivation, the presence of sense is all the more obvious, for the "inert" quality of moral reason by itself is one of the most frequent points that Kant discusses.[59] Matters here would be relatively simple if only Kant's theory of moral motivation could be explained merely in terms of the features of respect that have already been discussed. In some places, however, Kant's early lectures seem to suggest the suspicious, heteronomous doctrine that (as in Baumgarten) belief in God, and in his power to reward us, can be, or even must be, called upon to supplement the mere thought of duty in order to get us to carry out our obligations. It is passages allegedly to this effect from the Kaehler lectures that are the main source of Kuehn's argument that the pre-1780s Kant may have had a more "realistic" and properly "anthropological" motivational theory, one that, unlike what is found in the period of the *Critiques*, at least does not require human beings to act in ways that go fully beyond their sensory interests—although, ironically, it still could require, for self-serving reasons, that human beings be religious in a sense, that is, act out of fear of and devotion to divinity (Kuehn 2004, p. xxv). This is a very striking hypothesis because, among other things, it implies that right after—on Kuehn's own earlier account—having "made" morality "objective," Kant was retreating (in the mid 1770s) to base it on considerations that appear to make our concern for it less than necessary—indeed, on considerations that appear even more "heteronomous" than the perfectionist notions of 1770 or earlier.

Given these serious difficulties, I prefer to conclude that Kant's point here—as also much earlier in his career—is not that the thought of God (as the "enforcer" of the highest good) is meant oddly and improperly to substitute for the thought of duty in the direct course of our

59   See e.g., the Kaehler lectures' discussion of the "philosopher's stone," Kant 2004, p. 69.

moral motivation. Rather, Kant's point is the much less subversive one that the idea of God—and religion in general—might be used as a proper, indirect device to keep human beings who already have moral motivation from losing that motivation in the context of extremely difficult circumstances, including an understandable inability to imagine how else moral effort might really lead to a better world.[60]

Finally, with regard to the authority of morality, there is a way in which "sense" might be said to play a key, secondary role here as well, although only in a very extended sense. Consider Kant's late doctrine that for us it is ultimately a "fact of reason" (5:42)[61] or, more precisely, of pure practical reason, that the moral law holds. This doctrine clearly is not meant by Kant to be a move back to an empiricist or even dogmatic rationalist notion that we have some kind of sensible or intellectual intuition of the moral law, in a way that would remove all theoretical doubts about the absolute freedom that is its precondition.[62] Kant is simply stressing that our acceptance of (or "within") the "fact of reason" is a "fact" in that it is something that we actually take to be true in a way that is fundamentally "reasonable" but does not rest on a full and incontrovertible deduction. At this point, though, it would be very improper to say that Kant means that we know the truth of the law, that is, that pure practical reason is valid, just on the basis of some sense or feeling—even if that feeling is called "pure." This would be very misleading because, among other things, to the extent that the proper feeling is there, it is there (according to his theory of respect) only because of something more basic, namely one's free, rational, and non-sensory choice.[63] Nonetheless, insofar as the acceptance of morality on our part as sensible and willing beings brings with it factors that go beyond our mere intellectual nature, it is also understandable to say that, for Kant, as a fact of psychology, the experience of the authority of morality is not simply a matter of reason. So—in that extended sense—it could be said to be a matter of sense as well.

---

60 This notion is developed repeatedly in his late discussions of the postulates of pure practical reason, but it is also already anticipated in "Moral Herder" (27:19-25), and in a passage in the "Notes," which speaks of religion as needed to counteract situations of "great temptation," "injustices," and "compulsion" (Rischmüller, p. 22). As an analogy, consider how it is quite proper for mathematicians to seek a supportive environment in order to keep the "noise" of the outer world from disrupting their pure calculations—or even from thinking that such mere reflection is "pointless."

61 Cf. Ameriks 2003, Part II.

62 On Kant's relation to contemporary "intuitionism," see Audi 2001.

63 Degrees of this "acceptance" can be distinguished, since Kant believes that all human beings grant the validity of the law in some way, for no one has a devilish will.

Conclusion

In all four basic ways—with regard to possibility, content, motivation, and authority—Kant's account of morality was always concerned, not simply with expressing what ought to be, but also with explaining how morality fits the actual condition of human beings as sensible as well as reasonable creatures.

It should not be surprising, therefore, that the concerns of reality and religion overlap for him in each of these four moments, even if in quite different ways. First, the argument that morality is even possible—which must, of course, be the first step in any defense of its reality—requires, in Kant's view, transcendental considerations that—even if they do not directly establish God's existence or the value of religion—certainly lay out the fundamental preconditions for taking such matters seriously. Second, another Kantian way of addressing the "reality" of something is to fill out the full content of its notion, and here too there is an undeniable connection with religion. Without claiming that the existence of God must be known in order for us to know what the moral law is, Kant subscribes to the traditional view that there is a common moral law for divine and human rational agents, and that the notion of a perfectly rational being provides us with an essential standard. In rejecting what he calls "theological moralists," Kant is merely rejecting those who understand morality in terms of the "perfections" of a divine will that acts, on his description, in ways that aim *simply* at "power and vengefulness" (4:443)[64]

Third (to skip ahead to the topic of authority), it should be clear that, until Kant provides his account of the authority of morality, he has not addressed what for many of us is the most fundamental worry about morality's "reality." Even if we know what morality is meant to be, and what kind of agency and psychology it would have to involve, it can all seem idle until we understand why or how it can rationally be taken to be legitimate. It is true that Kant's basic account of our acceptance of moral authority does not directly invoke the thought of God (in part because he wants an ethical theory on which moral commands cannot be escaped by those who might, understandably, claim a lack of religious education). Nonetheless, precisely because even Kant's most persuasive grounds for holding to the authority of morality never claim to silence adamant skeptics, and because he also stresses that serious commitment to a moral life naturally brings along with it increasing worries about its historical pointlessness, it should not be surprising that

---

64   Cf. already "Moral Herder," 27:10.

Kant thinks an adequate treatment of the relevant authority of morality will need to face other issues as well, in particular the fourth and final fundamental issue of a realistic account of sustaining motivation. Kant repeatedly ties the "real relevance" of morality to its implications for how we can find rational motives to *persist* in a moral life without ignoring our inevitable concern with the general satisfaction of human nature as sensible. Precisely because Kant "realistically" does not assume that this sensible nature is antecedently disposed toward persistence in a moral direction, he is understandably concerned with religious responses to the problem of motivation that at least face up to its full difficulty, given our "crooked" and seemingly desperate situation. In other words, precisely because of the principle—which Kant stated in his earliest lecture announcement—that what we ought to be concerned with should not go beyond what, given our nature, we can *actually* be expected to stay committed to, Kant's religion can be understood as at root neither a form of otherworldly escapism, nor an inconsistent flirtation with ethical empiricism (i.e., an attempt to "curry favor" with a divine tyrant). Rather, it is based on distinctive, long-term, and genuinely "realistic" considerations (which, of course, may or may not be accurate) about the human condition, considerations rooted in an overall rationalist moral perspective.

I have not attempted to reconstruct, let alone evaluate or endorse, Kant's main argument that hope in divine assistance is the *only* way for us to proceed rationally, given the challenges of human moral life.[65] My aim has been to indicate reasons why a study of the development of Kant's thought does not force us to suppose that his ruminations on these topics, from the 1760s through the 1780s, are inconsistent or ever radically dogmatic or empiricist to the degree that some of the best Kant scholars appear to suggest. To the extent that there were basic changes in his thought, it can still be held that they came only from the theoretical innovations that marked his Critical turn, and that the maturation of his practical philosophy was dependent on what he understandably took to be a realistic appropriation of these innovations.

---

65 See especially Hare 1996, as well as Wood 1970; Adams 1979; and Moore 2003. For help on these topics I am especially indebted to colleagues from Notre Dame and to audiences at Houghton, Hertfordshire, Riverside, Portland, Spokane, and Salem.

CHAPTER 2

Moral Imperfection and Moral Phenomenology in Kant

Benjamin Lipscomb

In an essay largely hostile to Kant, Iris Murdoch remarks: "contemporary moral philosophy appears both unambitious and optimistic.... Such
attitudes contrast with the vanishing images of Christian theology
which represented goodness as almost impossibly difficult, and sin as
almost insuperable and certainly as a universal condition" (Murdoch
1970, p. 50-1). She quotes approvingly from Kierkegaard's *Fear and
Trembling*: "an ethic which ignores sin is an altogether useless science"
(*Ibid.*, p. 47). The point of ethics, she and Kierkegaard concur, is the
realization of goodness through a particular kind of life. If human beings are in various ways resistant to adopting this kind of life and an
ethical theory takes no notice of this fact, it will fail in its aim and de-
volve into, as Kierkegaard puts it, "a queer comedy" (Kierkegaard
1954, p. 108).

Murdoch regards it as obvious that we are resistant to living as we
ought. Whatever Freud's faults, she tells us,

> he presents us with a realistic and detailed picture of the fallen man.... He sees
> the psyche as an egocentric system of quasi-mechanical energy, largely deter-
> mined by its own individual history, whose natural attachments are sexual,
> ambiguous, and hard for the subject to understand or control. Introspection re-
> veals only the deep tissue of ambivalent motive, and fantasy is a stronger force
> than reason. Objectivity and unselfishness are not natural to human beings
> (Murdoch 1970, p. 51).

The conclusion philosophers should draw from Freudian and post-
Freudian psychology, Murdoch says, is that "in the moral life, the enemy is the fat relentless ego. Moral philosophy is properly...the discussion of this ego and of the techniques (if any) for its defeat" (*Ibid.*, p.
52). And, she adds, "neither the inspiring ideas of freedom, sincerity
and fiats of will, nor the plain wholesome concept of a rational dis-
cernment of duty, seem complex enough to do justice to what we really
are" (*Ibid.*, p. 54). The contrary view she attributes to the same contem-

porary moral philosophers she criticized in the quote with which I opened this section. The views of these philosophers she calls the "last dry distilment of Kant's views of the world" (*Ibid.*, p. 48).

A number of contemporary Kant scholars have objected to Murdoch's interpretation of the practical philosophy, which was as much indebted to an interpretation of Kant's ethics that dominated mid-century Anglo-American moral philosophy (an interpretation most fully developed by R.M. Hare) as to Kant himself.[1] What these critics have not pointed out is the extent to which Murdoch's view of the moral life is shared by Kant. For with the possible exception of the remark about the adequacy (practical as well as theoretical, we may assume) of a moral psychology centered on notions of freedom, reason, conscientiousness, and efforts of will, and with some (only slight) qualifications of the long passage characterizing human psychology from a post-Freudian perspective, Kant would have concurred in all the substantive claims quoted above. To see this is, moreover, to see a great deal about the structure and impetus of Kant's practical philosophy.

Let us begin by itemizing Murdoch's substantive claims about the moral life, to get a sense of the agreement I am claiming exists between Kant and Murdoch: Murdoch maintains that (1) the achievement of genuine goodness is almost impossibly difficult, because or insofar as (2) sinfulness is a universal condition among human beings, so far as we can see inextirpable within this life; (3) this sinfulness consists in an egoism that resists all attempts on the part of the individual to realize goodness in his or her life; (4) it is characteristic of sinful humans not only to prioritize their own gratification, but also to be opaque to themselves; (5) the point of an ethical code is the realization of goodness in human lives, both individually and collectively—the end is thus to improve our resistance to the wiles of sin; and, finally, (6) freedom, sincerity, force of will, and rational apprehension of duty are one and all inadequate as a theoretical basis for understanding and overcoming "the fat, relentless ego." To reiterate, I believe Kant agrees entirely with (1) through (5).[2] I have phrased each point in such a way as to highlight the

---

1   See O'Neill 1989, pp. 75-7. Allen Wood quotes O'Neill approvingly, and expands upon her critique, in Wood 1999 (pp. 373-4).

2   Someone might object (some *have* objected): are Murdoch's terms, "sin" and "sinfulness," appropriate in a discussion of Kant? Outside the *Religion*, these are not Kant's terms. Doesn't it court confusion to bring them into a discussion of Kant? Up to a point, I concur. Thus for the most part, I will use (and analyze) the subtle and shifting vocabulary with which Kant taxonomizes moral weakness, moral corruption, and the acts and patterns of action that characteristically emerge from such weakness and corruption. Nonetheless, I will occasionally, in a context like the above, allow myself the language of "sin" and "sinfulness." Why? Not only do these terms help one translate Kant's thought into Murdoch's terms and recognize the affinities between them; they supply

agreement, and have incorporated into the summary the minor qualifications I said would be necessary; but I do not think the itemized summary differs substantively, by addition or subtraction, from Murdoch's remarks. (6), as I said, may mark a point of disagreement.[3] In any event, Kant and Murdoch have interestingly different things to say about the matter—though it is beyond the scope of this essay to discuss the differences.

The significance of the agreement between Murdoch and Kant lies in the entry it gives us into Kant's understanding of the moral life. There are a number of familiar "skeleton keys" to Kant's ethical writings, concepts recommended by interpreters (and pressed into service by teachers of introductory courses) as opening the whole of the practical philosophy: universalization tests, the first-personal perspective, exceptionless duties, legislating for oneself. Without arguing that any of these other, more familiar interpretive keys is *not* helpful, I wish to propose that Kant's views on what Murdoch calls "sin," and Kant's moral phenomenology in general, are even more helpful for understanding his Critical moral philosophy, and how it fits into his Critical philosophy as a whole.

This can only be shown by example. The bulk of this essay, then, will consist of interpretations of central texts of the Critical period, highlighting how human moral imperfection and its attendant phenomenology (as Kant conceives these) comprehensively set the terms for Kant's mature practical philosophy. Along the way, we will have opportunity to explore the crucial Kantian notion of respect, the bridge between the noumenal self and its phenomenal experience, and to ask some questions about the possibility of moral purity—questions occasioned by Kant's moral phenomenology, which he nevertheless does not answer as clearly and satisfactorily as we might like.

---

covering terms for an aspect of our moral psychology that Kant regards—throughout his Critical corpus—as a complex unity, but for which he lacks a covering term, until the *Religion*. What the traditional religious terminology does—for me, as for Kant in the *Religion*—is permit us to name the *unity*, the shared basis and character of the acts, patterns of action, susceptibilities, and active tendencies that attend our bondage to what Kant calls, throughout the *Religion*, "the evil principle." But "sin" and its cognates are more versatile than "the evil principle." By "sin," when I use the term, I will mean the evil principle and what proceeds from it.

3   Kant's postulation of the availability of divine assistance to human beings in their moral striving problematizes the *prima facie* disagreement between him and Murdoch on this point.

Groundwork

Kant begins *Groundwork of the Metaphysics of Morals* with an extended attempt to proceed from "ordinary rational knowledge" of morality to the beginnings of a philosophical treatment of the same (4:392).[4] His idea is to limn, briefly, the common-sense moral outlook of his day and then to argue toward some conditions of intelligibility for this common-sense outlook.[5] The moral outlook in question, though one may quibble with this or that aspect, is recognizable in our day, and is far from losing its grip on our collective imagination. It includes, notably, the following truisms: there are some practical principles that one has to follow, regardless of what one contingently wants; these principles hold for everyone alike; in passing an overall judgment on a person, it is that person's intentions, not his or her success in bringing these (good or bad) intentions to fruition, that determine an appropriate overall judgment of the person; and so on. Again, although one might quibble with specific formulations in Kant's text, this picture of common-sense morality is no idiosyncratic fancy. It has deep roots in the Western intellectual tradition, and has retained its force long past Kant's time—that force strengthened no doubt by his influence, but certainly not wholly dependent on it.

The observations Kant makes in *Groundwork* 1 are interesting ones. From the start of the book, a single theme stands out: the concept of duty as the central concept of the common-sense moral outlook. Someone recalling the famous opening words of the book, concerning the unique, unconditional value of a good will, might object to this characterization. But in the course of the opening chapter, Kant quickly shifts his attention from the concept of a good will to that of duty which, he tells us, "contains that of a good will though under certain subjective limitations and hindrances, which…bring it out by contrast and make it shine forth all the more brightly" (4:397). What are these "subjective limitations and hindrances," which combine with the concept of a good will to produce that of duty? And where does this leave the relationship between the concept of duty and that of a good will? The definition of duty Kant provides shortly afterward helps us answer these questions.

---

4   On this point, I prefer James Ellington's translation (Kant 1993) to that of the Cambridge edition (Mary Gregor's). It seems to me to produce better English, without compromising the sense of the German: *gemeinen sittlichen Vernunfterkenntnis*.

5   My interpretation here is markedly similar to the interpretation Karl Ameriks applies to all of Kant's Critical works. See Ameriks 2003 and 2005.

Kant writes, "duty is the necessity of an action out of respect for the law" (4:400).[6] Duty, we may say, is the "mustness" (whatever this consists in) of action done from respect. "Respect" is the key term in this definition for, as Kant's clarificatory remarks make clear, to understand respect is to understand both the character of its necessitation and the fact that it must be directed toward law. We can only respect, Kant says, "what is connected with [our] will merely as ground and never as effect" (4:400). A proper object of respect must not be an *object* of action, a thing to be realized or possessed. It must direct our will without being a product of that will. He seems to take this too as a matter of "ordinary rational knowledge," requiring only articulation to gain assent. He does not argue for it.

In filling the specified role, the proper object of respect "does not serve my inclination but outweighs it or at least excludes it altogether from calculations in making a choice" (4:400). "Inclination," in Kant, is a species of desire, desire specifically for the contingent ends that our sensuous nature presents to the will as possible grounds of action. Simply as ends to be realized, these are unsuited to be objects of respect. A proper object of respect would direct our will, "outweighing" our ends or (better) "excluding" them from consideration.[7] Kant asserts that such an object would be, precisely by virtue of those qualities, a law to us. If there is such a law, respect follows upon recognition of this law. And the necessity or mustness accompanying action done from respect consists in the fact that it somehow trumps or excludes our inclinations. To claim that there is such a law, and that we can act out of respect for it, is to claim that the will can be determined by "the maxim of complying with such a law even if it thwarts all [our] inclinations" (4:400-1).[8] This "thwarting" is the mustness, the necessity (the necessitation, as Kant later puts it) of duty.

6　Amending Gregor's translation slightly. She has, "...from respect for law."

7　The language of exclusion seems more faithful to the overall cast of Kant's thought. It would be peculiar to suppose that the categorical character of moral obligation consisted in its being unusually weighty vis-à-vis the inclinations, 1) because this would leave room, in principle, for the relative weighting to shift, 2) because, if we were to understand practical deliberation on an analogy with mass, or physical force, it would frequently happen that the "weightier" consideration of duty failed to tip the scales of deliberation in its favor, and 3) because any such understanding of practical deliberation would conflict with Kant's views on human freedom. Andrews Reath stresses this last point in Reath 1989. Reath also notes the preponderance of metaphors of political sovereignty and allegiance over metaphors of weight or force in Kant's discussions of respect. The most searching exploration of what it means for one rational consideration to "exclude" another is surely Raz 1975.

8　Preferring Ellington's "thwarts" to Gregor's "infringes". A literal rendering of the German would be something like: "all my inclinations meet with cancellation [*mit Abbruch aller meiner Neigungen, Folge zu leisten*]."

We may now return to the questions we left hanging, two paragraphs back. There we noted Kant's claim that the concept of duty "contains" that of a good will, only subject to "certain subjective limitations and hindrances." These subjective limitations and hindrances, we can now see, are somehow connected to the inclinations, which appeal to the will but are (rationally) excluded by the law. Respect is, or follows upon, the recognition of this relationship, and duty is the necessitation accompanying this recognition. Kant is preparing us for this picture, in fact, from the first paragraphs of his preface to the *Groundwork*, where he describes moral laws (in contrast to natural-scientific laws) as "laws in accordance with which everything ought to happen...taking into account the conditions under which it very often does not happen" (4:388). These conditions are identical with the "subjective limitations and hindrances" that, added to the concept of a good will, yield the concept of duty. Both are in turn identical with some fact or facts concerning the inclinations. To understand exactly which facts these are, we must proceed further into the *Groundwork*. But we have already learned something non-negligible: a good will manifests itself in a distinctive form—the form of duty—in the life of beings subject in some way to sensuous inclinations.

In *Groundwork* 2, Kant offers an extended account of the "necessitation" relation that holds between beings subject in certain ways to inclinations and the principles of action constitutive of a good will. This account is intended to reveal "the point where the concept of duty arises" from "the practical faculty of reason" (4:412). The best way to approach this account, I think, is to quote the core of it in full, and then to work toward a satisfactory interpretation through commentary:

> Everything in nature works in accordance with laws. Only a rational being has the capacity to act in accordance with the representation of laws, that is, in accordance with principles, or has a will. Since reason is required for the derivation of actions from laws, the will is nothing other than practical reason. If reason infallibly determines the will, the actions of such a being that are cognized as objectively necessary are also subjectively necessary, that is, the will is a capacity to choose only that which reason independently of inclination cognizes as practically necessary, that is, as good. However, if reason solely by itself does not adequately determine the will; if the will is exposed also to subjective conditions...that are not always in accord with the objective ones; in a word, if the will is not in itself completely in conformity with reason (as is actually the case with human beings), then actions that are cognized as objectively necessary are subjectively contingent, and the determination of such a will in conformity with objective laws is necessitation.... The representation of an objective principle, insofar as it is necessitating for a will, is called a command (of reason), and the formula of the command is called an imperative. All imperatives are expressed by an *ought* and indicate by this the rela-

tion of an objective law of reason to a will that by its subjective constitution is
not necessarily determined by it (a necessitation). (4:412-3)

One thing we learn, early in this passage, is what makes a will good. A
good will, unsurprisingly, is a will that chooses well, allowing reason to
determine it "infallibly." Kant sometimes seems to suggest that, in the
ideal case, a good will would not be subject to any non-rational influence. But since the concept of a good will is supposed to be (in principle) realizable in a context of subjective limitations and hindrances, it
cannot be the case that only such an imperturbable will can be good.
Nonetheless, the main theme of the passage is that, insofar as a good
will is realized in a being subject to certain kinds of non-rational influence, it exists in a different relationship to the being in question than it
would if the being were not subject to these influences—and this difference is or gives rise to a difference in experience, in phenomenal representation.

What is this difference, and what kind or kinds of non-rational influence is it based upon? We may begin an answer to these questions by
considering again the limit case. It is at least conceivable that some
rational beings could be subject to no non-rational influence. In such a
case, Kant tells us, the objectively necessary (what reason prescribes)
would also be subjectively necessary (unchallenged—because unchal-
lengeable—in its determination of the will). There would be no possibility that apprehension of what reason prescribes would not be followed by a determination to act, or even that this determination would
be experienced (if "experienced" is the word) as a setting-aside or overcoming of contrary influence. But this is not how it is with us. The human will "is not in itself completely in conformity with reason."

This means two things, Kant suggests: first, that reason is insufficient to determine the human will apart from "subjective conditions."[9]
We are not merely rational, but rather require the presence of subjective
conditions (Kant later calls them "incentives") in order to act.[10] This is
put forward as a brute fact about our agency. Second, these subjective
conditions "are not always in accord with the objective ones." That is,
we are subject to influences that are not merely non-rational, but (in full

---

9   Some will regard this claim with bemusement or shock. But it appears to be what Kant
is saying in the long passage above. Further confirmation can be derived from passages
in the second *Critique*, passages I discuss below. There, Kant argues that reason must
be or become (among other things) an incentive. Why? Precisely because the will cannot be determined without an incentive. When I take up the second *Critique*, I will deal
with the obvious objection: that our actions are said to have moral worth only if the law
of reason "determine[s] the will immediately" (5:71). Kant's solution, to this problem
as to so many others, is transcendental idealism.

10 On this necessity of our constitution, and on the attendant contrast between our agency
and God's, see 28:1066.

context) contra-rational.[11] Some of what our subjective constitution recommends to us through sensuous inclination (the standard source of our incentives) opposes the prescriptions of reason. Thus what is "objectively necessary," appears to us as "subjectively contingent," as something that need not issue in determination to act (because other determining grounds of the will are available). Moreover, a determination to act resulting (in part) from a prescription of reason can be experienced by us as a setting-aside or overcoming of contrary influence. For we are subject to such influence, in the form of contra-rational inclinations.

The determination by reason of wills like ours, Kant says, is "necessitation." This term indicates a relation of "constraint" between the prescriptions of reason and the will.[12] A "perfectly good" will would be frictionlessly directed by reason (4:414). There would be no resistance on its part to the prescriptions of reason, and hence no constraint on reason's part of unruly tendencies in the will. It goes without saying, then, that no constraint would be apprehended by such a will. The human will, by contrast, is not perfectly good, and thus apprehends the voice of reason within as constraint, obligation, duty.

These are just a handful of the terms that Kant uses throughout his corpus to indicate the distinctive relation between the prescriptions of reason and the human will. Having indicated the character of the relation, he proceeds in the passage quoted earlier to introduce several more terms: the "representation" of a prescription of reason to a being like us, we are told, is a "command;" the "formula" of a command is an "imperative;" and an imperative is "expressed" by an "ought." Here again we may note a connection with the opening paragraphs of the preface, where Kant tells us that moral laws are those "in accordance with which everything ought to happen." "Ought" statements, Kant indicates, are just the most proximal step in the coming to expression in human deliberation of prescriptions of reason. What "ought" indicates

---

11   One of the members of a 2005 workshop at the University of Notre Dame suggested to me the term "contra-rational" as avoiding unwanted connotations of "irrational." I have forgotten who. At this point in the discussion, there is no basis for presuming either that the inclinations that in full context oppose the prescriptions of reason are contra-rational in themselves or that they are contra-rational merely in some contexts. Later, we will consider passages in the *Religion* where Kant indicates that we are subject to both kinds of contra-rational inclination. For present purposes, all that is relevant is the fact that we are subject to inclinations that oppose the prescriptions of reason.

12   This is Kant's description of the necessitation relation in the second *Critique*. See the next section for further discussion. Christine Korsgaard reflects at some length on the phenomenon in the opening chapter of Korsgaard 2009; for substantive reasons rather than exegetical ones, she resists the implication that necessitation goes hand in hand with sinfulness.

is that there are practical considerations that might conflict with our inclinations, but that have a claim on our adherence nevertheless. Reason presents itself to a will not perfectly good as, among other things, a burden or confinement.

What, then, is the relationship between a good will, duty, and inclination? Apparently this: a sense of duty is the manifestation of a good will in a being subject to contra-rational inclination. Attendant upon this manifestation is an apprehension of constraint. Duties, it seems, are principles of a good will, apprehended as constraint by a being subject to contra-rational inclination.

These reflections lead us directly (as they led Kant) to some distinctions among rational wills. For there are several ways a rational will might be related to sensuous inclinations. First, it might not be subject to any such inclinations. Second, it might be subject to inclinations that are perfectly conformed to reason, though they are not acts of reason. Finally, it might be subject to contra-rational inclinations. Kant designates the first kind of will "holy," the second "pure," and the third (by contrast with the second) "impure."[13] Human beings can presumably aspire to purity of will, though not holiness. We are creatures of need, and Kant explicitly links need with inclination, the latter being an expression of the former.

Kant says a number of things about holy wills, immediately after the long passage quoted above. Holy wills conform perfectly to the prescriptions of practical reason, but they do not apprehend themselves as constrained, because there is no conceivable tension between any aspect of their subjective constitution and what practical reason prescribes. Under these conditions, several features of our moral phenomenology drop out. Holy wills are not necessitated, and so cannot be dutiful. "No imperatives hold," Kant explains, "for a holy will: the 'ought' is out of place here, because the 'would' is of itself necessarily in accord with the law" (4:414).[14] Holy wills, having no capacity for rebellion against the prescriptions of reason, are not subject to any ought, imperative, command, necessitation, or duty. As we will see later, they also do not respect.

Before turning to some relevant passages in the *Critique of Practical Reason*, two final observations: first, Kant does *not* think that only

---

13   I am drawing here on the *Groundwork* and on the second *Critique*. In the *Religion*, Kant uses "impurity" in a different sense, to refer to a condition in which one cannot commit to morally required actions unless they serve one's inclination (6:29-30). One of the burdens of my later discussion will be to show how Kant could condemn such "impurity" and yet insist that the will requires incentives.

14   Following Ellington in bringing forward the parallelism between "*das Sollen*" and "*das Wollen*."

those beings whose adherence to law is subjectively contingent will apprehend the prescriptions of reason as law. The category of law (unlike those of imperative, command, or duty) does not imply anything about the constitution of those it governs. Indeed, according to Kant, law applies to "everything in nature." This raises a question: if the concept of law implies nothing about the constitution of the objects it governs, what is the connection between law in general and moral law?

Kant's description of a holy will suggests an answer: to be holy is to be like nature, except free. The stars are not *constrained* by the laws of physics, because there is nothing in them to resist the law. The law describes their behavior, but does not compel them; their "behavior" (so to speak) flows from their nature. Their conformity to law does not represent a setting-aside or overcoming of anything. Now observe: this is also a description of a holy will's relationship to the prescriptions of practical reason. A holy will, like the starry heavens above, has nothing within it to resist the law. The law describes its behavior, but does not compel it; its behavior flows from its nature.[15] Its conformity to law does not represent a setting-aside or overcoming of anything. As Kant says, "the 'ought' is out of place here, because the 'would' is of itself necessarily in accord with the law."

Bearing these points in mind, one can see comparisons between a holy will and unfree nature throughout Kant's Critical corpus. Consider again the opening paragraphs of the preface to the *Groundwork*, where Kant contrasts "the laws in accordance with which everything happens" with "the laws in accordance with which everything ought to happen..." (4:388). If a holy will is law-governed, but no "ought" applies to it, then holiness is a subjective condition in which one comes to relate to the prescriptions of practical reason as if they were the laws of physics and as if one were the Ring Nebula. Or, as I put it earlier, holiness is being like nature. This point, it seems to me, is too little observed in discussions of Kant's ethics.[16]

But there is a second observation to be made before we turn to the second *Critique*, one that complicates the picture we have been developing. We have so far discussed only holiness and the found human condition. But there is at least one intermediate possibility: purity. In

---

15 On the link between even a merely dutiful will—let alone a holy one—and its nature *qua* will, see Kain 2004.

16 Consider also, in this connection, the short section in the Analytic of the second *Critique* on "the typic of pure practical judgment" (5:67-71), the burden of which is to convince the reader that natural (scientific) law is something like a schema (a "type") for human moral judgment. This discussion would seem to justify a prominence for the *Groundwork*'s "formula of the law of nature" that one rarely sees it accorded.

describing the qualities of the human will that place it in a relation of necessitation to the prescriptions of practical reason, Kant identifies two features of our constitution: first, the fact that reason requires incentives in order to determine the will; and second, the fact that some of our incentives are not merely non-rational, but contra-rational. There is, however, no reason to presuppose that a human being couldn't (in principle) be characterized by the first quality, but not the second. In the second *Critique*, Kant gives us a name for this condition: purity. The possibility of purity is the possibility that a being requiring incentives to determine its will might nevertheless have no contra-rational incentives—that one might be a dependent creature and therefore subject to sensuous inclinations, and yet experience no tension between these inclinations and the prescriptions of practical reason.

The thing is possible. But what would be the proper account of such a being's subjective relationship to the prescriptions of practical reason? Two incompatible arguments can be constructed, based on two divergent understandings of the notion of possible resistance to the prescriptions of practical reason. One could note, on the one hand, that a pure will requires for its determination incentives, standardly rooted in non-rational inclination. Since our incentives are standardly rooted in non-rational inclination, they would be capable, in principle, of conflicting with the prescriptions of reason. They are a potentially competing source of motivation, without which the will cannot be determined. So a pure will could be understood as having within it an inextirpable capacity for resistance to reason, in the form of a heterogeneous source of motivation. Multiple, independent sources of motivation cannot be guaranteed *a priori* not to conflict, and apprehension of this fact by a pure will would manifest itself as apprehension of the prescriptions of reason as commands, imperatives, oughts.

There are passages suggesting that this is Kant's view of things. In discussing beings for whom "the 'ought' is out of place," Kant mentions only "the divine will and in general…a holy will" (4:414). And later in the *Groundwork*, when discussing God's place in the kingdom of ends, he suggests that creaturely dependence is sufficient to place one in a relation of necessitation to the prescriptions of reason:

> if maxims are not already of their nature in agreement with [the] objective principle…the necessity of an action in accordance with this principle is called practical necessitation, that is, duty. Duty does not apply to the sovereign in the kingdom of ends, but it does apply to every member…." (4:434)

Nevertheless, as I said, an alternative can be argued. This alternative would stress that the incentives of a pure will, by hypothesis, do not compete with or resist the prescriptions of reason. And such competition is the theoretical basis for distinguishing between the phenomenology associated with holy and impure wills, respectively. In developing his account of necessitation, Kant finds it necessary to introduce both the insufficiency of reason-absent-incentives to determine the human will, and the impurity of the human will. The latter condition he contrasts with the state of being "thoroughly good" or "perfectly good."

Nothing follows, then, about the phenomenology of a pure will, merely from the insufficiency of reason-absent-incentives to determine the human will. At the least, it would seem that a pure will, unlike an impure will, should not experience the prescriptions of practical reason as a burden or a confinement. If the condition of a pure will is not the same as that of a holy will, it is nevertheless crucially different from that of an impure will. Purity is, presumably, not an accident. And it would seem, in light of *Groundwork* 2, that this non-accidental fact could have phenomenological consequences.

Someone might regard such arguments as decisively rebutted, though, by the very passage in the second *Critique* where Kant introduces the notion of a pure will. For humans, he writes,

> the law has the form of an imperative, because in them, as rational beings, one can presuppose a pure will but, insofar as they are beings affected by needs and sensible motives, not a holy will, that is, such a will as would not be capable of any maxim conflicting with the moral law. …the relation of such a will to this law is dependence under the name of obligation, which signifies a necessitation. (5:32)

But we should not leap too quickly to conclusions. For the passage continues, "a choice that is pathologically affected…brings with it a wish arising from subjective causes, because of which it can often be opposed to the pure objective determining ground…" (*Ibid.*). Often, perhaps, but not, by hypothesis, in the case of a pure will. If there is such a thing as a pure will, this line of reasoning has no bearing on it.

Proceeding further in the same passage: after sketching again the notion of a holy will as elevated "not indeed above all practical laws, but rather above all practically restrictive laws and so above obligation and duty," Kant claims that holiness is "a practical idea, which must necessarily serve as a model to which all finite rational beings can only approximate without end…" (*Ibid.*). Kant cannot mean that we must take as a model the absence of inclination, for inclination goes with our nature. However desirable the condition might be, it is not ours. We cannot even work toward transcending "practically restrictive laws" unless this is (at least) an asymptotically approximable condition, something not ruled out by the kind of creatures we are, at our theoretical best. And even if we can only ever get close and progressively closer, mightn't that too have phenomenological consequences?

For now, let us set this puzzle aside and turn to another set of passages in the second *Critique* and, then, to the opening book of *Religion
within the Boundaries of Mere Reason*. A deeper understanding of these
texts will enable us—I think—to locate a kernel of truth in each of the
above arguments—that we should and that we shouldn't credit the possibility of purity and of a distinct phenomenology to match.

Critique

The parts of the second *Critique* of greatest interest for my purposes are
the third chapter of the Analytic, on "the incentives of pure practical
reason," and the discussion of immortality in the Dialectic. What these
texts provide is a fuller picture of the relation between the impure human will and the moral law, a picture that (when elaborated with the aid
of the *Religion*) can teach us a great deal that we could not have learned
from the *Groundwork* about the possibility and character of a pure will,
and about the moral phenomenology characteristic—even definitive—
of such a will.

    Chapter three of the Analytic takes its point of departure from a
puzzle about the account of motivation we encountered in the *Groundwork*. The puzzle is as follows: in the *Groundwork*, Kant tells us that
we ought to act "from duty" or "for the sake of duty"; in the second
Critique, he makes the point even more explicit ("what is essential to
any moral worth of actions is that the moral law determine the will
immediately" (5:71)). But he also tells us that reason, which teaches us
our duty, is insufficient to determine the human will without the cooperation of "subjective conditions" of a sensuous character, called "incentives." How then can the law of reason determine the human will
"directly," as it "ought" to do?

    It can do so, Kant explains, by becoming an incentive itself. The
name for this special incentive, which is supposed to be both identical
with the law of reason and yet sensuous in character, is "respect". To
show how respect can satisfy both of the above conditions, Kant resorts
to what we could call a phenomenological narrative. He cannot, he
admits, explain how reason can directly determine the will, simply by
presenting it with a law. Kant says that to explain this would be to explain how freedom works, which is impossible. We are here beyond the
speculative powers of human reason. But just as, in the *Critique of Pure
Reason*, Kant was able to dispel the air of paradox surrounding the notion of free causality by invoking the noumenal/phenomenal distinction,
so too he can dispel the air of paradox surrounding the "fact of reason,"

and show how it could manifest itself as something sensuous, by distinguishing between the inexplicable thing-in-itself and the appearance of
that thing in human experience.[17] He does this, as I said, through a phenomenological narrative.

Suppose then that reason does directly determine the will by presenting it with a law. How could that fact generate a feeling? The key to
Kant's response lies in this thought: if something squelches feeling, it
generates further feeling, even if what does the squelching is not itself
feeling.[18] Everyday examples of the phenomenon are not hard to come
by. Suppose I tell a student that he may not make up an examination on
which he has done badly. He will be frustrated, perhaps bitter. He came
to see me, we may suppose, with multiple desires and emotions. But
bitterness was not among them, not at first. What I articulate to him—
the words, or the quasi-legal reality they represent—is not itself feeling.
But because the words, or the reality they represent, dash his hopes,
they will have a felt force for him. They will generate a feeling simply
because they have a "negative effect on feeling."

This thought is at the heart of Kant's account of respect. When reason presents us with its law—however this happens—it strikes down
our "self-conceit." It squelches desires that are, in context, wicked, by
condemning a particular (wicked) way of relating to our desires. And
this "negative effect on feeling...is itself feeling" (5:73). We experience this condemnation of our inclinations as a negative sensation.

In order to adequately understand this account, we must clarify one
of its central terms: self-conceit. In the *Groundwork*, we encounter two
senses of the self-centeredness of human inclination—one pejorative,
the other a conceptual necessity. We will not fully understand the relationship between them until we turn to the *Religion*, but it is possible
already to distinguish them. Human inclination is self-centered as a
matter of conceptual necessity in that inclination expresses a want.
These wants are, of course, wants of the self, the subject. Inclinations
just are desires for ends, and inasmuch as these ends are our ends
(whatever else they may be), with our satisfaction riding on them, they
are self-centered. None of this, however, should be taken pejoratively.

---

17 For an account with similarities to my own, see Guevara 2000. Guevara too interprets
    Kant as claiming that all human willing involves incentives. And he too appeals to
    transcendental idealism to show Kant's account self-consistent.
18 What do I mean by the squelching of a feeling? A feeling is not squelched simply by
    being made to go away, like a headache. Feeling is squelched when it is successfully
    opposed, in such a way that the subject is (at some level) aware of the opposition. But
    this is not enough. The one whose feeling is squelched must not only be aware that his
    or her feeling is being successfully opposed; he or she must (at some level) identify
    with the feeling in question.

This is simply part of what it means to be a dependent being. And even if there is no such thing as a fulfilled desire that is not (among other things) a satisfaction to the person whose desire it was, desires can still be for objectively worthwhile ends.

There is, however, a further kind of self-centeredness. Its possibility is implicit in the remarks that seem to rule out close comparisons between the phenomenology of a pure will and that of a holy will. Because humans have heterogeneous sources of motivation—non-rational, (necessarily) self-centered inclination on the one hand and the prescriptions of practical reason on the other—we can be (and frequently are) put in the position of choosing between these motivations. And, without yet going into the causes of this, Kant believes humans universally and consistently privilege the demands of inclination over the demands of reason. Our inclinations are frequently contra-rational. And we opt to satisfy them even in these cases. In fact, we make a principle of it, whether or not we ever articulate that principle clearly to ourselves. This elevation of private preference over the precepts of practical reason Kant calls "self-conceit."[19]

This vicious self-centeredness is what is "struck down" when reason presents its law to the will. The self-conceited will, with its project of unlimited or only superficially restricted self-gratification, has its desires squelched by the law, which commands principled self-sacrifice, and which manifests its authority by exhibiting a connection between such behavior and moral worth.

The result of this confrontation is what Kant calls "humiliation." Our desires are opposed by the law. Moreover, the idea of ourselves that accompanies self-conceit—the idea that we *deserve* to have our preferences trump other considerations—is contradicted and condemned. At the same time, the manifest authority of the law forces us to concur in the verdict implicit in this opposition, contradiction, and condemnation. Because what is squelched is sensuous, so also is the experience of its being squelched. So in apprehending reason's law, we feel a species of pain, an initially simple frustration colored bitter and shameful by the fact that we are conscious of its justice: humiliation.

---

19 In thus interpreting self-conceit, I am disagreeing with one of the few other scholarly treatments of Kantian respect, Reath 1989. Reath applies what I say about self-conceit to self-love, offering a different (and, he admits, textually underdetermined) interpretation of self-conceit in its place. The difficulty for Reath's interpretation is that the apprehension of the moral law is supposed to merely "restrict" self-love, while it "strikes down" self-conceit. But the condition of prioritizing our own satisfactions over observance of the moral law is identified (most vividly in the *Religion*) as the essence of evil. This inversion of our proper practical priorities needs to be undone, not merely restricted. See my discussion of the *Religion*, below.

Again, the phenomenon is present in everyday experience. Opposition to one's desires frequently breeds frustration, even resentment. This is made more bitter (though this can express itself in many ways—from head-hanging shame to violent anger) to the extent that one sees the opposition as justified. Think of the ways people respond to artistic or intellectual criticism, or, in some cases, to standards of excellence *per se*. Think of the ways people treat referees and umpires.

Respect is not supposed to be merely or even primarily negative, though. Apprehension of reason's law also generates a positive feeling, an awe at what has humiliated us in our own sight. This works in two distinct ways. Kant claims, first, that anything that authoritatively humiliates us calls forth a kind of awe. Whatever humiliates us, apprehended as a source of sound direction—as something to which we ought to submit—awakens a new feeling, generated like humiliation by the antecedent effect upon feeling of something that is not itself feeling. This new feeling is respect proper.[20]

Again, illustrations of this "first path to respect" are readily available. When one is conscious of someone as superior to oneself in skill or wisdom, one will, *ceteris paribus*, feel a kind of teachable awe toward that person.[21] He or she is a source of authoritative direction—not merely an impressive figure, but one to whom it is appropriate to submit. The apprehension of that person, and the guidance he or she gives, are not feelings. But because they have certain definite relations to feelings, they reliably generate feelings at second hand.

There is a second way, too, in which apprehension of reason's law generates the positive feeling of respect. The awareness of a principle within that is capable of determining the will, even in the face of contrary inclination, is a source of inspiration, of moral uplift. Awareness of the fact of reason—precisely the checking of inclination and condemnation of self-conceit we have been discussing—lessens "the hindrance to pure practical reason" on the part of inclination (5:75). One can no longer persist in the delusion that one's inclinations ought to trump other considerations, for reason—one's own reason—has spoken. And "inasmuch as it moves resistance out of the way…this removal of a hindrance is esteemed equivalent to a positive furthering of its causality," and indirectly generates a familiar feeling: respect (*Ibid.*).

---

20 As others have remarked (e.g., Beck 1960), there is a close kinship between Kant's phenomenology of moral feeling and his phenomenology of the sublime (cf. especially 5:257). Space limitations forbid that I dwell on this kinship. For a helpful treatment of the "rhetoric of the sublime" in Kant's practical works, see Zuckert 2007.

21 In the *Religion*, Kant valorizes "the apprentice's feeling for the moral good" (6:48).

It might appear that, in this case, gratitude tempered with renewed confidence would be a better description than teachable awe for the consequent feeling. But Kant thinks that these feelings are the same. Perhaps we are to regard respect as bringing together both. Inspired gratitude, like teachable awe, looks up to a superior, and in each case construes what it looks up to as an authority. The gratitude in this case is for the authoritative condemnation of one's self-conceit, and the attendant inspiration is to follow the teachings of reason. So it is not implausible to suppose that newly confident gratitude and what I am calling teachable awe are two aspects of the same feeling.

Considering again the examples raised above, they can easily be viewed in this light. To see someone as a source of authoritative direction is to experience the direction one receives as a gift and as a challenge. But that is just the feeling here described.

What we are dealing with, regardless, is the phenomenal manifestation of an inexplicable noumenal fact: the fact of reason becoming practical and determining the will, making possible genuine moral worth. Reason is mysteriously capable of determining the will, and the feeling of respect is the manifestation in experience of that direct and sufficient determination. This does not contradict what Kant says in the *Groundwork*, because it remains the case that in any instance when the will is determined, reason does not determine it without a sensuous incentive. There is always an incentive involved; only in this case, the incentive is the phenomenal manifestation of a noumenal determination. "And so," Kant writes, "respect for the law is not the incentive to morality; instead *it is morality itself subjectively considered as an incentive...*" (5:76, my emphasis). This helps resolve what would otherwise be a puzzle: the fact that Kant speaks of respect both as the consequence of resisted inclination and overthrown self-conceit and also as a motive to resist inclination and self-conceit. As the phenomenal manifestation of the noumenal fact of reason, it can be regarded either way. Subjectively considered, it is a motive helping determine the will; but it is all the same the effect on feeling of the rational self-determination of the will.

All this accords with what we learned about respect in the *Groundwork*. Respect, we saw, is a feeling generated indirectly by the apprehension of a superior source of direction. Now recall Kant's discussion in *Groundwork* 1. One cannot respect that which one cognizes as an end one might bring about or possess; one can only respect the rational determining grounds of one's will. And what one respects must trump or exclude one's inclinations. But what is thereby described is precisely a source of direction, something that directs (i.e., determines) one's (inferior) will. It cannot be cognized as an object of one's will, but must be cognized instead as standing over against one's will. How could the inferior handiwork of an inferior craftsman seem to him or her to issue authoritative guidance? How could he or she stand before it with teachable awe, or regard him- or herself as the grateful recipient of its expert advice?[22]

It is instructive to examine the well-known footnote on respect in the *Groundwork*, which I did not quote earlier. "What I cognize immediately as a law for me," Kant writes, "I cognize with respect.... Respect is properly the representation of a worth that thwarts my self-love. Hence [it] is something that is regarded as an object neither of inclination nor of fear, though it has something analogous to both" (4:401n).[23] This participation of respect, the characteristic affect of one apprehending authority, in characteristics both of fear and of desire, without reducing to either, is reminiscent of the thought of a philosopher a century before Kant, whose influence on pre-Kantian German philosophy was as significant as it is underappreciated: Samuel Pufendorf.[24] For what Kant says about respect closely resembles what Pufendorf says about the affective dimension of obligation, its "necessitation."[25] For Pufendorf, as for Kant, this affective state arises in consequence of an objective relation of justified constraint and direction.[26]

---

22 This line of argument will provoke objections. Many would regard this way of talking about moral law ("a source of direction," "standing over against one's will") as heteronomous. Aren't we supposed to give the law to ourselves? How then can it stand over against us? Doesn't autonomy mean bowing to no external authority? How then can one look "up" at moral law, as something "superior" to and in any case distinct from the self? I would reply as follows: moral law is categorical. Its demands cannot be unmade or revised by us. We nevertheless give it to ourselves, in that the demand is presented to us by our reason, with which Kant strongly identifies us. And we obey its spirit only when the determining ground of our obedience is apprehension of its rationality (as against, say, threats). Nevertheless, it would scarcely be too strong to say that *what* reason prescribes does not depend upon us, except in that its context of application is determined by our circumstances and constitution. Returning to the immediate context of this essay: it is, I think, a datum for any interpretive approach to the texts I have been discussing that we are to regard the law with humility and awe. I suggest that the reason for this humility and awe is our imperfection, however that is best characterized, relative to the standard that our reason presents to us. So we are looking at something that stands, in some sense, over against us (even as, in another sense, it *is* us), and looking— in some sense—*up* at it. Hence, "a superior source of direction," "standing over against one's will," etc. It is of course crucial to note that the self referred to here is the phenomenal self, in all its imperfection. Still, the above seems to me the most consistent reading of the relevant texts. Cf. Hare 2001, Ameriks 2003, chapter 11, and Kain 2004.
23 Substituting, as before, "thwarts" for "infringes upon."
24 On Pufendorf's influence, mediated through the tradition of eclecticism, see Hochstrasser 2000.
25 I discuss this at length in Lipscomb 2005.
26 It is seldom observed that the German word *Achtung*, standardly translated "respect," carries a connotation not captured in the English: "beware." John Hare pointed this out to me.

One could spend more time examining Kant's account of respect, but a rough outline is now before us.[27] Can we summarize what it means for the conceptual and phenomenological relation between the prescriptions of practical reason and the impure human will?

The issues Kant addresses in the texts just discussed are closely connected to the issues with which I concluded my discussion the *Groundwork*: holiness, purity, and impurity. We may observe, first, that respect is impossible for a holy will. A holy will has nothing within it requiring constraint, and certainly nothing requiring condemnation. It expresses the prescriptions of practical reason in its actions, but is not subject to any independent principle, and so cannot regard these pre-scriptions as something standing over against itself. *A fortiori* it cannot regard them as something superior to itself, to which it must turn in awe and gratitude for guidance.

But what of the impure human will? All of us possess such a will, Kant thinks, and all of us are rational creatures. Indeed, the human will is not merely impure—i.e., subject to contra-rational inclinations; it is self-conceited, privileging the satisfaction of its inclinations over other considerations. Thus when we apprehend the law, whether as a concept arising within our reason or as something embodied in the life of an-other, we will feel respect. Respect as a positive emotion is necessarily accompanied by humility—by a sense of one's inferiority and need for direction. So respect involves recognition of ourselves as inferior to the holy standard, and as needing to submit ourselves to it. So long as we are impure, that is, we will experience ourselves as appropriately sub-ject to constraint, as beings apt to direct themselves clumsily (or worse) in the absence of an authoritative word. Here the connections between respect, authority, and duty come into view.

To apprehend the law as duty is to apprehend it with respect. Kant makes this clear in a testy response to anyone who thinks the prescrip-tions of reason could manifest themselves to us in a form other than that of duty: "to fail to recognize our inferior position...and to deny from self-conceit the authority of the holy law is already to defect from it in spirit, even though the letter of the law is fulfilled" (5:82-3). In this passage, note, Kant equates our apprehension of the prescriptions of reason as authoritative, as trumping other considerations, with our re-

---

27   There is a puzzle, arising out of the foregoing texts, that I will not attempt to solve here: Kant claims, as we have seen, that respect is the manifestation of reason's directly de-termining the will. And yet various passages in the *Critique* (and various plain facts) suggest that one can feel respect and yet do wrong (see e.g. 5:79-80). Well: did reason determine the will in these cases, or didn't it? I am confident that this puzzle can be sol-ved, perhaps by saying that once one has felt respect, one always feels it a little, even in the breach. But I do not wish to defend a view on the matter here.

spect for the law. To apprehend it otherwise would be "to deny [it] respect," which Kant can only attribute to the opposite of respect, "self-conceit."

What does the second *Critique* add to our understanding of the puzzle about human purity and alternate modes of apprehension of the prescriptions of reason? If nothing else, it makes clear the grounds of Kant's refusal to conduct any thought-experiment about a pure will and its phenomenological consequences. Kant writes, "If we already knew of ourselves what it is incumbent upon us to do and, moreover, were conscious of liking to do it, a command about it would be quite unnecessary" (5:83). His opposition to conceiving the moral life in other terms than duty surfaces out of a conviction that humans can never reach the point of knowing what to do and liking to do it. "Duty and obligation are the only names that we must give to our relation to the moral law," he says (5:82).[28]

But this does not resolve the perplexity we encountered at the end of the previous section; rather, it threatens to mystify completely why Kant ever admitted that "in [humans], as rational beings, one can presuppose a pure will...." For this opinion is apparently inconsistent with the following:

> if a rational creature could ever reach the stage of thoroughly liking to fulfill all moral laws, this would mean that there would not be in him even the possibility of a desire that would provoke him to deviate from them; for, to overcome such a desire always costs the subject some sacrifice and therefore requires self-constraint, that is, inner necessitation to what one does not altogether like to do. But no creature can ever reach this stage of moral disposition. (5:83-4)

It is evident from this passage (and from other, similar passages in the vicinity) that Kant's refusal to consider a pure will and its attendant phenomenology does not emerge from a conflation of purity with holiness and the absurd thought that the aim of the moral life is to become impassible.[29] He is thinking, as one would hope, about dependent rational beings whose inclinations, whatever their initial state, have been sculpted into consistent conformity with the prescriptions of reason. He seems to deny that such a thing can be ("no creature can ever reach this stage of moral disposition"). In the absence of this alternative, the relation of duty (accompanied by the feeling of respect) must be the sole relation between finite wills like ours and the prescriptions of practical reason.

---

28 Following Beck in preferring "obligation" to Gregor's "what is owed," as a translation of "*Schuldigkeit*".

29 Though he does regard it as an agreeable fantasy. See 5:118.

Kant does, however, paint a picture of asymptotic progress toward this goal, even as he denies that this progress affects our relation to the law. Immediately preceding the extended passage above, Kant tells us that although "as an ideal of holiness it is not attainable by any creature" (here Kant seems to veer toward the absurd standard), yet it is "the archetype which we should strive to approach and resemble in an uninterrupted but endless progress" (5:83).

Kant returns to these motifs in the Dialectic, in his treatment of the first postulate (5:122-4). Here is an interpretation of what Kant says there, one that at least solves the puzzle about striving for an unattainable goal: the ideal *is* a binary quality that we lack and, in a strong sense, *cannot* attain, viz., the in-principle impossibility of conflict between our subjective constitution and the prescriptions of reason. Nevertheless, this unattainable quality, which is only possessed by—or even possible for—a holy being, is susceptible of resemblance, through progressive purification. Kant seems to understand this purifying process as the formation of an ever-firmer resolve, strengthened through repeated action, to do nothing but what reason commands (the goal, he says, is "complete conformity of the *will* with the moral law" (5:122, my emphasis)). Kant does *not* seem to understand this, here, as involving any change in the character of our inclinations. They are only rendered more and more ineffective in their resistance to reason. Self-conceit is overturned, and reason comes to rule our will completely and reliably. The reason it is not nonsense to strive after such an ideal is because we can approach it asymptotically, and because an atemporal God (at least) could regard the whole series as equivalent to its perpetually deferred realization.

There is, however, a problem with this interpretation: if one concedes the incorrigibility of the inclinations, one renders inexplicable Kant's way of talking in the third chapter of the Analytic. There the thing we are told to suppose possible as the perpetually deferred culmination of an infinitely extended process *is* an improved state of inclination. It is the state of our inclinations that is repeatedly cited as the reason why human ethics must be and remain an ethics of duty. Unruly inclination is what prevents us from relating to the prescriptions of reason as a holy will would. And holiness is the condition, according to the third chapter of the Analytic, that we can never attain but must strive to approximate. So a puzzle remains.

Now, a variant of the interpretation suggested above could (in principle) be applied to a process of educating the inclinations. It could be stipulated that thoroughgoing, unmixed affection for what reason prescribes is impossible for us, but that we could asymptotically approach such pure affection over time. This asymptotic approach, like the other, could be regarded, from God's perspective, as equivalent to the attainment of its end. But because the approach is asymptotic and infinitely extended, reason will never in fact present its law to us in any mood other than the imperative.

Yet even with this interpretation in view and the puzzle about how anyone could strive for something unattainable resolved, we are left to wonder why Kant would think it impossible to love what reason prescribes, or to love it sufficiently that one's mode of apprehension would begin to change, even if only at particular times or in particular respects. For Kant clearly thinks this. Nothing exercises him more, in the second *Critique*, than the suggestion that purity of this sort could be realized, and that simple love of what reason prescribes could be a worthy motive, for any dependent being, at any time. He calls it, among other things, "blatant moral fanaticism," "an egotistical illusion," " a narrow moral fanaticism," and "exaggerated self-conceit."[30] Anyone not "fanatically" optimistic will, I think, see the sense in guarding against the supposition that one has achieved such purity. Rigorous self-examination, when it does not plainly contradict this supposition, at least reveals (to quote Murdoch) "the deep tissue of ambivalent motive." "We like to flatter ourselves with the false claim to a...noble motive," Kant writes in the *Groundwork*, but "in fact we can never, even by the most strenuous self-examination, get entirely behind our covert incentives.... ...if we look more closely at [our] intentions and aspirations...we everywhere come upon the dear self..." (4:407). Perhaps such a description of a person's motivational structure and mode of apprehension could only be given externally—perhaps only by God.

But as a claim doing substantive work for Kant, is this denial of the possibility of purity more than an educated surmise? Is there a principled basis for this pessimism? Because, functioning as it does, this anthropological claim does much more than caution the fanciful or arrogant. It rules out possibly fruitful inquiries into how the mode of apprehension of the prescriptions of reason might change for someone very far along the path of perfection. Kant allows that there is such a path, and that it takes us in some way closer to a state in which the prescriptions of reason would no longer present themselves as constraints. Yet Kant appears so apprehensive that people will take themselves to be further along the path than they are that he suppresses inquiries into the affective dimension(s) of character, habit, virtue, and so on. One would like a philosophical justification for any judgment with such significant consequences for a philosophical research program. Unsur-

---

30 For an analysis of Kant's views on practical fanaticism, see Rachel Zuckert's contribution to this volume.

prisingly, Kant has such a justification; it occupies the first book of the *Religion*.

Religion

In the second preface to the *Religion*, Kant denies that the book presumes knowledge of his earlier, Critical works. "Only common morality is needed to understand the essentials of this text," he declares (6:14). This may be so, but it is well to remember that the *Groundwork* begins from the same premise. Starting from common-sense morality and its conditions of intelligibility, it develops all the rudiments of Kant's practical philosophy. So we should not take Kant's remarks in the second preface to mean that the connections between his earlier works of practical philosophy and the *Religion* are not close and systematic. If both flow from the same source, we should expect them to be mutually supporting and interconnected in myriad ways.[31]

As the concept of duty dominates *Groundwork* 1, so the concept of radical evil dominates the first book of the *Religion*. Its importance for present purposes is the basis it provides for Kant's skepticism about any phenomenologically consequential approximation, among humans, of moral purity. By way of explaining the concept of radical evil, I will need to consider a small family of others. In order, they are: fundamental disposition, predisposition, and propensity.

Kant predicates "radical evil" of every member of the human race. What does this mean? It means that we all have or had an evil fundamental disposition, a disposition that underlies our whole practical existence. Every exercise of our will is affected by this fundamental disposition, so that even our morally licit acts do not fulfill the spirit of the law.[32]

This talk of the law's spirit may call to mind a passage quoted earlier (5:82-3), in which Kant identifies respectful submission as the only way for humans to fulfill the spirit of the law. It is helpful to bear that passage in mind in the present context, and to conjoin it, in reflection, with the nearby passage in which he contrasts respect with self-conceit. Self-conceit, recall, is the adopted principle of privileging one's desires over the prescriptions of reason. Respect, by contrast, is (or reflects) privileging the prescriptions of reason over one's desires: allowing the

---

31 For an elaborate and systematic treatment of these connections, see Sussman 2001.

32 Does this compromise human freedom? Not according to Kant, because the fundamental disposition is understood as freely chosen, albeit timelessly.

prescriptions of reason to trump or exclude one's desires in deliberation.

Radical evil, then, is a fundamental disposition to self-conceit, i.e.,
to privileging desire over the prescriptions of reason. Since what is in
view is the adoption of self-conceit as a principle, it is easy to see why
Kant would speak of the resulting disposition as "fundamental," and the
attendant evil as "radical." It is a disposition not to accord respect to
that which authoritatively directs us—indeed to do the opposite, to set
ourselves up as superior to the voice of reason.

This account raises numerous questions. Why suppose that one's
fundamental dispositions are unified in this way? Why suppose that
everyone's fundamental disposition is evil? Does the possession of an
evil fundamental disposition affect one's inclinations? If so, how? And
since we have it on the authority of the rest of Kant's practical philosophy that ought implies can, and that we ought to (and thus can) progress
toward purity, how do we overcome our evil fundamental disposition, if
every one of us at least began from such a disposition? Let us consider
these questions in the order in which they have suggested themselves.

First, why suppose that humans have such unified fundamental dispositions? Kant's answer has to do with the basic types into which the
possible determining grounds of the human will sort themselves. There
are two such types, he thinks—(innocently) self-centered inclination
and the prescriptions of practical reason. But as they are independent of
one another and can come into conflict, they sooner or later have to be
ranked, assuming there is no pre-established harmony between them.
Kant simply asserts that there is no such pre-established harmony—not
here and now, at least. It is simply not the case, in the world as we
know it, that we never become hungry (for example) at a moment when
it is objectively necessary to do something besides eat. We are all,
sooner or later, called upon to choose between inclination and the prescriptions of reason. This does not yet show that one could not rank the
two types of determining ground differently in different situations,
though.

To see why Kant thinks *this*, one must recall what respect involves:
submission to the law's authoritative direction. This is either a universal
principle, or it is nothing. If one elevates inclination over the prescriptions of reason part of the time, one elevates it in general, because one
declares oneself competent to dismiss the prescriptions of reason when
one sees fit. We may relate this to what Henry Allison dubs "the incorporation thesis" (Allison 1990, p. 5 and *passim*). Kant expresses the
thesis succinctly early in the first book of the *Religion*: a free agent
"cannot be determined to action through any incentive except so far as
[he] has incorporated it into his maxim (has made it into a universal

rule for himself, according to which he wills to conduct himself)..."
(6:24). This thesis is required by Kant's conception of freedom. For if
the will must be conceived, for practical purposes, as absolutely spontaneous, and yet as something more than a "random act generator," it
must give itself laws.[33] Thus, acting "under the idea of freedom"
(4:448), we must interpret our actions as the expression of self-given
laws; so interpreted, a single compromise between desire and the prescriptions of reason indicates that one has given oneself the law of self-
conceit—a law prioritizing the satisfaction of one's inclinations over
the prescriptions of reason.

But why not make a fresh start once one comes to oneself, like the
prodigal son at the feed trough? Why suppose that past compromises
determine future decision-making? This hopeful skepticism is, indeed,
the attitude one must take as one confronts new decision situations,
conscious though one may be of past failure. Kant insists, though, that a
single compromise radically corrupts the moral personality.

This is because it is stage-setting. Consider the hypothetical first
choice of an individual between the two types of determining ground
(Kant thinks the choice is in fact timeless). This choice, if it is free, will
fashion a law, an organizing principle for future decision-making. Either one treats the prescription of practical reason as a norm, "excluding
from consideration" one's self-interest, or one adopts the principle of
self-conceit, declaring that one may set aside the prescriptions of practical reason. Interestingly, one can make the latter choice even as one
opts for the external act that reason commands. One's internal dialogue
might play like this, for instance: "I will do the legal thing this time,
because there's not much to be gained by doing otherwise, and I could
be found out." Having made an original choice, though, one is left with
a "policy," a configuration of the will, and this has consequences for
future willing. Original choice is a choice as to what will count as decisive in situations of conflict.

One does not, then, confront the "next" decision situation as one
confronted the "first". For now one has a principle: a policy as to what
will count as decisive in situations of conflict. If one is to reverse the
prioritization, the configuration fashioned by one's original choice, one
cannot be *guided by* that choice, for it will never lead to its opposite.
But one *is* now guided by that prioritization, that configuration. That
was what was at stake in the original choice.

---

33 An argument that appears already in the Third Analogy. I remarked earlier on the re-
    semblance Kant sees between holiness and nature. Captivated as he was by Newtonian
    physics, Kant was arguably too quick to analogize laws of freedom to laws of nature.

This renders radical evil, according to Kant, inextirpable "through human forces, for this could only happen through good maxims—something that cannot take place if the subjective supreme ground of all maxims is presupposed to be corrupted" (6:37). An overthrowing of the original choice must occur, and this requires intervention from without the agent.

Returning again to our list of questions: why suppose everyone has made an original choice of self-conceit? Recognizing now that a single compromise implies, for Kant, incorporation of "the evil maxim," we are in a better position to understand the uncharacteristically loose and anecdotal argument Kant offers for the universality of radical evil. "[Skeptics about universal evil] must...hear out a long melancholy litany of charges against humankind," Kant writes:

> of secret falsity even in the most intimate friendship, so that a restraint on trust in the mutual confidence of even the best friends is reckoned a universal maxim of prudence in social dealings; of a propensity to hate him to whom we are indebted...which a benefactor must always heed; of a hearty goodwill that nonetheless admits the remark that "in the misfortunes of our best friends there is something that does not altogether displease us"; and of many other vices yet hidden under the appearance of virtue, let alone those of which no secret is made.... (6:33)

It is, I think, difficult to dismiss this list or its import, even if one regards Kant (as some do) as a foul-tempered little man, ridden by the hags of his pietist upbringing.[34] For one finds similar observations in writers of wildly diverse backgrounds. Aristotle, to cite just one, remarks at several points the human tendency to resent benefaction.[35] Unless one wishes to insist that there are some among us who have never preferred happiness to the prescriptions of reason, one who grants Kant's views on human agency is left to conclude with Kant that there is "a radical innate evil in human nature" (6:32). The argument, such as it is, *is* uncharacteristically loose and anecdotal. But it is credible enough.

One important fact that we have not yet touched upon is the mechanism by which the original use of the will alters our subjective constitution. No investigation of Kant's anthropological pessimism can be complete without an understanding of his views on what we might call the "affective consequences of evil." And so we must examine two

---

34 Kuehn (2001) laudably and compellingly combats the ugly caricatures Kant has attracted, almost since his death. In so doing, though, he underplays the significance of Kant's pietist upbringing for the structure and content of his practical philosophy.

35 Not only in his description of "the magnanimous man," but also in the friendship books. See *Nichomachean Ethics* 1167b18 and ff. Aristotle, true to his principle that the goal of life is self-realization through virtuous activity, *idealizes* this tendency.

more concepts not much discussed in summaries of Kant's practical philosophy: predispositions and propensities.

The concept of a predisposition, as Allen Wood explains, is a general one, taken from Kant's views on biology.[36] A predisposition, Wood says, is

> a feature of a living thing's nature that accounts for its developing in a certain way. Kant calls such a basic teleological feature of an organism…a 'predisposition' when it is a global feature of the organism, determining the relationships between its parts, hence its organic form as a whole. (Wood 1999, p. 211)

Predispositions are like seeds planted within an organism—seeds that, in the ordinary course of things, will grow into maturity, determining broad, formal characteristics of that organism.

Like Aristotle before him, Kant identifies different levels of human capacity—which he indexes to different predispositions—existing in a hierarchical and cumulative structure: an organism can exist at a lower level without existing at a higher level, but an organism cannot exist at a higher level without existing at all lower (preceding) levels. For Aristotle, these kinds or "levels" of soul are the nutritive, the appetitive, and the rational. For Kant, these levels—the predispositions—are animality, humanity, and personality. Our sensuous incentives are, every one, connected with one or another of these predispositions.

The first predisposition, animality, applies to each human "as a living being" (6:26). This covers all the tendencies and functions Aristotle included within his first two levels of ensoulment: those aspects of our nature that can exist apart from reason. Our impulses toward self-preservation, sex, and society (with their attendant incentives) all fall under animality, according to Kant, because they are shared with non-human animals. The second predisposition, humanity, applies to each human as a "rational being." I will say more about this in a moment, but first let me at least define the third and final disposition, personality. This, Kant tells us, applies to each human as a "responsible being."

What is the distinction between the predispositions to humanity and personality, both of which require reason? The first encompasses those rational tendencies that do not involve the direct determination of the will by the moral law. It encompasses, that is, all aspects of our rationality except the fact of reason, and is specifically responsible for impulses to secure dominance and recognition among our peers. These impulses (and their attendant incentives) are not merely animal but involve rational calculation. The second rational predisposition, person-

---

36 In his contribution to this volume, Lee Hardy describes the eighteenth-century embryological debate from which Kant adapted these terms and their corresponding concepts.

ality, presupposes humanity and encompasses our mysterious capacity for rational self-determination. It is associated with only one incentive: respect.

All three predispositions, like non-rational inclination as such, are innate, unchosen, and in themselves innocent (or better). The incentives to which the first two predispositions would give rise, in the absence of an evil original choice, would not *invariably* be appropriate to act upon, at the moment they suggest themselves. But neither would these incentives be *per se* incompatible with reason—such that they could never be appropriate to act upon.

Each of these predispositions gives rise to *essentially* contra-rational incentives, though, once the evil maxim is selected through the original use of the will. This exacerbates the conflict between the two determining grounds of the human will. Inclination, which as non-rational can suggest appropriate ends at inappropriate moments, suggests evil ends as a result of the evil maxim in us; gluttony, drunkenness, promiscuity, and "wild lawlessness" are "grafted" onto the pre-disposition to animality, while the "vices of culture" such as animosity, "envy, ingratitude, [and] joy in other's misfortunes" attach themselves to the predisposition to humanity, and are promoted by it (6:26-7).

How does this work, precisely? Kant does not give us as detailed an answer as we might like, but he does say something. He says there is a second variety of potential in the human being, like a predisposition except that its realization is not a matter of natural course. These "propensities," as he calls them, are tendencies toward evil that are animated, as it were, by the original choice of the evil maxim. These too are innate potentialities, but we are responsible for their actualization, because this actualization is consequent upon our original choice. Kant describes them at one point as conditional predispositions—predispositions "to desire an enjoyment which, when the subject has experienced it, arouses inclination to it" (6:29). Kant offers an example with enduring resonance: the propensity to addiction. One can have a latent tendency to alcoholism, he explains, which may never manifest itself, but which will come to life and oppress one ever after, if one begins to drink. The realization of this potential is only possible because of something innate in the potential alcoholic, but it can also be regarded, after the fact, as something brought upon the alcoholic by him- or herself. The phenomenon is not, I take it, unfamiliar.[37]

---

37 Still, Kant's views are not wholly intuitive. Kant holds, for instance, that the propensities are to be regarded as freely chosen evils—even before they are actualized in the context of a life. Philip Quinn pointed this out to me.

The propensities to evil are an interesting set, in light of the topics we have considered. We have propensities, Kant says, to frailty, impurity, and wickedness. The first is the tendency to succumb to inclinations experienced as irresistibly strong, even in the face of a prior, clear-sighted commitment to the prescriptions of reason. The second is the tendency to act on grounds other than duty, even when behaving in externally lawful ways.[38] The last propensity is a tendency to self-conceit, and can be regarded as a simple intensification of the direct result of the original choice of evil.

This is all most sobering, if true. Does Kant tell us anything, then, about how and to what extent recovery from the effects of these propensities is possible? Yes. In the first place, we are never abandoned by the commanding voice of reason. This is the point of saying that we have a predisposition to personality, i.e., to accountability. We each have a "seed of goodness" within us, in consequence of which reason continues its peremptory internal monologue, drawing our attention to the fact (which is its mark of authority) that moral worth and respect for the law are inseparable. Whatever the ill consequences of the original choice, these consequences should not to be understood to include "corruption of the morally legislative reason..." (6:35). Second, this very cognizance of reason's demand teaches us that our fundamental disposition can be changed. We cannot, perhaps, understand how this is possible, but the certainty that we ought to change assures us that it is possible, that we must strive toward self-transformation, and that whatever assistance we require in this is available to us. Finally, just as the propensities to frailty, impurity, and wickedness are actualized through the original choice of evil, so the transformation of the will's fundamental disposition, followed by an ever-extending series of dutiful actions performed in the face of contrary inclination, begins to loosen the power of contra-rational inclination over us, though contra-rational inclination is never eradicated. The transformation of the fundamental disposition, considered in itself, is as deeply inexplicable as any exercise of freedom. Somehow we change; that is all. But considered as appearance, the transformation of the fundamental disposition is "a gradual reformation" (6:47).

---

38 This is related to, but not identical with, the impurity elsewhere contrasted with purity of will. The propensity to impurity is a propensity to mingle considerations of inclination with considerations of duty, while impurity of will denotes, in the first instance, the presence of contra-rational inclinations within one's complete set and, by extension, a tendency to prefer these and other inclinations to duty in cases of conflict. But a tendency to base one's lawful behavior on inclination instead of respect will at least assist a tendency to prefer inclination to duty in cases of conflict.

In any event, it is clear why Kant is unwilling to entertain the possibility of phenomenologically significant human purity. Having once
sinned, humans set in motion a corruption of their subjective constitution that makes thoroughgoing education of inclination impossible. The
most we can hope for is a long progress from more resistant to less
resistant obedience to the voice of reason. Whether or not Kant's position is compelling in all its parts or on all its grounds, it is at least consistent and comprehensible. We can see more-or-less steadily and
whole the connections Kant wished to make between our tendencies to
moral failure and the manifestation of the prescriptions of reason as
commands.

Conclusion

What have we learned about Kant's view of human beings and their
conceptual and phenomenological relation to the prescriptions of reason? We may summarize as follows: while purity is conceivable for
human beings, it is impossible, for a variety of reasons—in the first
instance because there is no pre-established harmony between non-
rational desire and the prescriptions of reason, but also, and more
deeply, because of the propensities to evil animated by the (universal)
original choice of an evil disposition. The propensities to evil
strengthen the grip of contra-rational inclination upon us, muddy our
motives, and pull us into progressively deeper self-conceit. Undoing
their effects is an endless task.

Paradoxically, holy impassibility—though flatly inconsistent with
creatureliness—sets the standard for human striving, because it represents the ideal of a perfectly harmonious, perfectly good subjective
constitution. It is better not to think of our aim in terms of purity, although that is the strictly conceivable end, because we are apt to give
ourselves dangerous airs if we begin to think of the end of the moral
life in these terms. At one point, Kant goes so far as to say it is dangerous even to allow cooperation between motives of affection and respect
in promoting objectively appropriate actions (5:82). Nevertheless, our
aim could be described as a kind of purity. It is to combat the propensities to evil through repeated, disciplined willing of what reason prescribes, and thereby to experience progressively less (though always
some) tension between our subjective constitution and the prescriptions
of reason. So long as this tension remains, though, the prescriptions of
reason will always manifest themselves to us as duty—that is, as some-

thing obligatory, something imperative. In fact, the tension will remain forever.

For Kant thinks, as we have seen, that we all possess an evil second nature, grounded in the simple fact of non-rational desire but grown up, universally, into self-conceit—first a principle, then a set of dispositions to set aside objectivity and unselfishness in favor of private satisfaction. This unfolding of our propensities to evil involves, among other things, a conciliatory weakness in the face of evil desires, the presence of suspicious but opaque motives even in our best actions, and a tendency to an over-large picture of what we deserve. Kant posits a powerful and enduring conflict between our inclinations and the prescriptions of reason, on the basis of which he develops his notions of duty and respect. We dare not presume to have escaped this condition, and our only hope of becoming essentially good is to submit ourselves to the discipline and direction of something greater than ourselves, in order that our desires may slowly and gradually come to be ruled by reason, and our propensities to evil reduced.

The following, then, would seem to be a fair summary of Kant's thought: (1) the achievement of genuine goodness is almost impossibly difficult, because or insofar as (2) sinfulness is a universal condition among human beings, so far as we can see inextirpable within this life; (3) this sinfulness consists in an egoism that resists all attempts on the part of the individual to realize goodness in his or her life; (4) it is characteristic of sinful humans not only to prioritize their own gratification, but also to be opaque to themselves; (5) the point of an ethical code is the realization of goodness in human lives, both individually and collectively—the end is thus to improve our resistance to the wiles of sin. It is a set of theses we have encountered before.[39]

---

39 I acknowledge with gratitude the colleagues and students who have taken the time to read and talk with me about this essay and its arguments, and who have made suggestions for improving it. My largest debts are to Karl Ameriks, Heidi Chamberlin, Andrew Chignell, Patrick Frierson, John Hare, Lee Hardy, Patrick Kain, James Krueger, and Rachel Zuckert.

Section II

Interpreting Freedom

CHAPTER 3

Two Standpoints and the Problem of Moral Anthropology

Patrick Frierson

Kant's theory of freedom is famously described as a "compatibilism of compatibilism and incompatibilism" (Wood 1984, p. 74). On the one hand, Kant claims that human freedom is not a mere epiphenomenon of causally determined mental states. On the other hand, he seeks to reconcile this strong conception of freedom with thoroughgoing natural determinism of empirically observable actions of human agents. Equally famously, this theory of freedom has been given (at least) two different interpretations among Kantians. According to the "two-world" interpretation, human beings are free insofar as they exist in a noumenal world of things-in-themselves and determined insofar as they exist in a phenomenal world of mere appearances. According to the "two-standpoint" (or two-perspective) interpretation, humans are free insofar as they are thought of from a practical or deliberator's standpoint, and determined insofar as they are thought of from a scientific or observer's standpoint.[1] The two standpoints are not primarily distinguished by different beliefs, but by different tasks: from the theoretical standpoint one seeks to explain natural occurrences in terms of causal laws, while the practical standpoint is the standpoint from which human beings act in the world. But these different tasks have implications for belief. In particular, the practical standpoint requires thinking of agents as free, while the theoretical requires thinking of deeds as causally determined.

The two-standpoint interpretation has, in recent years, dominated discussions of Kant's theory of freedom, and it is at least implicit (and

---

1   See Ameriks 1982 for an overview of the debate, and Aquila 1979, Prauss 1983, Watkins 2005, and Allison 1983 and 1990, O'Neill 1989, and Korsgaard 1996. This paper was written long before the publication of Korsgaard 2009. In the light of that book, I would now use different terminology to make many of the points of this paper and could substantially enrich its final section.

84   Patrick Frierson

bodyoften explicit) in recent neo-Rawlsian versions of Kant's ethics. This two-standpoint interpretation has at least two important advantages over two-world accounts. First, it allows one to make use of Kant's insights about freedom from a practical point of view without making substantive metaphysical assumptions. Especially for those primarily interested in Kant as a moral philosopher, this advantage is considerable. Second, it helps one avoid difficult problems about how different worlds can relate—especially since Kant sometimes suggests that the only legitimate use one can make of concepts of relation (causality, interaction, etc) is when these are applied to the phenomenal world (B149, A139-40/B178-9).

    Whatever the merit of these advantages, the two-standpoint version of Kant's theory of freedom has recently come under fire. This paper examines three related objections to two-standpoint theories. First, two-standpoint theories seem to have a hard time making sense of the use of theoretical claims within practical deliberation, since such use seems to conflate two standpoints that are supposed to be distinct. Second, two-standpoint theories seem to lack a suitable answer to the question of whether human beings are *really* free. And finally, two-standpoint theories seem unable to make sense of Kant's deep commitment to what Eric Watkins has called the "grounding thesis," that "things in themselves, or the noumenal world, 'grounds' or 'underlies' appearance, or the sensible world" (Watkins 2005, p. 326). After articulating these objections, I show how two-standpoint approaches can adequately respond to them, where my solution to all three depends upon making sense of the grounding thesis in two-standpoint terms. In my conclusion, however, I suggest that this use of the grounding thesis opens two-standpoint theories to a new problem, the problem of moral anthropology. After briefly explaining how two-world theories might address this problem, I offer a conjectural beginning of a two-standpoint approach to moral anthropology.

The Theory-in-Deliberation Problem

On a two-standpoint interpretation of Kant's theory of freedom, a person can be regarded as free from one standpoint and as determined from another. For the purposes of this paper, I focus on the two-standpoint interpretations offered by Onora O'Neill and Christine Korsgaard. As they put it,

> We should…expect to find two accounts of action. The first, theoretical account would consider acts as natural events and would aim to explain their occurrence…. The second, practical account would consider acts as expressing

certain determinations of the will, and moral action as expressing certain sorts of determination of the will. (O'Neill 1989, p. 67)

> The deliberating agent, employing reason practically, views the world as it were from a noumenal standpoint.... The theorizing spectator, on the other hand, views the world as phenomena, mechanistic and fully determined. The interests of morality demand a different conceptual organization of the world than those of theoretical explanation.... Both interests are rational and legitimate. (Korsgaard 1996a, p. 173)

Korsgaard and O'Neill concur that "The two standpoints are to be thought of not as ontologically distinct realms between which human agents must switch, but as distinct, indispensable, yet mutually irreducible frameworks of thought" (O'Neill 1989, p. 68; see Korsgaard 1996a, pp. 160, 167-76). Korsgaard sometimes seems to associate the practical standpoint entirely with the *deliberative* or first-person perspective, although all that is strictly required is that one takes a standpoint according to which a person must be considered an *agent*, and this can occur whether one *deliberates* or is *evaluated* in a practical way. The point is that people have different reasons to give an account of a human action. Depending on the interests that motivate one's account, one assumes either a practical standpoint according to which the agent is the ultimate free cause of the action or a theoretical standpoint within which one traces natural causes of the action.

Recently, Dana Nelkin has summarized this view in a way that draws attention to the way that it helps Kant develop his unique sort of compatibilism between freedom and determinism. Nelkin explains,

> According to the two-standpoints account, the propositions to which reason commits us are indeed contradictory. But we are not irrational in believing that we are free and undetermined, on the one hand, and believing that we are determined and unfree, on the other, because we can hold apparently contradictory beliefs from different standpoints (Nelkin 2000, p. 567).

Within traditional compatibilism, freedom is demoted to a mere form of internal causation, so the claims of freedom and determinism do not even conflict. But Nelkin rightly highlights that *Kant's* compabilism does not do this; for Kant, human freedom is freedom from determination by natural causes, and *this* freedom exists along with a thoroughgoing natural determination of human actions. On two-standpoint interpretations of Kant, this conflict is only apparent because the claims that freedom is real and that natural determination is thoroughgoing are made from different standpoints.

Nelkin offers several objections to this two-standpoint account. In general, she raises the "difficulty of producing a criterion that sorts beliefs appropriately into those held from the deliberative standpoint and those held from the theoretical" (Nelkin 2000, p. 570). More par-

ticularly, Nelkin raises an objection based on the use of theoretical beliefs within the practical standpoint, an objection I refer to as the theory-in-deliberation problem. Nelkin argues,

> When we are engaged in deliberation, we often rely on theoretical or scientific
> beliefs. For example, if I am deliberating about whether to sound a fire alarm,
> one of the things I rely on is my belief about what effects that action is likely
> to have. Does this mean, then, that my belief about the causal role of alarm
> sounding is a belief from the standpoint of the deliberator? It certainly seems
> so, for the belief seems quite "relevant" to my deliberative task. And if so,
> then it would appear that either I have two beliefs with similar contents that
> are distinguished by the points of view from which they are held, or I have a
> single belief that floats freely back and forth between standpoints. In either
> case, there seems to be nothing in principle that prevents a belief that is held
> from one standpoint to be held from another. (Nelkin 2000, pp. 570-1; cf.
> Watkins 2005, p. 322)

The problem with taking theoretical claims into account in deliberation
is that it seems to obscure the distinction between standpoints. And if
there is no clear distinction between standpoints, then there does not
seem to be any reason to isolate the claim that one is unfree in a way
that one isolates no other theoretical claims. The use of theory in deliberation seems to break down the distinction needed to insulate the practical belief in freedom from theoretical refutation.

Nelkin's objection arises from interpreting the practical standpoint
of deliberation as fundamentally opposed to the postulation of causal
necessity in the world. But the practical standpoint of deliberation assumes no such thing. O'Neill insists that "the actions that agents perform assume a causally ordered and knowable world that provides the
arena for action" (O'Neill 1989, p. 68) and Korsgaard helpfully lays out
the structure of this practical standpoint: "the deliberating agent, employing reason practically, views the world...as an expression of the
wills of...rational agents" (Korsgaard 1996a, p. 173). The point is not
that one sees the world as free of causal influence when one views it
from a practical standpoint, but rather that one sees its causal relations
as tracing back to one's own, undetermined choices. It is perfectly reasonable, even required, to take into account natural connections between one's actions and their *effects*, but it does not make sense, from
the practical standpoint, to take into account natural connections between one's actions and their (sufficient) empirical *causes*.

Moreover, the *way* in which one takes into account natural connections is different, depending upon whether one is viewing the world
from the practical or the theoretical standpoint. From the practical
standpoint, the natural effects of pulling a fire alarm—panic, a rush of
people to leave the building, etc.—are important *reasons* for or against
action. Similar judgments about the effects of pulling a fire alarm could

be made from a theoretical standpoint, but here they would operate not as *reasons* for *action* but as *explanations* of *events*. From this theoretical standpoint, it might be relevant to ask not only about effects of pulling fire alarms, but about the causes that lead people to pull them. But in the context of practical deliberation, the effects of sounding the alarm are considered only as the *after*-effects of one's action, after-effects that are important in deliberation *because* they are after-effects *of one's action*. Thus when deliberating, one views the world "under the idea of freedom." One then *chooses* among options, all of which are largely constituted by objects the scientific properties of which may be relevant to one's choice. But the fact that scientific considerations are relevant to choice does not change the fact that one chooses.

First- and Second-Order Judgments and the Limits of Scientific Enquiry

The practical standpoint can accommodate judgments whose content is theoretical because, from a practical standpoint, one sees the world as a series of effects of one's choice, effects that begin in freedom but proceed in accordance with the order of nature. But Nelkin's theory-in-deliberation objection cannot be disposed of quite this easily. Given that scientific facts about the world can be reasons as well as explanations, Nelkin asks, "what is to prevent my taking th[e] theoretical belief [that I am unfree] into account in my deliberation just as I take into account other of my theoretical beliefs?" (Nelkin 2000, p. 571). If deliberation can take into account scientific facts about the world, why not take into account the fact that one is unfree?

As a preliminary response, we might turn to two related reasons that causes of choice should not be taken into account from a practical standpoint. First, as Korsgaard notes, causes of one's choices literally *cannot* function as reasons for choice. As she puts it, "imagine that you...know that your every move is programmed by an electronic device implanted in your brain.... In order to *do* anything, you must simply ignore the fact that you are programmed, and decide what to do— just as if you were free" (Korsgaard 1996a, pp. 162-3). Second, the practical standpoint is precisely the standpoint from which one holds oneself or others *responsible* for one's actions, and Kant insists that insofar as one is merely a secondary cause of one's action, one cannot be held responsible for that action (5:96). As soon as one introduces causal explanations of a particular human behavior, one has ceased to consider that behavior as a possible object of moral-practical evaluation, and one has thereby ceased to see that behavior from a practical standpoint. Unlike beliefs about natural effects of one's actions, there is—to use Nelkin's phrase—something "in principle" that precludes certain theoretical beliefs from being held (or at least, being relevant) within the practical standpoint.

But these points might seem only to make the problem more acute. What these responses show is that one *needs* to exclude in deliberation the thought that one is unfree, but they do not, in themselves, show why one is *entitled* to exclude that thought. What distinguishes the thought that one is unfree from other theoretical claims, such that one can rightfully exclude that thought but not others in deliberation?

To answer this question, it is crucial first to be clear about the status of claims about one's freedom. Within the standpoint of practical deliberation, one takes into account reasons for actions that include purely practical claims—"I should not cause needless suffering" or "I should not deceive others"—and empirical claims taken as reasons—"Pulling this fire alarm will cause panic" or "Pulling this fire alarm will make people wrongly believe that there is a fire." I call these sorts of judgments, which include any that function as reasons or parts of reasons for action, "first-order" practical judgments. Similarly, first-order theoretical judgments include any descriptive and explanatory claims about the world. When one explains the rush of people emerging from a building by saying that the immediate cause is a fire alarm, or explains that the cause of the ringing of the fire alarm is a pair of children seeking to cause trouble, one makes first-order theoretical judgments. First-order theoretical judgments can even include the psychological laws that lead children to pull alarms or people to respond to them, or the biological laws that explain certain predispositions in human nature, or the physical laws that explain the working of the alarm. The content of at least some of these first-order theoretical judgments will be present in at least some first-order practical judgments; "the sound of a fire alarm causes panic" could be either a theoretical or a practical judgment, depending on the context.

In addressing Nelkin's concern about the theoretical belief that I am not free, it is crucial to note that beliefs about human freedom do not occur among first-order beliefs in *either* the theoretical *or* the practical standpoints. One deliberates *as if* one is free, but one's freedom is not itself a reason for action.[2] Likewise one conducts theoretical investiga-

---

2   At least, freedom is not itself a reason for action in normal circumstances. Sometimes one's freedom might be part of a reason for a specific action. For instance, I might reason that since I am free, and this scientist tells me that he knows exactly what I will do next, I will do something totally random to spite him. In a much more complicated way, one's freedom might give one a reason to respect the moral law, although even here,

tions *as if* the objects of such investigations can be explained in terms of natural causes, but ultimate explicability in terms of causes is not itself a first-order scientific claim.[3] But for Kant (and for Korsgaard), there are also second-order judgments, some theoretical, some practical. These are not judgments made *within* a deliberative or theoretical standpoint, but judgments that articulate the philosophical presuppositions of each standpoint. As Korsgaard explains with respect to belief in freedom, this is "not about a [first-order] theoretical assumption necessary to decision, but about a fundamental feature of the standpoint from which decisions are made" (Korsgaard 1996a, p. 163). In Kantian terms, we might say that second-order judgments express the conditions of the possibility of legitimately making first-order judgments.

Korsgaard follows Kant's terminology in referring to second-order practical judgments as "postulates" of practical reason.[4] Korsgaard explains, "a postulate of practical reason is an object of rational belief, but the reasons for the belief are practical and moral.... Although these beliefs are theoretical in form—the will is free, there is a God—their basis and their function are practical" (Korsgaard 1996a, 172). Since both deliberation and evaluation require ascribing responsibility to oneself or others, one must always act (or judge) as if one is free. And since one must act as if one is free, one can philosophically justify the way one acts only if one maintains that one is free.[5] The belief that the will is free is a second-order judgment that articulates a presupposition underlying first-order practical judgments.[6] Similarly, the belief that all

---

one ought to obey this law because it is unconditionally binding, not because doing so confirms one's freedom.

3   At least, explicability in terms of natural causes is generally not given as a first-order scientific judgment. Insofar as universal explicability is presented as a scientific theory, it suffers from the problems of induction to which Hume famously drew attention in his *Treatise*, and which Kant further explained in the *Critique of Pure Reason*.

4   We might, consistent with Kant's terminology from the first *Critique*, refer to second-order theoretical judgments as "principles of pure understanding" (A148/B187).

5   This claim is based on Kant's conception of (moral) responsibility. It is not the purpose of this paper to evaluate Kant's arguments for freedom, but only to raise a problem for a particular way of interpreting freedom.

6   Korsgaard explains that a person "needs this belief" in order to deliberate properly, which in context means, to obey the moral law (Korsgaard 1996a, p. 172). Of course, a person can deliberate as if she is free, and even act from respect for the moral law, without actually affirming the practical postulate that the will is free. Kant insists that even "the most common and unpracticed understanding" is capable of acting in accordance with the moral law (5:36). Such a person need not have a philosophical understanding of the relationship between freedom and moral responsibility. Rather, ordinary people need only sufficient confidence in their abilities to act as if they are free. It might be difficult to maintain a commitment to the moral law, or even to serious deliberation, if one *denies* the postulates (cf. 5:452, Wood 1992), but even then, such a commitment remains possible in principle. The belief in freedom is a second-order belief, and thus

objects of nature are causally determined articulates a presupposition of first-order theoretical judgments.[7] As Hume eloquently showed, one has no empirical evidence *for* the claim that the world is governed by causal laws, but, as Kant (less eloquently) showed, this claim is a conceptual precondition of giving a coherent account of the world as we experience it. For that reason, Kant insists, "The correctness of the principle of the thoroughgoing connection of all occurrences in the world of sense according to invariable natural laws is...confirmed as a principle of the transcendental analytic," that is, as a principle that provides the condition for the possibility of experience itself (A536/B564).[8] And the ideal of an *exhaustive* or *sufficient* causal explanation of the world is neither an empirical claim nor even a necessary condition of experience, but a necessary *ideal* of theoretical reason.[9]

This distinction between first- and second-order judgments helps show how the belief in freedom can differ from what Nelkin describes as cases where it is "rational to be irrational." Nelkin considers an explanation of the "practical" belief in freedom based on a "justification criterion," according to which one justifies certain beliefs on practical grounds and others on theoretical grounds. She mentions as examples the

> sort of 'practical' justification which applies to Blaise Pascal's belief in the existence of God (because he stands to gain eternal happiness if he believes and his belief turns out true), or William James's belief that he can jump over a wide ravine (because he will have a better chance of succeeding if he believes than if he does not). (Nelkin 2000, pp. 573-4)

Nelkin describes these as cases in which it is "rational to be irrational," but the status of the practical postulate that one is free is fundamentally

---

    not *necessary* in order to act as if one is free. All that is necessary for rational action is good first-order beliefs. Nonetheless, one can *philosophically* make sense of deliberation only by accepting that one is free.

7   As in the case of second-order practical judgments, it is possible to believe various theoretical explanations of the world without formulating the explicit belief that everything has a prior cause. But the only way to make philosophical sense of one's investigations and explanations is to believe that the objects of those investigations and explanations can be explained by natural laws.

8   Kant adds that this principle "will suffer no violation," so "the only question is whether, despite this...freedom might not also take place" (A536/B564). In his B Preface, Kant adds that the correctness of the principle of universal determinism in accordance with natural law is so strong that, were freedom incompatible with it, "freedom and with it morality...would have to give way to the mechanism of nature" (Bxxix). For Kant, then, there is an important and underappreciated *epistemic* priority of the theoretical standpoint. For a contrast with Korsgaard, see note 18. For discussion of how to reconcile this priority with the "primacy of the practical," see note 25.

9   See the "Ideal of Pure Reason." For discussion, see Grier, 2001.

different from the "practical" beliefs of Pascal or James. The beliefs of Pascal and James are adopted as parts of ordinary practical judgments. Pascal reasons that he should believe that God exists, in order to attain ends that he thinks are good. Likewise James reasons that he should believe in his abilities to jump the ravine in order to increase his chances of success. Both of these are reasons for actions. In each case, one decides to hold a belief because holding that belief is good for one in some sense. But the belief that one is free is not in itself good for one, and it is not adopted because it is advantageous. Rather, it is a belief that is necessary in order to make sense of the fact that one can be practically rational at all. It is the conceptual presupposition of a standpoint that one must—as a rational agent—adopt.[10]

And now we can return to Nelkin's question: "what is to prevent my taking th[e] theoretical belief [that I am unfree] into account in my deliberation just as I take into account other of my theoretical beliefs?" (Nelkin 2000, p. 571). In deliberation, one takes the content of certain first-order theoretical beliefs into account as (partial) reasons for action. In doing so, one assumes that there is some causal regularity in the world, but—in contrast to one's standpoint in theorizing about the world—one need not assume that this causal regularity is universal. And the second-order belief in universal and sufficient causation is not a belief for which one has any justification; it merely articulates the presupposition of *another* standpoint on the world. So there is no reason why one would need—or even be entitled—to take it into account from a practical standpoint.[11] Given that if one attempts to take its con-

---

10 The "necessity" of adopting this standpoint is first and foremost practical. That is, if one considers whether or not to adopt the practical standpoint, one finds oneself always already committed to adopting that standpoint. From the theoretical standpoint, one can note that human beings have various cognitive and volitional capacities by virtue of which they hold themselves responsible for their actions, and thus can ascribe a sort of biological necessity to humans' adoption of the practical standpoint. Kant does this when he explains, in the context of his empirical accounts of human beings, that we have both higher volitional capacities—a *Willkühr*—and a moral predisposition. For further discussion of Kant's empirical account of human beings, see Frierson 2006.

11 At times, Kant does suggest that universal determinism is a condition of the possibility of belief in *any* particular causal relations (e.g., A188/B234, A536/B564). If this is correct, then even the ordinary use of causal reasoning in practical contexts may commit one to universal determinism, which would reintroduce a direct contradiction within the practical standpoint. Two considerations mitigate the impact of this concern. First, while *universal* determinism *does* seem to be a necessary presupposition of the empirical investigation of nature, all that is necessary in order to employ empirical reasoning in practical deliberation is that one see the possible *effects* of one's actions as determined in accordance with causal laws, not that one sees the whole world (including one's actions) as so determined. Second, Kant's defense of the universality of determination in accordance with causal laws is a claim about "the sequence of appearances," "all *occurrences*," and in particular "all *alteration*" (A188/B234, A536/B564, emphasis added).

tent as a practical belief (either first- or second-order), one finds that it conflicts with the practical standpoint, there is every reason *not* to take it into account. The difference between the belief that "the sound of a fire alarm causes panic" and "Everything (including myself) is unfree" is that the first is a first-order (theoretical and potentially practical) judgment and the second is a second-order (theoretical) judgment. And this difference justifies taking the first, but not the second, into account in deliberation.

In the form in which she phrased it, Nelkin's question has been answered, but there is a similar problem that arises even at the level of first-order theoretical judgments. In particular, there are some first-order theoretical judgments that might seem to conflict with the freedom presupposed by the practical standpoint, such as the claims that "my bad upbringing led me to be malicious and weak-willed," and "given these circumstances, my malicious disposition inclines me to pull this fire alarm," and "my weak will causes me to act on my inclinations." Of course, Kant—and two-standpoint theorists—admit the possibility of this kind of causal explanation of human behavior:

> Let us take a...malicious lie.... We endeavor to discover the motives to which it has been due.... [W]e trace the empirical character of the action to its sources, finding these in defective education, bad company, in part also in the viciousness of a natural disposition insensitive to shame.... We proceed in this enquiry just as we should in ascertaining for a given natural effect the series of its determining causes (A554/B582).

As with the generic claim of universal determinism, Korsgaard's example of the implanted brain-control device shows why judgments about particular determinants of one's choice cannot be taken into account in practical reasoning. But as previously noted, this begs the question against Nelkin's insistence that there is a real conflict between claims made from theoretical and practical standpoints. If one is *justified* in using in deliberation the claim that one's action is determined by one's upbringing (as the parallel with theoretical claims about the fire alarm suggests), and if the denial of this claim is required by the deliberative standpoint, then there is a contradiction *within the practical standpoint*, which is just what the two-standpoint theory is supposed to prevent. And unlike the second-order affirmation of universal determinism, the claim that a particular choice is determined by particular prior causes is a first-order scientific judgment for which one can have substantial

---

But from within the practical standpoint, one's choices are not themselves occurrences or alterations. One decides how the world should alter, but from within the practical standpoint, one's decision is not itself an "alteration," and thus even if everything *in the world* is subject to natural laws, the will of which that world is the expression (to use Korsgaard's phrase) is not.

empirical support. Thus we cannot dismiss these judgments as different in kind from judgments about the operation and likely consequences of the fire alarm. Both sets of judgments are first-order theoretical claims, and we take judgments about the fire alarm into account from a practical standpoint, but not judgments about ourselves.

So now the question is, does the claim that one's action is determined by one's upbringing preclude the sort of practical thinking that Korsgaard insists depends upon the idea of freedom? It would preclude this thinking *if* one's upbringing were taken as a *sufficient* cause of one's action. But *even from the theoretical standpoint*, no particular cause is fully sufficient to explain its effect, for two reasons. First, every cause itself has a prior cause (in time), so whenever a cause is posited as an explanation for the necessity of an effect, one can still ask what made that cause itself necessary. Second (and more importantly), every cause brings about its effect by virtue of an underlying law or causal power, and one can always ask why that causal law or power must be as it is.[12] O'Neill helpfully summarizes this limit of theoretical explanation:

> The important limitation is that all naturalistic explanations—even the most impressive explanations of some future neuroscience—are conditional explanations.... In a certain sense they are incomplete, for they can never explain that any natural law should take the form that it does. Even the most exhausting investigation cannot be exhaustive. Any explanations offered in terms of events and their effects is incomplete because it presupposes an account of the form of certain principles. Putting this in an old-fashioned way we might say that explanations under the heading of efficient causality presuppose explanations under the heading of formal causality. (O'Neill 1989, p. 68)

This theoretical limit on causal explanation provides room for practical deliberation. In practical deliberation, one can take into account "defective education, bad company, in part also . . . the viciousness of a natural disposition insensitive to shame" (A554/B582). One might reason, for instance, that telling the lie is not as bad for oneself as for another, since one has, after all, such a bad natural disposition, and people with dispositions like that tells lies; that's just what they do. But in the context of deliberation, these judgments are merely potential reasons for action. One must still *decide* whether to give one's natural disposition the weight that it typically has. One must decide whether these influences will have the causal power over oneself that they have been observed to have. And here, one *cannot* say, "well, it *has to* have that causal power over me," or rather, if one does say this, the "has to" will

---

12 Here (and throughout this paper), I use the term "cause" in a broadly Humean sense that Eric Watkins has recently claimed is inappropriate in interpreting Kant (see Watkins 2005, p. 384). For my response to Watkins, see Frierson 2006, p. 7, n. 16.

be a purely practical one, a decision about what one values, and not a decision "forced by the facts." One's deliberation would find no room for freedom only if one had either an *exhaustive* theoretical explanation of a particular act or a theoretical basis for claiming that there *is* such an exhaustive explanation available, though one does not (yet) have it. But at the level of first-order judgments, one lacks exhaustive theoretical explanations,[13] and the second-order commitment to such explanations need not, and indeed should not, matter from a practical standpoint.

It is important to highlight that the insufficiency of causal explanations of behavior does *not* imply that freedom should play a role in theoretical explanation. Insofar as one adopts a theoretical standpoint, the insufficiency of any particular causal explanation is a reason to look for further causal explanations, not a reason to posit freedom. The second-order theoretical belief in universal causation commits one to that pursuit. But insofar as one adopts a practical standpoint, one need not be committed to the possibility of complete causal explanations of phenomena, and one needs to be—and, without contradiction, can be—committed to freedom.

The Grounding Thesis and the Reality of Freedom

Two-standpoint interpretations of freedom can accommodate ordinary theoretical judgments as reasons for action because from the practical standpoint one sees the world as the effect of the choices of rational agents. Causal explanations are wholly appropriate as long as they are explanations of a series of effects of or considerations for choice rather than an exhaustive series of causes of choice. Moreover, because the theoretical belief that one is not free is a second-order belief, it is a way of making sense of the theoretical standpoint, rather than an insight *from* that standpoint that might be relevant for practical deliberation. So there is no reason to think that one *should* take *that* belief into account

---

13 One might, of course, have a theoretical explanation of the causal power of such a natural disposition, perhaps in terms of genetics. But then one will lack a theoretical explanation of why genes must function the way they do. The point is that at some level, one's theoretical explanations will come to an end, and then one will find room for deliberation. Note too that one need not explicitly think of one's choices in the way described here. That is, in deciding whether or not to have a cup of coffee, one need not make reference to one's genes. The fact that freedom to choose whether to give in to the inclination for coffee is translatable in terms of freedom to choose whether to let oneself be influenced by genes is a way of validating ordinary deliberation's appeal to freedom, not a reason to shift to a new way of deliberating.

and, in fact, one *cannot* take it into account in practical deliberation since it conflicts with practical deliberation's own second-order commitment to freedom.

But given that the theoretical and practical standpoints require apparently conflicting second-order judgments about human freedom, all of this may seem to beg the important question: is one *really* free? As Eric Watkins puts it,

> Regardless of whether or not two standpoints can be held at the same time, can they both be true or must one of them be illusory?.... That is, granted that we conceive of ourselves as free and as determined (albeit from different standpoints at different times), which of these conceptions contains a true description of how we are? (Watkins 2005, p. 322)

This question seems to be the one that most troubles objectors to the two-standpoint version of Kant's theory of freedom. The point is that there must be an answer to this simple, yes-no question, and however much we want to say "yes" from one standpoint and "no" from another, eventually we are entitled to ask, "and which standpoint gets it *right*?"

Following Allison, Watkins suggests one possible answer to the question of whether one is "really" free. As he explains,

> At this point, the proponent of the [two-standpoint] interpretation could claim...that this last set of questions is illegitimate, perhaps suggesting that one would have to adopt either a God's-eye viewpoint or stand outside of all standpoints so as to determine the accuracy or inaccuracy of each one. (Watkins 2005, p. 322; cf. Korsgaard 1996a, p. 176)

To some extent, this response is correct, in that one cannot have *knowledge*—in Kant's technical sense—about what the world is like "in itself," so if what is meant by "are we *really* free?" is "what can we *know* about what the self is like *in itself*?" then the answer is surely that we cannot *know* anything.

But this response is insufficient, for three fundamental reasons.[14] First, it ignores the fact that Kant *does* posit one standpoint as more fundamental than the other; one describes "things-in-themselves," while the other describes mere "appearances." Second, this response

---

14 Eric Watkins raises another problem with this response, suggesting that "the accuracy of a standpoint is not determined by any putatively divine meta-standpoint, but rather simply by the metaphysical facts of the matter" (Watkins 2005, p. 322-3). Ultimately, this need not be a problem for the two-standpoint theorist, since such a theorist can simply deny that we even know what the question of freedom would *mean* as a question about "metaphysical facts." Freedom has a clear meaning in terms of empirical causes and a clear meaning in terms of practical responsibility. Watkins seems to assume that it has a clear meaning "metaphysically." But this depends on the legitimacy of a "metaphysical standpoint" from which one can ask the question. Short of the legitimacy of such a standpoint, we don't even know what kind of "accuracy" a standpoint is supposed to have.

fails to distinguish the two-standpoint reading from the "wretched sub-terfuge" of compatibilism, according to which "freedom" is merely a word for an "effect, the determining natural ground of which lies *within* the acting being," a freedom that is no different than the freedom of "a projectile...in free motion" or a "turnspit" (5:96-7). Finally, this response fails to take seriously the nature of the practical standpoint itself, which is not merely a standpoint according to which one is free, but a standpoint from which one sees *the world of appearance* as the *effect of one's freedom*. That is, the practical standpoint posits a relationship between itself and the theoretical standpoint, according to which the theoretical standpoint is secondary. In order to make sense of the practical standpoint, one must posit that this standpoint sees things as they really are, and that the theoretical standpoint sees things *merely* as they appear. (As we will see later, the theoretical standpoint does not similarly prioritize itself.) Agnosticism about whether or not one is really free is thus unsatisfying.

Christine Korsgaard has suggested another way to think about whether or not one is really free: "Both interests [of theoretical and practical reason] are rational and legitimate" (Korsgaard 1996a, p. 173). Rather than agnosticism, Korsgaard offers a kind of syncretism: we *really* are both free and not free. There is a danger here of thinking that, on this interpretation, one's freedom amounts merely to a posture of deliberation, not something *real*. Some of Korsgaard's language provokes this concern, as when she says, "the point is not that you must *believe* that you are free, but that you must choose *as if* you were free" (Korsgaard 1996a, p. 162).[15] This way of putting it can make it seem as though freedom is *merely* the way we must think of ourselves for practical purposes, not the way we *really* are. But Korsgaard, following Kant, refuses to allow this interpretation of freedom. In *The Sources of Normativity*, Korsgaard responds to the point about "reality" as follows: "You will say that this means that our freedom is not 'real' only if you have defined the 'real' as what can be identified by scientists looking at things third-personally and from outside" (Korsgaard 1996b, p. 96).[16] In

---

15 Nelkin raises the question of how this passage relates to Korsgaard's statement later that "the standpoint from which you adopt the *belief in freedom* is that of the deliberating agent" (Nelkin 2000, p. 567, n7, citing Korsgaard 2006a, p. 174, my emphasis). As I read these passages, the first describes the view of the world constitutive of the deliberative standpoint. The later passage is part of Korsgaard's discussion of the postulates of practical reason. Because one *must* act *as if* one is free, one is (practically) justified in ascribing freedom to oneself. On this reading, then, Korsgaard's account does not raise the question about whether one is "really" free, though her language can *seem* to raise this question.

16 In her explanation of this argument, Korsgaard shifts her focus from freedom as such to the "reasons" that one offers within the practical point of view. Here "reasons" are first-

fact, the belief that one is free and the belief that one is determined by natural causes are symmetric. Each is a necessary presupposition of one standpoint,[17] and the question of which belief is "real" seems not to arise for either standpoint. Both beliefs are necessary—and in this sense "accurate"– because both standpoints are necessary (see Korsgaard 1996b, p. 96). While agnosticism denies the legitimacy of the question about whether or not one is really free by refusing to answer it, Korsgaard denies its legitimacy by answering it in two ways. The point is that questions about what is "really" the case always assume some conception of reality. If reality is limited to scientifically knowable things, then we are really unfree. But if reality is the world of practical concern, then we are really free.

Unfortunately, at least as stated so far, Korsgaard's solution falls into the same three problems that threaten the agnostic solution. As in the case of that solution, she fails to take seriously Kant's apparent prioritizing of things-in-themselves, she risks embracing the "wretched subterfuge" (5:96) of compatibilism that would make morality a "phantom" or "chimerical idea" (4:445; see too 4:456), and she fails to address the fact that the practical standpoint depends—at least for Kant—not merely upon the legitimacy of seeing oneself as free but upon the supremacy of the claim of freedom over claims about natural determination.

---

order practical beliefs. Why pull the fire alarm? Because pulling the fire alarm will notify people of the fire and thus increase the likelihood that they will escape the building uninjured, and I should do what I can to help people avoid unnecessary injury. In her discussion in *The Sources of Normativity*, Korsgaard's point is that this is no less "real" an explanation for pulling the fire alarm than one based on states of my brain, or the evolutionary development of sympathetic instincts, or theories of social conditioning. An explanation in terms of first-order practical reasons is not *scientific*, of course. But there is no reason to deny that these reasons are any less *real* than the scientific causes that figure in scientific accounts. As Korsgaard puts it, "reasons exist because we need them" (Korsgaard,1996b, p. 96). In the same way that first-order reasons "exist because we need them," the freedom that is postulated as the condition of deliberation exists because we need it.

Nonetheless, it is important to recognize here two important differences between Korsgaard's argument and Kant's own view about the relationship between the theoretical and practical standpoints. One, on which I focus in the main text, is that Kant ascribes a priority to the practical that Korsgaard underrates. The other, discussed above in note 8, is that Kant ascribes a sort of epistemic priority to theoretical reason, in that Kant takes the task of empirically cognizing the world to have priority over the task of choosing and evaluating actions in the light of moral responsibilities (Bxxix). Were it not for the fact that the theoretical standpoint leaves space for another standpoint, Kant claims that one would have to reject freedom (and with it the legitimacy of the practical standpoint).

17 Here I draw heavily from Kant's account in the first *Critique*. As far as I know, Korsgaard has not explicitly discussed the status of the belief that one is causally determined; as far as I can tell, there is no reason that she could not agree with Kant.

Both agnosticism and Korsgaard's symmetrical affirmation fail to take seriously the *asymmetry* upon which Kant insists as a way of avoiding crude compatibilism. What is needed is a way of articulating the supremacy of the practical standpoint over the theoretical, and neither agnosticism nor Korsgaard's syncretism seems capable of articulating this supremacy. And that, once again, raises the question of whether we are *really* free, but in a way that is particularly urgent from the practical standpoint.

The failure of the agnostic and syncretist answers to the question of the reality of freedom highlights the importance of what Eric Watkins has recently called the "grounding thesis." Watkins draws attention to the priority of freedom in a way that makes clear how it can solve the problem of whether one is "really" free, but that also seems to raise problems for two-standpoint theories. Watkins explains the grounding thesis as follows:

> In various works, Kant repeatedly suggests that things in themselves, or the noumenal world, "grounds" or "underlies" appearances, or the sensible world.... Despite the epistemic limitations Kant places on what we can know about how *specific* features of things in themselves might ground appearances, Kant makes several *general* claims about grounding. For one, Kant makes clear that the grounding relationship is one-way and not reciprocal.... Things in themselves ground appearances, but appearances do not ground things in themselves..... For another…not only does the noumenal world of things in themselves cause the *existence* of appearances…it is also responsible for the *laws* that govern appearances. (Watkins 2005, pp. 326, 328)

It should be clear how this helps with the question of the reality of freedom. Insofar as freedom is located at the level of things-in-themselves, free choices provide the grounds for the very causal laws of nature that are observed by theoretical reason (at least insofar as those laws bear on one's actions). Thus one is really free, but this freedom grounds a world governed by causal laws. Positing that free choices ground the laws of nature, one avoids the "wretched subterfuge" of compatibilism and provides legitimacy to the priority implied in the practical standpoint.[18] And this account is consonant with Kant's claims about the priority of things-in-themselves over appearances, which posed problems for agnostic and syncretist views. Thus the grounding thesis provides a coherent way of answering the question of whether one is really free.

But is this thesis compatible with a two-standpoint account of freedom and determinism? Watkins thinks not. He introduces his account of the grounding thesis as a way to arbitrate the dispute between two-

---

18   For a detailed explanation of a similar point, see Watkins 2005, pp. 329-39.

world and two-standpoint understandings of Kant's transcendental idealism:

> Despite the uncertainty and ambiguity that Kant's use of these two different understandings [as two worlds or two standpoints] of Transcendental Idealism creates at a general level, we can still turn to a particular aspect of Transcendental Idealism that is fundamental to his understanding of freedom and determinism, namely the issue of "grounding." (Watkins 2005, p. 325)

This objection might seem obvious. The description of the grounding thesis proposed by Watkins is permeated with two-world talk: "the noumenal world grounds...the sensible world," etc. And Watkins is surely correct that "the ontological, two-worlds interpretation of Transcendental Idealism...has no difficulties with the grounding thesis" (Watkins 2005, p. 329).[19] Moreover, a two-worlds interpretation provides a (relatively) straightforward interpretation of the priority of freedom as a metaphysical priority, the priority of a ground to its effect. But why is it impossible to make sense of this thesis on a two-standpoint interpretation? Watkins argues,

> [T]he assertion that "things in themselves ground appearances" is a claim that cannot be made from either standpoint. Assertions about things in themselves can be made only from the practical or deliberative standpoint, while claims about appearances can be made only from the theoretical or scientific standpoint. (Watkins 2005, pp. 328-9)

Phrased in this way, Watkins's problem with a two-standpoint interpretation of the grounding thesis is based on the same misunderstanding as the theory-in-deliberation objection. Insofar as the practical standpoint involves deliberation about action *in the world*, it can and must make claims about appearances. Moreover, as we saw the last section, insofar as "the deliberating agent, employing reason practically, views the world...as an expression of the wills of...rational agents" (Korsgaard 1996a, p. 173), the practical standpoint *commits* the deliberating agent to the grounding thesis. One who reasons practically precisely sees actions in the world—appearances—as the effects of the choices of a free—that is, "in-itself"—agent that determines—or grounds—those actions. Whereas the two-world interpretation treats the language of "effects" here more-or-less literally, the two-standpoint interpretation ascribes a purely practical meaning to such language. Rather than being a *metaphysical* ground of effects in the world, one is a *practical*

---

19 At least, the difficulties the two-worlds theory has are familiar ones, such as how to make sense of a causal relationship between things-in-themselves and appearances when the only conception of causation that we can understand is a schematized concept that applies only to appearances. For Watkins's response to this problem, see Watkins 2005, pp. 324-9.

ground, which is simply to say that one is (morally) *responsible* for one's actions and their effects.

The real challenge to the two-standpoint interpretation comes not from an inability to articulate the grounding thesis—since this can be done straightforwardly within the practical standpoint—but from particular *features* of the grounding relationship. Watkins draws attention to two features of Kant's use of the grounding thesis that enable him to avoid the "wretched subterfuge" of crude compatibilism. Of these, the more important is that "the grounding relationship is one-way and not reciprocal.... Things in themselves ground appearances, but appearances do not ground things in themselves" (Watkins 2005, p. 328).[20] One might be concerned that while the practical standpoint can assert its priority from *within* that standpoint, the theoretical standpoint could as easily assert *its* priority from within its own standpoint. In other words, we might think that when reasoning practically, we must think of our choices as determining the way the world will appear when we study it scientifically, while when reasoning scientifically, we must think of empirical causes as determining the way people choose. And if both standpoints are, as Korsgaard insists, "rational and legitimate" (Korsgaard 1996a, p. 173), then we are left either without a real grounding thesis or with a perfectly symmetrical one. Either way, we seem stuck with crude compatibilism and without an answer to the question about whether freedom is "real."

Fortunately, the apparent symmetry between standpoints does not stand up to scrutiny. While the practical standpoint does posit priority over the theoretical by postulating that it is (at least partially) responsible for the world as it appears, the theoretical does *not* similarly posit priority over the practical. In that sense, Watkins is partly correct in claiming that for two-standpoint theorists, "Assertions about things in themselves can be made only from the practical or deliberative standpoint" (Watkins 2005, p. 328). When Kant "den[ies] knowledge in order to make room for faith" (Bxxx), he thereby ensures at least that the theoretical standpoint is not in a position to challenge the priority that the practical ascribes to itself.

But we can go further. In two important respects, the theoretical standpoint asserts its own *subordination* to the practical (or at least, to some non-empirical standpoint). First, while the theoretical standpoint

---

20 In fact, Watkins specifically ties the problems two-standpoint theories have with the grounding thesis to these features of it. The second feature, that "not only does the noumenal world of things in themselves cause the *existence* of appearances . . ., it is also responsible for the *laws* that govern appearances" can also be accommodated on a two-standpoint interpretation, and my discussion of causal laws in the previous section suggests how this might be done.

cannot claim *knowledge* of "things-in-themselves," it posits things-in-themselves indirectly, as vaguely articulated ideals toward which scientific attempts at explanation aim. The incompleteness of science discussed earlier shows that within the theoretical standpoint itself, every particular explanation includes the recognition that something more needs to be said, that the explanation is incomplete. There is "a system of formal conditions that our understanding of the empirical world presupposes," and in the case of human beings, "we...not only see ourselves as parts of nature with a certain incompletely known empirical character; we...also see this empirical character as presupposing another, unknowable but *intelligible character*" (O'Neill 1989, p. 69). While theoretical reason cannot *posit* freedom to fill in those incomplete explanations, it implicitly recognizes its own always only partially formulated explanations as dependent upon something more fundamental, something that turns out to be the realm of freedom.[21] Second, even the theoretical standpoint is importantly practical in the sense that the theorizer sees herself as a free agent, capable of making judgments based on the best evidence, and not merely as a result of various causes. Thus the *practice* of science depends on freedom in a deeper way than the practice of morality depends on science: "The enterprise of naturalistic explanation itself depends on freedom" (O'Neill 1989, p. 69, cf. Korsgaard 1996a, p. 185, n18).[22]

For a two-standpoint theorist, there is no "absolute" standpoint from which to articulate the grounding thesis, but both theoretical and practical standpoints involve second-order claims about the relative priority of the standpoints. The "one-way and not reciprocal" aspect of the grounding thesis shows up in the fact that *both* the practical standpoint *and* the theoretical standpoint see the empirical descriptions given within the theoretical standpoint as *secondary*. *Both* standpoints, that is, affirm the "primacy of the practical." Now the *sense* of priority differs within each standpoint. The practical standpoint directly implies a second-order claim of the dependence of what can be observed on (among other things) the choices of human agents, where this "dependence" is understood in terms of ascriptions of responsibility. The theoretical

---

21 As Kant puts it, "*causa noumenon* with respect to the theoretical use of reason is, though a possible, thinkable concept, nevertheless an empty one.... Now, however...the concept is given significance in the moral law and consequently in its practical reference" (5:56, cf. 8:136-8).

22 The second sense in which the theoretical standpoint depends upon the practical is one about which Kant is much more wary than O'Neill and Korsgaard. While Kant suggests that the spontaneity of the transcendental synthesis of a manifold makes me "conscious of myself not as I appear to myself" (B157), he avoids concluding from this that one must, from a purely epistemic standpoint, see oneself as *free*.

standpoint does not imply *this* claim, but it implies the priority of the practical both in that the theoretical standpoint can find its ultimate satisfaction only in a standpoint that allows for an unconditioned ground of the conditioned effects that are its immediate objects of study and in that the theoretical standpoint involves a sort of practice invoking standards of epistemic responsibility that imply some sort of freedom.[23] Because *both* standpoints posit the grounding thesis in ways that mutually support one another, a two-standpoint account can make sense of the dependence of "appearances" on "things-in-themselves."[24]

Given the priority of the practical within both practical and theoretical standpoints, one could say that one is "really" free because, from all of the perspectives one can take on the issue, whenever one considers freedom, one must consider it to have priority over natural causes. Korsgaard herself, immediately after claiming that "Both interests [of theoretical and practical reason] are rational and legitimate" goes on to say, "Or, if either is privileged, it is the practical" (Korsgaard 1996a, p. 173). And this way of articulating the grounding thesis is just what one should expect—and all that is needed—from a two-standpoint theorist. Freedom is real, not merely in the sense that it is required from a practical standpoint, but also in the sense that this practical standpoint has priority—in both a practical and a theoretical sense—over the theoretical.[25] The grounding thesis, and the reality of freedom, are both captured in Kant's insistence on "the primacy of...practical reason" (5:119-21).

---

23 For discussion of the latter point, see Guevara 2000, pp. 64-8.

24 One might, of course, use a metaphysical account of two worlds, one of which grounds another, to make philosophical sense of the priority of the practical standpoint. The point of this paper is not to argue that the two-world account of freedom is incoherent or even wrong, only that it is not *necessary*. The priority of the practical can, for two-standpoint theorists, just be a basic fact about our standpoints, one that still lets us make sense of the grounding thesis.

25 This provides a way to reconcile Kant's different claims about the priority of the practical. On the one hand, Kant insists on the priority of practical reason (5:119ff.). On the other hand, Kant claims that if "speculative reason had proven that freedom cannot be thought...then the [moral] presupposition [of freedom]...would have to yield" to this speculative conclusion (Bxxix, cf. 4:456). On the two-standpoint account I have articulated, what Kant is saying is that *if* the theoretical standpoint were to claim priority for itself, we would have to accord it priority. But because the theoretical standpoint does not claim such priority, we can affirm the priority of the practical.

Theory-in-Deliberation Strikes Again: the problem of moral anthropology

This paper started with the problem of incorporating the content of scientific or theoretical claims into deliberation or, more generally, a practical standpoint on human actions. The key to solving that problem is seeing that the practical standpoint makes claims about the natural world, but only insofar as those claims are incorporated into reasons for action, either as consequences of action or as relevant contextual features. The practical standpoint is not a standpoint disconnected from the world of experience, but rather a standpoint that sees that world as the *effect* rather than the *cause* of choices. This characterization of the practical standpoint also allows for an answer to the question of the "reality" of freedom by providing a two-standpoint way of articulating what Eric Watkins has called the "grounding thesis." Thus two-standpoint theories can make sense of theory-in-deliberation, they can coherently claim that human beings are "really" free (while also, in a subsidiary sense, unfree), and they can make sense of the dependence of "appearances" on "things-in-themselves" in terms of the priority of practical reason.

Unfortunately, the asymmetry between standpoints that permits a two-standpoint account of dependency poses a new theory-in-deliberation problem in the context of certain *sorts* of theoretical claims that might play a role in certain sorts of deliberation. In particular, the grounding thesis claims that human freedom grounds the world as it appears, and that this grounding relationship is *not reciprocal*. This claim might seem problematic given that, scientifically speaking, there seem to be purely empirical causes of various human choices, but the necessary incompleteness of scientific explanation opens room within the deliberative standpoint for seeing "causal" preconditions as a *context* for choice rather than a *determinant* of choice. But a different problem arises when one seeks to make *use* of empirical claims about causes of human action from a *practical* standpoint. The sorts of theoretical claims that have the potential to raise a serious theory-in-deliberation problem are theoretical claims about causal influences on choices, where those theoretical claims are treated *as causal claims* and the choices are considered *as free choices*.

Unfortunately, there seem to be such theoretical claims.[26] For Kant, they arise explicitly in the context of what he calls "moral anthropology." As Kant explains in the *Metaphysics of Morals*,

> Moral anthropology...would deal...with the subjective conditions in human nature that hinder people or help them in fulfilling the laws of a metaphysics of morals. It would deal with the development, spreading, and strengthening of moral principles (in education in schools and in popular instruction). (6:217)

In cases such as moral education, one may seek to influence oneself or another through empirical causes, and influence oneself or another precisely insofar as one is a deliberative agent. In these cases, one reasons: "I will do action A in order to bring it about by a sequence of natural causes that person P does action B for reason R." Cases such as these seem to require viewing person P from both the practical and the theoretical-scientific standpoints at once and in the same respect. On the one hand, P must be viewed from the theoretical-scientific point of view, since one sees P's choice here as the result of a prior cause, action A. On the other hand, P must be viewed from the practical point of view, and hence as free, since one's goal is for P to act for a particular *reason*. The importance of "doing B for reason R" lies in the fact that one holds P *responsible* for acting in that particular way. If P were considered merely from a theoretical standpoint, one could seek to bring it about that P does B as a result of having a particular mental state, but one could not aim for P to do B for a particular *reason*.

The cases that raise conceptual problems for two-standpoint accounts of dependency must be distinguished from two similar but importantly different cases. One might treat another person as a mere object and seek to manipulate him through deceit, torture, or underhanded marketing. These forms of psychological manipulation are morally wrong, since they involve treating another as a mere thing, but they need not raise conceptual problems because one need not see the manipulated person as *both* manipulable *and* free.[27] One seeks to get another to do a particular action, but not for a particular *reason* (though perhaps as a result of particular psychological *causes*). The cases that raise difficulties for the grounding thesis should also be distinguished from ordinary cases of offering reasons to other agents. When I suggest a reason for you to do a particular action, I precisely see my action as

---

26   Elsewhere Kant adds that moral education and churches (5:151ff., 6:474ff.), politeness (6:473, 7:151-3), a cultivated aesthetic appreciation for the beautiful and sublime (5:268-9, 299, and 354-6) and even belief in the practical postulates can affect one's deliberation in morally positive ways.

27   To see what is *wrong* with these cases of manipulation, of course, one must in some sense see the agent as both determined and free. This problem also poses difficulties for the grounding thesis, but I do not focus on those here.

providing a context for choice, not being a cause of choice. I can aim for you to do a particular action for a particular reason, but not see your action for that reason as the causally necessitated effect of my action.

Sometimes, however, one seeks not merely to cause another to perform an action, nor merely to offer possible reasons for another to act, but to causally effect in another the state of acting for a particular reason. In *After Virtue*, Alasdair MacIntyre gives an example of the sort of consideration that causes this problem. In his discussion of teaching a child to value the goods internal to the practice of chess, MacIntyre says,

> Consider the example of a highly intelligent seven-year-old child whom I wish to teach to play chess, although the child has no particular desire to learn the game. The child does, however, have a very strong desire for candy and little chance of obtaining it. I therefore tell the child that if the child will play chess with me...I will give the child 50 cents worth of candy; moreover I tell the child that I will always play in such a way that it will be difficult, but not impossible, for the child to win, and that, if the child wins, the child will receive an extra 50 cents worth of candy. Thus motivated the child plays to win . . ..
> [T]here will come a time when the child will find in those goods specific to chess...a new set of reasons, reasons now not just for winning on a particular occasion, but for trying to excel in whatever way the game of chess demands. (MacIntyre, 1984, p. 188)

For the purposes of this paper, it is not necessary to get into the significance MacIntyre sees in this transformation. What is important here is that one seeks to change not only the sorts of decisions that the child makes, but even the sort of *reasons* that the child takes into account in deliberation. One would not start the process without believing that it is likely to give rise to the "new set of reasons" for which one aims, so it is not mere action at which one aims. And one seeks to get the child to play chess for the right reasons not by simply offering those reasons to the child, but by employing psychological tricks to eventually *cause* the child to see those reasons for herself.

From what standpoint is such a child considered? On the one hand, the child is clearly being viewed from the standpoint of theoretical-scientific reason, since one makes claims about how various empirical causes can influence the ultimate beliefs and actions of the child. On the other hand, one cares about the thoughts and actions of the child only insofar as one takes an evaluative, practical standpoint. One seeks to make the child better *as a deliberator*. One seeks to influence not merely the child's beliefs and desires, but the child's *reasons*, and one seeks to influence these reasons through natural-scientific causes. Moreover, one does not simply seek to change the mental states that *cause* the child to act in a particular way. One seeks to affect the sorts of *reasons* that the child takes into account in deliberation. Thus in this case, one seems required to think of the child at the same time and in the same respect as both free, since only as a free deliberator do the choices of the child have the relevant weight, and as unfree, since one seeks causal influence on those choices.

This problem arises in an even more poignant way with respect to moral development, since in this case one's concern with bringing about a particular sort of choice in another is more clearly dependent upon holding that person responsible. So imagine that one seeks to influence the future deliberation of oneself or another. One seeks to promote a commitment to acting rightly for the sake of acting rightly. In such a case, one might pursue certain sorts of moral education, or practices of discipline, with the goal of making oneself or another more likely to make morally worthy choices. One might even promote social and political structures to positively affect the moral development of those living within such structures. The goal of one's action is moral development, but in order to think of someone as *morally* better, one must think of that person as free. At the same time, though, in order to think of one's action as causing that end, one must think of the person as unfree. For the maxim: "do action A in order to bring about the moral development of person P" to be reasonable, one must think of P as *both* free *and* unfree.[28]

Decisions that promote volitional development, and especially those that promote moral development, involve considering people as at once free and unfree. Two-standpoint theories cannot easily dismiss the contradiction in such decisions because both ways of considering people enter into the reasons for performing actions that promote volitional development. Thus in these cases, Nelkin's general worry about a contradiction arising within a single standpoint does seem apt.

---

28   This kind of problem arises in non-moral cases, too, and even in cases in which one seeks to manipulate one's *own* behavior. For example, I might deeply enjoy going to the opera with my partner, and enjoy it for the sake of the opera and for my partner's company. Moreover, I might deeply desire to be the sort of person who goes to the opera for these reasons. But I often fail to consider going to the opera, or going to the opera seems like more trouble than it is worth when I consider it. But perhaps I know myself well enough to know that purchasing season tickets to the opera will make me more likely to decide to go. Having set dates ahead of time will effectively force me to consider going to the opera on the nights for which I have tickets. And having the tickets in hand will lead me to think that going is worth the trouble after all. One wouldn't want to waste the tickets, after all. Here it's important that the reason for going to the opera *not* be "to avoid wasting the tickets." Rather, the consideration that one would waste the tickets is merely a means for discounting the trouble involved in going to the opera, trouble that is usually exaggerated but in this case discounted. The reason for going to the opera is that I enjoy it, especially in the company of my partner. And I buy the season tickets because I want to be the sort of person who makes these sorts of choices. Again, I consider myself *qua deliberator* as susceptible to empirical causation.

Two Standpoints and Moral Anthropology

The problems with which this paper began were problems specifically for two-standpoint interpretations of Kant's transcendental idealism. The problem outlined in the last section is more general. Even with a two-world account of Kant's idealism, one will have to deal with a tension between the grounding thesis and the importance of having an influence upon the volitional (especially moral) development of oneself and others.

In *Freedom and Anthropology in Kant's Moral Philosophy*, I addressed a tension similar to that between the grounding thesis and moral anthropology in general,[29] but there I made liberal use of concepts and terminology drawn from a two-worlds interpretation of Kant's idealism. Put extremely briefly, my account there involved seeing that one's intelligible, noumenal character is expressed not merely in the individual, phenomenal actions of a moment, but in one's phenomenal life as a whole. The evidence from the empirical character of one's past suggests that one's intelligible choice in the noumenal world is not a pure choice of good, but includes a radically evil subordination of morality to non-moral inclinations, and the expression of this radical evil in the phenomenal world involves not merely evil choices but a deliberate propensity to evil. Insofar as one still has an obligation to *be* good (noumenally), this goodness can only mean a "revolution" against one's own radical evil, and the expression of this goodness (phenomenally) will be a life of constant struggle against one's own evil propensity. Moreover, because radical evil is (in part) social, this struggle must take place in the context of community; so one will not only struggle against one's own evil propensity but also seek to encourage others in their struggle against evil.[30] Thus promoting empirical states of affairs that strengthen the (empirical) wills of oneself and others against the propensity to evil is a way of expressing noumenal goodness-as-revolution.

However satisfying one finds this resolution to the tension between freedom and anthropology, it extensively uses two-world language, and one advantage of a two-world interpretation of Kant's idealism may be that it allows for a better articulation of a Kantian solution to the problem of moral anthropology than two-standpoint intrepretations. That

---

29 I articulate my version of the grounding thesis in chapter one, and lay out my solution to the tension posed above primarily in chapter five.

30 Cashing out the social nature of radical evil is challenging. For two different approaches, cf. Anderson-Gold 2001 and Frierson 2003, chapter 6.

said, the rest of this paper will sketch a Kantian[31] solution to the problem in strictly two-standpoint terms. The key elements of this solution
still lie in thinking of one's life *as a whole* as expressing free choice, in
recognizing the challenges posed by radical evil, and in seeing one's
struggle against evil as part of a social struggle.[32] The difference from
the two-world way of dealing with the problem is that a two-standpoint
interpretation is not entitled to the metaphysical speculations that underlie the articulation of these key elements in the previous paragraph.
But these elements can be developed through a richer conception of
what the "practical standpoint" involves. Typically, this standpoint is
described in terms of deliberation about (or evaluation of) a particular
action or choice, but the importance of moral anthropology forces a
revision of this typical description.

In this context, the implication of the first—life as a whole—
element is that deliberation and evaluation should not be seen primarily
as dealing with actions—what to do—but with character, who to be. In
deliberations at any given time, one should see oneself as constructing a
life, not merely as deciding on a particular action.[33] In a sense, of
course, one can only *immediately* determine one's choices in the present. But Kant's moral theory temporally extends these choices in two
important respects. First, genuine choices, for Kant, choices for which
one can be held responsible, are choices of *maxims*, which are *policies*
for action. As Korsgaard explains, these policies must been seen to be
at least somewhat temporally extended in order to constitute choices *of
an agent* (Korsgaard 1996b, pp. 231-2). What moral anthropology
forces is an expansion of what is always already a temporally extended

---

31 In part, the description "Kantian" is intended to highlight the role that radical evil plays
    in this account. One might develop a response to the problem of moral anthropology
    simply by shifting focus from individual acts to life as a whole. For Kant, however, the
    urgency of moral anthropology is due to the need to combat radical evil. Without radi-
    cal evil, it is not clear that the sorts of self-cultivation that pose *prima facie* problems
    for the grounding thesis would have an important role to play in Kant's ethics.
32 For a similar emphasis on seeing one's moral life as a whole, see David Sussman's
    contribution to this volume.
33 O'Neill explains, "We must not only see ourselves as parts of nature with a certain
    incompletely known empirical character; we must also see this empirical character as
    presupposing another, unknowable but *intelligible character*. This is the central
    claim...of the most difficult of all Kant's thoughts about the atemporal character of hu-
    man agency..." (O'Neill 1989, p. 69). The "atemporal" character of this agency is
    explained, in part, by the fact that the intelligible character for which we hold ourselves
    responsible is the presupposition of one's *whole* empirical character, that is, one's life
    as a whole. Similarly, when Korsgaard explains that "the deliberating agent...views the
    world...as an expression of the wills of God and other rational agents" (Korsgaard
    1996a, p. 173), the point is that the temporally extended world as a whole—not merely
    the way the world turns out *now*—is an expression of one's free choice.

account of particular choices. Second, insofar as we choose *a life* rather than merely an action, we make individual choices about what to do in the light of how these choices will form us into a particular sort of person. Cultivation of talents is morally required only because one is a temporally extended person, who will have a will in the future that can make use of the talents that one cultivates. Cultivation of moral resolve, similarly, is morally required because one is a temporally extended person who can express that resolve in the future.

The implication of the second element—the importance of radical evil—is that the practical standpoint is not *simply* the standpoint of freedom, but a standpoint that one might, following Jeanine Grenberg, call the standpoint of *humility*.[34] As Grenberg explains it, humility is "that meta-attitude which constitutes the moral agent's proper perspective on herself as a dependent and corrupt but capable and dignified rational agent" (Grenberg 2005, p. 133). Acting from the standpoint of humility is different from merely acting from a practical standpoint, and even different from acting from the standpoint of pure practical reason. From the standpoint of a morally responsible and dependent but noncorrupt agent, action is a free response to the condition of moral obligation in the face of temptations caused by inclinations. But the standpoint of *humility* that takes into account radical evil recognizes that one's real enemy is not mere temptation, which can "be sought in the natural inclinations," but a freely chosen "*malice* (of the human heart) which secretly undermines [one's] disposition with soul-corrupting principles" (6:57). This humility in the face of one's own corruption does not compromise the demands of morality. As Kant insists, it "is of no use in moral dogmatics, for the precepts of the latter...include the very same duties...whether there is in us an innate propensity to transgression or not" (6:50). Nonetheless, humility requires more of one than simple duty:

> In moral discipline...the thesis means...this: We cannot start out in the ethical training of our connatural moral predisposition to the good with an innocence which is natural to us but must rather begin with a presupposition of a depravity of our power of choice in adopting maxims contrary to the original ethical predisposition and ...with unremitting counteraction against [this depravity]. (6:51)

The standpoint of practical humility is a standpoint from which one sees one's life as a life of struggle against one's own self-wrought tendency to subordinate the moral law to one's inclinations. And from this standpoint, one must not only do what is right in a particular moment, but act in ways that will promote an increasingly good life overall.

---

34 In Frierson 2003, I refer to this as the "perspective of moral anthropology" (p. 132).

Finally, the third key element—that the struggle against evil is social—means that the humble, practical standpoint is not solely an individual one. Of course, the standpoint is individual in the sense that each
individual must decide how to act. But when an individual deliberates,
she should always see herself as part of a community. This requires
seeking to live out one's struggle against corruption *in community with
others*, and it involves seeing the ultimate consummation of that struggle in a new social condition. And that includes deliberately avoiding
creating unnecessary temptations for others, exercising caution in relationships with others to avoid using their actions as a pretext for one's
own corrupt desires, aiming to cultivate good choices in others, looking
to others for support and encouragement in one's own efforts to improve, and conscientiously cultivating the sorts of community that can
promote moral progress for all involved.

This two-standpoint solution to the problem of moral anthropology
is only a sketch, and considerably more detail would need to be filled
in. In the end, however, a two-standpoint interpretation of Kant's theory
of freedom would meet the challenges of theory-in-deliberation, even in
the case of moral anthropology, by developing a sufficiently rich account of the practical standpoint. The practical standpoint must attend
to the importance of character, radical evil, and humans' social nature.
It must also have "priority"; practical reasoning is not merely one sort
of reasoning among many, but the most fundamental perspective on a
world about which human beings think but also within which they live
and act. Nothing in this paper precludes making sense of these two
standpoints by appeal to two metaphysically distinct "worlds," but I
have argued that two-standpoint theorists do not *need* such an appeal.
What is required to make sense of freedom is not a new metaphysics,
but rather a certain sort of practical orientation, a form of life that takes
seriously both the priority and the complex nature of practical reason.[35]

35 I would like to thank James Krueger and Benjamin Lipscomb for their hard work put-
    ting together this volume and for inspiring me with ideas for this paper. I thank Alix
    Cohen for challenging me to better articulate the central claims of my book in two-
    standpoint language; this paper is a down payment on that challenge. I also thank Karl
    Ameriks, Andrew Chignell, John Hare, Lee Hardy, Patrick Kain, Houston Smit, Angela
    Smith, and Rachel Zuckert for comments and conversation that helped me revise early
    drafts of this paper. And finally, I owe more than mere thanks to Kyla Ebels-Duggan,
    Eric Watkins, and Dana Nelkin, all of whom have offered extremely penetrating com-
    ments and criticism on this paper, comments and criticism that have already substantial-
    ly improved this paper, but that I have only begun to address.

CHAPTER 4

In Search of the Phenomenal Face of Freedom

Jeanine Grenberg

Introduction

A debate about whether Kant is a compatibilist or an incompatibilist
has raged for at least twenty years now. In one corner, people like Allen
Wood, Ralf Meerbote and Hud Hudson have argued for a compatibilist
Kant of various stripes.[1] Although it was Wood who introduced the
now-familiar phrase, "the compatibility of compatibilism and incompatibilism" (Wood 1984, p. 239), to describe the awkward position of
the transcendental idealist trying to wrangle with the freedom problem,
he himself ultimately adopts a more straightforwardly compatibilist
interpretation. According to Wood's Kant, all action is determined,
either by reason or by inclination. It is just that the former version of
determination—determination by reason—is "compatible" with freedom *(Ibid.,* p. 247). Kant is, thus, a compatibilist, albeit of a rather different, and more metaphysically robust, sort than most contemporary
compatibilists (who, presumably, would demur at Kant's notion of rational as opposed to natural determinism). Meerbote's and Hudson's
Kant, by contrast, is committed to something like contemporary David-
sonian compatibilism, on which room for the mental is found in a naturalistic universe.

Henry Allison raises concerns about both Meerbote's and Wood's
interpretations, and seeks to retain an incompatibilist moment in Kant's
theory of freedom with his well-known Incorporation Thesis.[2] According to Allison's interpretation, an "action must be regarded as something the agent 'does' of itself, as opposed to being the result of something 'done' to the agent" (Allison 1990, p. 28). It is Kant's
commitment to this "activity requirement"—that is, to a robust conception of spontaneity—which, according to Allison, leads Kant ultimately

---

1 See Wood 1984, Meerbote 1984, and Hudson 1994.
2 See Allison 1990.

to an incompatibilist account of freedom with incorporation at its center (*Ibid.*, p. 38). A rational agent is not determined by desires or other incentives directly, but rather incorporates them into or "takes them as" reasons for action. According to Allison, if we don't admit such an incompatibilist moment in agency, we can't make sense of why Kant would have introduced the metaphysically complex (and unquestionably problematic) conception of "intelligible character" in the Third Antinomy.

In making this move, it is not that Allison entirely denies any compatibilist tendencies in Kant's texts. Indeed, he discusses how one can find the basis in Kant's texts for a "rich...compatibilist" *(Ibid.*, p. 29) account of freedom. His considered position, though, is that Kant ultimately finds a merely compatibilist solution to the problem of freedom inadequate. He suggests that "Kant's problematic begins just at the point at which the compatibilist analysis typically ends, namely, with the recognition that rational agency is integrated into the law-governed order of nature" (*Ibid.*, p. 81). That is, Kant's problem is not so much whether there is reason in nature; his problem is how to assure that such naturalized reason is also "compatible" with that higher, non-natural form of reason asserted within our intelligible character, the capacity to begin a series of events from oneself, independently of previous states in the natural order of things. Allison thus claims to be returning to and enhancing the position, introduced but abandoned by Wood, of the "compatibility of compatibilism and incompatibilism."

I accept Allison's more robust, and unapologetically incompatibilist, reading of Kant's theory of freedom. It seems to me, though, that we can do more than Allison thus far has to explain the overall unity of the being subject to both phenomenal and intelligible causality. Although Allison begins by articulating a compatibilist account of freedom and natural reason, his main concern is to keep the compatibilists at bay, and to convince us of the possibility of this other-worldly moment of incorporation issuing from our intelligible character. But once we accept his argument (as I do), further questions about the relation of this noumenal form of causality to the natural order arise.

Again, the story of naturalized freedom and reason that Allison provides[3] is articulated *previous* to his full account of incorporation, making it hard to determine what relationship this naturalized account has to intelligible character and its paradigmatic act of incorporation. Allison, in making room for this naturalized account of freedom, does

---

3   We find room "for freedom in a deterministic...universe by allowing for the description and explanation of human action in terms of the beliefs, desires and intentions of a-gents, that is, for a 'naturalized' version of the causality of reason." (Allison 1990, p. 34)

speak briefly of the idea that empirical character is "an expression or manifestation and not simply a result of an intelligible activity" (*Ibid.*, p. 32). But his concern to avoid an illicit "inference route from the empirical to the intelligible" leads him to limit what we can say about *how* empirical character is an expression of the intelligible.

The effect that this has on our understanding of the relationship of incorporation to the psychological details of our moral lives is unfortunate. We know that incorporation is incorporation *of* an empirical desire or incentive, but the limits of reason prevent us from saying any more about the relationship of the intelligible act to the empirical desire.[4] I think, however, that more can be said. And perhaps we need to clarify, or even abandon, the language of "compatibilism" to get at what is really at issue.

Our real concern is the old question that goes back to Kant's German Idealist critics: can we really say that a sensibly affected agent operating in the phenomenal world, yet guided by an other-worldly intelligible act, is a truly *unified* agent? Is this intelligible character with its act of incorporation of which I am not conscious—but which is asserted nonetheless as the source of my phenomenal acts, and the guide for my phenomenal desires, incentives and disposition—really *me*? If we can say nothing at all about how my intelligible self guides, or is expressed in, my phenomenal self, that intelligible self seems a ghostly shadow of me instead of, well, *me*.

Assertion of freedom in both the naturalized and intelligible senses without some further story about the relationship of intelligible and phenomenal activity threatens to break this agent apart. If one account of our freedom gives us 'A', and the other 'not-A' (which is what happens when we consider a sensibly affected agent as having both empirical and intelligible characters, the first of which is guided by natural causality and the second of which transcends this causality), we might hope at least for further reflection on why we should be happy with this paradox. Why should we be happy to describe as the *same thing* that which is asserted both to be free despite being determined by the causal series and also to have a freedom that transcends that causal series.

What is really at the heart of the question of whether Kant is both a compatibilist and an incompatibilist is thus revealed: to speak of an empirical, phenomenal, and admittedly compatibilist analogue to the incompatibilist free act of incorporation would be to affirm the *unity* of

---

4   Indeed, there are times when it seems that Allison wants to leave in the background, or set aside entirely, the "rich compatibilist" account he has provided, for example, when he suggests that "Kant *reject*[s]…a compatibilist solution to the free will problem and insist[s] *instead* on introducing the problematic notion of an intelligible character" (Allison 1990, p. 34, emphases added).

a being who is both intellectual and sensible. Without such resolution, we are left with the impression either that the sensibly affected rational agent is in a deeply paradoxical state, or that my intelligible character is not so much "me" as it is a foreign invader upon my phenomenal self.

I don't want to push this line of thought simply as a criticism of Allison. I am, as I've already indicated, in agreement with him about the importance of admitting an incompatibilist moment like incorporation into the freedom story, and I agree with him that the admission of such moments is just what makes Kant's account of freedom and human agency rich (if also more potentially paradoxical or mysterious). I only think that there is more to say about the unity of the subject whose agency can be described in both naturalized, empirical terms and in intelligible terms.

As Allison notes, intelligible and empirical character are claimed by Kant to have a relation to each other, in the Third Antinomy itself. Curiously, such a claim seems to go beyond Kant's own line on what the Third Antinomy is about. Kant asserts in the Third Antinomy that the only thing he wants to accomplish there is to prove the mere possibility of freedom (A536/B564). His assertion has guided many recent interpreters of this text[5]. But, in fact, much of Kant's discussion in the Third Antinomy (especially in the later parts, those that assert a relationship between intelligible and empirical character) goes further than assuring the mere possibility of freedom and seeks instead to bring a more substantial description to the relationship of intelligible and empirical expressions of freedom. I do not mean to argue that Kant is successful, in the Third Antinomy, in resolving these larger questions. I think instead, as will become clear, that these are questions more appropriately and adequately raised and answered within a practical as opposed to a theoretical discussion of freedom. Nonetheless, these passages in the Third Antinomy exist, in part because, when he wrote them, Kant was still in the middle of theorizing that new, practical use of reason, and didn't always recognize when, in his discussion of the central issue connecting the theoretical and the practical—viz., freedom—he was sliding subtly from aspects of the question of freedom best considered theoretically toward aspects of it more appropriately considered practically.

This makes the claims of the Third Antinomy difficult, but enticing. It is my intention in this paper to focus on one of those enticing claims—that empirical character is a sensible schema of intelligible character—to trace the development of Kant's ideas about the overall unity of the sensibly affected rational agent. It will be tempting to think that we can work out the overall unity of such a being on the level of

---

5   Wood (1984) and Eric Watkins (2005) are particularly guided by this constraint.

theoretical inquiry by appeal to something like schematism, a theoretical construct that helped Kant earlier in the *Critique of Pure Reason* to make apparently opposed things—concepts and intuitions—more amenable to each other in the construction of experience. What we will find, however, is that efforts to do so leave us in intractable contradictions. To resolve these issues, we—and Kant—must turn to a practical, instead of a theoretical, way of thinking about freedom. It is only by making this shift that the empirical and the intelligible can be tolerably integrated into a complex but unified life, the life of a finite, sensibly affected, but still genuinely rational being.

There is something lost by admitting that a more satisfying theoretical story about the relationship of intelligible and empirical character is not forthcoming. In abandoning such efforts, Kant is, really, abandoning the project that became the project of German Idealism, viz., the project of resolving theoretically the divide between nature and freedom. The turn to the practical will, in fact, be a more common-sense, action-guided way of resolving this problem, and it will not be satisfying to those seeking a clear, theoretical resolution of the tension. Hegel would be horrified. Yet the advantage of abandoning the effort at a theoretical resolution to the problem of the overall unity of a being who is both intelligible and phenomenal is that we can, ultimately, tell a more satisfying moral-psychological story about the lives of finite, sensibly affected rational agents.

In this paper, I limit myself to raising concerns about how Kant seeks to resolve the tensions inherent in asserting a schematizing relationship between intelligible and empirical character. My goal is thus to smooth the philosophical ground for later, practically oriented claims about this relationship. It is by saying more about the schematizing or expressive relationship asserted between intelligible and empirical character, and recognizing the intractable problems that the assertion of this relationship brings, that we can prepare the ground for a practical resolution.

Schematization as Applied to Intelligible and Empirical Character

Our concern, then, is to make sense of Kant's claim that the overall unity of a sensibly affected rational being can be assured by asserting that the empirical character is the phenomenal or "sensible schema" of the intelligible character (A553/B581). It is clear, in light of this claim, that we need to assert of the sensibly affected agent not only that she is subject to two characters, or laws of causality, but also that there is a hierarchical relation between these two characters In some yet-to-be-determined sense, the empirical character is dependent upon or grounded by the intelligible character.

This point does not escape Allison or Wood. And both focus primarily upon the analogy of schematism to understand the relation of intelligible and empirical character. Wood, for example, briefly considers the notion of empirical character as a schema of intelligible character when defending his compatibilist interpretation. For him, though, to say that empirical character is a schema of intelligible character is simply to say that it is transcendentally caused by the latter: "[e]mpirical causality regarding human actions is an *effect* of intelligible causality, which…is transcendentally free" (Wood 1984, p. 250, emphasis added). To say that empirical character is a "schema" of intelligible character is simply to say that it is an effect of it. Intelligible character is the cause, and empirical character the effect.

Although he does not make this point directly in response to Wood, Allison rejects the idea that empirical character could be a simple effect of intelligible character. Allison is concerned to "leave room for the attribution of an *empirical* character to the causality of *reason*," (Allison 1990, p. 32, emphasis added) and in order to do so, seeks a different understanding of the schematization of empirical character. For, if empirical character is the simple *effect* of the causality of reason, a mere "product" of the causality of reason, it does not itself exhibit such rational causality. For Allison, one's empirical character is not so much the *effect* of one's intelligible character, as a particular *expression* of it, here a specifically empirical or phenomenal expression *of* reason.[6] It is on this basis that Allison introduces the possibility of a genuine causality of reason on the empirical level, grounding a compatibilist conception of freedom.

Let us then reflect upon the challenges of asserting any sort of phenomenal expression of an intelligible idea, since such assertions push us up against the limits of reason. As Allison reminds us, we cannot admit an "inference route from the empirical to the intelligible" (*Ibid.*), but it seems we would be allowing just this if we try to say any more than Allison has about this relationship.

---

6 As he says, "Kant also speaks of the empirical character as the appearance or sensible schema of the intelligible character. Unlike the first [cause-effect] version of the relationship [of intelligible and empirical character], this view allows for the possibility that the causality of reason, although intelligible, might nonetheless be said to have an empirical character, namely, its phenomenal expression, appearance or schema" (Allison 1990, p. 32).

Consider again the schematism analogy suggested by Kant. If we were investigating the schematism of a pure concept of the understanding, we would know how to tell the story of its expression: it would be the story of the Transcendental Analytic, about how pure concepts combined with appropriate sensible intuitions yield knowledge of the phenomenal world. The pure concept would find its empirical intuition and be "expressed" as an object of experience.

This route is, of course, closed to us when it is the intelligible character of which we seek a sensible schematization. After all, to say that we have a sensible schema of intelligible character is, in the end, to say that we can schematize, or provide a phenomenal expression of, the law of freedom itself. To say that something has an intelligible "character" is to say that it has a particular "law of causality" (A539/B567). To say that this character is "intelligible" is, furthermore, to identify that law of causality as a causality of freedom, not nature. One's intelligible character is a "faculty of beginning a state from itself, the causality of which does not in turn stand under another cause determining it in time in accordance with the law of nature" (A533/B561). Such causality, freedom or "spontaneity" could "start to act from itself, without needing to be preceded by any other cause" (*Ibid.*).

This equation of freedom with a particular law of causality is a response to the argument of the Antithesis: that if you remove an action from under natural law, it must be lawless and chaotic. Freedom as we have just defined it, though exempt from natural law, is not thereby lawless; there is indeed a law or rule operative in free action, but it is different from the one that guides natural events. And this capacity to begin a series, this "law of freedom," just is one's "intelligible character".

Given all this, when we say that intelligible character is schematized as empirical character, we are asserting a schematization of the law of freedom itself.[7] And in asserting a sensible expression of that law, we are asserting the sensible expression of the causality of freedom. Given that this is what we are seeking, we cannot hope to provide a sensible intuition which will, together with a previously empty concept of freedom, yield either a full-fledged object of experience called "freedom", or strict knowledge of ourselves as free beings. To do so

---

7   In the *Critique of Practical Reason*, Kant speaks of finding a concrete form, not for intelligible character, nor strictly for the law of freedom (though he sometimes uses this language), but rather for the "*categories* of freedom" (5:65). We needn't be bothered by this slight shift in language from the "law of freedom" to the "categories of freedom." The law of freedom defines a rule (i.e., the rule governing the activity of freedom), just as a concept or category would, so the two phrases are essentially equivalent.

would be to violate the limits of reason, seeking an intuition for a transcendental idea instead of for a concept of the understanding.

Allison is aware of such constraints, which he articulates conversely as a concern that we avoid asserting an "inference route from
the empirical to the intelligible, a consequence that the 'critical' Kant
could hardly accept" (Allison 1990, p. 32). We cannot "construe…Kant
to be allowing for the possibility of inferring something about the nature of an intelligible activity or character from its empirical manifestation" *(Ibid.,* pp. 32-3).[8] Such constraints are part of what leads Allison
to describe that paradigmatic act of freedom, incorporation, as he does,
that is, as a purely intelligible act about which we can say little. We
cannot begin from some experience, and work our way back to a firm
assertion about the nature of the intelligible object that grounds the
experience. That is, we cannot identify an experience in the phenomenal world as the clear result of our activity of incorporation.

It is true that, in characterizing the phenomenal expression of intelligible character, we must not hope to begin with that phenomenal expression and trace our way back to complete knowledge of the intelligible character that grounded it. The limits of reason prevent us from
coming to straightforward knowledge of intelligible activity via the
phenomenal expression of that activity. Conversely, we cannot find an
object of experience that is a clear, complete, intuitively informed representation of freedom or intelligible character. Freedom is, after all, a
transcendental idea, and to seek a schematization of it seems to violate
the limits of reason.

Yet in his discussion of freedom, and indeed of all of the antinomies, Kant is careful to define a more limited theoretical context within
which we are not only permitted, but *obligated,* to pursue such questions. Having just affirmed the impossibility of finding an object of
experience for transcendental ideas, Kant insists, in the same opening
sections of the antinomies, that these questions internal to reason—
including the cosmological questions raised by transcendental ideas like
freedom—*need* some rational resolution. To try simply to abandon
them is to evade our epistemic obligation as knowers. Kant emphasizes
this point repeatedly:

> [W]e cannot evade the obligation of giving at least a critical resolution of the
> questions of reason before us by lamenting the narrow limits of our reason and
> confessing, with the appearance of a modest self-knowledge, that it lies be-
> yond our reason to settle whether…there is a generating and producing

8   In articulating the constraint in this way, Allison is referring implicitly to the work of
     Jürgen Henrichs (1968).

> through freedom or everything depends on the causal chain of the natural order. (A481/B509)

We cannot abandon the question of freedom when we recognize that there is no simple empirical manifestation of its idea. To do so is to engage in a false modesty. We need some other, more "critical" resolution of the matter. Despite being blocked by the traditional route to knowledge articulated in the Transcendental Analytic, we must nonetheless seek to say what we can about freedom, thereby fulfilling our epistemic obligation to make sense of those questions which reason poses to itself. Central among these questions is whether freedom as just defined could even find expression within a sensible, phenomenal world guided by the laws of nature.

The impression one gets from this section is that the source of our epistemic obligation here comes from reason itself. If reason cannot solve the problems inherent to itself, then we have good cause to distrust our reasoning capacities even in their task of articulating conditions for the possibility of experience. In resolving the problem of freedom (and other problems raised by transcendental ideas), we are fulfilling our obligation to show reason's overall coherence.

Kant's appeal to schematism in helping us understand the relationship of intelligible and empirical character is one of his first efforts to take on this obligation that reason imposes upon us. Even if the theoretical construct of schematism is not fully applicable to our problem, it may be that a more modest, but still theoretical appeal to it could help.

This more modest appeal to schematism would involve not full-fledged, entirely schematized empirical manifestations of our intelligible character, but more modest, empirical suggestions or indications of that character. This is entirely in keeping with Kant's admonition that we can "think" but not "know" the intelligible. Here, we are seeking to "think" the intelligible *via* its empirical expression, and in so doing to expand the ways in which we can think our intelligible character and its paradigmatic act of incorporation. Far from being illicit, such use of empirical means to think intelligible objects seems in keeping with the commitments of transcendental idealism: we are unavoidably phenomenal beings, so it makes sense that we would rely on phenomenal means to glimpse our intelligible selves.

We are, again, supported textually in making such an appeal. Kant claims, for example, that

> intelligible character could, of course, never be known [*gekannt*] immediately, because we cannot perceive anything except insofar as it appears, but it [i.e., intelligible character] would have to be *thought in conformity with the empirical character*. (A540/B568, emphasis added)

What is asserted here again is that it is not only possible but *necessary* (it "would *have* to be thought") to think of intelligible character via or "in conformity with" empirical means. Not only can we think the intelligible via the empirical; we must.

At a later point in the Third Antinomy, Kant makes a related claim, even as he confirms the "no inference route" point noted by Allison. According to Kant, on the one hand, the intelligible ground of appearances "does not touch the empirical questions at all, but may have to do merely with thinking in the pure understanding" (A545/B573). That is, we do not get knowledge of the intelligible via the investigation of empirical questions; and this is as it should be, since it is not necessary to appeal to intelligible causes to explain the course of things empirical, or even the laws of nature themselves. The intelligible has more to do with "thinking" than with "natural laws", and so is not required for an understanding of the latter.

Having just asserted this, though, Kant goes on to assert that the intelligible ground *has* to "touch" the empirical world in some way. Why? Because "the intelligible character…is the transcendental cause of the [empirical character]," and, as such, we should expect that the intelligible character be at least "*indicated* through the empirical character as only its sensible sign" (A546/B574, emphasis added). The language of "cause" here has already been rejected as the best way of describing the relationship between intelligible and empirical character, in favor of "schematization" And "expression." Nonetheless, if we accept (with Allison) that Kant seems unaware of this distinction in the text of the Third Antinomy, we can read this appeal to cause and effect through the lens of schematism and expression instead of as a strict cause-effect relationship. The exact nature of this relationship will need to be worked out further. For present purposes, however, we can simply assert that the intelligible does have to "touch" the empirical in some way because that very empirical realm is the schematized expression of the intelligible.

So, to continue with the passage: on the one hand, intelligible character, though it plays a yet-undetermined grounding role for our empirical character, "is passed over as entirely *unknown*" (A546/B574). But on the other hand (and this is a big 'but'), although the intelligible character is "entirely *unknown*" to us, it is not entirely *inaccessible* to us by lesser epistemic means. As Kant puts it, the intelligible character is "entirely unknown, *except* insofar as it is *indicated* through the empirical character as only its sensible sign" (*Ibid.*, emphasis added).

Finally, there is a third passage in which we have a clear indication that intelligible character must be explored via empirical means. "We are not acquainted with [the intelligible character]," says Kant, "but it is *indicated* through appearances, which really give only the mode of sense (the empirical character) for immediate cognition" (A551/B579, emphasis added). Once again, we find Kant asserting that the empirical world *does* provide a vehicle, not for *knowing*, but rather for *glimpsing*, the intelligible. The further implication in this passage is that such glimpses reveal intelligible character only in one particular "mode" of expression. Apparently then, intelligible character has varying "modes", viz., a "mode of sense" as opposed to its pure "mode of thought," and it is in its "mode of sense" that we gain glimpses of it.

It is clear from these passages that Kant—even the "critical" Kant—is happy to allow some epistemically constrained appreciation for the intelligible character via its schema of empirical character. And this makes sense: if intelligible character expresses itself as having an empirical face, then even if we don't have an object of experience for it per se, and even if we cannot tell a transcendental story which takes us back to conditions for the possibility of our being free, we can nonetheless read the empirical face of intelligible character (indeed, the empirical face of freedom itself) for signs of its intelligible heritage.

The approach Kant recommends—one in which, having begun by admitting that strict knowledge of these matters is impossible, the knower, instead of abandoning her project as pointless, approaches her questions with more modest epistemic goals—all this I would call an attitude of epistemic humility.[9] We should, therefore, seek a phenomenal expression of the intelligible and expect, as a result, that we will be capable of epistemically humble intimations of the intelligible from these phenomenal expressions. We should, that is, engage in a less epistemically ambitious, but still productive, pursuit of the intelligible via the empirical, and this precisely because the intelligible does "touch"— that is, express itself in—the empirical.

The question, though, is whether such an epistemically humble approach is possible while still on the grounds of theoretical philosophy. In abandoning the hope that we could have a fully schematized phenomenal expression of intelligible character because of the limits of reason, is there still room for genuinely theoretical reflection on this question? Or will it be necessary to look to a different context in order for these more epistemically humble claims to have purchase? As I have already suggested, the theoretical effort will ultimately fail. We will not be able to theorize empirical indications of the intelligible without falling into intractable contradictions. To find an experience that gives us a glimpse of the intelligible, we will need a new mode of reason. Understanding why Kant's theoretical effort had to fail can help

---

9   See Grenberg 2005 for further reflections on epistemic humility.

us to understand the motivation of his turn to a practical mode of reasoning.

Schematism as the Structure for Relating Intelligible and Empirical Characters

Let us turn now to consider with more care the epistemically humble application of the notion of schematism: what exactly would be asserted in claiming that empirical character is the schema of the intelligible?

It is, on the face of it, odd that Kant would use the language of schematism when explaining the expression of intelligible character as empirical character. Schematism is an important part of the transcendental story explaining the construction of objects of experience. But Kant has just asserted, as we have seen, that we need to reject the idea that a transcendental idea like freedom could refer to objects of experience (A483/B511). One cannot hope for a complete intuitive counterpart of freedom, for freedom (like other transcendental ideas) encompasses the "absolute whole" of a series of conditions, and that wholeness is precisely what is not offered to our intuitive perception. We cannot identify an object of experience that is freedom. But this is exactly what we would be seeking were we to seek a schematization of, and a sensible object of perception for, our intelligible character.

It is, therefore, curious that Kant appeals to schematism—an activity centrally involved in assuring that pure concepts or categories *will* find expression in objects of experience—in trying to answer the question of the relationship between intelligible and empirical character. To say that empirical character is the object of experience which intelligible character grounds, and of which it is a full expression, would be to violate the limits of reason. Whatever role schematization plays here, it must be a different and, as we have seen, more epistemically humble one than the role of helping construct an object of experience for our idea of freedom.

Yet there are other aspects of the construct of schematism to which we can appeal. We can even do so while remaining true to Kant's stated desire only to make sense of the mere possibility of freedom. Recall, first, Kant's assertion that, in the Third Antinomy, all he is seeking to do is to make room for freedom by showing its mere possibility:

> [T]hus the difficulty we encounter in the question about nature and freedom is only whether freedom is possible anywhere at all and if it is, whether it can exist together with the universality of the natural law of causality, hence whether

it is a correct disjunctive proposition that every effect in the world must arise either from nature or freedom, or whether instead both, each in a different relation, might be able to take place simultaneously in one and the same occurrence. (A536/B564)

What, however, is required to show the possibility of freedom? It is tempting simply to refer to "transcendental idealism": once we admit a distinction between appearances and things-in-themselves, we can grant that the law of natural causality and determinism applies to the world of appearances, but leave room for the causality of freedom in the noumenal realm.

This is a good move, as far as it goes, but to stop there would not prove even the possibility of freedom *in the relevant sense*. This is because we are trying to make sense of the possibility of freedom not in some realm distinct from that ruled by the natural law of causality, but rather, "in one and the same occurrence", that is, in the occurrence in the phenomenal realm. The need to prove the possibility of freedom for this realm is supported by other orienting points Kant makes in opening his resolution of the Third Antinomy. For example, Kant reminds us that to be concerned with the "intelligible" is to be concerned with "that *in an object of sense* which is not itself appearance" (A537/B566, 535, emphasis added). It is to the actions of sensibly affected beings that we seek to attribute the possibility of freedom. But to say that there might be room for freedom in the noumenal realm does nothing (or little) to assure its possibility in the actions of sensibly affected rational beings who must, clearly, act in the phenomenal realm. To show even the mere possibility of freedom for these beings, in *this* realm, we must assert more than simply the basic claim of transcendental idealism, and the possibility of noumenal freedom.

What more do we need to say, exactly? We need to show that the law of freedom, whatever its ultimate provenance, can find expression within the phenomenal realm, that is, within a realm guided by laws of nature. Or, more precisely: we need to show that *noumenal* freedom can be compatible in some way with the causal determinism of the phenomenal.

It turns out, then, that appeal to schematism is just what Kant needs in order to assert such a possibility. There are at least three potential candidates for relevant parallels between the role of schematism in the Transcendental Analytic and in the intelligible-empirical character relation:

1) schematism is the means by which intuitions are connected to concepts, thus assuring the applicability of said concepts to objects in the phenomenal world;

2) it does so by playing a harmonizing role between the otherwise heterogeneous elements of concepts and intuitions;

3) its ultimate product, a schema, is a precise determination of the intuition of
time in accordance with the relevant concept.

We have already seen that, given the limits of reason, we cannot hope
for any schematization of intelligible character that would yield an object of experience adequate to it. The first would-be role for schematism is thus precluded. But the means utilized in schematism on the way
to construction of objects of experience might still have relevance for
our more limited current purpose of assuring the mere possibility of
freedom for sensibly affected beings in the phenomenal world. That
schematism is intended to harmonize otherwise incompatible and heterogeneous elements, and that it yields, in addition to an object of experience, a more modest determination of time are both promising for
our current purpose of assuring the possibility of freedom. Let us consider each in turn.

Heterogeneity vs. Logical Contradiction

The activity of schematization works, Kant tells us, to assure "homoge-
neity" between two otherwise entirely heterogeneous things, namely,
concepts (or rules) and intuitions. As stated in the first sentence of the
Schematism: "In all subsumptions of an object under a concept the
representations of the former must be homogenous with the latter, i.e.,
the concept must contain that which is represented in the object that is
to be subsumed under it" (A137/B176). But there is a problem: "pure
concepts…in comparison with empirical (indeed in general sensible)
intuitions, are entirely unhomogeneous, and can never be encountered
in any intuition" (*Ibid.*). It is schematism that is introduced to help resolve this heterogeneity of the essential elements of knowledge. The
activity of schematization is what makes previously heterogeneous
things like concepts and intuitions more amenable to each other, more
able, if you will, to connect with each other.

Concepts and intuitions are not perfect parallels for intelligible and
empirical character. Both concepts and intuitions find their proper
realm of applicability in the phenomenal world.[10] They are indeed two

---

10   As Kant notes, "[T]he pure concepts of the understanding can never be of transcenden-
     tal, but always only of empirical use, and…the principles of pure understanding can be
     related to objects of the senses only in relation to the general conditions of a possible
     experience, but never to things in general (without taking regard of the way in which we
     might intuit them…[S]ince that which is not appearance cannot be an object of expe-

distinct roots of knowledge, but both roots are in their proper soil in the construction of objects of experience. The same cannot, however, be said about intelligible and empirical character. Indeed, the very issue we are struggling to resolve is how a character appropriate to one, noumenal, realm, could express itself in the foreign soil of the phenomenal.

Yet there is also an analogy to be drawn: just as concepts and intuitions are two distinct roots of knowledge, so too intelligible and empirical character are two distinct, apparently incompatible, laws of causality in need of harmonization.[11] These two characters are laws that appear to be not merely heterogeneous, but mutually exclusive. This is, after all, why consideration of their relation led us initially to an "antinomy". The law of causality which is the empirical character guides the states of the agent as produced via laws of nature and assures their overall coherence with the unity of experience. It is thus a causal force bound by a time-series: an object within this series cannot begin a further series of events by itself, but only through reference back, both causally and temporally, to some previous object or event in the time-series. But the law of causality of the intelligible character is a causality *not* bound by the time-series. An agent possessing such a law of causality thus *is* able to begin a series from itself. Indeed, the power to do so defines this form of causality.

But how could a causality not bound by a time-series schematize itself in a form compatible with natural causality which *is* bound by a time-series and unable to begin a series by itself? This is the heterogeneity of parts with which we are faced in making sense of the relationship of intelligible and empirical character; it is a heterogeneity which, like the dissimilarity of concepts and intuitions, *begs* for schematization.[12]

---

rience, [the understanding] can never overstep the limits of sensibility, within which alone objects are given to us. Its principles are merely principles of the exposition of appearances, and the proud name of an ontology, which presumes to offer synthetic a priori cognitions of things in general in a systematic doctrine (e.g., the principle of causality), must give way to the modest one of a mere analytic of the pure understanding" (A246-7/B303).

11   See, e.g., A540/B568.

12   Although this is not as central to our current concern, it is worth noting that such a story about natural causality depending upon intelligible causality grounds a potentially interesting interpretation of those apparently deterministic laws of nature that guide the empirical world. On this interpretation, the role intelligible character plays in grounding empirical character is analogous to the role the transcendental object plays in grounding objects of experience (A540/B568). There is something quite radical, and ironic, about the assertion that an intelligible form of causality grounds an empirical form of causality; the result is an explanation for natural causality quite different from most contemporary versions of it, and perhaps more in agreement with Allison's suggestion that a Kan-

Time-Determination

We can, at this point, turn to the second relevant parallel between our two situations, since it turns out that the harmonization of characters needs to be accomplished on the battleground of *time*. Indeed, to say that freedom needs to find an expression compatible with the phenomenal realm and its causal determinism is as much as to say that freedom needs to express itself temporally. As Kant puts it, the intelligible character needs to express itself "in conformity with the empirical character" (A540/B568), and this means taking on at least one of the forms of intuition of the empirical world, space or time.

Schematization is, once again, just what is called for here, for the product of the harmonizing activity of which we have just spoken is a "schema," and the schema is described as "a transcendental time-determination" (A138/B177). To say that this schema is a determined, or ordered, presentation of time is simply to affirm that the activity of schematization has been successful in resolving the problem at hand, viz. the problem of making two things previously heterogeneous to each other more amenable to each other. What this means is that something without temporal expression (viz., intelligible character) has been able to acquire it. Conversely, a mode of expression not amenable to expressing non-temporal things (viz., the empirical) has in fact been influenced by and enabled to express something foreign (viz., intelligible character).

The result of such harmonization, with concepts and intuitions, is a more precise ordering or rendering of the thing previously recalcitrant to such ordering, namely, "intuition" (here, specifically the intuition of time). Hence, the product of schematization is described as an ordering or "determination" of that intuition. Time is made more determinate by its successful connection with those concepts that can now order and synthesize it. For the construction of objects of experience, this further determination of time yields a more particular ordering of this intuition. Time has now, in virtue of its successful interaction with concepts and rules, a more precise flow, a content introduced into its progression, and a more precise ordering of those time contents in accordance with rules establishing substances and causal relations among substances (A145/B184-5).

In seeking to apply this determination of time to the relationship of intelligible and empirical character, we thus say that the law of freedom implicit in intelligible character must somehow act as the "concept"

---

tian determinism cannot be quite so determining as to preclude another form of causality (Allison 1990, pp. 43-4).

that orders and determines time. The progress of events in the phenomenal realm needs to be determined by some temporal, phenomenal expression of what is itself a timeless law, that is, the law of freedom. Kant repeatedly emphasizes this quality of the law of freedom, or of that "reason" which is its agent. What needs to happen in order for this timeless law to be "possible" within the phenomenal realm is for this timeless law to find an expression in time. Such an expression of the concept of freedom in a way compatible with the constraints of the phenomenal world thus needs to be a particular determination of the flow of time in that world via this noumenal idea. If such a thing can be identified, then we have proven the possibility of freedom in the relevant sense.

Applied to the concerns of the Third Antinomy, the activity of schematization is thus asserted to make intelligible character more amenable to the phenomenal world by finding one mode of its expression there, its "mode of sense" (A551/B579). Ultimately, via schematization, Kant asserts that a form of causality (i.e., the causality of freedom), in itself incompatible with the deterministic causality of the phenomenal world, *can* express itself within a sensibly affected rational agent in a way compatible with such determinism. In asserting a schematization of intelligible character, Kant is thus asserting the compatibility of an intelligible mode of freedom with the time-constraints of the phenomenal realm.

Searching for the Phenomenal Face of Freedom

Can we, though, make more precise sense of this possibility? What *is* the ordering or determination of time that results when intelligible character, this power of being first in a chain of causes without being caused, expresses itself sensibly, and thus temporally? How is the flow and/or content of time shaped in virtue of being an expression of intelligible character? This is precisely the problem in speaking of an intelligible character that expresses itself empirically. A character not subject to the conditions of time is now said to have its expression *in* time. Time must thus be determined by this timeless character. To push the paradox even further: in entering time, intelligible character—the law of *freedom*, a faculty which can start a series from itself—is entering the realm of natural causal *determinism*. What phenomenal experience, though, could ground our confidence in such a paradoxical claim?

There is one obvious candidate: an experience of being under an imperative such as Kant describes in the Gallows example in the *Cri-

tique of Practical Reason (5:30). In this example, a man faces the gallows in two different circumstances, first as punishment for indulging his lusts, and then as punishment for not telling a malicious lie. The point of this example is to show that there are imperatives that present themselves to an agent categorically. Whereas this agent believed his lusts were "irresistible," he discovers that the demand they place on him dissolves under the threat of death. But the demand to be honest (that is, not to tell a malicious lie) does *not* dissolve, even under the threat of death. It presents itself, that is, as a categorical demand upon him.

We could take this experience of an imperative as a schematized version of intelligible character—that is, as a particular determination or ordering of *time*—insofar as the recognition of the demand as compelling would need to find its causal force somewhere other than in natural causes. Events in time would thus be ordered by this new, non-natural cause. Or, as Kant points out when he raises a similar example within the Third Antinomy, when judging the actions of one who tells a malicious lie,

> one presupposes that it can be entirely set aside how that life [of one telling the malicious lie] was constituted, and that the series of conditions that transpired might not have been, but rather that this deed could be regarded as entirely unconditioned in regard to the previous state, *as though with that act the agent had started a series of consequences entirely from himself.* (A555/B583, emphasis added)

We can, that is, understand certain contents of time—human actions—as determined by a non-natural, intelligible law.

That Kant presents an example of someone telling a malicious lie within the Third Antinomy, suggesting that the force of the demand weighing upon him allows us to judge the action as though it started a series of consequences entirely from itself, gives further encouragement to the idea that we should take such an experience as the schematized version of the intelligible law of freedom in the phenomenal world. We find hints of the law of freedom operative in this world when we experience ourselves as obligated beings.

But although Kant does make such an appeal part of his apparently theoretical discussion of freedom in the Third Antinomy, he is not, at this point, entitled to such an appeal. There are several reasons for this. First, to define the law of freedom as a rational imperative is, surely, to go beyond the legitimate theoretical question of whether freedom is merely possible, for it begins to define the nature of that law of freedom more positively than being merely first in a chain of causes. This is the causality of reason at work, a causality that expresses itself in moral imperatives. But to describe intelligible character in this more robust form takes us beyond mere affirmation of possibility. More proof would be needed that this is the form that intelligible character takes.

More importantly, though, for assessing any purported experience of being obligated categorically within a theoretical discussion of freedom (that is, within a discussion in which our main concern is the question of knowledge), we would need to be able to describe that experience in Kant's language of knowledge and experience, that is via concepts of the understanding with corresponding intuitions. But, as we already know, this is not possible for the "concept" of freedom, and it is thus impossible for us to welcome this "experience" of being obligated into the realm of ordinary, theoretically constructed experience. Kant wants a more epistemically humble answer to this question, and baldly asserting an experience that violates the limits of reason is not satisfactory!

But without some phenomenal experience to ground Kant's formal suggestion that we can find something in the phenomenal world that hints at or indicates our intelligible character, we are left at sea. Recall, we are not trying simply to tolerate the melding of two heterogeneous things like concepts and intuitions (a resolution of A and B); we are trying to tolerate the co-presence of two things that appear to be in direct opposition to each other (A and ~A). To say that intelligible character expresses itself in time is to say that a *timeless* character expresses itself *in time*. It is to say that a cause that is not itself caused finds expression in a form in which it *does* have a previous cause. It is to seek a resolution not of A and B, but of A and ~A! Without something in our experience that would manifest the real possibility of what appears theoretically to be impossible, the logical tension is just too much to tolerate. Hegel might be happy to tell a story of a logical contradiction between thesis and antithesis resolved in a higher synthesis, but Kant's transcendental idealism leaves him no such option.

This effort to bring the conciliatory notion of schematism to two contradictory terms pushes the structure of schematism to the breaking point. Without a clear, theoretically articulable experience to ground it, a time-determined form of intelligible character seems nothing more than a contradiction that we are asked to accept as a mystery. The theoretically minded philosopher must reject this request to accept A and ~A.

This impasse is what forces Kant to a new epistemically humble territory, that of the practical. It is only on the territory of the practical that Kant *can* more successfully seek a phenomenal indication of a noumenal cause. Theoretically, we don't have a candidate for this more epistemically humble expression of our intelligible character. On the practical level, though, a temporal expression of the law of freedom would be just that temporal experience of imperatives considered earlier. Such an appeal on practical grounds is, furthermore, not subject to the same constraints as a theoretical appeal would be. The territory of practical reason is, after all, as Kant suggests at the opening of the second *Critique*[13], a territory in which reason is primarily concerned with doing, not with knowing. By loosening our demand for theoretical satisfaction in pursuit of the intelligibility of our actions; by setting aside the demand to articulate our experiences of action in terms of concepts of the understanding schematized via intuition; by furthermore realizing that the demands of the practical only heighten reason's original demand to resolve issues beyond what theoretical reason was able to resolve: by all these new considerations, Kant's movement toward the establishment of a new, specifically practically territory for the exercise of reason is given intellectual support. We *can* now say that we have found something in our this-worldly experience that hints or indicates our intelligible heritage if only we look at ourselves as doers and not simply as knowers. On this practical level, to experience an imperative would be an indication in our practical, but still temporal, experience of a law that holds in a different way than the laws of nature. Something presents itself as *necessary* to do, regardless of the state of natural causes in the world and, furthermore, as do-able by us autonomously, as an effect of our own willing.

There is much more to say about this practical resolution of the question of the unity of a being with both intelligible and empirical characters. Space constraints prevent me from considering those further questions here. The hope of affirming such unity is, however, possible only by turning to the practical. If one insists upon a more narrow, theoretical resolution to this conundrum, one is forced to less epistemically humble, Hegelian methods of resolution. The Kantian, however, in an effort to retain her epistemic humility toward the questions about freedom that she must ask, turns instead to practical reasoning.

---

13 "[I]f as pure reason it is really practical, it proves its reality and that of its concepts by what it does, and all subtle reasoning against the possibility of its being practical is futile" (5:3).

Section III

The Highest Good

CHAPTER 5

Something to Love: Kant and the Faith of Reason

David Sussman

Kant struggled throughout his career to provide a moral foundation for religious faith. Although the *Critique of Pure Reason* abandons all hope of a traditional metaphysical defense of the existence of God, the freedom of the will, or the immortality of the soul, Kant thinks that these claims can still be redeemed as "postulates of pure practical reason." In all of his major works and many of his minor ones, Kant argues that the moral law, in addition to establishing our particular obligations, assigns us an overall task: the attainment of the *summum bonum* or "highest good." For Kant, the highest good would be realized in a world whose members, having achieved perfect virtue, enjoy perfect happiness just because it is what they morally deserve. Kant argues that this goal can be reached only if we are free and immortal, and only if God exists. God is needed to properly assess our virtue and to order the laws of nature so that each of us ultimately receives the appropriate measure of happiness. We must be immortal in order to develop the perfect virtue that we supposedly cannot attain in any finite span of time. And we must be free if we are to be morally responsible and deserving creatures in the first place.

By denying the possibility of knowledge of supersensible matters, the first *Critique* established that we are entitled at least to hope that God, freedom, and immortality are real. It is not clear what practical faith is meant to add to such optimistic agnosticism. For Kant, the moral law's authority does not depend on any prior good that might be served by following it, nor does the law presuppose any authority distinct from our own reason. Morality has supreme authority over our choices just in case pure reason is practical in us, i.e., if and only if such moral judgment can be immediately motivating, independent of and even against all our inclinations, sentiments, and non-moral interests. Yet if morality neither needs nor allows anything distinct from pure reason to contribute to its normative or motivational grounds, why do we have to concern ourselves with the highest good at all? Of course, the demands of morality might be easier to bear if we sugar-coat them with the thought that we will never have to make a real sacrifice of our overall happiness. Yet this hardly shows that we have good reason to believe in God and immortality, any more than we would have reason to so believe in order to assuage our fear of death.

We might be tempted to conclude that Kant's account of rational faith is fundamentally confused and incompatible with the rest of his practical philosophy. Perhaps the whole approach stems from personal or philosophical preoccupations that Kant was unable to throw off even as his ethics and moral psychology outgrew them.[1] Such conclusions are difficult to resist so long as we consider only the arguments of the first two *Critiques*. However, in *Religion within the Boundaries of Mere Reason*, Kant connects faith to a new concern: the need of human beings to find something to love in morality. Admittedly, Kant is an unlikely guide to the moral and psychological subtleties of love. He usually presents love as either a kind of impersonal moral beneficence, or as a mere well-wishing or fondness for others. Kant seems to understand erotic love as little more than a natural appetite for contact with the genitalia of others (6:402, 6:277-8, 6:426). Nevertheless, in his later reflections on the moral significance of love, Kant offers at least the beginnings of a moral foundation for rational faith that need not conflict with either the authority or the motivational power of pure practical reason. Unfortunately, the relationship between love, faith, and reason is grounded in one of Kant's most obscure and unpopular doctrines: his account of timeless, noumenal self-constitution. In what follows, I argue that this doctrine is not metaphysically extravagant, and that it provides a way for rational faith to be something more interesting and defensible than either hopeful agnosticism or mere wishful thinking.

Opinion, Knowledge, and Pragmatic Belief

Kant's understanding of rational faith is especially puzzling because he never makes clear just what a "postulate of practical reason" is supposed to be, or what sort of doxastic commitment is involved in adopting one. The postulates resemble both theoretical and practical cognition in some respects, but cannot be wholly assimilated to either category. In the first and third *Critiques* as well as in "What Does it Mean to Orient Oneself in Thinking?" Kant contrasts rational faith with both "knowledge" and "opinion." Knowledge rests on grounds that are

---

1   See Rawls 2000, pp. 313-31.

sufficient both "objectively" and "subjectively," while the basis of opinion is both objectively and subjectively insufficient. We have knowledge when we believe something for what we recognize to be decisive reasons. In the case of opinion, we believe on grounds that we realize do not and should not allay all doubt. Rational faith is curiously intermediate between these two ways of "holding something to be true." In faith, I recognize that while my belief might be reasonably challenged by someone else, no such worries can be live options for me. While I acknowledge that the claim may well be doubted, this fact does not touch my own confidence: "I must not even say '*It is* morally certain that there is a God, etc.', but rather '*I am* morally certain, etc.'" (A829/B857, Kant's emphasis).

For Kant, knowledge and opinion are both held on the basis of reasons that are recognized as being epistemically relevant, whether or not they settle the issue. In principle, an opinion could always "gradually be supplemented by the same kind of grounds and finally become a knowing"[2] (8:141). In contrast, faith is not any kind of claim to knowledge, either partial or complete, even though it is properly expressed through existential propositions about supersensible entities. Kant insists that rational faith involves a kind of belief that is completely different from that involved in our knowledge of "matters of fact," be they scientific or moral. Even so, such faith involves an equally strong commitment from us: "this holding true (if only the person is morally good) is not inferior in degree to knowing, even though it is completely different from it in kind" (8:141-2).[3] Although rational faith has purely moral grounds, its postulates do not seem to be merely regulative principles to guide practical deliberation. If faith comprised only such moral heuristics, it would be compatible with the denial that God and immortality are real (freedom remains a special case, insofar as it can be directly "deduced" from the moral law itself). Yet Kant insists that while faith involves no claim to knowledge, it is nevertheless inconsistent with "dogmatic unbelief" in God, freedom, or immortality (5:472-3).

It is tempting to understand rational faith as the sort of "pragmatic belief" that Kant illustrates with the example of a doctor who, confronted with an urgent but uncertain case, must decide on some definite course of treatment.[4] Absent decisive evidence one way or another, the doctor proceeds on the working assumption that her patient has tuber-

---

2   Kant's example is his own opinion that life exists on other planets. See also A820-31/B848-59, 5:467).

3   Kant defines matters of fact (*scibilia*) to include not just scientific knowledge, but also our grasp of the moral law, the sole basic moral matter of fact (5:467-75).

4   See e.g., Beiser 2006.

culosis, although she might believe that this is probably not the case. She may think it more likely that the patient is merely suffering from a bad cold but still treat for tuberculosis because of the greater threat it poses. Similarly, the doctor may think it more likely that the patient is really suffering from advanced lung cancer, but treat for tuberculosis because it the only thing she has any real chance of affecting.

In such cases the doctor is not just acting "as if" her patient were consumptive, as she might when giving a demonstration to medical students. Although the doctor need not believe that tuberculosis is the most likely diagnosis, she must at least think that such a diagnosis is a real possibility. If tuberculosis could be conclusively ruled out, then the doctor could no longer guide herself by that assumption. Even so, the doctor's practical deliberations need not show the same sensitivity to evidence as would a disinterested scientific evaluation. If it turns out that the patient is suffering from tuberculosis but that little can be done, or that there is an even more dire possibility that might be more effectively treated, then the doctor's working assumption would have to be revised in light of these practical concerns, despite a balance of evidence in favor of tuberculosis.

Kant's rational faith often sounds like the doctor's merely pragmatic belief, distinguished only by the fact that the concerns that motivate rational faith are moral in character. Yet it is hard to see how faith in God, freedom, and immorality is supposed to inform our practical deliberations in anything like the way the presumption of tuberculosis guides the doctor. A diagnosis of tuberculosis bears on what treatments the doctor selects, how she interprets symptoms, and what side-effects or other difficulties she anticipates. Under this operating assumption, the doctor's practical reasoning is importantly different from how it would be if she did not assume this diagnosis. Yet Kant never suggests that rational faith might enter into our moral reasoning like this. The highest good requires that we develop our own virtue, support the development of others' virtue, and perhaps promote the permissible happiness of others. Yet these are all obligations that we should already recognize prior to consideration of the highest good.[5] As Kant observes in the *Religion*: "[T]his end does not increase the number of morality's virtues but rather provides these with a special point of reference for the unification of all ends" (6:5). Even though we must trust that God will ultimately apportion happiness to desert, Kant does not conclude that we need not worry about helping or harming others. Nor does he suggest that we should be less concerned with matters of life and death (e.g., murder, suicide, war, rescue) given our practical confidence in the

_____

5   See Beck 1960, pp. 244-5.

immortality of the soul. Kant does insist that we must deliberate "under the idea of freedom" (4:448) and treat others as free and responsible beings, but these real deliberative consequences stem from freedom's unique status as not merely an object of rational faith, but as the *ratio essendi* of the moral law itself.

Faith in the *Critique of Pure Reason*

In the first *Critique*, Kant argues that rational faith is needed not to properly guide our moral deliberations, but to motivate us to act in ways that properly follow from such thought. Here Kant claims that without the prospect of reward or punishment associated with the highest good, the moral law could not address us as an imperative, let alone a categorical one:

> Hence also everyone regards the moral laws as *commands*; which however they could not be if they did not connect appropriate consequences with their rule *a priori*, and thus carry with them *promises* and *threats*. This however they could not do if they did not lie in a necessary being, as the highest good, which alone can make possible such purposive unity. (A811-2/B839-40, Kant's emphasis)

Kant is clear that even without such promises and threats, the moral law would still provide the rationally appropriate standpoint to judge human action. Yet this standpoint would be a purely spectatorial or evaluative one, instead of one that could immediately govern our deliberations and choices. Kant concludes:

> Thus without a God and a world that is now not visible to us but is hoped for, the majestic ideas of morality are, to be sure, objects of approbation and admiration but not incentives for resolve and realization. (A813/B841)

Here Kant seems still to be operating with a largely Humean moral psychology. Although the first *Critique* allows that reason can motivate us (and hence distinguishes our wills from those of instinct-driven animals), our exercise of this ability seems to be largely indirect. Kant suggests that reason does not immediately determine our choices in the act of judgment, but instead motivates us by creating new inclinations in us by means of a special kind of representation. It is these rationally produced inclinations, pushing against those stemming from our sensible nature, that are the immediate causes of our rational acts:

> For it is not merely that which stimulates the senses, i.e., immediately affects them, that determines human choice, but we have a capacity to overcome impressions on our sensory faculty of desire by representations of that which is useful or injurious even in a more remote way; but these considerations about

> that which in regard to our whole condition is desirable, i.e., good and useful, depend on reason. (A802/B830)

Such a will possesses "practical freedom" in that, although it is not determined immediately by rational judgment, it can still be "determined independently of *sensory* impulses" (A802/B830, my emphasis), i.e., by impulses arising from the rational representation of something as good or bad in some respect. Yet since rational judgment does not determine the will immediately but only through some distinct psychological mechanism, "that which with respect to sensory impulses is called freedom" might still "with regard to higher and more remote efficient causes be nature" (A803/B831).

In the first *Critique*, Kant seems to think that this merely "comparative" or compatibilistic freedom is enough for the purposes of moral philosophy. Kant never doubts that morality is justified without any reference to inclination. However, he thinks that reason might need to present us with the prospect of reward or punishment in order to supply, if not our original moral incentive, then at least a motivational counterweight heavy enough to overcome competing inclinations. Kant remarks that although "the human mind takes…a natural interest in morality" this interest "is not undivided and practically overwhelming" (A830/B858n). Although pure reason brings us to approve of the moral law *in foro interno*, a truly effective commitment to morality presupposes an external power that guarantees we will not ultimately suffer any overall loss of happiness by living up to this commitment. Unfortunately, such an account of faith presupposes a possible divergence between the authority and motivational power of reason that Kant decisively rejects as his moral philosophy progresses.

Faith in the *Critique of Practical Reason*

In the second *Critique,* Kant offers what is usually taken to be his mature account of moral faith, freed from the still partially heteronomous understanding of the will at work in the first *Critique.* In the second *Critique,* Kant insists that pure reason can be immediately practical in recognizing and being motivated by the moral law, a law with an authority we grasp as an underived and unconditional "Fact of Reason." The moral law is the fundamental commitment of any truly free and autonomous agent, who is thereby able to act not only in independence of any particular sensibly-based desire, but in opposition to the entire economy of her inclinations.

In the first *Critique,* Kant considered the will only insofar as it possesses a kind of psychologistic "practical freedom" that leaves open the possibility that the motivating power of reason might fall short of its normative demands. In the second *Critique*, Kant instead claims that the law applies to us only if we are transcendentally free, so that we can act with complete spontaneity, regardless of our entire psychological character and history. Kant offers the example of a man who is threatened with death or torture if he refuses to perjure himself, and concludes that he

> must admit without hesitation that it would be possible for him [to refuse]. He judges, therefore, that he can do something because he is aware that he ought to do it and cognizes freedom within him which, without the moral law, would have remained unknown to him. (5:30-1)[6]

Since Kant holds that morality binds us just because our wills are autonomous in this way, there can never be any motivational gap between judgment and action that faith might be needed to close.[7] We may often pretend to such infirmity when we succumb to temptation, but such pleas, however familiar, can be little more than hypocrisy or bad faith.

Instead of appealing to motivational concerns, the second *Critique* argues that, without rational faith, we could not recognize the validity of the moral law in the first place. Kant presents the practical postulates as part of the resolution of a supposed antinomy that arises as practical reason moves past its fundamental constitutive principle (the moral law), and considers how to integrate all of its criteria of judgment into a complete system. Kant argues that although morality and happiness are fundamentally distinct concerns, reason still seeks to systematize them by articulating a necessary connection or ordering between their basic principles. For Kant, any such necessary connection between two distinct concepts counts as a kind of cause:

---

6   See also 5:158-9.

7   This consideration is neglected by John Hare, who argues that the function of moral faith "is to give the victory in the internal battle to [one's] moral commitment, though this will not be the end of the war" (Hare 1996, p. 78). Hare claims that "One premise in Kant's own argument is… 'psychological eudaimonism,' the view that humans always act with their own happiness in mind." (p. 87). Kant does hold that happiness is an inherently rational concern. Yet this does not mean that prudential interests can never be overridden or "silenced" by moral considerations. Hare seems to have confused an aspect of the fundamental maxim of our timeless moral disposition (which does include an ineliminable concern for happiness as such) with features of the lower-level maxims of particular actions (which may not). As finite rational beings, we must always have a general interest in our own happiness. However, this does not mean that, in each of our actions, we must be acting in a way that is at least partially motivated by such self-love.

> Two determinations *necessarily* combined in one concept must be connected
> as ground and consequent, and so connected that this *unity* is considered either
> as *analytic* (logical connection) or as synthetic (real *connection*), the former in
> accordance with the law of identity, the latter in accordance with the law of
> causality. (5:111)

Because virtue and happiness are supposedly "extremely heterogeneous" concepts, Kant concludes that their necessary connection can only
be one of cause and effect, a conclusion that generates the "antinomy of
practical reason." The thesis of this antinomy is that virtue is the "efficient cause" of happiness, the antithesis that "the desire for happiness
must be the motive to maxims of virtue" (apparently a gloss on "happiness causes virtue") (5:111). This latter alternative, that we are motivated to act virtuously out of concern for some prior conception of happiness, is not a live option for Kant. With the dismissal of the antithesis,
we are left with only the thesis, that virtue must somehow be the cause
of happiness.

Kant is well aware that in this life, people do not always get what
they morally deserve. To defend the thesis, Kant argues that there must
be more to causality than the efficient causation of nature established in
the Second Analogy. As free creatures, creatures who can be virtuous
or vicious, we must have an intelligible aspect distinct from our sensible existence. We can sustain the thesis if there is a kind of causation
appropriate to the intelligible realm that does not stand under the conditions of time. Supposedly, virtue can be the cause of happiness only if
there is more to our lives than the span we see,[8] and only if there is an
"intelligible author of nature" who is able to both assess our virtue and
mete out happiness accordingly (5:115). If there is to be a highest good,
there must be a morally perfect mind that is also the basis of nature, a
role Kant thinks could only be fulfilled by the God of theism. Since the
required proportioning of happiness to virtue is clearly not happening in
this life, there must be some afterlife in which our personal accounts are
properly settled.

Unfortunately, the resolution of this antinomy seems to rest on an
equivocation about causation. Kant holds that any necessary connection
between two distinct concepts constitutes a sort of causal relation. He
goes on to construe this relation in terms of *efficient* causation, the causation characteristic of the world as it might be described and known by
natural science. Only insofar as the connection is posed in terms of such
efficient causation does a problem emerge that can only be solved by

---

8   All this consideration gets us is an afterlife, not immortality. To show that our afterlife
     must be unlimited, Kant has to bring in further considerations, which are not yet in play
     in the initial presentation of the antinomy.

appeal to divine agency, as a power that can be active in both the moral and natural orders.

However, for Kant, a necessary connection between two distinct concepts constitutes a cause only formally. In a logical sense, a cause is just the antecedent of any ground-to-consequent relation, in which appeal to the ground serves to explain or justify its consequent. Efficient causation, the causation characteristic of the natural world, is just one instance of this general ground-to-consequent relation, an instance in which we might explain or predict some natural state of affairs by reference to some preceding state. In this case, the logical form of causality has been "schematized" in a way appropriate to distinct spatio-temporal events. Yet this particular interpretation of the logical relation of causality does not render the original, unschematized form unavailable for reinterpretation in ways better suited for different domains of judgment. On Kant's own terms, we should be able to say that virtue "causes" or is the ground of happiness in the unsurprising sense that only our virtue can conclusively justify our being happy (just as only our vice can call our happiness into question).

The resources of Kant's logic allow him to resolve the practical antinomy in much the same way as he did the dynamical antinomies of the first *Critique*: by understanding both the thesis and the antithesis to be true and mutually consistent when properly interpreted in terms of the limited domains to which they properly apply. The claim that virtue is the cause of happiness is true of the intelligible world, as a proposition about desert that properly governs our first-personal, practical deliberations and our moral evaluations of ourselves as free beings. The claim that happiness is the cause of virtue can then be sustained as a putative truth of empirical psychology. Since freedom cannot be empirically cognized, such psychology might only be able to understand our moral motivation as an instance of some more general drive for pleasure or happiness.

We might still argue that reason must take an interest in the attainment of the highest good simply as the complete and systematic fulfillment of our appropriately qualified duties of beneficence and moral self-perfection. The highest good would then fail to be anything more than a general ideal for our striving, something that we must recognize a duty to "promote" even if we could not completely achieve it at any point in time.[9] However, if the highest good is only a goal that we must approximate as closely as we can, then rational faith turns out to be a

---

9   This would be so whether this duty is interpreted as applying directly to individuals, or primarily to humanity as a whole, making its satisfaction necessarily a collective endeavor.

very anemic commitment. It may be true that if I intend to bring about some end, I must take that end to be possible (or I must at least not take it to be impossible). However, no such confidence is needed for an end to serve as an ideal. I may strive to be the perfect parent or teacher without believing that either goal could ever be fully realized by anyone at any particular time, at least if that would mean that no further improvement would be possible. In these cases, rational commitment requires only that I have an ideal coherent enough to determine what would count as getting closer to or further away from it at any given time.[10] If my duty is merely to approximate the highest good as best I can, then even without God and immortality, I could do so whenever I morally improve myself or remove impediments to the improvement of others, or when I advance the permissible happiness of those who deserve it.[11] Kant has given us no reason to suppose that, without faith in God and immortality, we would be so practically disoriented as to be unable to recognize anything as constituting even relative success or failure in such efforts to morally improve the world.

Faith in *Religion within the Boundaries of Mere Reason*

In the *Religion*, Kant finally surrenders the claim that either the authority or motivational power of morality is at stake in matters of faith. He frankly admits that:

> All human beings could sufficiently partake of this [moral] incentive too if they just adhered (as they should) to the rule of pure reason in the law: What need have they to know of the outcome of their doings and non-doings that the world's course will bring about? It suffices for them that they do their duty, even if everything were to end with life in this world, and in this life too happiness and desert perhaps never converge. (6:7n)

Kant no longer presents attainment of the highest good as a demand made by the moral law at all. Instead, our commitment to the highest good is offered as the one instance where "practical reason reaches beyond the law," and adapts the law to "one of the inescapable limitations of human beings and of their practical faculty of reason" (6:7n). Kant explains:

---

10   If so, then Kant's arguments do not even establish the "hopeful agnosticism" that Allen Wood thinks is their only proper conclusion. See Wood 1992.

11   Although, due to epistemic and moral limitations, there is very little we can or should do about apportioning happiness to virtue, beyond supporting morally permissible and mutually compatible conceptions of happiness generally.

Now, in this end human beings seek something that they can love, even though it is being proposed to them through reason alone. Hence the law that only inspires respect in them, though it does not recognize this sought-after something as [its own] need, nonetheless extends itself on its behalf to include the moral ultimate end of reason.... (6:7n)

This surprising appeal to love may not seem to be of much help, particularly in light of the impoverished understanding of love Kant often employs. In the *Groundwork*, Kant presents love as having "practical" and "pathological" forms. For something to be an object of practical love in its most general sense is just for it to be an object of sincere rational concern. Morality does not need to appeal to the highest good to provide us with an object of love in this sense. For Kant, the moral law immediately defines the basic object of practical concern as "humanity," understood as the most basic "material" of the moral law. Humanity is an object of love in that it is a substantial guiding concern, the underlying point of our obligations that makes morality something more than a fetishistic concern with "duty for duty's sake." Insofar as love in general involves positive concern for others, a kind of morally motivated love is realized in the duty of beneficence, by which we are directed to care about and promote the happiness of others, simply for their own sake as rational, self-governing agents.

The love Kant speaks of in the *Religion* seems closer to what he sometimes calls "pathological" love—that is, a love that fully integrates our feelings, our imagination, and our attention around a particular object of concern. The moral law never pretended to give us something to love in this sense. Proper moral motivation, at least in particular instances, can lack these richer affective aspects, as the *Groundwork's* opening discussion of the motive of duty famously illustrates. What moral need do we have to love something in this way? More important, how could such a need entitle us to believe in the eventual attainment of the highest good and in the reality of God, freedom, and immortality?

Admittedly, such an inspiring object of love might make the demands of morality seem less onerous, and thereby remove many temptations and occasions for transgressions. Kant does suggest just such a therapeutic role for love in "The End of All Things":

[L]ove, as a free assumption of the will of another into one's maxims, is an indispensable complement to the imperfection of human nature (of having to be necessitated to that which reason prescribes through the law). For what one does not do with liking he does in such a niggardly fashion—also probably with sophistical evasions from the command of duty—that the latter as an incentive, without the contribution of the former, is not very much to be counted on. (8:338)[12]

An aspiration that inspires moral love could be ethically useful, if only by weakening the motives that either compete with morality or provide occasions for self-deception about what the law requires.[13] But none of this would establish that sincere moral commitment and action would be *impossible* without the edifying picture that rational faith presents, only that such commitment would be more difficult or less stable.

In any event, there is nothing in this appeal that would pick out the practical postulates as the uniquely appropriate objects of rational faith. Most normal people might indeed find that trust in the highest good is what best shores up their commitment to morality. But insofar as the issue here is purely one of motivational effectiveness, then any of a wide range of fantasies might have morally salutary effects, given the right background psychology. Of course, some fantasies might conflict with what can be empirically known (e.g., the prospect of an earthly reward for virtue), or with what can be morally tolerated (delight in the torture of the damned). Yet within these bounds, the objects of rational faith could range as widely as the desires and temperaments of individual human beings. Nor is it clear that this sort of rational faith could survive a clear understanding of its own basis. How could I sincerely trust in God, freedom, and immortality once I acknowledge that these ideas have no grounds beyond their useful effects on my shaky resolve?

Coming to Love the Law

For love to do the work that Kant assigns to it, it has to be more than a peculiar psychological state, however pleasant or motivationally power-

---

12 In the *Critique of Judgment*, Kant similarly suggests that faith serves only to psychologically buttress failing moral resolve. Kant considers the case of Spinoza, who "actively reveres the moral law" but is nevertheless an atheist: "Suppose...he wants to continue to adhere to the call of his inner moral vocation, and that he does not want his respect for the moral law, by which this law directly inspires him to obey it, to be weakened, as would result from the nullity of the one ideal final purpose that is adequate to this respect's high demand (such weakening of his respect would inevitably impair his moral attitude): In that case he must...assume the existence of a moral author of the world (5:452-3).

13 For an interpretation of the Highest Good along these lines, see Guyer 2000a. Guyer argues that practical reason only requires that we act *as if* the postulates were true. However, our psychology is such that we start to really believe in them, and such belief is to be encouraged as a way of effectively coping with the non-rational elements of our sensibility. As Guyer presents it, rational faith seems to be a kind of morally-motivated self-manipulation.

ful. Instead, love must be closely akin to reason itself: not a buttress to moral commitment, but a particular way of being committed to morality. In the *Religion*, Kant argues that all of a person's maxims must ultimately be embraced by one fundamental maxim or moral "disposition" that determines the relative importance of the claims of morality and those of self-love. Kant claims that this basic maxim is established by a kind of intelligible choice that occurs outside of the conditions of time, but which still finds expression in all of our ordinary deliberations and actions. Kant insists that, for each life, there can be only one such ultimate maxim. Our basic disposition is not something that we choose at one point in time, only to revise or reject it at some other point, as we might some more ordinary commitment.[14] Kant considers our ordinary deliberation and striving to be the empirical expression of our intelligible choice, but leaves the sense of "expression" here almost completely mysterious. What is clear is that if intelligible choice is treated as an event ontologically distinct from ordinary thought and action, then profound problems about practical self-knowledge and imputation immediately emerge.

These problems can be avoided if we do not take our intelligible and empirical choices to be distinct events, one natural and one supernatural. Kant suggests that a person's ultimate maxim is identical with the entirety of her ordinary choices taken as a kind of whole. For each person, there is a basic fact about what she is most deeply committed to, a fact established by what all her strivings amount to when considered as "a unitary phenomenon."[15] A morally good agent is one whose life, as a totality, takes the form of one long decision in favor of what's right over what is most pleasing. Here the *virtus noumenon*, the fundamental choice of morality, manifests itself in time as the *virtus phenomenon,* an endless progress in our empirical character in which our moral commitments gradually gain power over our non-moral interests. The intelligible decision is prior to our empirical choices, not temporally, but in the sense that we must make sense of the meaning of empirical choices as a totality before we can assign a determinate character to any such choice taken individually.

---

14   Kant does insist on the possibility of a "revolution" in our character in which our fundamental disposition would seem to change. Nevertheless, he also denies that one part of my life might be governed by one disposition, and a later part by another. Kant seems to think that any revolution in our character retroactively changes the prior character of our disposition. As long as we live, our disposition is not so much changeable but indeterminate, taking on a definite shape only in the timeless perspective of God.

15   "For the moral subjective principle of the *disposition* by which our life is to be judged is…not of the kind that its existence can be thought as divisible into temporal segments but rather only as an absolute unity" (6:70n).

What has all this to do with love? In the *Religion*, Kant observes,

> Now, if we ask, "What is the aesthetic constitution, the temperament so to
> speak of virtue: is it courageous and hence joyous, or weighed down by fear
> and dejected?" an answer is hardly necessary. The latter slavish frame of mind
> can never be found without a hidden *hatred* of the law, whereas a heart joyous
> in the *compliance* with its duty…is the sign of genuineness in virtuous disposi-
> tion…. This resolve, encouraged by good progress, must needs effect a joyous
> frame of mind, without which one is never certain of having gained also a love
> for the good, i.e., of having incorporated the good into one's maxim. (6:23n)

It is unlikely that Kant is claiming that it is impossible for moral action
to be properly motivated if it is done reluctantly or joylessly. If this
were Kant's point, he would be summarily rejecting in a footnote the
Groundwork's central analysis of the motive of duty insofar as it was
supposed to reveal the distinctive commitments of a good will.

We can avoid reading Kant as abandoning his characteristic position about the motive of duty if we realize that his claim about the "aesthetic temperament of virtue" concerns the character of one's practical
life as a whole, a topic that was not under consideration in the first
chapter of the *Groundwork*. For Kant, a person's fundamental temperament is not something episodic, like a yen or a mood. The accounts
of the motive of duty in the *Religion* and the *Groundwork* are compatible if we allow that proper characteristics of the whole need not be realized in each of its parts. Kant's point may be that a person's practical
life taken as a totality counts as a fundamental decision in favor of morality only if such moral striving is experienced overall not as a burden,
but as something undertaken happily.

To ultimately realize the right sort of *virtus phenomenon*, I must
generally understand morality as something that enriches my life, as
something I accept gladly, even if I find it burdensome on occasion.
This attitude is not merely an effect of my having made the right intelligible choice. Instead, it is part of the phenomenal aspect of that choice
itself, being an essential part of what sincere adoption of the moral disposition comes to in temporal, embodied creatures such as ourselves.
None of this means that a morally committed agent could never properly do her duty reluctantly or joylessly. Indeed, some duties are such
that they should not be performed gladly, as when we inflict just punishment, or neglect the needs of one person in order to tend to the more
pressing needs of another.

However, our proper relationship to morality as a whole has a different character, something more like what is involved in loving or
coming to love a person. If I am truly devoted to my child, then I will
generally see the demands she makes on me not as a chore or a duty,
but rather as part of what my life is about. While I realize that good

parenting requires that I give up many objectively valuable things, this realization does not touch my commitment to my children, or dilute what they bring to my life. I understand that a person might reasonably decide not to have children precisely because of these costs, but even so I am not open to such worries. What I impersonally recognize to be costs I do not experience as costs to me, but as essential aspects of being a parent. However, none of this means that I have to be thrilled when my daughter needs her diaper changed at 3:00 a.m. We might worry that anyone who was enthusiastic about this chore had passed from love into obsession or monomania. Yet while I may often experience what my child requires as onerous, this does not entail that I experience her (or my love for her) as anything like a burden in my life (even one for which I am vastly overcompensated). Looking at my life as a whole, I would not wish for it to be different even if at this moment I might also wish that I could have gotten a few more hours' sleep.

Our ordinary decisions do not require reference to any object of moral love such as the highest good. The law commands unconditionally, and as autonomous creatures we are capable of recognizing this command and being immediately motivated by it. No special object of love is required for us to perform these obligations as we should, so long as these actions are considered in isolation from the rest of our doings. However, it is a feature of human agency that our choices must be understood not just episodically, but as parts of our ongoing careers as agents who must exist and make sense of themselves over time. We must concern ourselves not just with the right decision to make here and now, but also with what, ultimately, we stand for. If Kant is right, then the true nature of our overall commitments cannot be pieced together from the qualities of our particular choices taken severally. While any particular act of a morally committed agent may be done joylessly, it is not possible that all or even most of them may be. A properly devoted parent might change diapers reluctantly, but insofar as he is sincerely committed to his child, this attitude must be exceptional, disappearing from view when he considers his overall relationship to her and her place in his life.

In the *Religion*, Kant explains that in faith human beings "are seeking something…that might serve them as an end and even prove the purity of their intention" (6:7n). A life in which our moral actions were typically done reluctantly or joylessly would be the life of a person with at best a very incomplete understanding of or commitment to morality, even though no fault might be found with any of her choices considered by itself. For our overall relation to morality to be a joyous, wholehearted one, we may need to recognize more than just the authority of the moral law. We may also need to sustain a teleological vision of our efforts that makes our relation to morality, demanding as it usually is, something we can gladly affirm as a whole. To maintain such gladness in the face of frustration and disappointment, we need more than just the hope that we are moving toward the highest good in some way. We need a deeper confidence that we are part of the collective achievement of this goal, just as medieval masons took for granted that a cathedral would result from their efforts, even if none expected to live to see its completion. Kant's thought may be that only when morality is presented in terms of such a narrative are human beings able to embrace it, not just with respect to this or that action, but as a guiding principle that can integrate an entire course of life.

What if we failed to see morality in light of a broader teleological picture oriented toward the highest good? The consequence could not be that the moral law would cease to be binding, given that it would remain an unconditional principle of pure practical reason. But our commitment to morality, while real, might still be fundamentally ambivalent. The moral law can become the unifying principle of an entire human life only if we can represent its basic concerns in ways that engage our narrative self-understanding. Kant need not be saying that we must believe in the postulates in such a way that they become premises in our practical reasoning. Instead, the postulates may only serve to establish a background picture against which we can unreflectively understand our particular strivings and our relations to one another as parts of a common moral endeavor. This faith would not change the way we reason, but it would profoundly inform how we conceive of our relationship to our own reason and that of others, making us capable of an overall commitment to morality that is neither alienated or ambivalent, but something that could count as sincere devotion. In form, our timeless, intelligible choice of moral disposition may then be less like our ordinary practical decisions than it is like realizing that we have fallen in love.[16]

---

16 In this respect, faith is needed not to sustain morality as a demand of reason, but to present this demand in a way that can serve as the sort of "ground project" that Bernard Williams thinks we need: "Life has to have substance if anything is to have sense, including adherence to the impartial system...." See Williams 1981, p. 19.

CHAPTER 6

Duties, Ends and the Divine Corporation

James Krueger

In "The Divine Corporation and the History of Ethics," J. B. Schneewind argues that "we can best explain the development of modern ethics by seeing it as resulting from attempts to defend belief in the reality of the moral world, viewed as a just cooperative venture, while accommodating changes in, or departures from, the religious underpinnings of that belief" (Schneewind 1984, p. 180). Kant is given an important, if "profoundly ambivalent" role in this history (*Ibid.*, p. 189). Schneewind argues that while Kant himself was unable to fully escape believing that the moral world requires religious underpinnings, he did point the way to such an escape. At least in part, he accomplished this by increasingly treating "the moral world as a historical task rather than as a metaphysical or religious assurance" (*Ibid.*, p. 191).

Criticizing the place given to Kant in this historical narrative is not a simple task. For one, given the claim advanced by Schneewind, it is not enough simply to point out that Kant insisted on the moral necessity of religious faith throughout his writings. One has to further conclude that he was right to do so. One must argue that his discussions of world-historical progress cannot serve as a replacement for religious faith, that he was right to insist on the need for such faith.

Complicating the discussion even further, the interpretive task is a challenging one. Kant's arguments for the necessity of religious belief are often far from clear. They depend on his account of the highest good, a notion that poses its own interpretive challenges. In the *Critique of Practical Reason*, Kant identifies the highest good as "happiness distributed in exact proportion to morality" (5:110). He goes on to argue:

> since the promotion of the highest good, which contains this connection in its concept, is an *a priori* necessary object of our will and inseparably bound up with the moral law, the impossibility of the first must also prove the falsity of the second. If, therefore, the highest good is impossible in accordance with practical rules, then the moral law, which commands us to promote it, must be

fantastic and directed to empty imaginary ends and must therefore itself be
false. (5:114)

Many have wondered, reading such passages, why strict proportionality
between virtue and happiness is the highest good. More general concerns about Kant's notion of the highest good often center on the question of what (if anything) it adds to his moral view. Does the introduction of happiness into the highest good undermine his strict
condemnations of heteronomy?[1] If there is a duty to promote the highest good, as he repeatedly insists, it could seem to require that we esti-
mate the moral worth of others, and apportion happiness to them accordingly. But Kant famously argues that we can not know the moral
worth of others (see, for example, 4:406-7). How, then, can we have a
duty to promote the highest good? How, moreover, could the impossibility of the highest good imply the "falsity" of the moral law? Kant has
argued elsewhere for the reality of the moral law and its bindingness.
What is missing, so that a further argument is required to secure the
"truth" of the moral law?

Rather than looking first at these interpretive issues, however, I
want to come at the problem from another direction. Those, such as
Schneewind, who suggest that historical progress is sufficient to ground
Kant's moral view accept that such progress is needed to fill *some* role.
In other words, even on Schneewind's interpretation, *something* we
might call "the highest good" is required to ground morality; otherwise
he would follow those who simply dismiss Kant's discussions of the
highest good and the practical postulates. Starting with a clear understanding of the problems that Schneewind and others are responding to,
we might be able to work backward to an understanding of these passages in Kant.[2] At the very least, understanding the problem should
help us to evaluate the prospects for historical progress as an alternative
to religious faith in grounding morality.

The Problem for the Secular Moralist

One difficulty in beginning with contemporary writers is that there
seem to be important differences in how they conceive the problem to
which they are responding. Thus, presenting an account of *the* problem
that requires faith in historical progress involves its own challenges.
There might not be just one problem. Nonetheless, I believe there are

---

1   See Beck 1960, p. 244.
2   Of course, any such understanding would need to be shown consistent with the relevant
     texts in order to stand as a viable interpretation.

threads that run through work of a number of contemporary interpreters that can help us understand what might be driving Kant's arguments concerning the highest good and the practical postulates.

One of the most general discussions of the problems that face a moral atheist can be found in Annette Baier's "Secular Faith." Baier is directly confronting what she sees as one problem that a religious view seems to easily solve, but with which a secular moral view must grapple. In a manner consistent with Schneewind's understanding of Kant's historical role, she locates in Kant the resources for a secular solution to that problem.

Put simply, Baier wonders if atheism can undermine one's "expectation that unilateral virtue will bring happiness" (Baier 1980, pp. 131-2). She writes:

> The theist might believe, in his cool hour, that unilateral, or minority, or exploited majority morality will not procure ultimate ruin, that all things will work together for good, but what consolation can a secular philosopher offer for the cool, thoughtful hour, in the absence of God? (Baier 1980, p.132)

The religious person can always hope that God will set things right. Heaven and hell might ensure that everyone gets his or her just deserts in the end. What can the atheist rely on? What can he or she hope for?

Baier raises this question as one of general philosophical interest and turns to Kant for an answer. Andrews Reath starts within the Kantian framework, and argues for a (secular) conception of the highest good as Kant's own. He argues:

> The doctrine of the Highest Good is one place where Kant can begin to address the problems raised by the fact we live in a morally imperfect world, which is not conducive to fully rational conduct. Simply put, we live in circumstances in which we cannot count on others to adhere to moral principles and act as they ought. The result is that different people's choices taken together create conflicts to which there may be no completely acceptable solution, and that situations arise which seem to make it impossible to act from moral principles. The problem which this poses for Kant is that, in many situations, it may become (or appear to become) irrational for individuals to act from what they recognize as their duties. (Reath 1988, p. 618)

In some respects, Reath's problem is the same as Baier's (the fact that the immorality of others can lead to their taking advantage of the scrupulously moral), though Reath's problem is more specific. It is not just the threat of unhappiness, but the way in which the failure to achieve happiness can make uncompromisingly moral action seem impossible.

Reath does not provide much detail as to how circumstances could make it such that it would "seem impossible to act from moral principles." He does, however, point to Christine Korsgaard's discussion of lying in "The Right to Lie: Kant on Dealing with Evil" where she spells out how such an argument might go.

Korsgaard focuses on the familiar case where a murderer comes to one's house, seeking to know the location of a neighbor he intends to kill. One concern voiced by Korsgaard is that Kant's moral view does not provide resources for responding to such cases, that his rigorist interpretation of our moral duties leads him to insist that we must tell the truth despite the horrific results we might sometimes expect from doing so. Korsgaard thinks Kant's response to this concern is found (at least in part) in remarks he makes about the responsibility we have for the negative outcomes that follow our actions when we act morally. In "On a Supposed Right to Lie from Philanthropy," Kant writes,

> if you have *by a lie* prevented someone just now bent on murder from committing the deed, then you are legally responsible for all the consequences that might arise from it. But if you have kept strictly to the truth, then public justice can hold nothing against you, whatever the unforeseen consequences might be. (8:427)

The choice not to lie protects one from responsibility for what follows, where the choice to lie makes one responsible for all the negative results, no matter if they are unforeseen. As Korsgaard puts it, "The advantage of the Kantian approach is the definite sphere of responsibility.... If you act as you ought, bad outcomes are not your responsibility" (Korsgaard 1996a, p. 150). Thus, the moral person need not feel any guilt at an innocent death that, in some sense, results from his choice, for the responsibility for the killing lies solely with the murderer. And the moral importance of failing to achieve happiness through moral action would be blocked, for it is not the moral actions that bring about the negative outcomes, it is (in this case) the immoral choices of another.

However, as Korsgaard argues, this cannot be an adequate account of our moral obligations. "The trouble is," she observes, "it is grotesque to simply say that I have done my part by telling the truth and the end results are not my responsibility" (*Ibid.*, p.150). In the case of the murderer at the door, we have essentially decided to sacrifice the life of another by telling the truth, and simply denying responsibility for the death does not show truth-telling, in these circumstances, to be consistent with the requirements of morality. The decision to tell the truth would seem to amount to using one's neighbor as a mere means to the attainment of one's own freedom from responsibility. As such, we do not yet have a description of what the truth-teller is doing that makes this particular action consistent with our moral obligations. Saying that the truth-teller is trying to avoid responsibility for the death that results seems to make the choice morally questionable, rather than securing its moral intelligibility.

This is so even if we agree, in advance, that truth-telling is always morally required of us. What we seek is not a justification for the *general* prohibition against lying. That we may possess. What is missing is some understanding of how we can *live out* that general requirement that we not lie, in this particular set of circumstances, in a way that maintains the consistency of our action with broader moral requirements, requirements that might also provided us with that very justification for the general prohibition. As noted, if we seek to avoid responsibility through our choice not to lie, we may be keeping to a general prohibition against lying, but in a way that does, nonetheless, run afoul of our moral obligations.

This is because, to put the point simply, ends are relevant to the moral worth of actions. Without some end, an action is not intelligible as properly human. Moreover, without a fairly specified end, we don't have a proper description of what someone is doing, not one adequate for moral analysis of the person's actions. Thus, without some understanding of what the truth-teller is seeking, we don't yet know how to describe his or her action (including its end) in a way consistent with the requirements of the morality (however construed). If the end sought is not consistent with the requirements of morality, it is hard to see how an action aimed at that end can pass moral muster. Thus, Reath's concern is with the necessity of ends for action that can make our actions morally intelligible. Even if I already know that (for example) lying is never morally permissible, I might still want to know what my action *is*, what it is aimed at, when I tell the truth. That end had better be consistent with the requirements of morality if the action is to be morally intelligible. If no end is available as a possible end for me that is consistent with what virtue requires, then living according to the moral law seems impossible.

Despite the difference in the way the problem is formulated, we can nonetheless see it as related to Baier's concern. Baier began from the fact that one cannot expect unilateral virtue to lead to happiness. On Reath's account, by contrast, it is the lack of some end consistent with what morality requires (whether or not that be construed as constituting, or even being consistent with, happiness) that is the problem. Without the guarantee of there being such an end, consistent with morality in all possible circumstances, the moral person is at risk of being put into positions where no course of action is morally intelligible. However, given Reath's claim that the highest good (with its reference to happiness) is required to solve this problem, we can connect the two accounts. What this suggests is that the core of the problem is the same for both. In both cases, it is that happiness (in some sense) is, in some circumstances, impossible as the result of moral action. What Reath's analysis allows us to do, however, is state the problem in a way that does not start from a worry about realizing happiness. We can note, first, that morality requires an end consistent with its requirements if an action is to be morally intelligible. The crucial link to the possibility of achieving happiness only emerges later once we recognize that the highest good is necessary to guarantee such ends.[3]

It is important to be able to state the problem in this way because, for Kant, there cannot be a simple argument from the absence of happiness to the moral unintelligibility of an action. Such an argument would seem to assume heteronomy. However, it is surely the case that the moral law requires that the ends we seek be consistent with its requirements. Thus we can see that the absence of an end of the right sort can call into question whether moral action is intelligible. If happiness is, in some sense, a morally necessary end and if the absence of happiness as a consistently plausible end is what generates the problems discussed here, then we can make the link to happiness in a way that does not threaten the purity of the moral law.

There are, nonetheless, certain textual challenges that must be confronted in order to defend this as an interpretation of Kant. For example, in the preface to the first edition of *Religion within the Boundaries of Mere Reason*, Kant writes:

> morality needs absolutely no material determining ground of the free power of choice, that is no end, either in order to recognize what duty is or to impel its performance; on the contrary, when duty is the issue, morality can perfectly well abstract from ends all together, and ought to do so. For example, to know whether I should (or even can) be truthful in my testimony before a court of justice or faithful when someone else's goods entrusted to me are being reclaimed, there is no need to demand an end which I might perhaps propose to myself to realize by my declaration, for what sort of end this might be does not matter at all; rather, one who still finds it necessary to look around for some end when his testimony is rightfully demanded of him, is in this respect already contemptible. (6:4)

This would seem to suggest that arguments such as the one just sketched, which demand some end in order to evaluate the moral status of a course of action, are making a profound mistake. Individuals who "look around for some end" in order to know they are doing the right thing are "already contemptible."

---

3   Obviously, I have not yet shown that the highest good *is* necessary to guarantee such ends. That crucial link, tying the different understandings of the problems together, requires a detailed discussion of what, in fact, is necessary to solve the problems identified here. For the moment, I simply want to suggest that since Reath, for example, sees the highest good as essential to the solution, we can assign a certain level of plausibility to the claim that the problems Baier and Reath are discussing are connected. The arguments needed to establish this with more certainty will be discussed below.

However, Kant goes on to claim that "although on its own behalf, morality does not need the representation of an end which would have to precede the determination of the will," nonetheless "it may well be that it has a necessary reference to such an end, not as the ground of its maxims, but as a necessary consequence accepted in conformity to them" (6:4). This is so because, "in the absence of all reference to an end no determination of the will can take place in human beings at all" (*Ibid.*).

This helps to clarify exactly how the problem identified above arises. In one sense, morality is completely independent of considerations of ends. As we said regarding the case of the murderer at the door, we might possess an argument which shows us that we must never lie and yet still wonder how we can live out that requirement, in a way consistent with morality, in the world as we encounter it. In this sense, the moral law does not require "on its own behalf" (for its validity) reference to an end. What is at risk is our ability to *live out the requirements of the moral law in the world*. Without an end consistent with the requirements of the moral law, the moral law stands, but it is impossible to guarantee that the law can be applied. It would seem that, in cases like that of the murderer at the door, every possible action (every possible end we could seek) is morally questionable. If every possible action (every possible end) is morally questionable, how can we act according to the requirements of the moral law? If we seek to act from duty, in such circumstances, what do we do? What do we seek?

For human beings, our dual nature as both rational and sensible impacts our ability to live out the requirements of the moral law. As rational beings, we do not need to "look around for some end" to discern our moral obligations. I know I must not lie because of the contradiction that such a course of action creates in the will, no matter what specific end I seek. Nonetheless, as human, as a sensible being, I always act for some specific end. I have no choice but seek something when I act. That end is clearly relevant to what I am doing when I act. That end, then, must be consistent with the requirements of morality if my action is to be morally intelligible. I do not need to invoke an end to know I must give true testimony before a court. I need to invoke an end to know how my choice to do so is morally intelligible, in full context. As Stephen Engstrom argues, "although the moral law does not depend on any material for its *validity*, it does depend upon or presuppose material for its *employment*" (Engstrom 1992, p. 752, original emphasis).

Importantly, then, this passage from the *Religion* suggests a restriction on possible solutions to the problem identified here. In order to maintain the purity of the moral law, the end in question must be a "necessary consequence" of moral maxims. In other words, the end in question must, in some sense, have its source in the moral law. Otherwise, the moral law would require some contingent, external (i.e., alien) condition, in order to secure its universal applicability. Rather than depending on such a condition, in Kant's view, the moral law necessitates an end that we must conceive as possible through virtuous action, regardless of how the world might appear. The moral law can necessitate certain beliefs about what is possible through virtuous action (so long as the contents of those beliefs are not themselves impossible). As Engstrom observes,

> Practical reason determines what its ends can be by empirically ascertaining what its powers of agency are … pure practical reason, because its ends are necessary rather than contingent, reverses this order of determination: it postulates the powers of agency … needed to realize its necessary ends. (Engstrom 1992, p. 774)

The empirical world (and our empirical nature) does not constrain the validity of the moral law (beyond broad constraints about what is really possible); rather, the moral law necessitates an understanding of what ends we must seek as human beings.

Thus far, we have seen that a problem can arise for an individual seeking to live according to the requirements of the moral law. In particular, such a person may confront circumstances in which it seems that no end is available that is consistent with virtue. Solving the problem requires a guarantee that some end, grounded in the moral law, is available, regardless of the circumstances in which one is acting, and regardless of whether others are acting virtuously. The lack of such a guarantee would mean it is possible for circumstances to arise in which no end, and thus no course of action, is consistent with the requirements of morality. In such circumstances, the requirements of the moral law would be impossible to live out, a conclusion that would make moral requirements, in such circumstances, illusory. We have also seen hints that happiness plays an important role here. What remains to be seen is if we can show the necessity of happiness to any solution of the problem and, in particular, if secular accounts focused on historical progress can provide that solution. Let us turn, now, to consider how a secular account might go. The necessity of the link to happiness will begin to become more clear as we consider how proposed solutions to the problem function.

Secular Faith

In order to provide some consolation to the moral atheist in circumstances where the immorality of others seems to put her at risk, Baier argues that what is needed is a kind of faith. She argues "faith, not knowledge [is] what is needed to support those 'plain duties' whose unilateral observation sometimes appears to procure the dutiful person's ruin" (Baier 1980, p. 133). By faith, she does not mean blind or irrational acceptance of particular beliefs. Rather, she is clear that "faith, for rational persons, must appear reasonable before it can be sustained" (*Ibid.*). In other words, it "must not fly in the face of inductive evidence" even though it may go beyond what such evidence, strictly construed, supports (*Ibid.*). It cannot be just any end that is introduced; that end must be somehow connected with the action and its circumstances, so that it plausibly can be an end for that action, and so that we can make sense of the notion that the action is capable of securing that end. We don't have to know, with any certainty, that our action will secure the end. But we do have to have grounds for hope that it will (or could), given the circumstances. In addition, the end in question has to be such that the viciousness of others cannot result in the unintelligibility of our action as directed to that end. Remember, as Baier sets up the problem, her concern is that the moral person is in danger of being exploited; thus the possibility of the end has to be unassailable by the immorality of others.

To find a candidate that can meet these requirements, she turns to Kant. She writes:

> Kant says that although a rational being, when he acts on the maxim he can will as a universal law, "cannot for that reason expect every other rational being to be true to it; nor can he expect the realm of nature and its orderly design to harmonize with him as a fitting member of a realm of ends which is possible through himself. That is, he cannot count on its favoring his expectations of happiness. Still the law: Act according to the maxims of a universally legislative member of a merely potential realm of ends, remains in full force, because it commands categorically. And just in this lies the paradox, that merely the dignity of humanity as rational nature without any end or advantage to be gained by it, and the respect for a mere idea, should serve as the inflexible precept of the will. There is the further paradox that the sublimity and worthiness of every rational subject to be a legislative member in the realm of ends consists precisely in independence of maxims from all such incentives." (Baier 1980, pp. 145-6, see 4:438-9[4])

Baier reads this passage as asserting that

> The willingness to act *as if* one is a member of an actual kingdom of ends, when one knows that one is in fact a member of a society that falls short of this ideal, alone makes one worthy to be a legislating member of an actual kingdom of ends or just society. (Baier 1980, p. 146, original emphasis)

The kingdom of ends is itself "possible thorough oneself" because "the existence of persons with the ability to act from respect for that 'mere

---

4   Baier is quoting Kant 1978b.

idea' is … one condition for the idea's actualization" (*Ibid.*). Thus, when we act morally, we keep alive "the assurance of the possibility of qualified members for a just society" (*Ibid.*). Our action demonstrates the reasonableness of faith in a kingdom of ends. We show that it is possible for human beings to act from duty, thus showing that it remains possible for there to be a society in which all persons act in this way.

Similar accounts can be found in the work of a number of contemporary writiers. In each case the moral community (or demonstrated worthiness for membership in such a community, or progress toward such a community) comes to replace religious faith as guaranteeing an intelligible end for any moral action. In Schneewind's view, according to Kant:

> We are to think of ourselves as like God in one respect. We are required to make the world into a just moral community. The moral law shows us the conditions to which it must comply if it is to be one in which we as rational agents can willingly participate…. Kant did not really think we could leave it up to God. (Schneewind 1984, p. 191)

Reath argues in a similar vein, distinguishing a secular from a theological understanding of the highest good in Kant's works. The theological version recognizes virtue as worthiness to be happy, focusing on proportionality "between the virtue of an individual's character and that individual's happiness" (Reath 1988, p. 605). On the secular version, "happiness is subordinated [to virtue] by making the permissibility of an end the condition of its satisfaction or value" (*Ibid.*). On this second understanding, a just moral community becomes the condition that allows the person to achieve the morally permissible ends that he or she seeks (his or her happiness as conditioned by the moral law). Reath argues that, given the existence of the right kind of moral community, "It is not implausible that individuals would by and large be successful in achieving their ends" (*Ibid.*, p. 616). Thus we seek such a community precisely in order to make possible a world in which action consistent with what morality requires is always morally intelligible. There is no need to rely on God to secure this intelligibility. The political community, rightly ordered, is capable of insuring that ends consistent with the requirements of morality are available to us.

Thus, on such accounts, faith in the possibility of a merely human kingdom of ends (or worthiness for membership in such a kingdom) replaces religious faith, and is put forward to resolve the problems identified in the previous section. The question remains, however, whether or not such accounts can deliver on this promise. Can such accounts secure the intelligibility of morally required action, regardless of the circumstances? There are at least three ways to interpret the end being put forward. It could be: 1) demonstrating one's own worthiness to be a member of the kingdom of ends; 2) demonstrating the possibility of the worthiness of humanity in general; or 3) demonstrating actual progress toward the creation of the kingdom of ends. Consider each possibility in turn.

First, one might focus on one's own worthiness to be a legislating member of the kingdom of ends. Even if the immoral actions of others prevent a person from achieving every other possible good, she could still demonstrate, through her action, that she is worthy of such membership. It is not hard to see that such an account will not help when the harm that results from one's action is harm to a third party.[5] I might sacrifice my own happiness in the name of my moral worth, but may I sacrifice the happiness of another on this ground? May I sacrifice, say, someone's life in order to secure my virtue? To act in this way seems grotesque, just as Korsgaard says. It amounts to using others as mere means, as objects in relation to which I demonstrate my moral character. As Allen Wood puts it, to act in this way is to recommend "an indifference to human welfare, and a smug introverted preoccupation with the purity of one's own intentions" (Wood 1970, p. 63). One's personal virtue cannot itself serve as the guarantor of the moral intelligibility of one's acts, because an excessive focus on one's personal virtue is itself a form of vice. I take it this is part of the importance of seeing the moral world as a cooperative venture. To conceive of the moral world as simply a place for me to demonstrate my excellence is to get something horribly wrong about the nature of our moral obligations. It is, ultimately, self-defeating. Thus, this end ultimately cannot serve to make actions morally intelligible in all possible circumstances, and thus cannot solve our problem.

A second option focuses on the possibility of moral worthiness for humanity generally. Instead of resting content with the idea that virtuous action demonstrates something good about me, it focuses instead on how it demonstrates the possibility, for humanity generally, of virtuous action, of living out the demands of our rational nature. By focusing on this possibility, this account seems to avoid the objectionable self-centeredness of the first account. We are not just interested in demonstrating our own worthiness, showcasing our supposed virtue; we seek to demonstrate for and about humanity in general the possibility of worthiness.

We exhibit our worthiness through exhibiting our humanity, our ability to act from reason. We can see, then, a connection between demonstrating worthiness as an end, and our humanity as an end. In the *Groundwork for the Metaphysics of Morals*, Kant discusses our humanity as an end. The problem, however, is that it is not an end in the sense

---

5   Baier herself notes the greater difficulty of such cases, see 1980, p. 146n10.

of a good to be brought about in the world. While it is true that rational nature is "the matter of every good will," it is also the case that "the end must here be thought not as an end to be effected but as an *independently existing* end, and hence thought only negatively, that is, as that which must never be acted against" (4:437). Korsgaard's discussion of the formula of humanity is instructive. She observes that "there are two different roles an end can play in the determination of conduct; it can serve as a purpose pursued, or it can play a negative role and serve as something one must not act against" (Korsgaard 1996a, p. 108). Humanity is of the second sort. It is not a positive end, something to bring about, but only something we must not act against. Korsgaard uses an analogy to illustrate the point: "we do not often get into situations where self-preservation serves as a positive incentive to any action, but it might quite frequently keep us from taking undue risks in the pursuit of our other ends" (*Ibid.*).

In the case we are considering, we still confront the question of what "other ends" are available, consistent with our humanity (with our worthiness to be members of a kingdom of ends). We know we must not treat humanity as a mere means, but we do not yet know what specific ends we could pursue that would guarantee the moral intelligibility of our actions. We thus see that the question of our particular end remains. The end offered here is not something we seek directly: "The capacity for rational choice is not a purpose that we can realize or something we can bring into existence" (Korsgaard 1996a, p. 125). Until we have something that can serve as an end in that way, we are left with the question of what we are trying to accomplish, and whether what we are doing is consistent with the requirements of the moral law.

If this argument is correct, both the first two possibilities fail because they are not ends of the right sort. Without such an end, it is not clear how to guarantee the moral intelligibility of our actions. A third possibility, providing the grounds for possible historical progress, or even making actual progress, toward the existence of the kingdom of ends, might allow us to avoid this problem since it is an end we can pursue. Such an account would allow us to say we are making progress (or showing the possibility of progress) toward an actual end, related to the requirements of the moral law, but nonetheless going beyond the possibility of virtue. Baier, for example, argues, "The secular faith which the just live by is, then, a faith in the possibility of a society for membership in which their just action theoretically qualifies them" (Baier 1980, p. 147). In this way, demonstrating worthiness for membership becomes the basis for progress toward a kingdom of ends. She writes, "The actions of individuals who ... act for the sake of justice do not necessarily hasten the coming of a just society, but they do rule out one ground on which it might be feared impossible" (*Ibid.*, p. 146). They do this by demonstrating the possibility that human beings can act from duty, that human virtue is possible. This itself then constitutes a kind of support for progress.

The difficulty, however, is that Baier's account seems to require that we know our action is from duty. It isn't just *consistency* with duty that is required. We need to know that we are acting *from* duty, undetermined by any sensible impulse. As mentioned earlier, however, one of the problems for understanding a duty to promote the highest good is Kant's repeated assertion that we cannot have knowledge of our own moral goodness (let alone anyone else's). In other words, while we might be able to demonstrate the possible "independence of maxims from all such incentives" by conceiving the possibility of a categorical imperative, we will not have shown the actual possibility that human beings can be worthy members of a kingdom of ends in the sense required unless we know that, in this case, a person really did act from reason alone. It isn't enough to show the possibility of a categorical imperative in the abstract, or even to prove that the pure reason *can* be an incentive to action, all by itself. Without knowing that I am acting from duty, I cannot know if my action demonstrates worthiness to be a member of the kingdom of ends and I cannot know whether I am, in fact, demonstrating the possibility of membership in a kingdom of ends.

We might, then, take a different tack. Instead of focusing on actual action from virtue as demonstrating progress toward a kingdom of ends, we might instead flesh out the idea of the kingdom of ends itself, and argue that we are making progress toward such an end on other, independent grounds. For example, one might follow Rawls and point out that Kant identifies "the political organization of a realm of ends" as "a peaceful international society (or confederation) of peoples, each people organized as a state with some kind of constitutionally representative regime" (Rawls 2000, p. 321). The object of our faith might then be "that the course of human history is progressively improving" and that "we may not unreasonably hope to discern a plan of nature to force mankind ... to form a confederation of constitutional democratic states, which will then ensure perpetual peace and encourage the free development of culture and the arts" (*Ibid.*, pp. 319-20). Could progress toward this end make virtuous action morally intelligible, even in the kinds of circumstances considered here?

If one follows this route, one encounters a different difficulty, namely that the danger that the specified end will pull apart from what is possible in the circumstances in which we act. In other words, circumstances could conspire to make it hard to understand how any of the available courses of action can result in progress toward the goal.

Take the case of the murderer at the door. It is unclear how refusing to lie to the murderer would count as progress toward the creation of such an international political order. Perhaps it demonstrates the possibility of honest dealings, which might be seen as a prerequisite to any such order. This suggestion, however, either collapses the account back into Baier's, with all its problems, or it confronts the fact that honesty, in this case, is exploited by the immorality of another in a way that could undermine one's sense of progress. In other words, we must either know that we are acting virtuously (and hence demonstrating progress toward such a political order) or we must show that our action affects some concrete progress toward such a political order. We simply have no reason to believe that such a society will always be available as a rationally defensible hope. We need some basis for believing that moral action can always aim at this end. Faith that, overall, human history is progressive is not enough; one must be able to understand one's action as, in some sense, contributing to that end.

But perhaps this is construing the role of the political community in the wrong way. Perhaps the political community is not, itself, the end we seek. Rather, perhaps we seek to bring about the political community because of the other ends it makes possible. Reath identifies the secular conception of the highest good as requiring that we are capable of achieving our morally permissible ends. We seek this capacity by seeking the kind of political community that makes this possible. What the political community does, then, is make it possible to achieve the ends we seek (on the condition that they are moral ends).

Thus, as we already saw, Reath argues, "It is not implausible that individuals would by and large be successful in achieving their ends" within the right sort of moral community (Reath 1988, p. 616). He writes:

> General adherence to the duties of justice would lead people to pursue their own ends in ways that do not interfere with the legitimate interests of others. Moreover, it would likely have an effect on people's desires that promoted, rather than hindered, their satisfaction. As individuals would be guided by moral concerns, they would be less inclined to pursue ends that are divisive, or harmful to others, and would be willing to accept resolutions to any conflicts that might arise when these resolutions accord with publicly accepted principles. Beyond that, the duties of virtue would lead individuals to take a positive interest in the happiness of others, as well as a concern for the common good (the proper functioning of the social system). Having a virtuous character would include, in addition to adherence to public moral principles, a willingness to do one's share in maintaining this system. Overall one could expect an atmosphere of mutual respect and shared concern for the interests of all, as well as the high degree of social cooperation needed to make this system work. (*Ibid.*)

On this account, the kingdom of ends is not sought just for its own sake; it is also sought because such a community is the condition under which each of us can achieve a morally bounded happiness. In part, then, the kingdom of ends ensures that there are no murderers to come to our door and put us in the kind of circumstances that could call into question the intelligibility of moral action. In this way, the role of the kingdom of ends is not to be, itself, the end of moral action, but rather to ensure that moral action is always possible by ensuring the possibility of the highest good.

There are at least two reasons to worry about such an account. First, it doesn't make our actions morally intelligible in the circumstances we actually find ourselves in. Even if we accept the claims advanced by Reath, the most that they show is that the world could be changed so that such circumstances do not arise. The argument does not show that we can make progress toward such a world in the circumstances we actually confront in the world as it is currently constituted. At best, it shows that moral action would always be possible in a kingdom of ends. It does not show that moral action is always possible in a world that falls short of that kingdom. It would only accomplish the latter if it could demonstrate that it is always possible to make progress toward such a world in the circumstances we confront; but that is to return us to the account just considered and the problems just discussed.

Second, it is not clear that a just moral community could, by itself, secure even the possibility of acheiving our morally permissible ends. One would not be in danger of being exploited by the immorality of others if everyone adhered to the requirements of such a moral and political order (in this way, we might address Baier's concern). However the threat to the moral intelligibility of our actions need not arise just because of the immorality of others. While the right political arrangements might mitigate the suffering caused by hurricanes, tornadoes, the death of a loved one and so on, they certainly could not prevent it. No matter how fair and efficient the distribution of aid after a disaster, it cannot entirely stop the suffering that is visited even on the most virtuous. Moreover, there are all manner of ends that a political order could not help bring about, even if each and every one is morally permissible. There is no guarantee that an individual will find a loving spouse, give birth to a healthy child, find employment in his or her desired field, live a long life, or achieve any of a wide range of other innocent goals, even if the individual is scrupulous about his or her moral duties, and no matter the political structure in place. The most moral people can live lives of bitter, unfulfilled hardship, and many of the causes have nothing to do with world-historical progress, the distribution of virtue in society or the details of political arrangements.

Perhaps, however, this is too quick. Might it not be like seeking, for example, perfection at some skill or profession, something which we may never realistically achieve, but which we can nonetheless see ourselves as approaching ever closer through our own efforts? While one might seek to be perfect in some regard, or perhaps the best in a particular field, even though it is extremely unlikely one will succeed, such strivings are fundamentally dissimilar to what is required to realize the highest good. The capacities we seek to extend in those cases remain within us, within our power. They are the abilities, skills and knowledge necessary for carrying out the project in question. The achievement doesn't require any change that is not, in some respect, internal to the striving individual (or group of individuals). The fact, however, that the natural order takes no account of moral worth is not amenable to change through human effort. It is not some ability of ours we can seek to develop or refine. Insofar as moral character is beyond human knowledge, all we can do is attempt to encourage virtue and attempt to secure general happiness. We are not capable, as those who have objected to the idea of a duty to realize the highest good have urged, of making the link ourselves.[6] What is needed is something that, in principle, we cannot affect. We cannot affect whether the natural order takes account of moral worth, no matter what we do.

What this means is that political progress cannot provide the hope required to solve the problem. If a just political order could be seen as making it possible for us to achieve happiness, and if acting as required by the moral law could always be seen as helping to bring about such a political order, then the solution would work. However, as it turns out, there is little reason to believe either condition holds in the world as we confront it.

Importantly, these final considerations lead to a different understanding of the problem than we developed above. We started with Baier and the worry that the moral person could be exploited by the immorality of others. Now it is clear that the problem created by the possible immorality of others can arise from other sources as well. We can see that the problem arises, too, because the natural order takes no account of morality. This way of understanding the problem has the virtue of fitting Kant's discussions of the highest good. In the *Critique of Judgment*, for example, Kant points out that the virtuous are still subject to all the evils of "poverty, illness and untimely death" because nature "pays no attention" to the moral worth of persons (5:452). This means that whatever ends we seek, whether or not those ends are con-

---

6   See, for example, Beck 1960, pp. 244-5. Reath endorses this argument from Beck; see Reath 1988, pp. 609-10.

sistent with morality, there is no guarantee that we can achieve them. This remains true if we limit ourselves to morally acceptable actions. Nature simply does not care if we act as morality demands. It does not notice one way or another. It is simply the case that "no necessary connection of happiness with virtue in the world, adequate to the highest good, can be expected from the most meticulous observance of moral laws" (5:113). Even in the passage Baier identifies as the inspiration for her proposed solution, Kant observes not only that one cannot count on the morality of others, but also that one cannot count on the cooperation of nature (4:438). It is because of this disconnect between the natural and moral order that circumstances of the kind we have discussed can arise. This is the problem to be solved.

There are, then, several reasons to think that accounts that focus on world-historical progress will be inadequate to solve the problem. If the focus is on actual progress to some worldly state of affairs, it is unclear that such a goal is always going to line up with what is possible in our circumstances. Since this lack of fit between the world of experience and what morality requires can be understood as the source of the problematic cases we need to address, we can see why such accounts are not likely to offer a solution. That lack of fit, political progress cannot remedy. Further, the reason that the natural order is not responsive to morality is not simply because of the possibility of exploitation by others. Even in a world where everyone acts according to the strictures of the moral law, even in a world of perfect virtue, circumstances of the kind identified here can arise and present problems for the moral person.[7] They present the same challenge, though they do not depend on the immorality of others. If we focus instead on worthiness to be a member of such a political order, we encounter a different problem. Such accounts fall short because they either fail to provide an end we could seek to bring about, or they require us to know our moral character in a way that Kant argues is impossible.

Kant and the Consolation of the Religious Moralist

The question remains, then, whether religious belief is required to solve the problem (and why, precisely, happiness is essential to any solution).

---

7   Certain trolley cases illustrate this point. Again, the moral person could seem to take a callous, instrumental view of those at risk (here, from the runaway car). They are sacrificed as a means of demonstrating or safeguarding the moral person's (supposed) purity. But acting in this way seems, in Korsgaard's words, grotesque. Such cases do not depend on the immoral action of others.

At first glance, there is reason to be skeptical that a religious account could do better than the secular accounts just considered. It is hard to see how the possibility of one's otherworldly happiness could justify sacrificing the happiness of another. This appears just as grotesque as sacrificing one's neighbor's happiness to demonstrate one's supposed virtue. The discussion so far has highlighted several ways in which a justification for conscientious behavior can go wrong. We can use those identified failings, though, to craft an account that successfully avoids such pitfalls.

An account can go wrong if the end offered is not, in some sense, shared. If the good that I seek is conceived as good only for me—if it is not an actual end for those affected by my action (an end they share with me)—then the proposed end will fall victim to Korsgaard's grotesqueness objection. Moreover, since the one affected by my action could be any rational being at all, it must be shared by any rational being as such. It must be recognized as, in some sense, a good for all such beings by its very nature. In Schneewind's terms, we see here the importance of viewing morality as a cooperative venture.

What candidate ends can meet this requirement, can legitimately be seen as shared in the sense that is necessary? There are two ends that we know are actual for all persons. Those are virtue (one's moral perfection) and happiness (the satisfaction of one's desires). We have already seen that the first alone cannot serve, for it does not have sufficient empirical content; it is not an object or state of affairs that we can bring about. The second fails as well. I may desire my own happiness, but conceived as the satisfaction of my contingent desires, it is not, by the mere fact of being such, a universally shared end. Put another way, a particular person's happiness is not unconditionally good. It may be a good for me, or (by extension) for those who are my friends and family and thus share in my projects, but what could make it such that it would be a good for any rational being whatsoever? What could make it constitute an end for all, by its very nature? Something else is required in order to transform my personal happiness into a shared end, an end that makes claims on all.

The solution is in the proper relationship between these two universal ends. Happiness provides the end, the thing to be brought about, while virtue secures the goodness of happiness, the conditions on which it can constitute a shared end. Consider the following passage from Engstrom, where he reconstructs Kant's argument that virtue is required for the goodness of happiness:

> Assume first that one's end of happiness is good. Then the claim of self-love is valid; and one's end of happiness, according to this claim, is a necessary object of desire according to a principle of reason. Since self-love is the ground

of the claim, this end can be necessary according to a principle of reason only if it has been made the object of a universal attitude that recognizes the claims of others' self-love also and hence both restricts this end so as to render it compatible with all the ends of others that have been similarly restricted, and moreover adopts all such ends of others as its own. Therefore, this end of happiness is the object of a universal attitude. The universal attitude is the attitude of virtue, so virtue is necessary for the goodness of happiness. (Engstrom 1992, p. 764)

It is through the requirements of virtue that the objects of desire become goods, objects that must be regarded by all as good and that make claims on all of us. The highest good, then, considered as "the whole and complete good as the object of the faculty of desire of rational finite beings" must include happiness, but not "merely in the eyes of a person who makes himself an end but even in the judgment of an impartial reason, which regards a person in the world generally as an end in itself" (5:110).

From this we can see why happiness is required as part of any solution. It is an end we can seek to bring about (a happy world) and, conditioned by morality, it is a shared end making claims upon all rational beings. It is, then, the fact that general happiness sometimes seems impossible, that generates the problem. Moreover, this shows the link between the problem identified by Baier, and that discussed by Reath. Both discussions rest on the fact that the natural world fails to take account of the requirements of morality, resulting in the possibility that happiness can pull apart from morality and threaten the moral intelligibility of actions.

We have not, however, solved the problem. We may have identified a shared end, but is it always available, no matter the circumstances we confront? Can it really serve to make moral action intelligible, in every possible circumstance? Clearly not. The cases considered above illustrate how a happy world cannot be guaranteed. Moreover, we have seen that human political arrangements cannot supply this guarantee. Forging a link between morality and happiness, quite simply, requires more-than-human power. No change that humanity alone could bring about can guarantee a happy world as a possible end of every moral action. The problem is that the world does not take any account of morality, so that confluences of natural events can always undermine our ability to achieve the shared end of happiness through moral action.

This is, of course, how Kant introduces religious faith as a necessary postulate of pure practical reason. It is not, on Kant's view, that God directly ensures the happiness of the virtuous. Rather, the "*kingdom of God*" is such that "nature and morals come into harmony, foreign to each of them of itself, through a holy author who makes the highest good possible" (5:128). God brings the laws of nature and the laws of morality into harmony, such that the satisfaction of our desires is always compossible with moral action. It is in the capacity of "cause of all nature" (5:125) that God is able to bring about the kind of happy world that is required in order to secure the general intelligibility of moral action across all possible circumstances. From the *Critique of Pure Reason*, we know that reason cannot rule out the possibility of God's existence. Now we see that it is only by postulating the existence of God, of a being capable of bending the natural order to take into account the requirements of morality, that we can guarantee that moral action is always intelligible as such.

Kant's argument (not surprisingly) is formally similar to that offered by Reath. The major difference is simply that God (rather than the moral community) is what rules out the problem we have been considering. That means, however, that this account faces some of the same challenges as Reath's. For one, how is it that the possibility of realizing the highest good at some future time can make my act, today, morally intelligible? Don't I need to believe that my act today contributes to bringing about a happy world, not just that God may, someday, bring about a world in which the realization of happiness is possible through obedience to the moral law? How can this be consistent with the argument above that the conditions necessary for the highest good cannot be established by me (or even by all of humanity acting in concert) and are not operative in the world as I experience it?

Of course this problem could be solved if one of the conditions of a happy world is itself a goal we can seek. In that way, we could seek to bring about a happy world through working to bring about one of the conditions of its realization. But this leads directly to a second, related, problem. Because divine intervention is necessary to make the end possible, it is not clear that *we* can seek that end. If general happiness is only possible on the condition of a specific kind of divine intervention, how is it an end *for us*? As Reath argues, if we see the highest good as dependent on divine action, we face a problem: "it makes no sense to view the Highest Good as an end we are to promote unless it is a state of affairs that we can envision as the result of our conduct" (Reath 1988, p. 607). Since we *cannot* see the basis for a happy world as possible through human action alone, the argument would go, the end in question cannot be an end for us, and we have failed to locate what we need to solve the problem. The kingdom of ends *is* possible through human action, so (Reath argues) the secular conception of the highest good is preferable to the theological.

We seem to be caught on the horns of a dilemma. Either we focus on those things that human action can bring about, and face the fact that these will never guarantee the intelligibility of moral action, or we rely on divine intervention, but at the cost of making the end that guarantees the intelligibility of moral action no longer an end for us. Is there any way to resolve the dilemma?

We can move toward a solution if we recognize that the need for another's assistance in pursuing an end does not *ipso facto* prevent an end being an end for me. To illustrate, consider some common examples. If I seek a promotion, or a new job, the achievement of the end is not directly within my power. Ultimately, the action of another is necessary for me to achieve the end. But it would be odd to say that I cannot seek a promotion, or seek a new job. What does seem to be necessary is that there are things I can do that somehow contribute to achieving the end. While getting the job or the promotion ultimately depends upon another, I can submit résumés or take extra care with the quality of my work. I undertake these tasks precisely in hope that they will contribute to my getting the promotion or job.

The same analysis allows us to say that the kingdom of ends is, in some sense, an end for each of us individually. Of course I cannot bring about, through my action alone, the kingdom of ends. This requires the cooperation of others, in fact the cooperation of the whole of humanity. Yet, the kingdom of ends is clearly also an end for me. I do my part to bring it about insofar as I seek to act virtuously. In that sense, my efforts to do what duty requires are my efforts to bring about such a community even though the bringing about of such a community is strictly speaking beyond my power.[8]

The arguments offered by Baier, Reath and Schneewind thus capture important aspects of Kant's arguments concerning the highest good. The connections to historical progress, and to our striving to live out the requirements of the moral law, are real and crucial. Without the possibility of the kind of progress central to such accounts, there would be no sense in which we could be understood as pursuing the highest good. However, for reasons we have seen, such accounts are incomplete. They do not solve the problem that threatens the moral intelligibility of certain acts of virtue. To solve this problem, we must strive for something beyond our own virtuous character, and beyond a particular kind of moral and political community. We have to see our pursuit of this as the pursuit of a world in which moral action is the route to general happiness. We cannot bring about that world by ourselves, but our

---

8   Notice, unlike some accounts considered earlier, this does not require that I actually know I have made progress. My striving to live a moral life is a striving after the end in question, even if I do not know which particular acts (if any) actually contribute to progress.

pursuit of a moral community, and of our own virtue, is a necessary condition for the realization of such a world. If we are to achieve a happy world, we have to achieve a moral community, for if virtue is the condition for the goodness of happiness, the best world (the highest good) will be found in a virtuous world where that virtue is what brings general happiness.[9]

We can make this clearer by a further example. There are researchers who try to detect signals from extraterrestrial life. They take concrete steps in pursuit of that goal (building radio telescopes and analyzing the data from them, for example). The intelligibility of their goal, however, presupposes the possibility of extraterrestrial life, the possibility that such life could create (say) radio signals, and that we could detect them. The first two of those conditions, in particular, we are incapable of doing anything about. They are things we must postulate (believe) in order to make these actions intelligible. Yet, if we deny that they are possible, it makes no sense to say that anyone seeks evidence of extraterrestrial life. In a similar way, we have to believe in a being capable of bringing about a connection between virtue and the laws of the natural order (such that virtue leads to happiness). To bring about such a connection is not within our power (just as to bring about the existence of aliens capable of creating radio signals is not within our power). At the same time, though, there are concrete actions that we need to take in order to help bring about the highest good. In particular, we need to be virtuous and to seek general happiness (insofar as this is required by benevolence). Promoting the ideal political community, the kingdom of ends, is what human beings can do (akin to building and using radio telescopes); the realization of the end, however, is dependent on something we cannot control (just as we cannot create alien life). But that does not block us from seeking the goal in question, any more than our inability to create alien life blocks us from seeking to detect such life.

Even so, there is one further objection to be considered. Reath argues that there is a further reason the theological conception of the

---

9   Notice that this does not change the earlier argument that what is required for the realization of the highest good is beyond our power. In seeking virtue, or the right kind of political structures, we do what we can to bring about the highest good. We seek one necessary condition for its realization. However, our striving is not sufficient, and never can be, for what else is required for achieving the highest good is beyond our power. While hard work may be a necessary condition for my achieving a promotion, it is not sufficient in and of itself because of the role that the actions of another (my boss) must play in the realization of that end. That hard work is necessary is important, for it allows me to contribute, through my action, to the achieving of the end, even though the other conditions for achieving it remain outside of my control and even though my hard work could never be sufficient for achieving the promotion.

highest good (the conception that depends on divine action for its realization) cannot be an end for us. He contends that this conception identifies the highest good as "a state of affairs *that comes about in another
world* through the activity of God" (Reath 1988, p. 601). Since the
highest good does not come about in the world of sense, it is fundamentally beyond our capacity to bring about. Our actions belong to the
natural order, and hence cannot make a causal contribution to something that only comes about in *another* world. Divine action alone is
responsible for the realization of the highest good. If this is correct, we
have not escaped the dilemma sketched above.

I think there are several reasons, however, for rejecting the suggestion that the highest good, in its theological form, requires "another
world," so divorced from the empirical world that our actions can have
no bearing on it. First, if the highest good, in its theological form, requires a particular relation between virtue and happiness, it seems clear
that any "other world" in which the highest good is to be realized has to
be empirical. Our desires are due to our empirical nature. The satisfaction of our desires constitutes happiness. Thus, if the world in which the
highest good is to be realized is not an *empirical* world, the concept of
the highest good becomes nonsensical. In order for happiness to exist in
that world, it has to be empirical, a world in which we have desires and
those desires are satisfied.

Now, clearly, an empirical world in which the highest good could
be realized differs, in crucial respects, from the empirical world as it
appears to us. It differs, in particular, in that the empirical world as it
appears to us takes no account of the character of the persons within it,
while the world in which the highest good is possible must make morality a condition for the achievement of happiness. But, as empirical, it is
not really a *different* world, or even a different *sort* of world. It is the
empirical world, the world we know, but shaped by divine action. The
sense, then, in which the world we seek is different from the one we
inhabit does not undermine our ability to work toward that world.
Whenever I create something there is a sense in which I have changed
the world. After I build a house, I live in the world in which that house
exists. Yet it is the *empirical* world that is affected by my action, and
there is no sense in which that which I seek is found beyond the world
where my actions have effect. God does not bring about the highest
good in any world other than the empirical. That world is not the world
as I experience it currently, but it is the empirical world as I may hope
to experience it.

What about passages where Kant seems to indicate that the highest
good is only realized in another world? I see no reason to believe those
passages inconsistent with the view just sketched. For example, Reath

points to passages from the *Critique of Practical Reason* to support the contention that the highest good (on a theological conception) is realized in another world. Kant writes,

> the possibility of such a connection of the conditioned with its condition belongs wholly to the supersensible relation of things and cannot be given according to the laws of the sensible world, although the practical results of this idea—namely actions that aim at realizing the highest good—belong to the sensible world... (5:119)

What this asserts is not that the highest good only comes into existence in another world, different from the world in which we act. All it asserts is that the basis for the connection constitutive of the highest good cannot be demonstrated in terms of the laws of the sensible world as they are. In other words, we cannot show such a connection empirically. We need recourse to God's existence, not an object of sense, to provide a basis for such a connection. The basis for the connection to be realized in the highest good is located in the supersensible; that does not mean the highest good is to be realized in anything other than the empirical world.

Reath also points to an earlier passage where Kant writes,

> When we find ourselves compelled to go so far, namely to the connection with an intelligible world, to seek the possibility of the highest good which reason points out to all rational beings as the goal of their moral wishes, it must seem strange that philosophers both of ancient and modern times could nevertheless have found happiness in precise proportion to virtue already in *this life* (in the sensible world), or persuaded themselves that they were conscious of it. (5:115)

What Kant is objecting to here is the belief that virtue is already linked to happiness in the world as we experience it. In other words, Kant is arguing against those who do not recognize the practical antinomy as a real problem, who argue that virtue itself *is* happiness. In objecting to such accounts, Kant is merely suggesting that the world as we experience it does not contain the basis for belief that moral worth is always accompanied by happiness. This does not mean that God cannot or does not bring about this connection in the world of experience. It only means the connection is not present in the empirical world as we experience it presently.

Thus, I think there is no reason to believe that the highest good, even on a theological conception, is brought about in another world, a non-empirical world divorced from human action. It seems that we can seek the general happiness via moral action, insofar as the highest good is possible, even though the highest good requires divine action to be realized. Divine action can change the empirical world, even as human action changes it.

Conclusion

Schneewind argues that while Kant does not, himself, give up on the idea of a religious foundation for ethics, he points the way to such an escape by increasingly focusing on the moral world as a historical task realizable by human action alone. Defending such an account requires showing that historical progress can serve as an adequate solution to the problem Kant saw as necessitating divine action. Here, I have attempted to give an account of that problem, drawing first on contemporary commentators who agree that *something* is wrong. The problem is that, given the independence of the natural and moral orders, it is always possible for the two to pull apart and undermine the moral intelligibility of action. The moral law is valid, yet in its application to the world of experience, in our efforts to live according to its dictates, there must always be ends available that are consistent with what the moral law requires. If a set of circumstances is such that no end consistent with morality can be found, then we have reason to doubt that the requirements of the moral law can be lived out in the world as we confront it.

While historical progress, and individual virtue, contribute to a solution to this problem, they cannot solve it. A link between what is possible according to natural law and what morality requires simply cannot be secured by human action alone. Ultimately, divine action is required to change the way the empirical world operates so that it accounts for what morality requires. Thus, the insights offered by accounts that focus on political and moral developments within our grasp are important, but not adequate to secure the general intelligibility of moral action. It is thus essential, for Kant, that the world remains a divine corporation.[10]

---

10 I owe thanks to Karl Ameriks, Andrew Chignell, Patrick Frierson, John Hare, Patrick Kain, Houston Smit, Angela Smith, Christopher Toner and Rachel Zuckert for helpful comments and discussion. Thanks also to audiences at the Society of Christian Philosophers Eastern Meeting (Houghton College, May 2006) and the inaugural meeting of the Midwest Ethics Society (Columbia College, April 2007). Special thanks are owed to Benjamin Lipscomb, for tireless work and thoughtful comments at every stage of my work on this project.

Section IV

Epistemology and the Supersensible

CHAPTER 7

Real Repugnance and Belief about Things-in-Themselves:A Problem and Kant's Three Solutions[1]

Andrew Chignell

Identifying the Problem

Kant famously claims that it can be rational to accept propositions on the basis of non-epistemic or broadly practical considerations, under certain circumstances, even if those propositions include "transcendental ideas" of supersensible objects. But he also worries about how such "ideas" (of freedom, the soul, noumenal grounds, God, the kingdom of ends, things-in-themselves generally) acquire positive content in the absence of an appropriate connection to intuitional experience. How can we be sure that the ideas are not empty "thought-entities [*Gedankendinge*]"—that is, speculative fancies that do not and perhaps even cannot have referents in reality (A771/B799)?

This is a fair question, and when he is focused on it Kant often issues dire warnings about the casual employment of "empty" ideas, especially in metaphysical speculation:

> Representations that are devoid of all intuition (to which, as concepts, no corresponding intuition can be given) are absolutely empty (without cognition of their object). (8:214)

> How can two people conduct a dispute about a matter the reality of which neither of them can exhibit in an actual or even in a merely possible experience, about the idea of which [they] only brood in order to bring forth from it something *more* than an idea, namely the actuality of the object [*Gegenstand*] itself? (A750/B778)

> To demonstrate the reality of our concepts, intuitions are always required. If they are empirical concepts, then the latter are called *examples*. If they are pure concepts of the understanding, then the latter are called *schemata*. But if

1 A small portion of the material in this paper is drawn from two related pieces recently published by DeGruyter: Chignell 2008 and 2010. I am grateful to the editors of those volumes, and to the Press, for permission to re-publish that material here.

one demands that the objective reality of the concepts of reason, i.e., of the
ideas, be demonstrated, and moreover for the sake of theoretical cognition of
them, then one desires something impossible, since no intuition adequate to
them can be given at all. (5:351)

The concepts of reason are, as we have said, mere ideas, and of course have no
object [*Gegenstand*] in any sort of experience, but also do not on that account
designate objects that are made-up and at the same time thereby assumed to be
possible. They are merely thought problematically... mere thought-entities
[*Gedankendinge*] the possibility of which is not demonstrable, and which cannot therefore be used to ground the explanation of actual appearances through
an hypothesis. (A771/B799)

Note that in the last two passages, Kant says that showing that a concept is not "empty" in the relevant sense involves demonstrating or
exhibiting its "objective reality," and that this in turn involves appealing to an empirical example or a schema. In the last passage he also
explicitly associates these issues about positive conceptual content and
"objective reality" with the problem of demonstrating that the concept
has a really possible object.

It thus appears that there are at least four distinct problems with respect to the transcendental ideas of reason (hereafter simply "ideas"):

(1) The problem of finding *rational grounds* for assents involving
    ideas.
(2) The problem of finding *positive content* for ideas.
(3) The problem of establishing the *objective reality* of ideas.
(4) The problem of proving the *real possibility* of objects of ideas.

I have offered an account of Kant's answer to (1) elsewhere (Chignell
2007a, b). The grounds are non-epistemic or "subjective" in Kant's
special sense: they correspond to various pragmatic, theoretical, or
moral interests, and they are sufficient to license rational "assent"
(*Fürwahrhalten*) for certain subjects under certain conditions.[2]

Problems (2), (3), and (4) appear to be distinct, but Kant often suggests that they can be answered together, or even equated. In some passages, such as the first one above, from "On a Discovery," he appears
to link (3) with (2) by claiming that an idea with no objective reality is
"absolutely empty" (8:214). Elsewhere he assimilates (3) and (4): in the
Critique of Practical Reason, for instance, we're told that reflection on
the conditions of willing the highest good lead us to

presuppose three theoretical concepts (for which, because they are only pure
rational concepts, no corresponding intuition can be found and consequently,

---

2   Note that Kant's "holding-for-true" or "assent" is a somewhat more expansive concept
     than our contemporary concept of "belief." For instance, very weak opinions or hunches
     that we would not consider beliefs would still count as assents for Kant.

by the theoretical path, no objective reality): namely, freedom, immortality, and God. Thus by the practical law that commands the existence of the highest good possible in a world, the *possibility of those objects of pure speculative reason, the objective reality which the latter could not assure them, is postulated.* (5:134, my emphasis)

The main claim here is that practical considerations license us in "presupposing" the ideas of God, freedom, and immortality. And this is said to be equivalent to postulating their *objective reality* as well as the *real possibility* of their objects.

But *are* problems (2), (3), and (4) really equivalent? Consider (2) and (4) first in conjunction with a familiar example from contemporary metaphysics. Zombies are typically defined as beings that are physically qualitatively identical to human beings but lack consciousness. Now suppose that we know something about the content of the predicates involved: that is, something about what a human body is, what consciousness is, and thus what the absence of consciousness is, and so forth. Obviously the concept has some positive content for us, even if no empirical example of it can be identified. But is a zombie really possible? That is a different (and much harder) question, one that persists even after we answer the question of whether the concept has positive content.

It should be clear that conceiving of the central problem here as one about *content* or *sense*, on any normal understanding of those terms, is a dead end. Kant obviously does not take ideas of the supersensible to be *nonsensical*. On the contrary, they are content-rich concepts that we can entertain, analyze, and successfully rid of logical contradictions. True, they are also "empty," but for Kant that is a technical notion: it involves, among other things, being "without an object [*Gegenstand*]" that we could sensibly intuit (A290/B347). Thus in the second *Critique* he characterizes the idea of a "*causa noumenon*" as a "possible, thinkable concept [which is] nevertheless an empty one." In other words, the idea of a noumenal cause has some positive content, but is still "empty" in the technical sense of being "without any intuition which is appropriate to it" (5:55-6; cf. 8:214). Such an "empty" idea has no *Objekt* or *Gegenstand* in empirical reality, then, but it may still be profitably entertained and analyzed, and it may even pick out a supersensible *Ding*.

In some passages (such as the fourth one in the list above (A771/B799)), Kant's real worry about the ideas of reason is more clearly expressed. The real worry (I submit) is that even when they *do* have sufficient determinate content, the positive predicates involved may, for all we know, be "really repugnant" in a way that makes their objects "really impossible." In other words, their content may be such that they can be thought, entertained, analyzed, and shown to be logi-

cally consistent, but still be such that no corresponding object even
could obtain. (Note that some contemporary physicalists say precisely
that about the concept of a zombie: i.e, that it is logically/conceptually
but not metaphysically possible for there to be an entity that coinstanti-
ates the predicates *being physically qualitatively identical to a human
person* and *not having consciousness*). Thus it looks as though, for
Kant, there is no way to know through mere conception and analysis
whether the positive predicates of an idea are "really harmonious"
rather than "really repugnant." The confusion arises when we mistake
Kant's concern about how ideas acquire *this* sort of content—really
harmonious content—for concern about how they acquire *any* positive
content whatsoever.

The best way to keep all of this straight is to add yet another problem to our list:

(2') The problem of finding *really harmonious positive content* for
ideas.

(2') is different from (2) since, as we have seen, "empty" ideas may
have *some* positive content, even if it is not harmonious content. (2') is
equivalent to (3), however: a concept can be shown to have objective
reality, in Kant's sense, just in case we can prove that its content is
really harmonious.[3] And it should be obvious that if an idea has really
harmonious content, then its object will be really possible in the internal or "absolute" sense that is of interest here. After all, its predicates
are logically consistent *and* really harmonious: there is nothing in the
concept or nature of the thing that stands in the way of its being real.[4]
Thus Kant says that establishing the objective reality of an idea a-
mounts to showing "that an object corresponding to it is possible" [*daß*

---

3   Kant uses the term "objective reality" in a very loose fashion: sometimes it means that
    the concept has an actual instance (5:5, 28:1015); sometimes it means merely that an in-
    stance is *logically* possible (5:54). Typically, however, it means that an instance of the
    concept is *really* possible, and that's how I use it here. Adding to the confusion is the
    fact that Kant thinks the *knowledge* of something's real possibility is often inferred from
    knowledge of its actuality (see A231-2/B284). But this epistemological connection does
    not entail a conceptual collapse; real possibility and actuality are distinct modal notions.
4   Of course, the object might *still* fail to be really possible in some extended sense by
    failing to have an external ground in reality, or by being metaphysically incompatible
    with something else that necessarily exists. Leibniz as well as later Leibnizeans (Wolff,
    Baumgarten, and Meier) distinguished between what is "internally," "per se," or "abso-
    lutely" really possible, and what is "externally" or "relatively" really possible *given
    God's necessary existence and essential willing of the best*. The latter, of course, is a
    much narrower domain than the former—indeed, it may include only one maximal set
    of compossible essences. This external or relative kind of real possibility is not so-
    mething that we can "prove" since we are incapable of knowing *a priori* which combi-
    nation of essences is the best. By "real possibility" in what follows I will mean "absolute"
    or "per se" real possibility unless otherwise noted.

[*daß ihm gemäß ein Objekt möglich sei*] (5:396). This means that a solution to (2') and (3) is *ipso facto* a solution to (4), and vice versa. In what follows, then, I propose to focus primarily on (4)—the problem of how to know whether the objects of ideas are really possible. My goal is to discern whether Kant has resources to reply to criticisms (raised in his own day and ours[5]) that he violates the epistemological and/or semantic strictures of his own critique by recommending Belief in (or even discussing!) supersensible objects of transcendental ideas.

Harmonious Content and Real Possibility: a modal condition on knowledge

In *The Only Possible Basis for a Demonstration of God's Existence* (1763)—where Kant first makes extensive use of the logical vs. real modality distinction—something's real possibility is said to be "given" in its very representation. In other words, the early Kant assumed that by carefully analyzing an idea, we are able to see whether it refers to something really possible, or whether some of its constituent predicates are really repugnant. The fact that real possibilities are "given" to thought in this way—in conjunction with a rationalist commitment to explaining such modal facts—led Kant to posit the necessary existence of a most real being (*ens realissimum*) whose predicates ground or explain these facts (2:77-86).[6]

In the critical period, Kant becomes much more concerned about epistemological issues, and no longer presumes that real possibility is "given" to us in reflective analysis. Instead, he seeks to understand *how* we know that a thing is really possible—i.e. how we know that the positive predicates (or "realities") composing its concept are really harmonious and not just logically consistent. With respect to the idea of an *ens realissimum*, for instance, Kant now says that we "must be able to know that the effects of the realities do not cancel one another" before using it in an explanation (28:1015-6).

Such modal-epistemological questions can't be answered by appeal to some external ground; rather, we have to consider the nature and limits of our intellectual faculties. Furthermore, an appeal to our consistent *thought* of a thing won't be enough, since mere thought (in the critical period) tracks logical possibility rather than real possibility (Bxxvi, 5:136, 8:137). Thus, Kant suggests, we have to make a connec-

---

5   See, for example, the appendix to the second edition of Jacobi 1787, as well as Bennett 1974, p. 52, Strawson 1966, pp. 11-12, and Höffe 1992.

6   For a detailed reconstruction of this argument, see Chignell 2009.

tion between the thing and possible experience if we want to be sure that our idea is not a mere thought-entity:

> In a word: it is only possible for our reason to use the conditions of possible experience as conditions of the possibility of things [*Sachen*]; but it is by no means possible for it as it were to create new ones independent of those conditions, for concepts of the latter sort, although free of contradiction, would nevertheless also be without any object [*Gegenstand*]. (A771/B799)

The claim here is that the *only* way we can be justified in taking something to be really possible is by being justified in holding that it is an actual or possible object of *our* experiential cognition. The realm of *knowable* real possibility is thus restricted to what can in principle be sensibly experienced. Kant calls this the realm of "empirical real possibility" and says that it is co-extensive with the realm of knowable actuality (A232/B285, "Metaphysics L$_2$" (25:558)).

Of course, it is not always easy to determine whether this condition is satisfied. Are we in principle able to experience water that is XYZ rather than H$_2$O, or Parfit's post-fission person, or a zombie of the sort mentioned earlier? And in discerning this, must we appeal to minds with our limitations or can we consider minds analogous to ours but with enhanced faculties or other abilities? I leave these issues to the side for now, but it should be clear that by taking cognizability to be the "proof" of real possibility, we do not thereby acquire answers to all of the interesting metaphysical questions. Indeed, for Kant, the fact that something is really possible is not even *explained* by the fact that we can cognize it. When he's being careful, he keeps the epistemology and the metaphysics separate—even in the critical period—and leaves plenty of logical space for objects to *be* really possible, even though we could never *know* that they are.[7] Cognizability is a reliable guide to, but not an analysis of, a subset of the domain of real possibility; there are still "absolute real possibilities" that are, necessarily, beyond our cognitive ken (again, see A232ff/B285ff).[8]

The important point for present purposes is that the critical Kant thinks it is not *epistemically* justified to assent to propositions—even

---

7   Kant makes this point by saying that the problem with our ideas of such objects is not that they *don't* have objective reality (how could we know *that*?), but rather that they are "concepts into whose objective reality there can be no insight" (A473/B501). Note that if this is correct, it works against Henry Allison's claim that the "objective reality" of a concept is equivalent to its "empirical significance" (Allison 1983, p. 61). The "significance" or referent (*Bedeutung*) of an objectively real concept might well be non-empirical.

8   Kant holds that God and the immortal soul are *actual*, as he makes clear in the practical works. Thus he must think that they are really possible in some sense, even though he consistently denies that we can even in principle hope to have theoretical cognition of them.

propositions that fall out of otherwise good arguments—without being able to "demonstrate" or "prove" that the objects of all the concepts they refer to are really possible (5:398, Bxxivn, A602/B630). In other words, even if we have a valid argument with apparently plausible premises, the conclusion does not count as knowledge (*Wissen*) unless we can also be *certain* that there is no real repugnance amongst any of the predicates of the concepts involved. Kant's claim can be captured in the following necessary condition:

> *Modal Condition*: **Necessarily, S knows that *p* only if S is in a position to prove the real possibility of the objects referred to in *p*.**[9]

Positive Applications of the Modal Condition

With respect to what Kant calls "empirically certain" knowledge, the Modal Condition is satisfied by way of the subject being able to appeal to her own perceptual or memorial experiences, or to known causal laws connecting the object with something she has experienced. The very same experiences and causal connections are the objective grounds that allow the relevant assents to satisfy other conditions on knowledge as well. In such cases, we might say, the proof of (empirical) real possibility comes along for free by way of the trivial inference from actuality to possibility (cf. 28:557). Likewise for "intuitively certain" synthetic a priori knowledge in mathematics: the mathematician is able to ground her assent by constructing an example of the relevant object in pure intuition, and so the Modal Condition is easily satisfied if and when the other justification conditions are satisfied.

The case of synthetic a priori philosophical knowledge is somewhat more complex. The only assents that are epistemically justified in this context, for Kant, are based on "transcendental" arguments—i.e., inferences from some known fact to the "only possible basis" of that fact (call these "inference-to-only-possible-explanation" (IOPE) arguments for short).[10] Here is a crude simplification of the argument of the Second Analogy:

---

9   The "in a position to prove" operator here makes the Modal Condition weak enough to be at least somewhat plausible. Kant himself typically speaks of being "able to prove real possibility."

10   With respect to the pure concepts of the understanding, Kant says that "their objective reality is founded solely on the fact that because they constitute the intellectual form of all experience, it must always be possible to show their application in experience" (A310/B367). This is of course what Kant spends much of the Transcendental Deduction trying to establish. Conversely, in the third *Critique* he says that the idea of a teleological causality in nature "can of course be thought without contradiction, but it is not

(1) Necessarily, we have cognitive experience only if every phenomenal event has a phenomenal cause.

(2) We have cognitive experience.

Thus,

(3) Necessarily, every phenomenal event has a phenomenal cause.

(1) says that the truth of the causal principle in (3) is part of the only possible explanation of a fact we take for granted—namely, (2). But given the Modal Condition, knowing that (1) requires that we be in a position to prove the real possibility of all the objects referred to, and thus to prove that

(0) A phenomenal cause is really possible.

Because "cause" is an a priori category, the truth of (0) can only be proved by appeal to the sort of pure example that Kant calls a "schema," as noted in a passage cited earlier (5:351; cf. 5:69). Thus the availability of schemata allows the synthetic principles generated from the categories to meet the Modal Condition and to count as a priori knowledge. Conversely, the unavailability of schemata for "ideas" prevents them from figuring into items of knowledge.

So in transcendental IOPE arguments like (0)-(3), the real possibility of the object referred to in the conclusion again comes along for free, as part of the basis for the conclusion itself. Without at least implicitly containing a premise like (0), however, the argument would be valid but epistemically impotent—thanks to the Modal Condition—and thus result at most in rational Belief (Glaube).

Probabilistic empirical knowledge works somewhat differently (note that Kant thinks of direct perceptual knowledge as "empirically certain" and not probabilistic (8:70)). Consider the following inference-to-best-explanation (IBE) argument, where p is the proposition that the universe contains phlogiston.

(1) We have observed phenomena X.

(2) The best explanation of X, given our current knowledge of causal laws and our best empirical theories, is that p.

Thus,

(3) Probably, p.

This is again a crude simplification of a complex inference. The important point for present purposes is that the IBE referred to in (2) is not

good for any dogmatic [i.e. epistemic] designations, because since it cannot be drawn from experience and is not *required* for the possibility of experience its objective reality cannot be required by anything" (5:397). So there is no theoretical IOPE argument for its objective reality (and thus for the real possibility of natural teleology).

sufficient to license empirical certainty that p, and so even if p is true, our knowledge of it is probabilistic, as stated in (3). This means that our grounds for holding that p do not all by themselves provide full-blown "proof" of the real possibility of phlogiston in the way that, say, an observation or deductive proof of the existence of phlogiston would. Proof of real possibility does not come along for free in the case of IBE. But can't we still know propositions such as p on the basis of such arguments?

John Locke's rather stern answer to the question would be "no," if we are talking about the high-level knowledge (*scientia*) he valorizes in the Essay. Our assent to p will at best be able to count as "right judgment," or "Belief," or "hypothesis," for Locke, precisely because we cannot prove through mere thought and IBE-style reasoning that the quality-combinations referred to in our complex idea of phlogiston are really possible (Locke 1700, IV.xiv).[11]

Kant seems to depart from Locke in allowing propositions like (3) to count as knowledge. But his argument on this score constitutes, I submit, a serious weakness in his overall account. When discussing this kind of empirical assent that is not "certain" because it is not based on direct observation or demonstrative inference, Kant suddenly appeals to a broader conception of real possibility—one that he calls "formal possibility" in one place (A127), though I will call it "formal real possibility" in order to distinguish it from merely "formal" or logical possibility.[12] If we know that the objects referred to in p would be appearances—i.e. located in the spatio-temporal-causal nexus that is governed by the "forms" of intuition and the general principles of pure understanding—then, says Kant, we know that p is consistent with the formal conditions of our experience. Moreover, that alone is sufficient to allow assent like (3) to satisfy the Modal Condition and count, if true and otherwise justified, as knowledge. In general, then, for Kant the conclusions of IBEs and other probabilistic inferences do satisfy the Modal Condition, as long as they refer exclusively to appearances that we can prove to be formally really possible.

This seems like a weakness in the account because is not clear why conceiving of something as part of the spatio-temporal-causal nexus proves that it is not afflicted by subject-canceling real repugnance. Consider in this connection some familiar examples from contemporary metaphysics: a donkey that is an orange, Queen Elizabeth I with a father who isn't Henry VIII, water that is XYZ rather than H_2O, a zombie, and so forth. Insofar as we successfully conceive of these things at

---

11   See Chignell 2010 for further discussion of the origin of this problem in Locke.
12   For discussion of the various types of possibility in Kant, see Chignell/Stang 2010.

all, we conceive of them as being in space and time and governed by the general principles of pure understanding (cause-effect, substance-property, reciprocity, etc.). So they count as "formally really possible" on Kant's view, and thus do satisfy the Modal Condition. But surely there is still a serious question about whether such things are really possible! Without some independent account of why anything that is governed by the axioms and the principles cannot suffer from subject-canceling real repugnance, then, Kant's appeal to formal real possibility as a way of satisfying the Modal Condition seems decidedly ad hoc. Satisfying those conditions does not—at least not obviously—remove the worries that motivated the Modal Condition in the first place.

By contrast, the much stricter notion of "empirical real possibility"—i.e., conformity to spatio-temporal axioms, the principles of pure understanding, and the empirical laws and facts—is such that by satisfying its conditions a thing is guaranteed to be exempt from real repugnance. That's because, as we have seen, something that is empirically really possible is in principle perceptible in this world and thus actual. If we can know that all the objects referred to in p are empirically really possible then we have obviously and richly satisfied the Modal Condition.[13]

Given all of this, it seems that Locke has the more consistent, albeit more restrictive, position on this issue. If we agree that knowledge requires proof of real possibility, and if subject-canceling real repugnance is not ipso facto ruled out by spatio-temporal-categorial conformity (and it is hard to see why it should be), then scientific theories that postulate quality combinations that aren't proved to be empirically really possible can at most deliver "right judgment" or "rational hypothesis," just as Locke says. Of course, this result may lead those with lower epistemological standards than either Kant or Locke to think that there is something wrong with the Modal Condition in general.

---

13   Kant occasionally seeks out yet another middle position by appeal to analogy. If we know that certain predicate combinations are really possible, and we can draw analogies between those combinations and the ones we're theorizing about, then perhaps we can count as responding, in some extended and analogical fashion, to the concerns underlying the Modal Condition. Kant is clearly committed to something like this with respect to Belief (cf. the discussion of the Third Solution below), but he also occasionally suggests it in discussions of natural-scientific knowledge. See for example "On the Use of Teleological Principles in Philosophy" (1788), where Kant says that we can seek "the connection between certain present properties of the things of nature and their causes in an earlier time," and then go ahead and postulate those causes but "only so far as permitted by analogy" with what we observe (8:160-2). This passage is highlighted in Kain 2009, 72ff. Perhaps this occasional reference to analogy in scientific contexts can make the explicit appeals to analogy in the context of Belief seem less out-of-the-blue.

Negative Applications of the Modal Condition

When he turns to cases of the supersensible—the realm beyond all possible empirical awareness—Kant joins Locke in holding that the Modal Condition prevents otherwise reasonable assents from counting as knowledge. Consider by way of (admittedly anachronistic) illustration the following argument against physicalism:

> (1) If physicalism is true, then it is necessary that physical properties of such-and-such a configuration are accompanied by consciousness.

> (2) It is really possible that there is a zombie, i.e. a being with physical properties of such-and-such a configuration but without consciousness.

Thus,

> (3) Physicalism is not true.

The argument is valid and (1) is merely a statement of the physicalist's position in the form of a conditional (where "such-and-such" is a placeholder for some complicated physical description). (2) explicitly *asserts* the real possibility of zombies. So even though this argument appeals to a strange metaphysical entity, the relevant qualities of which (let's grant) are not even in principle perceptible, the satisfaction of the Modal Condition will come along for free *if* the premises are known.

The problem, of course, is that it not clear where we would find independent proof of (2), given that mere thinking tracks the contours of logical rather than real possibility.[14] In the absence of such, however, the argument will not be sound, and there will be no armchair way (here at least) of proving the falsehood of physicalism. Reflection on this case shows that and why Kant would not be a friend of the "conceivability" arguments popular in contemporary metaphysics.

There is another kind of argument involving the supersensible that requires examination, one that does not explicitly premise a claim about real possibility:

> (1) If we are causally responsible for our actions, then our will is incompatibilistically free.

> (2) We are causally responsible for our actions.

> Thus,

---

14 This is obviously true if by "real possibility" in (2) we mean *absolute* real possibility. But it is also true if we mean Kant's "formal real possibility." For as we have seen, the latter requires coherence with the formal conditions of experience—viz., the forms of intuition and the categories. But if, as the physicalist suggests, mental states are identical to or strongly supervene on brain states, then there will be no world (even one in which the causal laws and initial conditions differ) in which there is a zombie. According to physicalism, a zombie is not really possible in any sense.

(3) Our will is incompatibilistically free.

Grant for the sake of argument that we theoretically know (2) some-how. [15] Can we appeal to (1) to ground knowledge of (3)? Kant's an-swer is "no," and his reason is that (1) and (3) contain the idea of super-sensible freedom. And though there is *some* positive content in the (let's suppose) logically consistent concept of a free will, we still lack theoretical proof that

(0) An incompatibilistically free will is really possible.[16]

Thus (1) is not a candidate for theoretical knowledge, and neither is (3).

This is also Kant's problem with his speculative theistic proof from 1763. In the critical period he still thinks that the argument is formally valid, but holds that there is no way to ground the assumption that an *ens realissimum* is really possible. Thus the Modal Condition is no more satisfied with respect to the idea of God than it is with respect to the idea of freedom of the idea of a zombie: again, such ideas are of "mere thought-things [*Gedankendinge*], the possibility of which is not demonstrable, and which thus cannot be used to ground the explanation of actual appearances" (A771/B799). It is when dealing with ideas of deities, free wills, souls, afterlives, zombies, worlds, and so forth, that the problem of real repugnance becomes a real problem.

What, if anything, can we make of the Modal Condition from a contemporary point of view? Although I can't defend this at length here, the claim that the objects referred to in our positive propositional attitudes need to be demonstrably really possible has something by way of appeal. It smacks of bald stipulation or wish-fulfillment to postulate something on the basis of a probabilistic causal argument or inference-to-best-explanation when we're not independently sure that such a be-ing is really possible. Indeed, our *prior* sense of what is really possible is often what marks out the domain of explanations that we take to be candidates for the "best."

Needless to say, there are competing accounts of what this prior sense of what is really possible amounts to, and some of them do not

---

15 In early lectures, and even in the A-edition of the *Critique of Pure Reason* and the *Groundwork* (cf. 4:451-3), there are passages where Kant suggests that there *is* a theore-tical proof of transcendental freedom. In the B-edition as well as the second *Critique*, however, Kant clearly holds that the only valid argument for transcendental freedom is practical. Such an argument produces "practical knowledge" at best. (For discussion of the development of Kant's views here, see Ameriks 2003, chapters 6-9 and Allison 2006).

16 In the second *Critique*, Kant explicitly says that we can't have theoretical insight into "how freedom is even possible" (5:133). Karl Ameriks cautions, however (in conversa-tion) that "insight" into "how" something is possible might be a more complex and dif-ficult-to-achieve state than mere knowledge *that* something is really possible.

require appeal to intuition or experience. Perhaps the most familiar account says that we know a thing is really possible if we can positively *conceive* of it; there is lively debate over what it means positively to conceive of something.[17] Kant's account, on the other hand, seeks to divide and conquer: he develops a very stringent policy regarding theoretical *knowledge* (*Wissen*) and a much less stringent policy regarding what he calls "Belief" (*Glaube*).[18] With respect to the former, mere conceiving, imagining, or thinking is not enough; there has to be some appropriate and demonstrable connection to intuition. With respect to the latter, the story is more complicated. The Modal Condition doesn't apply to Belief: we don't have to be able to *prove* the real possibility of the objects involved. But Kant is not willing to relinquish the demand represented in the Modal Condition altogether, even with respect to assents based on practical or other non-epistemic grounds. In other words, Kant seems convinced that *some* response to the problem of real repugnance is needed if Belief (practical or theoretical) is to be legitimate from a rational point of view. Again, the motivation for this is presumably the conviction—expressed in the passages quoted earlier—that it isn't rational to assent to propositions about objects which may, for all we can tell, be really impossible.

Kant offers three solutions to this problem of real repugnance vis-à-vis Belief—solutions that are different but not incompatible. We will examine each of these in the sections that follow, but here is a brief overview. The First Solution (prominent in the first *Critique* as well as in "What Does it Mean to Orient Oneself in Thinking?" (1786)) appeals to the non-sensible "matter," "content," or "data" provided by the very same needs and interests of reason that justify the Belief itself. Presumably what this means is that if we have subjective grounds for holding that an object is actual, then we also have subjective grounds (the same ones!) for holding that it is really possible. Here, as in the case of *a priori* and empirically certain knowledge, the proof of real possibility comes along for free when the other justification conditions are satisfied.

The Second Solution (prominent in the second *Critique* and other ethical writings) appeals to a non-sensible "practical cognition" that provides the basis for justified Belief or even "practical knowledge" about specific things-in-themselves. The latter state is different from

---

17   See the introduction to Gendler and Hawthorne 2002, as well as Chalmers 2002 in the same volume.

18   Though it may be that the policy regarding "practical knowledge" falls somewhere between these two. See Patrick Kain's contribution to the present volume for more on this elusive but intriguing notion in Kant.

theoretical knowledge in important ways, as we will see. But like the First, the Second Solution appeals to the principle that actuality entails possibility: if we practically know that the thing is actual, then we also practically know that it is really possible. The solution to the problem of real repugnance comes along for free, though in a practical rather than a theoretical mode.

The Third Solution (prominent in the late 1780s, the "Real Progress" essay, the *Critique of the Power of Judgment*, and beyond) seeks to forge a much stronger connection between sensibility and ideas by invoking the notion of "symbolism" or "schematism by analogy." Even if we can't exhibit or schematize an idea, Kant thinks we may be able to *symbolize it* in order to gain a fragmentary grasp on what it would be like for it to have an actual object. The process of symbolization thus gives us some sensible indication—a "trace or sign," as Kant says in one place (5:300)—that the content of the idea is really harmonious rather than really repugnant, and goes at least some way toward attaching genuine intuitional content to the marks included in the ideas.

First Solution: rational needs

Kant's First Solution to the problem of real repugnance for Belief involves an appeal to the legitimate (though in a technical sense "subjective") needs, interests, and propensities that make a particular Belief rationally acceptable for certain subjects in certain situations. These needs, issuing from the very "womb of reason" itself, justify the assumption that the objects referred to in the Beliefs they ground are actual. And if those objects are actual, of course, then they are really possible.

At times, Kant conceives of the appeal to these rational needs as a kind of transcendental argument. Just as the official Deduction establishes the objective validity of the principles of pure understanding, an appeal to the needs of reason establishes the objective validity of articles of rational Belief. In the Appendix to the Transcendental Dialectic we're told that

> the ideas of reason, of course, do not permit of any deduction of the same kind as the categories; but if they are to have the least objective validity, even if it is only an indeterminate one, and are not to represent merely empty thought-entities (*enti rationis ratiocinantis*), then *a deduction of them must definitely be possible*, granted that it must also diverge quite far from the deduction one can carry out in the case of the categories. (A669-70/B697-8, my emphasis)

This striking passage, coming on the heels of the sustained assault on speculative metaphysics in the Dialectic, explicitly says that there *is* a sort of deduction that can be carried out for the ideas of reason, although the objective validity of the resulting postulates will remain "indeterminate."[19] The argument that Kant goes on to provide deals primarily with a theoretical kind of Belief about entities like the *ens realissimum* or the ultimate ground of reality. The argument is also confusing because Kant sometimes seems to conflate the demand for the "validity" (i.e. sufficiency or justification) of assents with the demand for "reality" (i.e. really harmonious content) in their constituent concepts (cf. Bxxvin). But it is reasonably clear that when Kant talks about "indeterminate objective validity" in passages like the one just quoted, he is referring to the status of having what he elsewhere calls "subjective sufficiency"—a broadly practical or subjective kind of justification for an assent (A820ff/B848ff).

Note, however, that in the case of the categories, Kant thinks the Deduction has to be supplemented by the Schematism in order for the Modal Condition to be satisfied. In other words, we have to show not just that the relevant principles have good grounds, but that the temporally structured versions of their constituent concepts have objective reality (see the "Schematism" chapter in the first *Critique* as well as the third *Critique*, 5:351). As far as the First Solution is concerned, Kant doesn't seem to offer any counterpart to schematization with respect to Belief involving rational ideas. If he says anything at all, it is that the problem of real repugnance is *also* solved by appeal to reason's various needs and desires (perhaps this helps explain the conflation mentioned in the last paragraph). Such an appeal assures the metaphysician that she is not dealing with "merely empty thought-entities" because the same subjective grounds that render Belief subjectively valid or sufficient also show that the ideas involved "have their reality and are by no means merely figments of the brain" (A314/B371). Kant puts his position this way in the context of a discussion of moral Belief:

> (T)here is a ground of assent that is, in comparison with speculative reason, merely *subjective* but that is yet *objectively* valid for a reason equally pure but practical ... objective reality is given to the ideas of God and immortality and a warrant [*Befugnis*], indeed a subjective necessity (a need of pure reason) is provided to accept [*anzunehmen*] them, although reason is not thereby ex-

---

19 Likewise at the beginning of the Dialectic Kant says that "No *objective deduction* of these transcendental ideas is really possible, such as we could provide for the categories. For just because they are ideas, they have in fact no relation to any object [*Objekt*] that could be given congruent to them. But we can undertake a subjective derivation [*Ableitung*] of them from the nature of our reason, and this is to be accomplished in the present section" (A336/B393). Erdmann's text reads "*Ableitung*" here, though other editions insert "*Anleitung*" ("introduction"). In light of the quotation just provided in the body of the text, however, it seems that "*Ableitung*" is more adequate to Kant's intentions.

tended in theoretical cognition and, instead, all that is given is that their [real] possibility, which was hitherto only a *problem*, here becomes an *assertion* and so the practical use of reason is connected with the elements of the theoretical. (5:4-5)

Genuine moral activity requires Belief in freedom, God, and immortality, and thus our practical commitments allow us rationally to accept and assert that these objects are actual and really possible. There is no separate argument that would seek to meet an analogue of the Modal Condition.

If this reading is correct, then the First Solution is effectively an attempt to make Belief function like *a priori* knowledge and non-probabilistic empirical knowledge with respect to the problem of real repugnance. In the case of those kinds of knowledge, as we have seen, the grounds that justify assent to the actuality of the objects also simultaneously establish the real possibility of those objects. The First Solution likewise says that if a need of reason provides S with subjectively sufficient grounds for Belief in an object O, then it also grounds Belief in O's real possibility. Elsewhere Kant varies his terminology and says that an appeal to rational needs and interests establishes the "*subjective reality*" of the ideas (A339/B397) and the "practical possibility" of their objects (5:115).[20] But the overall picture is the same.

An objector might worry that this is ill-gotten gain. Even if we agree that a rational need pushes us to adopt a Belief that refers to some object O, how does this tell us *anything* about whether O is really possible? How does appeal to a need (of reason or anything else) tell us something about what can or cannot find a footing in reality? Again, there are no sensible intuitions involved here, no appeal to the forms of intuition, and no constructions, images, or schemata. There is thus a

---

20 Kant also uses "objective practical reality" to refer to this property or status, especially in the second *Critique* (e.g. 5:48-9). But that term, too, has advantages and disadvantages. On the one hand, "objective practical reality" makes the fact that it is a kind of harmonious content or "objective reality" explicit. On the other hand, it makes it sound as though the considerations that ground our confidence in the object's real possibility must always be strictly "practical." And while it's certainly true that Kant relegates the considerations that support *Belief* to the realm of the "practical," this is potentially misleading because it can sound as though he's speaking of strictly *pragmatic* or *moral* considerations. There are *broadly* "practical" considerations which are neither pragmatic nor moral under the usual definitions, and which can ground a kind of *theoretical Belief* in particular (see Chignell 2007a). "Subjective reality" nicely establishes a parallel to the "subjective sufficiency" discussed in the Canon of Pure Reason, and also makes clear that our confidence in a transcendent object's real possibility has an important subjective aspect that our confidence in the "objective reality" of an object of our experience does not. Alas, Kant doesn't stick to this terminology, and so I continue to use "objective reality."

serious disanalogy between the deduction of the categories and the deduction of the ideas, a disanalogy that Kant ignores in these texts.

One strategy here is to emphasize the parallels between the transcendental arguments that justify the pure categories of the understanding and the "deduction" of ideas by appeal to rational needs. In both cases, it is a *rational* need for something like explanation, rather than some irrational need, that underwrites the principles involved. I'm not sure there is much more to do by way of defending Kant, except to emphasize again that we are talking about mere Belief rather than theoretical knowledge. Meeting a legitimate need of reason in the right way (via a metaphysical argument that provides "completeness," say, or a moral argument that heads off a kind of absurdity in our moral vocation) makes a firm Belief (theoretical or moral) fully legitimate from a rational point of view. And if a Belief that *p* entails Belief that O exists, then it trivially entails Belief that O is really possible. Such Beliefs—especially the theoretical ones—will in many cases be tentative and defeasible: if someone can show that the object of the Belief is really *im*possible, or logically impossible, or that the grounds on which the Belief is based are faulty, or that there are stronger grounds for a logically incompatible proposition, then we will have to re-evaluate our assent. But in the absence of such defeaters, the Belief that *p* will be consistent with what we know by way of theoretical reason, and our rational needs will make O a legitimate part of our picture of the world.[21]

It is worth reemphasizing that a consequence of Kant's First Solution is that metaphysical arguments that start from the bald postulation of the real possibility of something (such as the zombie argument against physicalism above) are unacceptable. For according to the First Solution, the real possibility of an object of speculative metaphysics is something that we accept only because we have independent grounds to Believe that the object is *actual*. Thus we accept the real possibility of free wills or God because we already have an argument (albeit on "subjective" grounds) for their actuality. An argument that simply *starts* with the real possibility of a bodiless soul or a soulless body will lack

---

21 "It is clear that, even if from the [speculative] perspective [reason's] capacity does not extend to establishing certain propositions [about supersensibles] affirmatively, although they do not contradict it, *as soon as these propositions belong inseparably to the practical interest* of pure reason it must accept them—indeed as something offered to it from another source, which has not grown on its land but yet is sufficiently authenticated—and try to compare and connect them with everything that it has within its power as speculative reason, being mindful, however, that these are not its insights but are yet extensions of its use from another, namely a practical perspective; and this is not in the least opposed to its interest, which consists in the restriction of speculative mischief" (5:121).

grounds for its initial premise: there is no rational need that pushes directly for this modal assumption, and the critical Kant doesn't think we have a faculty that "clearly and distinctly perceives" (or, to use Chalmers' language, "ideally positively conceives") real possibility in a reliable way (see Chalmers 2002). Kant's own argument for the soul, of course, goes from the rational need to avoid practical absurdity to Belief in an afterlife, and from there to a Belief in the "future life" of the soul (which may or may not be immaterial). So although Kant has no problem with *some* traditional metaphysical propositions construed as objects of Belief, he would reject speculative arguments that simply *start* with the putative real possibility of some supersensible entity (an immaterial soul, a zombie, a being than which none greater can be conceived, and so forth).

Early in the critical period, Kant often makes recourse to the First Solution to the problem of real repugnance regarding Belief. But he also gestures in the direction of a Second Solution, one that becomes more prominent later in the 1780s. Perhaps Kant began to feel that the First Solution was somehow unsatisfactory: as we have seen, even though he talks about "transcendentally deducing" the ideas, what he is really doing is showing that various subjective aspects of our rational vocations as speculating, inquiring, and acting creatures lead us to generate those ideas and, perhaps, to accept that their objects exist. In the absence of a Modal Condition on Belief, the postulates can seem like mere projections of our rational needs onto the screen of our worldview, projections whose real possibility is dubious. Switching metaphors, the seeds that would be cultivated later by James (in a positive light) and Feuerbach (in a negative one) are already sown in this theory, and Kant may have sensed that something stronger and more closely connected to cognition or sensibility would be preferable.[22]

Second Solution: practical data

The Second Solution is largely focused on one idea—the idea of freedom—though Kant sometimes applies it to other postulates of practical

---

22 We needn't wait for the 19th century to see the Feuerbachian sort of objection arise. Kant himself refers to criticisms put forward by Wizenmann in a 1787 article in the *Deutsches Museum*: "he disputes the authorization to conclude from a need to the objective reality of its object and illustrates the point by the example of a *man in love*, who, having fooled himself into an idea of beauty that is merely a chimera of his own brain, would like to conclude that such an object really exists somewhere." Kant responds by distinguishing between assent based on mere inclination, and assent based on needs of *reason* (5:144n). Cf. Wizenmann 1787.

reason as well. After turning away from Leibnizean compatibilism in the late 1760s, Kant appears to have thought for a time that there is a *theoretical proof* of the reality of the incompatibilist freedom of the will (see, e.g., Metaphysik L_1, 28:269).[23] But by the mid-1780s, he had relegated assents about transcendental freedom to the status of things we can only hold on subjective grounds. Still, Kant seems to say that our assent about freedom is somehow stronger or more secure than the assents about God and the afterlife that are based on rational needs and count as practical and theoretical Belief. So we find him—seldom in the A edition but often in the B edition—speaking of "practical cognition" (*praktische Erkenntnis*) of the supersensible. Here is a suggestive passage from the B Preface:

> Now after speculative reason has been denied all advance in this field of the supersensible, what still remains for us is to attempt to see whether data is to be found in its practical cognition [*in ihrer praktischen Erkenntniß Data finden*], for determining that transcendent rational concept of the unconditioned, in such a way as to reach beyond the boundaries of all possible experience, in accordance with the wishes of metaphysics, cognitions *a priori* that are possible, but only from a practical point of view [*Absicht*]. (Bxxi)

Practical cognition "determines" the idea of freedom somehow, and this allows us to go beyond Belief, though still only from a practical point of view.

In the second *Critique*, we're told more about the nature of practical cognition. It turns out that it is not *bona fide* cognition at all, if by the latter we mean the bringing of pure or sensible *intuitions* under concepts. Rather, it appears to be the result of an *inferential* conclusion from what Kant calls the "fact of reason"—i.e., our fundamental awareness of the moral law and our subjection to it as rational beings. If we are subject to the moral law, the inference goes, then we must be able to follow it (and to disobey it), and thus we must be incompatibilistically free. Ought implies can here in a substantive metaphysical way (cf. 5:89-106). Indeed, in some places Kant refers to the conclusion of this argument as full-blown "practical knowledge [*Wissen*]" (5:4, for instance).

Setting this argument aside, note that in the logic lectures we're told that "practical cognition" has at least three different uses (9:86ff). First and most strictly, it refers to cognition of what we *ought* to do— knowledge involving hypothetical or categorical imperatives. But it can also refer, second, to cognition of what *exists* just in case that existence has clear implications for what we ought to do. For instance, speculative cognition that there is a God (supposing we could achieve it) would

---

23   See Ameriks 2003, chapters 6 and 9 and Allison 2006.

count as practical cognition insofar as it would lead us to try to discover that being's commands. Clearly this second sort of practical cognition is practical only in its application, however; it could very well be theoretical cognition "in itself," so to speak.

Third, "practical cognition" can refer to an existence-claim *derived* from an ought-claim. Such cognition presupposes a commitment to the principle that ought implies can, and the most significant case of it is the argument for transcendental freedom. Once I *practically cognize* that I ought to follow the moral law, I can infer that I am transcendentally free as another item of practical cognition or knowledge. This is not a mere "as-if" attitude: Kant often calls it "assertoric" rather than "problematic," though he always qualifies it as assertoric "from a practical perspective" or "in a practical respect" (5:105).

Kant's mid-1780s adherence to the Second Solution is confirmed by an important footnote in the B Preface that I've mentioned but not quoted at length. The note is attached to Kant's assertion, in the body of the text, that although we cannot cognize things-in-themselves, we can at least *think* of them. Kant glosses this claim starting with the now-familiar point that "to cognize an object, it is required that I be able to prove its possibility (whether by the testimony of experience from its actuality or *a priori* through reason)" (Bxxvin). Kant is obviously talking about real possibility here; the claim is that, in order to count as theoretically cognizing an object, I must be able to *prove* that it is really possible by forging some sort of connection between it and possible experience. He also explicitly says that this will often take a route "from [the object's] actuality" to its real possibility.

Having made this point with respect to theoretical knowledge, Kant notes that

> I can *think* whatever I like, as long as I do not contradict myself, i.e., as long as my concept is a possible thought, even if I cannot give any assurance as to whether or not there is a corresponding object [*Objekt*] somewhere within the sum total of all possibilities. But in order to ascribe objective validity to such a concept (real possibility, for the first sort of possibility was merely logical) something more is required. This "more," however, need not be sought in theoretical sources of cognition; it may also lie in practical ones. (*Ibid.*)

Discursive "thought" is guided by the principles of general logic and, more specifically, the logical forms of judgment that correlate with the unschematized categories (cf. 5:136). Thus, as already noted, the sort of possibility that "thought" tracks, for the critical Kant, is logical rather than real, and *mere* thought-entities do not have objective reality. This means that in order to guarantee objective reality for ideas and real possibility for their objects, "something more is required."[24] Kant's rather oblique claim about finding that "something more" in the practical "sources of cognition" is, I suggest, a gesture at the practical cognition of freedom that is central to the Second Solution.

Although Kant calls our awareness of the fact of reason "practical *cognition*," there is an important disanalogy between the structure of this cognition and that of its theoretical counterpart. On most interpretations of the fact of reason, the awareness of the moral law that constitutes it is intellectual and not sensible: it doesn't involve inner or outer intuitions from sensibility. This means that despite Kant's metaphorical talk of "data" in the passage cited earlier, our awareness of our status as obligated beings doesn't provide any *intuitional* content determinable by the application of a concept. Any "data" that rational ideas acquire from this sort of cognition will thus be markedly less determinate or "material" when compared to the intuitional content of our empirical concepts. So it is hard to see, in the end, how practical cognition and knowledge of our freedom is anything more than a very distant cousin of the cognition of objects that we get in the theoretical/empirical context.[25]

This difference, I think, is what motivates Kant to develop yet one more response to the problem of real repugnance with respect to ideas—a response that reflects our situation as sensible, intuiting beings, and not just Gradgrindian rational inquirers. It is in the Third Solution to the problem of real repugnance (and especially the part of it that appeals to beauty in art and nature) that we see Kant's concern that intuitional "indications" of the reality of ideas be provided—if not as evidence, exactly, then at least as accommodations to our sensible nature and its central role in guiding assent.

Third Solution: sensible symbols

In writings on the problem of real repugnance at the end of the 1780s, Kant makes a slight but discernible shift toward an approach that is different from, though compatible with, those already discussed. It is

---

24 In this passage, Kant again seems to use "objective validity" to refer to what he usually calls "objective reality." In general, however, *objective validity* is the property that attaches to propositions when they have a truth value and objectively sufficient grounds. *Objective reality* is the property that attaches to concepts when their objects are really possible.

25 Not necessarily an illegitimate cousin, however. Again, see Patrick Kain's essay in this volume for an engaging discussion of how practical cognition might provide substantive (albeit still "practical") knowledge of the objects of ideas.

not that he abandons the first two approaches, exactly: references to both can be found in texts throughout Kant's career. But for whatever reason, toward the end of his career he starts appealing to a special kind of *sensible* experience as a source of positive content for ideas. His technical term for this ersatz mode of supplying content is "symbolization." The claim is that even if we can't prove, demonstrate, or exhibit that a rational idea can have an object in reality, we can still *symbolize* the object in order to gain a fragmentary grasp on what it would be like for it to have an actual instance.[26] Because this mode of "indicating" real possibility involves appeal to some sort of experience, it is structurally closer to Kant's method for proving real possibility in the case of knowledge (empirical and *a priori*). The symbolic analogue of a schema gives us a sense (though not a proof) that the content of an idea is really harmonious rather than really repugnant, and thereby goes at least some way toward legitimating our use of that idea. Symbolization is thus an important part of Kant's philosophy—one that has been largely neglected in the literature.[27]

The Third Solution in *Real Progress*

By the late 1780s, Kant was feeling pressure from critics (e.g. Jacobi, Wizenmann, and Eberhard) who had accused him of violating (in the Appendix to the Dialectic, the Canon, and the practical works of the mid-1780s) his own policies regarding what we can and cannot say or know about things beyond the bounds of possible experience.[28] The First and Second Solutions had failed to quiet these critics—as well, perhaps, as the nagging critic within. The account of symbolization in an essay from that period—namely, *What Real Progress has been Made in Metaphysics since the Time of Leibniz and Wolff?*—is thus meant to show *both* that Kant's philosophy had progressed beyond Leibniz's and Wolff's uncritical adherence to the Principle of Sufficient Reason *and* that it can account, on its own terms, for the legitimacy of talk about ideas and rational Belief in their objects.

The main section to consider is in the middle of the essay, where Kant is discussing what he calls "practical dogmatic assent." This atti-

---

26 Note that this is quite different from the Leibnizian-Wolffian conception of a "symbol" as a more-or-less arbitrary sign. See Leibniz 1989, p. 25.

27 Important exceptions include Kang 1985 and, with respect to the practical philosophy, Bielefeldt 2001.

28 Again, see Jacobi 1787, Wizenmann 1787, and the second *Critique* at 5:144n. Eberhard's critique of Kant can be found in the first volume of *Philosophisches Magazin* (1788-9) and in Allison 1973.

tude appears to be the same as what he elsewhere calls "Belief": it is assent (*Fürwahrhalten*), typically about supersensibles, that is objectively unjustified but yet subjectively "sufficient" (justified) by way of responding to certain needs or interests of reason itself. The title of the section raises the worry at the heart of our discussion here, namely, "How to Confer Objective Reality on the Pure Concepts of Understanding and Reason."

The pure concepts (or categories) of the understanding, Kant says, acquire objective reality via schematization—"objective reality is accorded to the concept directly (*directe*) through the intuition that corresponds to it, i.e. the concept is immediately presented" (20:279, cf. A310/B367). A transcendental idea of the supersensible, on the other hand, "cannot be presented immediately, but only in its consequences [*indirecte*], [and] may be called the symbolization of the concept" (20:280). Symbolization, Kant then explains,

> is an expedient [*Nothülfe*] for concepts of the supersensible which are therefore not truly presented, and can be given in no possible experience, though they still necessarily appertain to a cognition, even if it were possible merely as a practical one. (*Ibid.*)

Note that here Kant seems to link the Second Solution—according to which we can practically cognize freedom through our awareness of the moral law—with the Third Solution, which appeals to the "expedient" of sensible symbolization. The latter is said to be the *only* sort of presentation available for supersensibles, *including* the freedom that we practically cognize by inference from the fact of reason (cf. 5:43ff). So by 1790, Kant is apparently thinking of the Third Solution as a complement to the Second. But the Third Solution also goes further than the Second, since symbolization is available for many ideas whose objects we don't practically cognize at all.[29]

So what *is* symbolization anyway, and how is it accomplished?

> The symbol of an idea (or a concept of reason) is a representation by analogy, i.e., by the same relationship to certain consequences as that which is attributed to the object in respect of its own consequences, even though the objects themselves are of entirely different kinds. (20:280)

---

29   Guyer suggests that Kant introduces the *Nothülfe* because "the rationalism of the *Critique of Practical Reason* was too austere even for Kant himself" and the fact that we are embodied, sensing beings "makes it necessary not just that the constraints but also that the attractions of morality be accessible to our senses as well as our intellect." One of the main "attractions" of morality, according to Guyer, is that it entails us being truly, transcendentally free (Guyer 2005, p. 225). I suggest below that the attempt to appeal to our sensible nature potentially includes all of the ideas—and many different kinds of symbols—rather than just the ideas of freedom and morality.

This is opaque, but Kant provides an example to illustrate what he means:

> I conceive of certain products of Nature, such as organized things, animals or plants, in a relation to their cause like that of a clock to man, as its maker, viz., in a relationship of causality as such … which is the same in both cases, albeit that the subject of this relation remains unknown to me in its inner nature, so that only the one can be presented, and the other not at all… (*Ibid.*)

The claim seems to be that we can get a limited sense of whether a thing is really possible by drawing an analogy between *its* relationship to something we know to be really possible, and the relationship between two *other* things that we already know to be really possible.[30] In doing this, symbolization allows us to import some intuitional or even imagistic content into our idea of a thing. As Kant says in an earlier *Reflexion*: "A *symbolum* is an indirect intuition [*indirecte Anschauung*]. Words are not *symbola*, because they don't provide a picture [*Bild*]" (25:710).

With this in mind, consider Kant's example of God and the clockmaker (and note that he is writing before Paley). We see that the clock is an organized system, and know that it has an intelligent designer. But nature as a whole, too, seems to be an organized system. Thus we can take the two organized systems to be analogous "consequences" of analogous causes and conclude that, just as the watch has a maker, so too it might make sense to think of the world-whole as having an intelligent author (*Welturheber*).

Kant is not implausibly suggesting that this analogy somehow demonstrates that a world-author *in fact* exists, or even that we can univocally ascribe predicates to our concept of such a being.[31] But he does think it gives us an indication of whether the idea has positive harmonious content—i.e., of whether it describes something that could find a footing in reality: "For just as in the world one thing is regarded as the

---

30 Compare this quotation from the third *Critique*: "All *hypotyposis* (presentation, *subjecto sub adspectum*), as making something sensible, is of one of two kinds: either *schematic*, where to a concept grasped by the understanding the corresponding intuition is given *a priori*; or *symbolic*, where to a concept which only reason can think, and to which no sensible intuition can be adequate, an intuition is attributed with which the power of judgment proceeds in a way merely analogous to that which it observes in schematization, i.e., it is merely the rule of this procedure, not of the intuition itself, and thus merely the form of the reflection, not the content which corresponds to the concept" (5:351; cf. 5:464n). This is a bit misleading, insofar as it is not *merely* the formal activity of mind that is similar in both cases; rather, the contents of the states are themselves analogous and thus symbolically related. See Chignell 2006 for an argument along these lines.

31 Kant warns in *Religion within the Boundaries of Mere Reason* against the illegitimate "*metabasis eis allo genos*" (a switch from one genus to another) that results from univocal ascriptions of sensible predicates to a supersensible like God (see 6:65).

cause of another thing when it contains the ground of this thing, so in the same way we regard the whole world as a consequence of its ground *in God*, and argue from the analogy" (28:1023).[32]

Another caveat: clearly such methods are not going to demonstrate or prove the real possibility of a thing in the same way that establishing a connection to experience would. But where proof is not available, Kant suggests that symbolization can provide at least a sense of what it would be for the object of the idea to exist—even as a thing-in-itself— by drawing analogies to objects and relations with which we are acquainted. Schemas and examples give us proof of real possibility; symbolizations give us intimations of such.[33] Limitations notwithstanding, it is crucial that such symbolization of rational ideas take place, since otherwise those who accept various articles of Belief could be accused, on Kant's principles, of trafficking in incoherent concepts of really impossible objects:

> As far as reality is concerned, it is evidently intrinsically forbidden to think it *in concreto* without getting help from experience, because it can only pertain to sensation, as the matter of experience, and does not concern the form of the relation that one can always play with in fictions. (A223/B270)

Rational people will thus have a strong interest in anything that can provide sensible content, however symbolic, to rational ideas.

The Third Solution in the Third *Critique*

The fact that Kant thinks that the symbolization of ideas is useful for handling the problem of real repugnance comes out just as clearly in the major work written around the same time as the *Real Progress* essay— the *Critique of the Power of Judgment* (1790). At the end of the section on aesthetics, Kant suggests that many artworks—and perhaps some aspects of nature—are valuable to us insofar as they symbolize that which cannot be directly presented or exhibited, viz., the transcendent

---

32 For another prominent example of symbolization, see the analogy Kant draws between divine love of creatures and a parent's love of a child in *Prolegomena to any Future Metaphysics* (4:358n).

33 Symbols are also supposed to be available for specifically Kantian ideas such as the idea of the "unity of reason" in which all the concepts and principles of the understanding are somehow systematically combined into a "unity." With respect to this idea, Kant says that "although no schema can be found in *intuition* for the thoroughgoing systematic unity of all concepts of the understanding, an *analogue* of such a schema can and must be given, which is the idea of the *maximum* of division and unification of the understanding's cognition in one principle" (A665/B693). It would be worth deciphering exactly what this analogical relationship is and how it is supposed to work, but I don't propose to attempt that here.

objects of rational ideas. In an unpublished reflection he goes so far as to suggest that we should find beautiful *only* those works and natural vistas that somehow symbolize rational ideas: "The entire use of the beautiful arts is that they set moral propositions of reason in their full glory and powerfully support them" (25:33).

This last claim is in tension with Kant's position early on in the third *Critique* according to which curlicues on wallpaper, crustaceans, birdsongs, and the like can count as beautiful solely on account of their "purposive form." Without trying to resolve the tension here, I think we can at least say that *one* important function that beautiful art plays for Kant is that of exhibiting, in fragmentary fashion, objects which are officially "unexhibitable." Kant also thinks that beauty in *nature* can "indicate" that certain rational ideas have objective reality;[34] in other words, it can "show some trace or give a sign" that their content is not metaphysically incoherent. Moreover, "reason must take an interest in every manifestation in nature of a correspondence similar to this; consequently, the mind cannot reflect on the beauty of *nature* without finding itself at the same time to be interested in it" (5:300). Given that reason "needs" to accept articles of Belief involving ideas, Kant says that it is crucial for us to have experiences that suggest that these ideas are coherent and may have objects. Indeed, taking an interest in beautiful art and nature is the sign of a good soul, since many of the ideas are *moral* ideas, and someone who is looking for their objects is also likely to have a strong predisposition to morality.[35]

"Taste" on this picture, becomes "basically a faculty for judging the sensible rendering [*Versinnlichung*] of … ideas by means of a certain analogy" (5:356). Making an aesthetic judgment, of course, is an *active* process of assent-formation, but it is preceded by a pleasurable representational response to the object as it is beheld, a response which Kant sometimes dubs an "aesthetic idea." It is appropriate to call such aesthetic responses *ideas*, Kant says, because in the process of having them our mind

> strives toward something lying beyond the bounds of experience, and thus seeks to approximate a presentation of concepts of reason (intellectual ideas), which gives them the appearance of an objective reality. (5:314)

---

34 "Indicate" (*anzeigen*) is from *Reflexion* 1820a at 16:127. Kant says there that "Beautiful things indicate that the human being fits into the world"—that is, that the natural world is also what Leibniz calls a "moral world."

35 "[H]e who takes such an interest in the beautiful in nature can do so only insofar as he has already firmly established his interest in the morally good. We thus have cause at least to suspect a predisposition to a good moral disposition in one who is immediately interested in the beauty in nature" (5:300-1).

In other words, our aesthetic response to certain objects involves imaginative "striving" toward the supersensible, presumably because there is something in the objects that we associate with ideas of the latter. The associative chain of representations that "yield" (*geben*) such an aesthetic idea in us will never adequately exhibit a rational idea, of course, since by definition the latter cannot be exhibited (cf. 5:315). But aesthetic ideas are accompanied by a fragmentary, symbolic, intriguing sense—which we can think of as a kind of confirmation or indication— that rational ideas *could* have a real object.

Kant notes that literature, in particular, often contains explicit attempts to exhibit rational ideas:

> The poet ventures to make sensible rational ideas of invisible beings, the kingdom of the blessed, the kingdom of hell, eternity, creation, etc., as well as to make that of which there are examples in experience, e.g., death, envy, and all sorts of vices, as well as love, fame, etc., sensible beyond the limits of experience, with a completeness that goes beyond anything of which there is an example in nature, by means of an imagination that emulates the precedent of reason in attaining to a maximum. (5:314)

Because literature, more than any of the other arts, is often guided by the explicit desire to symbolize ideas such as these, Kant says that "it is really the art of poetry in which the faculty of aesthetic ideas can reveal itself in its full measure" (*Ibid.*).

It is important to reiterate that Kant would *not* say that the fact that a work of art depicts the supersensible in some fragmentary way is what *grounds* positive aesthetic judgments about it. A number of commentators have tried to salvage Kant's Deduction of Taste by developing an interpretation along these lines[36] and, admittedly, Kant himself seems to suggest this in places (again see 25:33). But I think this is an interpretive mistake, since it conflicts with the overarching doctrine that the normativity of judgments of taste cannot stem from *any* intellectual interest that we have in rational ideas (5:204-5).

What Kant offers us, on the contrary, is a subtle theory according to which aspects of art or nature symbolize rational ideas for us and thus occasion the sort of mental episode ("aesthetic idea," "free play of the faculties") that is itself the source of aesthetic pleasure and the proper "subjective" basis for a judgment of taste. So the symbolic content of the object may be important for grounding a judgment of taste, but only indirectly—i.e., it is one aspect of an object or vista that may lead beholders to have the form of characteristically aesthetic experience that

---

36 For example, Crawford 1974 and Savile 1993.

is itself the only legitimate basis for aesthetic judgment.[37] A central task of the Kantian critic would thus be to draw our attention to the way in which an artwork can be "closely or remotely" associated with particular rational ideas (5:326) and to try to decrypt the "cipher by means of which nature figuratively speaks to us in its beautiful forms" (5:301).

Interestingly, Kant plays the critic himself at one point, and offers a specific (albeit politically suspect) example of the way that symbolization in art occurs:

> When the great king [i.e. Friedrich the Great] expresses himself in one of his poems thus:
>
> *Let us depart from life without grumbling and without regretting anything, leaving the world behind us replete with good deeds. Thus does the sun, after it has completed its daily course, still spread a gentle light across the heavens; and the last rays that it sends forth into the sky are its last sighs for the well-being of the world,*[38]
>
> he animates [*belebt*] his idea of reason of a cosmopolitan disposition even at the end of life by means of an attribute that the imagination (in the recollection of everything agreeable in a beautiful summer day, drawn to a close, which bright evening calls to mind) associated with that representation, and which arouses a multitude of sensations and supplementary representations for which no expression is found. (5:315-6)

Whether Kant is seriously recommending Friedrich's poetry here is not the main issue; the point, rather, is that part of the poem's value is said to consist in its ability to "animate" an idea of reason—in this case, the moral idea of a perfect cosmopolitan or stoic disposition.[39] The poem gives some positive content to this idea by drawing an analogy to a late summer's sunset—it says, in effect (and what follows is a flat-footed gloss), "look at the way the sun sets and casts its rays gently and generously across the world as it departs—that is an analogue of the way that the ideal cosmopolitan sage feels and acts when approaching the end of

---

37 For different views on how to work this out, see Allison 2001, chapters 10-12 and Guyer 1998, as well as my own suggestion in Chignell 2007c.
38 Kant is loosely rendering this poem, which Friedrich wrote in French:
    Oui, finissons sans trouble, et mourons sans regrets,
    En laissant l'Univers comblé de nos bienfaits.
    Ainsi l'Astre du jour, au bout de sa carrière,
    Répand sur l'horizon une douce lumière,
    Et les derniers rayons qu'il darde dans les airs
    Sont ses derniers soupirs qu'il donne à l'Univers.
39 Kant does not deny that some people of particularly good character can *partially* exhibit certain moral ideas of virtue. He admits that such an "idea of practical reason can always actually be given *in concreto*, though only partially" (A328/B385) but emphasizes that "no human being will ever act adequately to what the pure idea of virtue contains," which is why it still counts as an idea (A315/B372).

his or her time on earth." For Kant, this poem has aesthetic value because it excites aesthetic response in us *by way of* symbolizing that
moral idea.

Someone might worry that Kant's theory of taste here threatens to
be too narrow—ascribing aesthetic value only to those works or vistas
that we somehow associate with rational ideas. Like Plato in the *Sym-
posium*, it might be suggested, Kant on the present interpretation is so
fixated on transcendental ideas that he sidelines the important this-
worldly aspects of art and nature, aspects which clearly contribute to
their aesthetic value. This worry, however, rests on a misunderstanding.
Although the connection to ideas is, for Kant, *one* of the aspects of an
object that can evoke aesthetic response from us, there are other aspects
that can do so as well. I have already mentioned Kant's extended discussion, earlier in the third *Critique*, of the aesthetic merits of mere
"form"—lines, metric form, shapes, and so forth.

Furthermore, Kant's use of Friedrich's poem highlights the fact that
the domain of rational ideas, for him, is large. It is not that all great art
points narrowly to God or the Good, as some readings of the *Sympo-
sium* suggest; rather, there is a vast array of moral, religious, and metaphysical ideas that can be symbolized in art, and all such symbolizations can serve as the occasion for aesthetic response. Thus (and this
too will be crude and flat-footed from an art-critical point of view)
some of Wagner's music might give symbolic content to the metaphysical idea of an *unconditioned totality*, whereas Holst's *The Planets*
might provide a musical analogue for our cosmological idea of the
world-whole. The characters in *Sense and Sensibility* clearly provide
symbolic content to the moral idea of *decorum*, whereas Iago symbol-
izes *envy* and Ivan Karamazov *intellectual honesty*. Michelangelo's
David could symbolize the ideal of perfect (masculine) human beauty,
and perhaps the Petronas Towers are symbols of the idea of *transcen-
dence* generally.[40] Finally, the literary portrait in the Gospels is said by
Kant to approximate "the ideal of humanity pleasing to God (hence of
such moral perfection as is possible to a being pertaining to this world
and dependent on needs and inclinations)" (6:61; cf. 6:65n). Clearly,

---

40 I take comfort from the fact that Kant's description of how symbolization works in
    nature is almost as flat-footed as my description of how it works in art:
    Thus the white color of the lily seems to dispose the mind to ideas of innocence, and
    the seven colors, in their order from red to violet, to the ideas of (1) sublimity, (2) au-
    dacity, (3) of candor, (4) of friendliness, (5) of modesty, (6) of steadfastness, (7) of
    tenderness. The song of the bird proclaims joyfulness and contentment with its exis-
    tence. At least this is how we interpret nature, whether anything of the sort is its inten-
    tion or not. (5:302)

the possibilities for symbolizing ideas are wide-ranging, and this is not a narrow Platonism about aesthetic value.

Having said that, I should admit that there is an unmistakably Platonic flavor to the theory. Kant is suggesting that one of the main goals of art- and nature-appreciation is to help us catch sight, so to speak, of the transcendent objects of rational ideas. Kant's language is that of both aesthetic appreciation and Platonic *eros* when he asks: "Why has Providence set many objects, although they are intimately connected with our highest interest, so high that it is barely granted to us to encounter them in an indistinct perception, doubted even by ourselves, through which our searching glance is more enticed than satisfied?" (A743-4/B771-2). One answer to the question might be: so that we would make beautiful art, and learn to appreciate beautiful nature. Beauty entices us by giving us symbols—indistinct perceptions, doubted even by ourselves—of transcendental ideas.

Three final remarks about symbolization in the third *Critique*: (i) First, it is crucial to distinguish the instances of symbolization I have just been discussing from another and better known instance in this text. In section 59, Kant claims that the *way* we make aesthetic judgments (i.e. the way the faculties of imagination and understanding freely "harmonize") *itself* provides a symbol or analogue of the way that rational agents make moral judgments (i.e., the way the faculties of reason and will freely "harmonize"). It is in this way that "beauty is a symbol of morality," as the title of section 59 announces, or that "taste is an *analogon* of perfection—it is in intuition what morality is in reason" (25:196). This means that in a genuine aesthetic judgment, there may well be two different symbolization-relations obtaining. First, the *content* of the artwork or the natural object itself may symbolize for the beholder some idea of reason. And, second, the *form* that aesthetic judgment assumes in the mind of the beholder will symbolize the form of an authentic moral judgment. My sense is that commentators have focused largely on the second sort of symbolization and neglected the importance of the first.

(ii) Kant is apparently willing to use "cognition" (*Erkenntnis*) even to describe the kind of transaction with the supersensible that mere symbolization affords. But he usually includes an explicit denial that it is *theoretical* cognition, since the latter involves a straightforward empirical or schematic exhibition of concepts, rather than an analogical one. Instead, symbols provide us with or are involved in *practical* cognition (*praktische Erkenntnis*) of ideas. This use of "practical" can be misleading, however, because the process we are talking about can involve not just narrowly *moral* ideas, but other ideas as well. The metaphysical idea of a noumenal ground or an *ens realissimum*, just as much as the moral idea of a cosmopolitan sage, can be symbolized in beautiful art and nature.[41] So it is important to note that while the considerations that ground the relevant assents may be broadly speaking "practical," the ideas involved need not be.

This provides another indication that around 1790 Kant starts to conflate or at least link the Second Solution to the problem of real repugnance with the Third Solution. It also suggests that Kant's considered view is that practical cognition can *either* constitute (or perhaps ground) "practical knowledge"[42] of the supersensible *or* provide a non-standard kind of positive or material content to ideas for the purposes of mere *Belief*, depending on the content of the assents involved.

(iii) Third, lest there be any doubt that the role that Kant assigns to symbolization in rational inquiry is an important one, it is worth noting that it is *the* main mode of giving positive content to many of our most important philosophical concepts:

> Our language is full of such indirect presentations, in accordance with an analogy, where the expression does not contain the actual schema for the concept but only a symbol for reflection. Examples are the words *ground* (support, basis), *depend* (be held from above), from which *flow* (instead of follow), *substance* (as Locke expresses it: the bearer of accidents), and innumerable other nonschematic but symbolic hypotyposes and expressions for concepts not by means of a direct intuition, but only in accordance with an analogy with it, i.e., the transportation of the reflection on one object of intuition to another, quite different concept, to which perhaps no intuition can ever directly correspond. (5:352)

This passage is puzzling because in the first *Critique* Kant says that at least some of these ideas (substance, ground, etc.) can be schematized for use in an *a priori* metaphysics of experience. Setting this aside, it is certainly clear that the theoretical Belief—which for Kant is the only rational result of what the tradition called *special* metaphysics—will traffic in a great deal of symbolization. In particular, the idea of God is clearly "merely symbolic, and anyone who takes it, along with the properties of understanding, will, etc., which prove their objective real-

---

41   In notes he made for the *Real Progress* essay, Kant reflects on the problem of real repugnance specifically with respect to the idea of the *ens realissimum* (which is a metaphysical rather than an explicitly moral idea). He says there that, in general, we can resort to "either the real schematism (transcendental), or the schematism by analogy (symbolic). The objective reality of the categories is theoretical, that of the idea is only practical" (20:332). It seems clear from this that some very broad notion of "practical" can be used to refer to all of the transcendental ideas, including speculative metaphysical ideas like that of an *ens realissimum*. But this is not a narrow, morality-focused sense of "practical." See also 5:353.

42   Cf. the talk of practical knowledge (*Wissen*) at 5:4 and of the "*scibilia*" at 5:467-8.

ity only in beings within the world, as schematic, lapses into anthropo-morphism" (5:353).

In the account of symbolization in the third *Critique* and *Real Progress,* then, we have the groundwork for a *via analogia* account of metaphysical and religious concepts in general. Kant continues to build on this in the subsequent decade (e.g. at 28:1023, 1048ff), and thus joins a long tradition of holding that ideas of the supersensible get much of their content by making analogies to beings and properties we experience in the terrestrial sphere: "We always need a certain analogy with natural being in order to make supersensible characteristics comprehensible to us," Kant writes in the *Religion* (6:65n). Or, in a later German philosopher's more colorful phrase: "The more abstract the truth you want to teach, the more you must seduce the senses to it" (Nietzsche 2002, §128).

Conclusion

The problem of real repugnance with respect to articles of rational Belief—moral and theoretical—is a serious one for Kant, but he thinks that he has the resources to respond. His First Solution appeals to the "needs" of reason, his Second to an intellectual awareness of the "fact of reason," and his Third to sensible experience of an analogical/symbolic sort. The third *Critique*'s version of the Third Solution focus on the way sensory experience of beautiful objects or vistas, in particular, can symbolize the objects of "unexhibitable" rational ideas.

It is important to note, finally, that for Kant it's not worth symbolizing just *any* idea in the manner of the Third Solution. There are certainly objects that can't be given to us empirically or schematically, but that also don't have a connection to any of the practical or theoretical "needs of reason." In the first *Critique*, Kant provides the example of an entire series of effects of a given cause. Such a series "has no transcendental use" and if we nevertheless "make for ourselves an idea of an absolute totality of such a synthesis … then this is just a thing of thought (an *ens rationis*), which is thought up only arbitrarily, and not presupposed by reason" (A337/B394). Thus here we encounter a crucial division among concepts that cannot be intuitively exhibited: on the one hand, there are the genuine ideas of reason that we are naturally predisposed to generate and for which we postulate objects on the basis of "subjective grounds." These are the ideas that raise the problem of how to find really harmonious content for them, even if it can only be symbolic.

On the other hand, there are the concepts that "idle brains" dream up, reflection on which "makes the spirit dull, the object gradually disgusting, and the mind dissatisfied with itself and moody because it judges that in reason's judgment its disposition is contrapurposive" (5:326). The latter are just empty thought-entities: of no important use to reason, metaphysically repugnant for all we know, and liable to lead us into the blind alleys of mystical "enthusiasm" or speculative "pedantry" in which Kant thought so many of his predecessors had been lost (5:70-1, A486/B514). For concepts such as these, the problem of real repugnance has no solution.[43]

43 My thanks are owed to Karl Ameriks, Frederick Beiser, C. Rich Booher, Richard Boyd, Ernesto Garcia, Gordon Graham, Lee Hardy, John Hare, Desmond Hogan, Anja Jauernig, Patrick Frierson, Patrick Kain, Rae Langton, Derk Pereboom, Karl Schafer, Houston Smit, Angela Smith, Nicholas Stang, Eric Watkins, Allen Wood, Rachel Zuckert, and the editors of this volume for helpful discussion and feedback on earlier drafts. Thanks also to audiences and workshops at Syracuse University, the Princeton Institute for Advanced Study, Universidade de São Paulo, Houghton College, Instituto de Filosofía de Granada, Princeton Theological Seminary, and the University of Notre Dame.

CHAPTER 8

Practical Cognition, Intuition, and the Fact of Reason

Patrick Kain

With the wane of excessively positivistic interpretations and appropria-
tions of Kant's philosophy, the charge that Kant's talk of noumena,
things-in-themselves, or the "supersensible" must be, on his own terms,
meaningless, has been largely abandoned. Yet Kant's claims about
supersensible objects, and his account of the epistemic status of such
claims, remain neglected and poorly understood, to the detriment of our
understanding of Kant's metaphysical and epistemological system. It is
with good reason that Kant's account of theoretical cognition has been
examined as closely as it has, but unfortunate that his account of practical cognition, and of its relationship to theoretical cognition, has been
so little studied.

In the *Critique of Practical Reason*, and again in the *Critique of the
Power of Judgment*, Kant claims that we have practical cognition (*Erkenntnis*) and knowledge (*Wissen*) of the moral law and of our supersensible freedom; that this cognition and knowledge cohere with, yet go
beyond the limits of, our theoretical cognition; and that this knowledge
grounds rational belief (*Vernunftglaube*) in the existence of God, the
immortality of the soul, and the real possibility of the "highest good."[1]
This essay is intended to untangle some of these claims about practical
cognition, practical knowledge, and practical belief and their relation to
Kant's account of theoretical cognition and theoretical knowledge. I
will argue that there is a core conception of cognition and knowledge
underlying the accounts of theoretical cognition and practical cognition,

---

1   On the translation of *Glaube* as "belief," see Chignell 2007a, p. 335, and 2007b. One
    limitation of this translation is that Kant's term connotes *warranted* belief. For an excel-
    lent discussion of Kant's conception of "doctrinal" or theoretical belief, see Chignell
    2007a, pp. 345-54. Chignell suggests that "acceptance" may be better than "belief" be-
    cause the characteristic phenomenology of belief may be missing from *Glaube* (2007a,
    pp. 341-3, 359-60). I'm not convinced Kant thinks this about the case of the practical
    postulates, but that must be considered another day.

one which allows for a principled distinction between cases of practical knowledge and practical belief. Kant's doctrine of the "fact of reason" turns out to be crucial to his claims about the legitimacy of and distinction between the two forms of practical cognition, one of which constitutes knowledge and another which cannot.

Intuition, Theoretical Cognition, and Knowledge

Kant's theoretical philosophy aims to provide an account of our empirical knowledge and of the *a priori* principles that make such empirical knowledge possible. In its theoretical employment, reason (or understanding) seeks extensive, rich, distinct, systematic, convincing, certain, and true representations of objects (9:33-90, A707-855/B735-883). Kant developed and deployed some technical terminology to classify our representations and their epistemically significant characteristics and relationships. Cognition (*Erkenntnis*) is an objective perception or representation that refers to an object (A320/B376), an acquaintance with something with some consciousness of its similarity and difference from other things (9:65).[2] Knowledge (*Wissen*) is a sufficiently convincing and sufficiently certain representation of an object's "constitution" or determinations, a cognition based on objectively sufficient, if fallible, grounds, grounds in principle available to all and ultimately "resting on" or "grounded in" the object and its constitution (A821-2/B849-51, Refl. 2446, 16:371).[3] On Kant's account, all knowledge may be cognition, but not all cognition, not even all warranted and true cognition, constitutes knowledge in Kant's sense.[4]

Kant famously insisted that humans have two distinct sources for our representations, sensibility and understanding, and that this distinc-

---

2   This is not to deny that Kant sometimes uses the word *Erkenntnis* quite loosely, to refer, for example, to virtually any mental representation "of something" (9:65) or to refer to the elements of a cognition, such as an intuition or a concept in their own right (A320/B376). Even in the sense indicated in the text, cognition comes in degrees. "What it [the principle of thoroughgoing determination] means is that in order to cognize a thing completely one has to cognize everything possible and determine the thing through it, whether affirmatively or negatively" (A573/B601). For more on the relationship between these senses of cognition, see Smit 2000, pp. 239-47.

3   For a more thorough analysis of Kant's conception of knowledge, see Chignell 2007a and 2007b. Chignell prefers to say that cognition can ground knowledge, rather than that it can be or constitute knowledge (2007a, p. 348).

4   This is one of several ways in which Kant's usage differs from contemporary English usage. I here set aside questions about whether Kant allows a form of *Wissen* that is not *Wissen* of objects and so does not presuppose genuine *Erkenntnis*, such as possible *Wissen* of propositions about things-in-themselves. See Smit, n.d.

tion between sources supports the distinct, yet complementary, roles that the resulting representations play in our cognitive economy (A15/B29, A50/B74, Caygill 2003). In order to cognize [*erkennen*] something, that is, to be acquainted with something with consciousness of its similarity and difference from other things, finite subjects like us who represent objects discursively, that is by means of partial or incomplete representations or "marks" (9:58), must employ representations that, on the one hand, relate to the object directly and in its singularity and representations that, on the other hand, relate to the object mediately and by means of some common mark or marks which facilitate its comparison with other objects. Kant calls representations that facilitate immediate and singular relation to an object "intuitions"; representations that relate to objects indirectly and in virtue of their generality he calls "concepts" (A320/B376).[5] So Kant's claim is that our cognition must involve both intuitions and concepts.

> Our cognition arises from two fundamental sources in the mind, the first of which is the reception of representations (the receptivity of impressions), the second the faculty for cognizing an object by means of these representations (spontaneity of concepts); through the former an object is *given* to us, through the latter it is *thought* in relation to that representation (as a mere determination of the mind). Intuition and concepts therefore constitute the elements of all our cognition, so that neither concepts without intuition corresponding to them in some way nor intuition without concepts can yield a cognition. ... It comes along with our nature that *intuition* can never be other than *sensible*, i.e., that it contains only the way in which we are affected by objects. ... Without sensibility no object would be given to us, and without understanding none would be thought. Thoughts without content are empty, intuitions without concepts are blind. It is thus just as necessary to make the mind's concepts sensible (i.e., to add an object to them in intuition) as it is to make its intuitions understandable (i.e., to bring them under concepts). (A50/B74ff)[6]

Kant's claim is that it is through sensible intuition that objects "are given to us;" without intuition we have mere thought. To properly grasp the significance of intuition in cognition and knowledge, it is important to sketch several of the distinct roles played by intuition in the generation of theoretical cognition.

First, in sensible intuition, a subject is affected by an object and receives certain sensations, representations with qualitative features such as a certain degree of warmth, a particular texture, or a particular color or odor.[7] These qualitative features provide the *matter* of intuition and may be or indicate information about the constitution of an object, its

---

5   For an important discussion of "marks," see Smit 2000.
6   Cf. also A15/B29, B146, and 20:296, 325.
7   The principle of the anticipations of perception is that sensation, or its phenomenal object, has intensive magnitude.(A165/B207)

features and causal powers. By touching an object and receiving sensations of warmth and smoothness, for example, I am in a position to
represent an object as warm and smooth (and to employ such representations, once acquired, in other ways and other contexts). Our representations with this sort of qualitative content, Kant insists, must be derived from sensible intuition (A28-9/B44). Perceptual experience
provides us with much of the content that can be ascribed to objects; it
is the source of our concepts of sensible qualities and the matter of our
empirical concepts of objects.

Second, sensible intuition plays a crucial role in establishing what
Kant calls the "real possibility" of various kinds of object. Some concepts explicitly contradict other concepts and a combination of such
contradictories cannot genuinely be thought, e.g., quadrangular trian-
gles are absolutely impossible (2:77). While the absence of such contradiction is sufficient for a (possible) thought, Kant contends that it is
not sufficient to establish the real possibility of a corresponding object.

> I can think whatever I like, as long as I do not contradict myself, i.e., as long
> as my concept is a possible thought, even if I cannot give any assurance
> whether or not there is a corresponding object somewhere within the sum total
> of all possibilities. But in order to ascribe objective validity to such a concept
> (real possibility, for the first sort of possibility was merely logical) something
> more is required. This "more," however, need not be sought in theoretical
> sources of cognition; it may also lie in practical ones. (Bxxvi, n)

For example,

> to have the opinion that there are pure, bodiless, thinking spirits in the material
> universe…is fiction, not a matter of opinion at all, but a mere idea left over if
> one takes everything material away from a thinking being but still leaves it the
> power of thought. But whether in that case thought remains…we cannot de-
> termine. (5:467)

Or,

> in the concept of a figure that is enclosed between two straight lines there is no
> contradiction, for the concepts of two straight lines and their intersection con-
> tain no negation of a figure; rather the impossibility rests not on the concept in
> itself, but on its construction in space… (A220/B268)[8]

In the latter case, Kant contends, the "more" that allows determinations
of real possibility or real impossibility comes from the *a priori* form of
spatial intuition. The real impossibility of a figure enclosed by only two
straight lines, Kant claims, can be established by an examination of the
conditions and determinations of space, which preclude such an exhibition. The real possibility of a figure enclosed by three straight lines can

---

8   Cf. A47/B65. Another example of something logically possible that is (or can be shown
     to be) really impossible: a triangle where one side is greater than the sum of the other
     two sides (A25/B39). Cf. A716/B744.

be exhibited in a geometrical construction (A47/B65). Similarly, our perceptions can establish the real possibility of certain kinds of substances, forces, and interactions by exhibiting, within experience, that the relevant qualities can be copresent in a unified object of experience (A221/B268ff, A770/B798, 8:161-2, 179).

Third, Kant argues that the spatio-temporal form of our intuition grounds the validity of a set of determinate *a priori* principles for experience. Because everything we can intuit or experience can only be experienced in time and/or space, certain characteristics of time and/or space can be known *a priori* to determine any such experience and render the pure concepts of the understanding, the categories (which are themselves independent of intuition and experience), applicable to experience in determinate ways (A147/B186). For example, the pure forms of intuition play a crucial role in grounding the "Analogies of Experience," the claims that, in experience, substance persists, alterations occur in accordance with the law of cause and effect, and simultaneously existing substances are in thoroughgoing interaction (A176/B218ff). The determinacy and certainty of such principles of possible experience, principles necessary for any empirical knowledge, are tied to the *a priori* form of intuition.

Fourth, intuition plays a crucial role in validating claims about the *actuality* of an empirical object or force and in securing reference to such objects. When representations are given to us in intuition, and are properly synthesized in experience (in accord with the principles of possible experience), they may constitute knowledge of the actuality of an object or power with the relevant qualities (if subsumable under laws or a system of laws). "Whatever is connected with a perception according to empirical laws, is actual" (A376). The qualitative features of perceptual experience resulting from more-or-less direct and discernibly law-like effects of objects on us can provide us with "reliable information about the 'constitution of the object'" or its powers, and the causal connection can ground the reference of these representations to those objects and powers (Chignell 2007b, p. 39, quoting A821/B849).[9] For example, my cognition and knowledge that *the sun is warming the stone* depend upon the sun, the stone, the sun warming the stone, and my perception of those things (though it is also crucially dependent upon the range of perceptions that support the relevant empirical laws and the analogies of experience that underlie all empirical laws) (4:301n, 305n, 312).[10] When such objects and perceptions actually

---

9   On questions of reference, see Hanna 2004/2009.

10 Other examples: "all bodies are heavy" (A8/B11); sunlight melts wax, but hardens clay (A766/B794).

ground such judgments of experience, we may have the combination of objectively sufficient grounds resting on the object and subjective conviction that can constitute empirical knowledge.[11]

Because of the crucial roles of sensation (and perception) and the forms of our sensible intuition in generating knowledge, Kant famously claims that we cannot have theoretical cognition of supersensibles, beings whose nature would preclude them from being presented in sensible intuition. Our thoughts of supersensible "objects" lack qualitative matter and determinacy (i.e., are sparse in representational content), are incapable of having their real possibility as objects established, cannot be assumed to be subject to the principles of possible experience or other *a priori* principles, and lack a comprehensible mode of reference to actual and knowable objects.

> We cannot think any object except through categories; we cannot cognize any object that is thought except through intuitions that correspond to those concepts. Now all our intuitions are sensible, and this cognition, so far as its object is given, is empirical. Empirical cognition, however, is experience. Consequently no *a priori* cognition is possible for us except solely of objects of possible experience. (B165-6)[12]

The absence of possible sensible intuition precludes theoretical cognition of supersensible objects and *ipso facto* theoretical cognition with sufficient objective grounds, or theoretical knowledge, of such conceivable objects.

In the Dialectic of the first *Critique*, Kant elaborates the implications of this doctrine for the Ideas of an immortal soul, free agency, and God. In the Paralogisms, Kant argues that the "I think," which may accompany any of my representations, has no content and is no more determinate than the unschematized pure concept of substance (A381). In the Antinomies, Kant emphasizes how the concept of (noumenal) freedom and intelligible character is purely negative and no more determinate than the unschematized pure concept of a ground (A541/B569, A546/B574). In the critique of speculative theology, Kant raises concerns about the content of the concept of God: for example,

---

11 Again, see Chignell 2007b, p. 47. On the role of the object in objective or logical grounds and objective or logical certainty, see 9:72, A829/B857, 5:461, 24:198, 234). I emphasize, more than Chignell does, that objective grounds or logical grounds required for knowledge should ultimately "rest on" or be "grounded in" or connected to the object or its constitution. Cf. Chignell 2007b, pp. 41-2 and 2007a, pp. 327, 337, 349. Depending upon how this is specified, it may build a "truth condition" into the notion of an objectively sufficient ground. Compare 2007a, p. 330.

12 *A priori* cognition in mathematics is, in the first instance, of schemata, such as the schema of a triangle, rather than of any image of a triangle or any triangular object of possible experience (A141/B180). Nonetheless, all of our theoretical cognition "is in the end related to possible intuitions…" (A720/B748; cf. B147).

the concept of an *ens realissimum* cannot contain the concept of existence, the concept of an absolutely necessary existent contains no real content, and the teleological concept of God as architect lacks the determinacy of the concept of a creator (A592-630/B620-58). The critique of pure reason in its theoretical employment teaches us "of our unavoidable ignorance [*Unwissenheit*] in respect of the things in themselves and [limits] everything that we can cognize theoretically to mere appearances" (Bxxix). There can be no theoretical cognition or knowledge beyond the bounds of possible experience.

Practical Knowledge: understanding the fact of reason

Kant's account of the role of intuition in theoretical cognition and the famous boundary condition that he infers from it appear, at first glance, to preclude any and all cognition or knowledge of supersensibles. However, Kant persistently rejects this further conclusion. For example, late in the first *Critique*, right after re-articulating the boundary condition, Kant suggests that, "nevertheless, there must somewhere be a source of positive cognitions that belong in the domain of pure reason," namely in pure reason's "practical use" (A796/B824).[13] Kant suggests that in addition to intuition, an indispensable source of theoretical cognition, there may be "practical data," "practical sources" of cognition (B xxi, xxvi n). Similarly, in his never-completed essay on the "real progress of metaphysics," after summarizing the results of his critique of pure reason, Kant noted that it remained an open question "whether, in spite of that, there could not be a practico-dogmatic cognition of these supersensibles" (20:296).[14]

Throughout much of the first *Critique*, Kant is less conscientious than he could be about reminding his readers that the restriction of cognition to the domain of possible experience, i.e. to the "sensible," is a

---

13 Cf. Bxxi. The first edition of the first *Critique* is, especially early on, less than clear that it is focused on pure reason in only one of its uses, the theoretical. The earliest mention of the theoretical/practical distinction in this edition (A14-5) is confused, and the practical use of pure reason is hardly mentioned again until the Dialectic (A314-29, A366, A470, A589, A796ff.) The second edition Preface and Introduction are somewhat better on this point (Bx, xxi, xxvi, B29) but the Aesthetic and Analytic remain silent on this point. See also 5:6-8. Kant suggests that some of the most puzzling issues in his system stem from the fact that, prior to the second *Critique*, the practical use of reason was "known only by name" (5:5).
14 It is only in 1786, in "What does it mean to orient oneself in thinking?", that Kant begins writing extensively about "cognition of the supersensible" and metaphysics as "the science of progressing by reason from cognition of the sensible to that of the supersensible" (20:260, Schwaiger 2004, p. 333).

restriction of *speculative* cognition, a limit of pure reason in its theo-retical use.[15] Especially in the first edition of the first *Critique*, it can be easy to miss or fail to see the significance of Kant's claim that reason, indeed *pure* reason, has a practical as well as a theoretical use; besides being concerned with determining its concept of a given or sensible object, reason may also be concerned with the determining grounds of the will, with determining objects to make actual (Bx, 5:15).[16] In the first instance, pure reason in its practical use is concerned with *a priori*, objectively valid principles of rational willing.

Kant's contention, in the second *Critique* and thereafter, is that "as soon as we draw up maxims of the will for ourselves," "we become immediately conscious" that certain things are to be done, regardless of our desires (5:29). In this sole "fact of reason," we cognize with "apo-deictic certainty"; we "know" that there is an "undeniable" moral law to which we are subject (5:4, 29, 32, 47, 105; A823/B851, 9:70, 8:396n, 418). But practical cognition can be of both imperatives and of "the grounds of possible imperatives," which might include free and immor-tal finite beings and God (9:86, 24:251, 751, 901). Kant contends that we also have practical cognition and knowledge of our freedom—the "condition of the moral law" (5:4).[17] The fact of reason "points to a pure world of the understanding and, indeed, even *determines* it posi-*tively* and lets us cognize something of it, namely a law" (5:43). This moral law, which we know, is supposed to provide the basis for our knowledge of our freedom:

> Freedom is real, for this idea reveals itself through the moral law. But among all the ideas of speculative reason freedom is… the only one the possibility of which we know [*wissen*] *a priori*, though without having insight into it, be-cause it is the condition of the moral law, which we do know [*wissen*]. (5:4)

Our consciousness of the moral law, in the fact of reason, is the "*ratio cognoscendi*" of our freedom (5:4n) and, as Kant explains in the third *Critique*, this makes freedom "the only one among all the ideas of pure reason whose object is a fact and which must be counted among the *scibilia* [knowable]" (5:468). Our cognition of freedom and the moral

---

15 This weakness is perhaps most obvious in the chapter on "Phenomena and Noumena" (A235-60/B294-315) which includes no explicit qualifications.
16 Cf. 5:46, 89
17 Kant does sometimes seem to equate *Wissen* with (one of the highest forms of) specula-tive or theoretical *Erkenntnis* (Bxxx, A799/B827, A805/B833, 5:475, 8:420-1). At least in the first *Critique*, Kant may have been thinking that practical freedom is as good as empirically-theoretically established (A802f/B830f); in contrast, he explicitly denies knowledge of God and immortality (A805/B833, A828/B857), and in *Groundwork of the Metaphysics of Morals*, he suggests a theoretical deduction of freedom. On either of those accounts, the putative cases of practical *Wissen* fit the theoretical model.

law is thus to be specifically distinguished from "matters of belief [*Glaube*]" such as the existence of God and the immortality of the soul.[18] The question is whether and how the characteristics of cognition and knowledge can be present in the absence of intuition.[19] Much of the answer depends upon Kant's account of the nature and role of the fact of reason.

In one sense, Kant's descriptions of the *content* of the fact of reason are quite fluid, suggesting that the fact of reason is the moral law, or the categorical imperative, or consciousness of the moral law (and its un-conditional validity), or consciousness of freedom.[20] Nonetheless, cer-tain aspects of its content are clear. As stated in the second *Critique*, the fundamental law of pure practical reason contained in the fact of reason is, in its imperatival form, "So act that the maxim of your will could always hold at the same time as a principle in a giving of universal law" (5:30). Kant contends that this principle is an objective law that gov-erns, indeed the only law that could govern, the will of every rational being. It is also a "determinate law" for the will (5:474); it can serve as the "determining ground of the will" (5:15, 28, 42, 50, 89, 105). This law, though formal, has genuine content, sufficient in principle to de-liver a verdict of permissibility or impermissibility on any maxim.[21] On Kant's analysis, it is this *a priori* principle that makes possible the cog-nition of the moral status of particular maxims.

The determinacy and determinate use of this principle, however, cannot come from intuition. We have no "supersensible," "intellectual" or non-sensible intuition; and no sensible intuition or data, empirical or pure, could adequately present the categorical validity of the moral law (5:31, 43, 91). This is one of the most fundamental ways in which prac-tical cognition differs from theoretical cognition, which must begin

---

18 See also 9:93, 20:295, 300-1, 310-1. This seems contrary to Allison's suggestion that all three supersensibles (God, freedom, and immortality) are matters of belief "rather than knowledge." But as Allison notes, there are two distinct senses of freedom operative in these contexts (Allison 2002, p. 344, Allison 1990, 285n35).

19 For an earlier account that raises some of these issues in a complementary way, see Ameriks 2003, esp. pp. 251, 258.

20 On the relationship amongst Kant's various formulations, see Beck 1960, pp. 166-7; Allison emphasizes "consciousness of standing under the moral law and the recognition of this law 'by every natural human reason as the supreme law of its will' [5:91]" (Alli-son 1990, pp. 231-3, 283n12). Proops emphasizes that the moral law has a pure origin, and suggests that the other formulations are linked by related objective and subjective senses of legal evidence (Proops 2003, pp. 225, 228). Willaschek suggests that the act of "making conscious" of the validity of the moral law is central, and that other variati-ons are connected by the looseness in action and consequence descriptions (Willaschek 1991, p. 460-1). See also Rauscher 2002, pp. 486-7 and Kain 2006, pp. 453-4.

21 Even if Kant himself sometimes exaggerates the ease with which such verdicts may be delivered (see, e.g., 5:36).

from pure and empirical intuition, from sensible data (5:42, 91). Yet Kant is insistent that the fact of reason is itself something "given," itself "data," though of a unique sort (5:31, 47, 55, 66, 91, 105; 5:468, 8:396n, 403)[22] What is first given to us is not an intuition or a relation to an intuited individual, but rather a *principle*, indeed the categorical principle to which we are subject (5:91, 42, 46, 29-30, 65, 104-5). We are immediately confronted with a determinate constraint on our action—at least initially, we do not experience this as a constraint of our own making or of our own nature. My proposal is that Kant's persistent characterization of the fact of reason as a "fact," "given," and "data" is intended to position it, within practical cognition, as an analogue of sensible intuition within the account of theoretical cognition: as an immediately received, non-derivative source of content, a source that might provide the determinacy, reference, and subjective and objective sufficiency sufficient to constitute knowledge.[23]

Several recent commentators, however, have challenged apparent assertions of the "givenness" of the fact of reason, arguing that the fact of reason is intended as, first and foremost, an act or deed of reason, perhaps even as a "willful" and "violent" act, rather than as a given *datum* (Franks 1997, pp. 318-20).[24] First, it has been noted that Kant's German term *"Factum"* is derived from the Latin *"facere,"* meaning "to make," and that Kant himself uses both the German term and its Latin cognates, in at least some contexts, to refer specifically to imputable deeds.[25] Similarly, the German term *"Thatsache"* (cf. 5:468) can be applied to either deeds or generic states of affairs, as long as they are taken to be well-established (Willaschek 1991; Franks 1997, p. 318). Some also place particular emphasis upon Kant's allusion to Juvenal's *"sic volo, sic jubeo"* ("What I will, I command") in his description of

---

22 On "practical data," "practical sources of cognition," or "data of pure reason" more generally, see 5:91, Bxxi, xxvin, xxviii, A795/B823, 5:468, 8:141.

23 For a similar suggestion, see Adams 1997, p. 814; Beck 1960, p. 273n (quoted below). Elements of this analogy can be found in Refl. 7201 (19:274-6), for example. But we should not forget the way Kant distances himself from too literal an interpretation of the parallels between the pure intuition of space and time and the principle of morality in the second *Critique* (5:42-3, 91, Allison 1990, pp. 234-5; Beck 1960, p. 166). There are disanalogies: the moral law is not sensibly given (though it does have an effect on feeling/sense), consciousness of it is not itself of an individual, and it allegedly possesses absolute universality and certainty.

24 For earlier responses to Franks, see Proops 2003, p. 227 and Kain 2006, p. 454.

25 Willaschek 1991, Sussman 2001, p. 111, O'Neill 1989, p. 65, O'Neill 2003, p. 363n3, Lukow 1993, Engstrom 2002, p. xlii. See 6:23, 8:255, 19:159. One could add Kant's discussion of "made concepts (*factitii*)" and "given concepts" in the *Logic* (9:93).

the "sole fact of pure reason which, by it, announces itself as originally lawgiving" (5:31, Franks 1997, p. 320).[26]

In response, first, one must acknowledge the ambiguities in the relevant terms as they are found in general use, but Kant's repeated assertions (cited above) that the fact of reason is something "given" and amounts to "data" reduce such ambiguities in the present case. Second, Kant's allusion to Juvenal, understood in fuller context, can be reconciled with the proposed reading. In its original context in *Satire* 6.223, the line certainly connotes arbitrariness, willfulness, and violence: a demand for a slave's execution is put beyond question by the declaration, "*sit pro ratione voluntatis*" ("Let my will take the place of reason"). Given Kant's taste for the Latin classics and his other allusions to Juvenal, he might well have been familiar with these connotations.[27] Yet, these lines also have a long history in legal and political discussions that is somewhat independent of their original context. Canonists, legists, and jurists of the late twelfth and thirteenth centuries employed the phrase "*pro ratione voluntas*" without implications of arbitrary, willful, or unlimited absolutism (Post 1972). While also associated with the absolutism of Louis XIV, the line's absolutist implications are qualified in the early modern period by Pufendorf (Postema 2001, p. 483).[28] Most significantly, Kant's invocation of "*sic volo, sic jubeo*" in the second *Critique* must be understood in immediate relation to the provocation of an astute reviewer of the *Groundwork*, H. A. Pistorius. Pistorius had objected that legislation independent of all prior interest is indistinguishable from arbitrary legislation [*eigenmächtige Gesetzgebung*] and appears to be a blind procedure [*ein blindes Verfahren*], indistinguishable from "*stat pro ratione voluntatis*" (Pistorius 1786, p. 461).[29] Kant's "*sic volo, sic jubeo*" cleverly invokes and embraces the other half of the thought, and only that half, in order to clarify his position, asserting that it is the unconditionality of the command which allows reason, as opposed to some arbitrary or irrational volition, to

---

26 See also Schicker 1991.

27 On Kant's Latin training, see Kuehn 2001, pp. 47-50. Kant also alludes to Juvenal's *Satire* 8.79-84 (5:158, 6:49n, 6:334) and *Satire* 1.74 (5:160). Kant explicitly names Juvenal in *Anthropology from a Pragmatic Point of View* (7:197), but that reference is to Persius's *Satires* 3.78 (Louden 2007, p. 516n47).

28 Pufendorf was commenting on Hobbes's allusion (Pufendorf 1672, § I.6.1; Hobbes 1642, §XIV.1). See also Leibniz, 1702-1703, §1 (Leibniz 1988, p. 46), Locke 1689, Book I, §51, and Voltaire 1765, "Liberté".

29 In the second *Critique*, Kant specifically admires Pistorius's anonymous review of the *Groundwork* (5:8-9). See also Kant's "Vorarbeit" (21:416). Kant was informed of Pistorius's identity as the author in a letter from Daniel Jenisch (14 May 1787), 10:486.

"announce itself as originally lawgiving" (5:31).[30] Understood in this context, the point of Kant's allusion is to emphasize the epistemic ultimacy of this fact, this consciousness of the moral law, and the limits of its comprehensibility.[31]

One concern with such a construal of the fact of reason is its seemingly arbitrary or dogmatic implications. It does appear to represent a significant philosophical retreat from the grand ambition of a deduction of the moral law found in the *Groundwork*. This construal of the fact of reason as a given or brute fact need not, however, entail that it need not or cannot be defended or supported or confirmed.[32] Just as the legitimacy of elements classified as experiential or intuitional within the theoretical domain may be subject to defeat and challenge against which it might be defended, the legitimacy of the fact of reason may require defense. Proops has recently suggested, for example, that Kant's appeals to ordinary people's pangs of conscience and feelings of respect (5:32, 88, 91) may offer "proof," in the legal sense of defeasible evidence, for the fact of reason (Proops 2003, pp. 225-7).[33] Rawls has emphasized Kant's suggestion that the "fit" between the determinate practical conception of freedom and the negative theoretical conception may serve as a "credential," "authentication," warrant, or confirmation of the former (Rawls 2000, pp. 253-72, emphasizing 5:46-57)[34] Even if these suggestions increase the plausibility of the account, they by no means preclude all forms of skepticism; though Kant himself seemed to think he had systematic reason for discounting any serious threats to (the certainty of) the fact of reason and the freedom it reveals. An assessment of the systematic adequacy of this position is beyond the scope of this paper. Our present concern is with how such an alleged fact, supposing its warrant is certain or at least undefeated, could constitute knowledge, in Kant's sense of the term.

If we are to classify our cognition of the moral law and of freedom as knowledge, the real possibility and objective grounds of these cognitions must be identified. It is at this point that the epistemological

---

30 Hobbes famously noted that, absent the latter phrase, the implications of the former remained ambiguous. (Hobbes 1650, §XIII.6). In his review of the second *Critique*, Pistorius refers to Kant's "*sic volo, sic jubeo*" twice and chooses to contest only the determinacy of Kant's moral principle and its arbitrariness in application, conceding its unconditionality, which seems to confirm my reading of the exchange (Pistorius 1794, pp. 81, 91).

31 Cf. the rare other cases of this allusion in Kant: in a similar context, in *Opus postumum* (21:23, 28) and concerning mathematical definitions, in Refl. 2930 (16:579).

32 It may, however, limit its availability for radical constructivist, anti-realist interpretations such as those of O'Neill and Lukow. See Kain 2006, pp. 451-2.

33 Proops builds upon Allison's emphasis on such experiences. Allison 1990, pp. 233-9.

34 Cf. 5:5-6, 106. But see Timmermann 2007.

"givenness" of the fact of reason must be linked to reason's role in the law's ontological foundation. Kant's analysis of categorical obligation is intended to reveal that the moral law should be understood, once it is acknowledged, as a principle that is self-imposed, given, or legislated by a free rational being (Kain 2004). Only a free being can be unconditionally subject to a practical principle or act out of respect for such a principle, and a free being can only be categorically obliged by a law given by pure practical reason itself (5:28-9, 33). Analysis of this determinate law thereby reveals its own relatively determinate *ratio essendi* or ontological grounding, that is, something determinate about the noumenal self of any agent bound by the law: the law gives determinate positive content to the concept of ourselves as *causa noumenon* (5:48, 50, 55, 105). Freedom is thus "the condition of the moral law... [its] *ratio essendi*.... [W]ere there no freedom, the moral law would *not be encountered* at all in ourselves" (5:4n). The givenness of the law—and the real possibility and actuality it must be granted if its warrant remains undefeated—can itself underwrite the real possibility and actuality of its ontological grounds, as long as they can be determinately thought.[35]

Kant considers it important to stress that we encounter the moral law in ourselves and that the supersensible reality it (first) reveals is not "outside us." This

> principle does not need to be searched for or invented; it has long been present in the reason of all human beings and incorporated in their being.... The concept of freedom alone allows us to find the unconditioned and intelligible for the conditioned and sensible without going outside ourselves. For it is our reason itself which by means of the supreme and unconditional practical law cognizes itself and the being that is conscious of this law (our own person) as belonging to the pure world of understanding and even determines the way in which, as such, it can be active. (5:105-6)

"We have in ourselves a principle that is capable of determining the idea of the supersensible in us," freedom (5:474).[36] Because each may find the principle within her own reason and that principle reveals something about her own self, at least one referent of this determinate concept of a *causa noumenon* is unproblematic—what is designated is the subject herself (5:56).[37]

---

35 At least this: if the ontological grounds of such a "given" are determinately thought, we have significantly "more" than a merely logically possible thought.

36 Cf. 5:195, 20:295.

37 This might address a disanalogy with empirical cognition: in practical cognition, the fact of reason does generate reference to a particular *causa noumenon*, something not possible in empirical theoretical cognition.

Moreover, the grounds of this representation of the law, and of one-self as a *causa noumenon*, allow us to make sense of the claim that they constitute or indicate the presence of sufficient objective grounds "resting on" or grounded in the object in question. First, the grounds are not merely subjeictve in the sense that they are not idiosyncratic to an individual or subset of individuals. Each rational agent has relevantly similar grounds for these representations of herself. Second, they may provide objective grounds in the stronger sense that they purport to be, or be ontologically dependent upon, the constitution of or determinations of the object under consideration (the obligated being, the free being him- or herself), rather than being merely features of the subject, distinct from the object. This is significantly aided by the fact that in this case, the rational agent is herself the object under consideration—the requisite connection can be granted without positing additional substances or relations between them. If this account is correct, then it turns out that we cognize our freedom *in virtue of* our freedom, because it is in virtue of our freedom that we are subject to the moral law that reveals our freedom to us. This is what allows Kant to classify these cognitions as knowledge.

While Kant seems to contend that in this case the reality of freedom is "proved by an apodictic law of practical reason," without the need for any intuition (5:3, cf. 5:66), he also contends that the proof of the reality of any matter of fact, including the fact of reason and the freedom it reveals directly, requires the help of "some intuition corresponding to the concept," or at least some possible intuition or possible experience (5:468). Kant points to moral actions, unperformed yet obligatory actions, moral dispositions, and feelings of respect or guilt as possible empirical manifestations of the reality of the moral law and freedom of the will, and of their applicability to the world of sense. In the case of the fact of reason, the reality is established "through practical laws of pure reason and, in accordance with these, in real actions, and thus in experience" (5:468).[38] While there can be "no fully corresponding intuition" (5:66) that would allow us to infer the reality of freedom or the moral law simply from the observation of events in the sensible world, possibly intuited events can be properly regarded as ultimately grounded in such freedom.

The immediacy of the fact of reason, and the identification of its *ratio essendi* in the agent herself are integral to Kant's account of the givenness, determinateness, real possibility, actuality, objective grounding and apodeictic certainty that accompany such representations, the very qualities that allow them to be classified not only as practical cog-

---

38   Cf. 5:66-71, A317/B374, A328/B385, A802/B830, A807/B835, 20:300, 8:403, 8:416.

nition but also as practical knowledge, even though neither can be directly intuited.

Practical Belief: firm cognition without *knowledge*

I have argued that Kant's doctrine of the fact of reason is intended to manifest the possibility of a distinctively practical form of cognition that could constitute knowledge, namely practical knowledge of the moral law and of our freedom. Now I will argue that this same fact is also intended to reveal the possibility of another sort of practical cognition, namely practical "belief" which cannot constitute knowledge.[39]

Kant's various enumerations of examples of this sort of practical cognition can be somewhat confusing: sometimes he explicitly insists that there are only two such objects, namely God and immortality (A830/B858); other times he explicitly claims there are only three, the highest good, God, and immortality (5:469, 20:299) or God, "freedom in its practical aspect," and immortality (20:298); yet other times he suggests that freedom, perhaps understood as virtue (or "autocracy") (20:295), or a propensity toward virtue, or a "moral order" morally progressing, or an intelligible world (20:299, 306-7; 5:137, 143; 4:462) be included. Particularly puzzling in this context is the apparent suggestion that the reality of freedom may itself be a matter of belief rather than of practical knowledge, suggested most prominently by seemingly competing accounts of the postulate of freedom in the Analytic and Dialectic of the second *Critique* (5:94,132). These confusions are best understood as a result of ambiguous terminology, such as the multiple senses of freedom, complex relationships between the various items, and insufficient precision in certain contexts. At least with respect to freedom, however, clearer passages suggest both a distinction, and—more important for our purposes—principled reasons for distinguishing between objects of practical knowledge and those of practical belief.[40] To avoid some of these distracting details, we will focus primarily, as Kant himself typically does, on the postulate of God's existence.

---

39 I do not mean to imply that all forms of belief (*Glaube*) involve cognition. Kant insists that theoretical or doctrinal belief is not cognition (Chignell 2007a, p. 351). But Kant insists that genuine moral belief is cognition. My suggestion in what follows is that the fact of reason provides positive content for moral belief; this would appear to be lacking in theoretical or doctrinal belief.

40 On the distinction between freedom as autonomy and as autocracy and its relevance to this question, see Caswell 2003, pp. 214-6, Allison 1990, p. 285n35, Allison 2002, p. 346, and Beck 1960, pp. 207-8.

Since, on Kant's account, rational agency involves the choice of one's character (*Gesinnung*) or single fundamental maxim, and finite rational agents possess an interest in both happiness and the worthiness to be happy, then every possible fundamental maxim must include both elements; the only morally permissible way to relate these two elements is in terms of the highest good, the systematic union of virtue and happiness in proportion to it.[41] Thus, while Kant's moral theory requires that the moral law, rather than some further end, be the fundamental criterion for and motivating ground of a good will, finite rational beings ought, nonetheless, to intend to promote the highest good; it is a rationally required end. This analysis reveals one respect in which the resulting postulates rest on "subjective grounds" (A829/B857): this grounding applies only to *finite* rational agents. Relying upon his conception of real possibility, Kant supposes that rational agents can rationally will an end, in this case the highest good, only if they can rationally consider it to be *really possible* (Guyer 2000a, pp. 345-7). This leads to a second set of subjective factors: as finite beings with needs and cognitive limitations, living in a world where the proportionality between virtue and happiness is not guaranteed by observable natural laws, we lack grounds in theoretical cognition for thinking that the highest good is really possible. In light of these factors, Kant concludes that the existence of God (along with the other postulates) is the only condition we can rationally consider adequate for the real possibility of the highest good, which we are required to promote. Kant concludes that we "must postulate the *existence of God* as belonging necessarily to the possibility of the highest good (which object of our will is necessarily connected with the lawgiving of pure reason)" (5:124).[42]

We have already seen Kant's suggestion that the putatively rational demand of the moral law is part of what legitimates the assumptions of the real possibility of freedom and the moral law: the fact of reason provides "determinacy" for the concepts of freedom and the moral law, and the "proper" self it reveals purports to be the object of these concepts (5:105, 4:457–8, 461). This practical cognition and knowledge is

---

41 I have discussed this point in Kain 2006, pp. 456-7. See also Caswell 2006; cf. Kain 2003 and Engstrom 1992.

42 For useful elaboration of and analysis of this argument, see e.g. Wood 1970 and 1978, Kuehn 1985, Hare 1996, pp. 69-96, and O'Neill 1997. Sussman and Caswell have recently emphasized how Kant's argument may be buttressed by bringing in an additional "subjective" factor: his doctrine of the human propensity to evil (Caswell 2006, Sussman 2001, pp. 144ff.). Kant repeatedly asserts that the *existence* of God is linked to the real possibility of highest good. The existence of God is considered to be a necessary though not sufficient condition for the highest good. Contra Ferreira 1983 (pp. 78-9), the actuality of God would not directly *entail* the realization of the "complete" highest good in the relevant sense, since it does not entail that we attain virtue.

supposed to provide part of the basis of the practical cognition of the postulates: their determinate content and real possibility, and sufficient warranted confidence (or conviction) in their actuality.[43]

The content of the highest good that finite rational beings ought to intend (the systematic union of virtue and happiness) is determined by the moral law and the structure of finite practical reasoning (5:110ff, 5:450).[44] The concept of God is then determined in relation to the highest good: God must be a being with sufficient intellect, power, and will to render the highest good possible, which Kant contends amounts to omniscience, omnipotence, and all-beneficence (5:129, 140, 5:474, 481). The real possibility of the moral law and of freedom is also supposed to legitimate our assertion of the real possibility of the highest good and, through it, of the real possibility and actuality of God.[45]

> The ideas of God and immortality...are not conditions of the moral law but only conditions of the necessary object of a will determined by this law.... They are... conditions of applying the morally determined will to its object given to it a priori (the highest good). ... By means of the concept of freedom objective reality is given to the ideas of God and immortality and a warrant, indeed a subjective necessity (a need of pure reason) is given to assume them, although reason is not thereby extended in theoretical cognition. (5:4–5)

How does the (alleged) real possibility of the moral law and of freedom legitimate these claims? By providing an example of a supersensible object (myself as *causa noumenon*) whose real possibility and actuality we can practically cognize, the fact of reason adds something to the merely logical possibility of other conceivable supersensible objects. They are supersensible ideas tied to this practically known supersensible agency. Moreover, we have a "rational need" to acknowledge their real possibility in relation to our rational agency. The postulates of God and immortality purport to make explicit what we must consider to actually be the case, ontologically, supposing that the moral law is real and its object (the highest good) is really possible: they are the "physical or metaphysical conditions—in a word, those [conditions] which lie in the nature of things—of the possibility of the highest good" (5:143). The result is supposed to be a warranted assent with a firmness or sta-

---

43 If veridical, it may also suffice for meaningful reference to ourselves as free and immortal finite beings, and to God.

44 While some of Kant's works focus on the promotion of more limited goals such as "perpetual peace" or an ideal "ethical commonwealth" which may not require as strong a set of postulates, there is no obvious incompatibility between these specific and more "secular" or "historical" components of the highest good and the larger whole of virtue and happiness, nor is there a clear shift in Kant's focus away from such a whole (Caswell 2003, Mariña 2000, and Kain 2005, pp. 132, 143, discussing suggestions in Reath 1988, Yovel 1980, and Pogge 1997).

45 For a similar contention, see Adams 1997, pp. 814-5.

bility comparable in degree to that found in knowledge (8:141, 9:72, 16:371).[46]

For our purposes, what is equally important is that even though this account may show how the existence of God (and the other postulates) can be matters for firm practical cognition, Kant takes it to simultaneously preclude such cognitions from constituting practical knowledge. Recall that this latter point is not itself entailed by the nature of all practical cognition: Kant insists we have practical *knowledge* of the moral law and our freedom. One thing Kant often emphasizes is that our cognition of the highest good and of God's existence is dependent upon our cognition of our freedom and ultimately the fact of reason (5:4, 105). But this is not decisive either, because the dependency of one cognition on another need not preclude a dependent cognition from being knowledge, at least if what if it depends on is knowledge.

Two other hints Kant provides are somewhat more promising. Kant insists that in the case of the objects of practical belief, there is something more subjective about their grounds and that the route to those objects involves reference to something external to us and to the moral law. Some rational agents (if only an infinite one) may not be obligated to promote the highest good or may be able to cognize its real possibility directly or at least without any additional postulates. Moreover, within any subject who must postulate any of these things, the commitment to the moral law and the rational need to cognize the real possibility of one's intentions are crucial to these postulations. At the same time, what is postulated (God or one's own immortality) is neither the ontological ground of the moral law that we encounter in the fact of reason nor is it represented as identical with the subject as directly revealed by the moral law.[47] The highest good, Kant insists, is the object of volition under the moral law, not the ontological ground of the law, and its realization consists in much more than the volitional state of a single agent. Similarly, God is represented as a partial ground of the real possibility of the highest good, rather than as the ground of the moral law, and is represented as something distinct from the finite agent herself. The idea of God is the idea of a "supersensible above us"

---

46 I have argued elsewhere that these claims are best interpreted as involving full-blown cognitive assent with genuine ontological commitment (Kain 2006, pp. 458-9). See also Chignell 2007a, pp. 341-3. For a different view, see Guyer 2000a, p. 364-71 and 2000b, p. 41, Sussman 2001, pp. 117ff., and Caswell 2003, pp. 225ff.

47 Though, as I have suggested elsewhere, some of Kant's comments do suggest that in the special case of agents like us, the postulates may constitute an ontological ground of the *full rational authority* of the moral law or of its command to promote the highest good (Kain 2005, esp. n. 30).

or "outside of us" (20:295, 5:105, 5:474).[48] While the concepts we have of the highest good and of God are determined, they are determined by, "derived from," and "drawn from" our conception of ourselves as moral agents, rather than being derived or drawn from those external objects themselves (20:300, 305, 309).[49] This is all in marked contrast to the case of freedom: freedom is the ontological ground, the *ratio essendi*, of the moral law itself, and freedom is represented as the supersensible in the agent herself, from which the concept itself is drawn.

What remains to be clarified is how these contrasts fit with and exemplify the distinction between practical knowledge and practical belief. In typical cases where the object of a cognition purports to be distinct from the agent or subject (or to be accessed by such a distinct object), one would expect the object to play a significant role in generating the cognition, at least if there is to be knowledge. On Kant's account of the cognitions in question, it turns out to be determinations and rational needs of the subject that predominate. What we believe to be true of these objects is grounded in our rational agency, without even purporting to be grounded in any effect of these realities on us.[50] On this account, we cognize the highest good's real possibility but not *in virtue of* its real possibility. On this account, we cognize God's existence but not *in virtue of* God's existence.[51] Kant contends that such belief is rational and warranted cognition, but that it should be distinguished from cases of theoretical and practical knowledge. While there is no reason to dismiss such belief as illusory, it is an illusion to consider such cognitions knowledge, even if they are true (20:298, 300).[52]

---

48 Though we may, in a slightly different context, also need to represent God as ontological ground, i.e., creator of free beings. The postulates of immortality and of freedom conceived as autocracy may turn out to be more problematic on this score—they seem to be grounds for the real possibility of complete moral adequacy itself (i.e., of the supreme element in the highest good rather than only of highest good as a whole) and they are represented as determinations of the agent herself (though not necessarily ones immediately revealed by the mere fact of obligation—they may involve, for example, the assumption of radical evil).

49 These objects cannot be presented in experience, nor can more experience properly contribute greater determination to our cognitions of them, as if by empirical progression. In the case of "supersensibles," there is no possible (empirical) progression to the determination of concept (5:483). We cannot even fill in much about our contribution to the highest good, in contrast and in relation to God's contribution to it, though there is some discussion of this in *Religion*.

50 Indeed, Kant thinks it is morally important that God and our immortality do not directly effect our cognition of them (5:147).

51 At least in the case of this argument. A successful cosmological argument, or an argument from the dependent nature of finite rational agency that bypassed reference to the highest good might turn out differently.

52 Cf. A473-4/B501-2.

Even if they are true, and the account of our cognition of them is correct, the cognition lacks an objective ground "resting on" or "grounded in" the object and its constitution, which is a requirement for knowledge in Kant's sense.

A Common Concept of Cognition and Knowledge

Cognition, whether practical or theoretical, must involve the representation of a relatively determinate, really possible object. Kant contends that this determinacy and real possibility, in both practical and theoretical cognition, must derive from something given. In the case of theoretical cognition, sensible intuition and its pure form are required. The fact of reason, our immediate awareness of the moral law, is supposed to function analogously. Knowledge, whether practical or theoretical, requires sufficient objective grounds. Kant claims that the relationship between freedom and the fact of reason allows us to cognize their sufficient objective grounds and consider them knowledge, but that the different relationship between the fact of reason, the highest good, and God provides subjective grounds for firm assertoric cognition and confident belief, but cannot provide the objective grounding required for knowledge.

As Lewis White Beck once observed in passing, "the fact of pure reason is the practical corollary of intuition…in converting mere concepts of the logically possible into cognitions that the logically possible is really possible… (Beck 1960, p. 273n).[53] We can add that this fact's differential relationship with other cognitions, its ability or inability to indicate sufficient objective grounds for those cognitions, provides a key for distinguishing between practical knowledge and practical belief, as two forms of warranted practical cognition.[54]

---

53 Cf. p. 173
54 I would like to thank Karl Ameriks, Andrew Chignell, and the editors of this volume for valuable comments on this project.

Section V

Epistemology and Religion

CHAPTER 9

Kant's Reidianism: The Role of Common Sense in Kant's Epistemology of Religious Belief

Lee Hardy

> "It is absolutely necessary that one should con-
> vince oneself that God exists; *that His existence
> should be demonstrated, however, is not so nec-
> essary.*"
>
> Kant, "The Only Possible Ground of Proof for a
> Demonstration of God's Existence" (2:163)

In the circles of reformed epistemology, rarely is an appreciative word
spoken of Immanuel Kant. He is usually cast as the father of modern
"creative anti-realism," and left to stand in that singular role for those
of realist convictions to abhor (see Plantinga 1990, pp. 14-7). Thomas
Reid, on the other hand, enjoys good press in these same circles, for
Reid broke with the demands of classical foundationalism and thus
paved the way to a non-evidentialist account of religious belief. Reid
held that many of our common beliefs are justified not by inferential
procedures, but rather by the native dispositions that spontaneously
produce them. Following this cue, Alvin Plantinga and other reformed
epistemologists have developed a Reidian account of religious belief,
maintaining that belief in God too receives its warrant not from arguments produced by the faculty of reason, but from the proper functioning of a specific belief-producing disposition.

Given his unique role in the recent development of religious epistemology, it is something of a historical irony that Reid himself did not
exploit his dispositional account of basic belief formation in order to
construct a robust, non-evidentialist theory of religious belief. Most of
his discussions of religious belief refer us not to a *sensus divinitatis*, but
rather to the standard arguments for God's existence drawn from the
tradition of natural theology (Tuggy 2004, Helm 2004). In this paper I
want to double this irony by pointing out that while Reid failed to de-

velop a Reidian account of religious belief, the *bête noire* of reformed epistemology, Immanuel Kant, did.

To demonstrate that Kant subscribes to a broadly dispositional account of religious belief, I will have to establish (at least) the following two claims: (1) that, on Kant's view, belief in God is commonly produced by a native disposition; and (2) that the native disposition responsible for belief in God also lends primary warrant to that belief. Given that Kant expends a great deal of philosophical energy attacking the standard speculative arguments for God's existence, and a comparable amount of energy constructing a moral argument for God's existence, I should add a third claim that in effect amplifies the second: (3) the primary warrant for belief in God is secured apart from proof or argument. This is to say that the absence of valid speculative arguments for God's existence does not deprive belief in God of its primary warrant; and conversely, that the primary warrant for belief in God does not depend on the presence of moral arguments for God's existence. This last point will have to be finessed, given that the presence of potential speculative defeaters of religious belief may call for a critical defeater of those defeaters. Thus, what could be called the secondary warrant for belief in God may in some way depend on the success of the critical defeater. For some persons in some contexts, then, the justification of religious belief may depend upon arguments both theoretical and moral.

The third claim deserves a preliminary comment. Presupposed in the notion that the primary warrant for religious belief is independent of philosophical argument is a distinction between what is required for the justification of philosophical knowledge claims and what is required for the justification of common belief. Descartes made a distinction between standards of justification—a distinction between the metaphysical certainty required for philosophical knowledge and the practical certainty that suffices for the conduct of life (Descartes 1985, pp. 289-90). By the time of Locke, it seems, many philosophers were committed to giving a one-size-fits-all evidentialist account of justified belief.[1] I think Kant is best read on the assumption that he allows for different standards of justification and that those standards vary with respect to the type or purpose of belief. Here the relevant distinction is between the kind of justification required for the construction of a system of

---

1   "Reason must be our last judge and guide in everything." So claims Locke in his *Essay Concerning Human Understanding* (Locke 1700, IV.xix.14). Knowledge is generated on the basis of reason's insight into necessary relations between abstract ideas, and is, for that reason, fairly restricted in scope. The vast domain of opinion, which operates on probabilities, must nonetheless be regulated by reason. The firmness of belief in matters of opinion must be proportioned to reason's insight into the probability of that belief being true on available evidence (see Wolterstorff 1996).

theoretical knowledge and the kind of justification required for beliefs we find necessary in practice. In the Transcendental Doctrine of Method, toward the end of the *Critique of Pure Reason*, Kant notes that, "In regard to its practical use reason still has the right to assume something which it would in no way be warranted in presupposing in the field of mere speculation without sufficient grounds of proof.... There it thus has a possession the legitimacy of which need not be proved, and the proof of which it could not in fact give" (A776/B804). Certain kinds of practical belief, then, can be warranted without proof. In this paper I will argue that the source of their warrant lies, ultimately, in the dispositional arrangements of common sense or common human understanding.[2] Kant does not demand that common sense beliefs justify themselves according to the standards of theoretical knowledge; neither does he let the speculative philosopher get by with anything short of apodictic certainty (Axv, A781/B809). Philosophical knowledge and common belief have their own distinct standards and sources of legitimacy.

The legitimate religious beliefs of the common understanding, however, do not count as knowledge in Kant's book. Knowledge, for Kant, always requires the givenness of the relevant object in experience (or transcendental reflection on the possibility of an object being given in experience) (A782-3/B810-1). This requirement cannot be met, Kant holds, in the case of God or the afterlife. The religious beliefs of the common understanding draw upon subjective, not objective, sources, and for that reason will never count as knowledge even though they are justified. For Kant, then, not all forms of justified belief are knowledge. Knowledge must meet strict standards of evidence and demonstration, yielding apodictic certainty. But there are other kinds of justification, and indeed other kinds of certainty.

From Speculation to Practice

I begin with an extended passage from the B Preface to the first *Critique* that opens up the possibility of a dispositional account of common religious belief:

---

2   In *Anthropology from a Pragmatic Point of View*, Kant says that the judgments of "common sense" do not come from sense, but from the understanding—the "real, though obscure, deliberations of the understanding" (7:145; I am using the Victor Lyle Dowdell translation, Kant 1978b); later he says that "sound human understanding is also called common sense" (*Ibid.*, 7:168). So I take the two terms to be equivalent in Kant, although he holds "common understanding" to be the more accurate of the two.

I ask the most inflexible dogmatist whether the proof of the continuation of
our soul after death drawn from the simplicity of substance, or the proof of
freedom of the will against universal mechanism drawn from the subtle though
powerless distinctions between subjective and objective practical necessity, or
the proof of the existence of God drawn from the concept of a most real being
(or from the contingency of what is alterable and the necessity of a first
mover), have ever, after originating in the schools, been able to reach the public or have the least influence over its convictions? If that has never happened,
and if it can never be expected to happen, owing to the unsuitability of the
common human understanding [*des gemeinen Menschenverstandes*] for such
subtle speculations; if rather the conviction that one finds widespread throughout the public, insofar as it rests on rational grounds, has to be effected by
something else—namely, as regards the first point, on that remarkable predisposition of our nature [*Anlage seine Natur*], noticeable to every human being,
never to be capable of being satisfied by what is temporal (since the temporal
is always insufficient for the predispositions of our whole vocation) leading us
to the hope of a future life; in respect of the second point, the mere clear exposition of our duties in opposition to all claims of the inclinations leading to the
consciousness of freedom; and finally, touching on the third point, the splendid order, beauty, and providence shown forth everywhere in nature leading to
the faith in a wise and great author of the world—then this possession not only
remains undisturbed, but it even gains in respect through the fact that now the
schools are instructed to pretend to no higher or more comprehensive insight
on any point touching the universal human concerns than the insight that is accessible to the great multitude (who are always worthy of our respect) and to
limit themselves to the cultivation of those grounds of proof [*Beweisgründe*]
alone that can be grasped universally and are sufficient from a moral standpoint. (Bxxxii-xxxiii, translation modified[3])

Here Kant is preparing the dogmatists for the loss they will suffer at the
hands of his unsparing criticism of natural theology. If the speculative
arguments for central religious beliefs are one and all fallacious, and if
their logical inadequacies are exposed to the public—as they will be in
the Transcendental Dialectic—should we then anticipate the imminent
collapse of religion? Will the demolition of natural theology open the
floodgates of atheism? Not at all, Kant maintains. For common religious beliefs never were held on speculative grounds, nor could they
be; the arguments are too subtle, too refined and complicated, to serve
as their basis. Later, in his discussion of the philosophical argument for
the immortality of the soul, Kant claims that this "merely speculative

---

3   The Guyer and Wood translation of this passage has religious convictions "reaching"
     the public on the basis of our predispositions together with our consciousness of the
     moral law and the splendid order of creation. The German verb translated as "reaches"
     is not *gelangen* but *sich verbreiten*. Thus I modify the translation as follows: "the con-
     viction that one finds widespread throughout the public." This is important for my the-
     sis, since I want to claim that warrant here does not reach the public from the outside,
     but is rather generated within the public on the basis of indigenous dispositions.

proof has never been able to have an influence on common human reason [*die gemeine Menschenvernunft*]. It so turns on a hairsplitting point that even the schools can retain it only as long as they can keep it standing there spinning around ceaselessly like a top, and thus even in their own eyes it provides no persisting foundation on which anything could be built" (B424). If we are searching for adequate and enduring grounds of religious belief, clearly we must look elsewhere.

The elimination of speculative argument as a basis for religious belief leaves us with two options: either belief in God is based on non-speculative arguments, or it is not based on arguments at all. In his *Lectures on the Philosophical Doctrine of Religion*, Kant claims that "it is impossible for speculative reason to demonstrate the existence of such a being [God] with apodictic certainty; but he [the theist] is nevertheless firmly convinced of the existence of this being, and he has faith beyond all doubt on practical grounds. The foundation on which he builds his faith is unshakeable and it can never be overthrown..." (28:1011). There are legitimate, stable and pervasive grounds for religious belief; but they are to be found in the practical sphere rather than the speculative. The question I want to address in this study is the following: are the practical grounds for religious belief primarily evidential or dispositional?[4] Is basic religious belief in the first instance grounded in the moral argument for God's existence, or is it grounded in what Kant sometimes calls the "moral predisposition," a predisposition that inclines us to believe in the existence of God upon experience of the moral law or the manifest order of the universe? The first option holds that Kant wishes to base religious belief on argument: not on speculative argument, but on moral argument. Presumably the moral argument would be a more suitable support for general belief because its premises are more accessible to the masses and because the argument itself is simpler, so simple that even the inferentially challenged can grasp its persuasive power. Although there are textual bases for thinking Kant goes in this direction, I will argue that he takes the dispositional option instead. I will do so on the basis of three considerations: first, the language of compulsion and immediacy we find in Kant's phenomenology of common religious belief; second, what I shall call Kant's populism; and third, the secondary role Kant assigns to philosophical argument in securing warrant for religious belief.

---

4   In the common-sense tradition, reason also counts as a disposition. From the perspective of this tradition, then, the contrast I want to make would be between two kinds of dispositions: reason, which moves us to belief on the basis of evidential relations between propositions explicitly apprehended; and others kinds of belief-producing dispositions, which take us from certain kinds of experience to certain beliefs without the mediation of inference.

If Kant holds that common human understanding moves from experiential grounds to beliefs by way of a disposition, and that the beliefs in question are warranted just by virtue of being produced in this way, then Kant holds to a broadly Reidian account of common religious belief even though he remains interested in constructing moral arguments for core religious convictions. On this reading, the moral arguments are not needed to prop up religious belief in the absence of the support formerly provided by speculative arguments. All that is needed for common religious belief are certain experiential grounds plus a certain disposition—a moral disposition (*moralische Gesinnung*) in which religious beliefs are "interwoven" (*verwebt*) (A829/B827). Granted, in the extended quote above, Kant recommends arguments for common religious convictions whose grounds of proof (*Beweisgründe*) are accessible to the public. But he says that the schools, not the public, should cultivate the arguments based on those grounds. In Kant's view, expressed in *Groundwork of the Metaphysics of Morals*, philosophical arguments are for philosophers, and for all those who have been adversely affected by errant philosophical arguments (see 4:404-6).

The interpretive picture of Kant I want to develop, then, is this: common human understanding naturally moves from certain experiential grounds to certain religious beliefs by way of a moral predisposition; these beliefs are fully warranted just by virtue of being generated in this way; but the philosopher can construct—or reconstruct— practically sufficient arguments from those same grounds (taken as premises) to the same religious beliefs (which will now count as conclusions). Thus the rational cultivation of the *Beweisgründe* in the development of the moral argument is best understood as an explication of the common human understanding—an explication that is required for the justification of religious belief, I will argue, only in special circumstances.

The Design Argument

I should point to one curiosity in the extended passage from the B Preface quoted above. In his list of speculative arguments marked for demolition, Kant does not mention the design argument, what he calls, in the Transcendental Dialectic, the "physico-theological proof." This argument for God's existence, along with the ontological and cosmological arguments, is roundly criticized in the first *Critique*. Why is it absent from the hit list in the preface? And why does this argument, or, at least, the grounds of this argument (the experience of splendid order in the universe) appear in the list of legitimate grounds for religious belief, grounds awaiting philosophical cultivation? The answer, I think, is threefold. First, Kant maintains that the grounds of this argument are commonly accessible. The ontological argument presupposes acquaintance with the metaphysical idea of God as the *ens realissimum*—hardly an everyday concept. The cosmological argument trades on the distinction between necessary and contingent existence—again, a distinction we are rarely motivated to draw in everyday life (2:124). But all of us have experienced and, Kant would add, marveled at the "majesty of the world's architecture" (A625/B652). This is a relevant consideration if one holds that Kant, in developing his arguments for God's existence, is doing little more than explicating what is already available in common human understanding. Second, it is possible, in Kant's view, to construct an argument from the experience of order to the existence of God that is sufficient for the purposes of practical life. So, although the design argument for God's existence fails as a speculative argument for all the reasons Hume points out, its conclusion gets a second chance as a warranted practical hypothesis. Again, Kant has a differentiated theory of justification. What fails to meet the requirements of theoretical proof may meet the requirements of legitimate belief in the practical sphere. Third, even apart from an explicitly formulated practical argument, common human reason has an innate tendency to move from the experience of order to the belief in an intelligent cause. For this reason, Kant says, the design argument should always be mentioned with respect, not because it is deductively valid, but because it is the "most appropriate to common human reason" (A623/B651).

The epistemic status of belief in God as the intelligent cause of the universe is best apprehended in the context of Kant's general taxonomy of belief. In the third section of the Canon of Pure Reason, Kant marks out two bases for holding something to be true: objective grounds (*Gründen*) and subjective causes (*Ursachen*) (A821/B849). Objective grounds are, as one might suspect, rooted in the nature of the object given in experience, and for that reason capable of compelling intersubjective agreement. Subjective causes are rooted in the nature of the doxastic subject. Both bases can be either sufficient or insufficient. Sufficient subjective causes of belief must be rooted in the common structure of the human mind, or "reason" in the broad sense, if the resultant beliefs are to express the generically human take on the world, not a merely individual take. They answer to the "needs of reason," as Kant puts it in "What Does it Mean to Orient Oneself in Thinking?" (8:139). Beliefs produced by such causes compel consensus, not because they refer to an intersubjectively accessible object given in experience, but because they are required by the universal structure of human rationality. Holding something to be true on the basis of insufficient objective grounds and insufficient subjective causes is mere opinion. Holding something to be true on the basis of sufficient objective grounds and sufficient subjective causes counts as knowledge. Legitimate belief, in contrast to both opinion and knowledge, is based upon insufficient objective grounds and sufficient subjective causes. Belief in God falls into this category.

Or, at least, into a sub-species of this category. Never one to shy away from distinctions, Kant identifies three species of legitimate belief: pragmatic, doctrinal, and moral. All three have to do with what we must assume, but cannot prove, in the course of practical life. We cannot prove God's existence, but we are nonetheless compelled as moral agents to believe that God exists because God is the condition of the possibility of realizing the end we necessarily will as subjects of the moral law. For this reason Kant says that belief in God, while objectively indemonstrable, is subjectively well-founded (A827/B855). Although belief in God as the intelligent cause of the world also has an important role to play in any coherent moral life (see the discussion of teleological judgment in section 87 of the *Critique of the Power of Judgment*), Kant first discusses this belief in the Canon with respect to more exclusively theoretical concerns. There is an analogue to the moral postulate of God's existence within the theoretical domain (A825/B853). In this context, belief in God counts as a doctrinal belief, not a moral belief. A doctrinal belief is theoretical, in that it is a belief about an object that exists independently of what we do; nonetheless this belief serves as the basis for doing something. While it is not itself a practical belief, it plays a role in theoretical practice. The practice of theory, Kant maintains, requires that we believe that the world has a purposive unity, and that this unity has its origin in an intelligent cause. Although with respect to the body of theoretical knowledge about nature, I am under no obligation to posit the existence of God, nevertheless,

> purposive unity is still so important a condition of the application of reason to nature that I cannot pass it by, especially since experience liberally supplies examples of it. But I know no other condition for this unity that could serve me as a clue for the investigation of nature except insofar as I presuppose that a highest intelligence has arranged everything in accordance with the wisest ends. Consequently, the presupposition of a wise author of the world is a condition of an aim which is, to be sure, contingent but yet not inconsiderable, namely that of having a guide for the investigation of nature. The outcome of my experiments also so often confirms the usefulness of the presupposition, and nothing can be decisively said against it, so that I would say too little if I called my taking it to be true merely having an opinion, but rather even in this theoretical relation it can be said that I firmly believe in God; but in this case

> this belief must not strictly be called practical, but must be called a doctrinal belief, which the theology of nature (physico-theology) must everywhere necessarily produce. (A826-7/B854-5)

Again, by Kant's lights, we cannot prove that there is an intelligent cause of the world. The grounds for this belief are objectively insufficient. But we must assume that there is such a cause if we are to attempt a coherent theoretical explanation of the world—especially the biological world—as an orderly system of reciprocal causes and functions (A317-8/B374). Hence the belief is subjectively required. The belief in an intelligent cause of the universe motivates the search for order beyond that presently known or experienced; and the subsequent discovery of ever-increasing fields of order in turn reinforces the belief in an intelligent cause—to the point that, as Kant notes in the Transcendental Dialectic, "it becomes an irresistible conviction" (A624/B652).

Thus, in Kant's view, objections to the design argument drawn from "abstract speculation" will do little to dislodge the well-entrenched belief that stands at its conclusion (A624/B652). But that's not because Kant is willing to give a wink and a nod to the irrational forces of common belief-formation. On the contrary, he says he has "nothing to object against the rationality and utility of this procedure" (A624/B652). This may seem an odd admission, however, since he is about to show that the design argument is a bad one. The apparent tension in Kant's attitudes can be resolved if we remind ourselves that he only intends to show that the design argument is a bad deductive argument. The procedure of common human reason and its extension in the sciences does not derive God's existence as the conclusion of a deductive argument, but posits it as an explanatory hypothesis, a hypothesis that receives fresh confirmation everywhere experience and research conducted under its auspices turn. So the "proof" here is powerful, but "only empirical" (A624/B652). It has its own kind of hypothetical-deductive rationality. Kant's criticism of the design argument seeks only to deflate it as a deductive argument, pointing out that the proof of an intelligent cause will always fall short of the "apodictic certainty" required for knowledge (A624/B652).

The Moral Argument

Moral belief in the existence of God, as opposed to doctrinal belief, is subjectively stronger, for the practical end served by the belief is not contingent, but necessary. I may or may not engage in an attempt to understand and explain the workings of the natural world. That end is optional. But the moral end is not optional—I ought to "fulfill the moral law in all points" (A828/B856). Therefore positing the condition under which alone that end is possible is not optional either: "The end here is inescapably fixed, and according to all my insight there is possible only a single condition under which this end is consistent with all ends together and thereby has practical validity, namely, that there be a God and a future world" (A828/B856). So, "I will inexorably believe in the existence of God and a future life, and I am sure that nothing can make these beliefs unstable, since my moral principles themselves, which I cannot renounce without becoming contemptible in my own eyes, would thereby be subverted" (A828/B856). Again, the existence of God cannot be proven: "Pure *rational faith* can never be transformed into knowledge by any natural data of reason and experience, because here the ground of holding true is merely subjective, namely a necessary need of reason (and as long as we are human beings it will always remain a need) to *presuppose* the existence of a highest being, but not to demonstrate it" (8:141). Moral belief in the existence of God is not the conclusion of a speculative argument. It is not a theoretical hypothesis confirmed in the course of empirical research. It is, as Kant maintains in the *Critique of Practical Reason*, a necessary postulate of the moral life (5:143).

The moral argument for God's existence proceeds from practical grounds—from the experience of the moral law and the good it enjoins us to promote—to the condition of the possibility of realizing that good. Kant holds that the good we are to envision insofar as our will is determined by the moral law is the perfect and proportionate convergence of virtue and happiness. Since we, as finite agents, are not in a position to bring about this good, we must assume the existence of a being who both wills that good and is powerful and intelligent enough to bring it about. That being is the God of classical theism (see A815/B843):

> Morality in itself constitutes a system, but happiness does not, except insofar as it is distributed precisely in accordance with morality. This, however, is possible only in the intelligible world, under a wise author and regent. Reason sees itself as compelled either to assume such a thing, together with life in such a world, which we must regard as a future one, or else to regard the moral laws as empty figments of the brain, since without that presupposition their necessary success, which the same reason connects with them, would have to disappear. (A811/B839; see also 5:114)

The moral argument, then, is not an apodictic demonstration of God's existence. Morality, for all we know, could be an empty figment of the human brain. But the argument does show us what we must believe if we are to make sense of our moral experience and commitments, "thereby making it [the belief in God] into not a demonstrated dogma

but yet an absolutely necessary presupposition for reason's most essential ends" (A818/B846).

Belief by Disposition

The postulation of God's existence is subjectively necessary on the part
of a finite moral agent. It is required if practical reason is to be coherent. Despite that necessity, belief in God falls short of knowledge
(A829/B827). The conviction of God's existence is a matter of moral
certainty, not logical certainty; it trades on the requirements of practical
life, not the achievements of natural theology (A829/B827). But when
it comes to the justification of religious belief, are we only contrasting
the merits of two different kinds of argument: the theoretical and the
moral, the objectively sufficient and the subjectively sufficient? I think
not. For Kant holds that beneath the level of philosophical argumentation, the moral certainty of belief in God finds ample support in the
subjective grounds (*subjektiven Gründen*) of our moral disposition
(*moralischen Gesinnung*) (A829/B857). In fact, this belief is so deeply
embedded in our moral constitution that it is unlikely to be dislodged
by any philosophical considerations: "The belief in a God and another
world is so interwoven with my moral disposition [*moralischen Gesinnung*] that I am in as little danger of ever surrendering the former as I
am worried that the latter can ever be torn away from me"
(A829/B857). Granted, the concepts of God and the immortality of the
soul are concepts, "the possibility of which no human understanding
will ever fathom." Nonetheless, "no sophistry will ever convince even
the most common human being that they are not true concepts" (5:133-
4).
 I read these passages as claiming that the moral disposition generates the beliefs necessary for making sense of the moral life, and that
such beliefs have legitimacy by virtue of being so generated. Of course,
philosophers can produce an argument for belief in God and a future
life on moral grounds. But, Kant says, "this much common human understanding [*der gemeine Verstand*] could also have accomplished
without taking advice from the philosophers" (A830/B858). This comment indicates that, in Kant's estimation, the moral argument for God's
existence is not an artifact of the common human understanding.
Rather, it is the work of the schools. Nonetheless the common understanding does produce belief in God and a future life. Does it do so by
way of another, simpler argument, or by way of some dispositional
arrangement? Kant does not refer to another argument. But he does

refer to dispositions, dispositions with which religious beliefs are, as he says, "interwoven." And in describing the work of these dispositions, he often uses the language of feeling, compulsion, and immediacy, not inference. In *Religion within the Boundaries of Mere Reason*, Kant claims that belief in an afterlife, a basic element of religious belief, "*imposes itself* upon [*dringt sich auf*] everyone by virtue of the universal moral predisposition [*Anlage*] in human nature" (6:126, my emphasis). In the third *Critique*, he states that "even the most common human reason is *compelled* to give *immediate* assent" to the existence of a supreme intelligent cause that wills the creation of a human community bound by the moral law (5:447, my emphasis). Elsewhere Kant speaks of cases whereupon having a certain kind of experience, the human mind "feels a need" to form a certain belief (5:445); or in which we "feel an inner conviction on *practical grounds* that *a God must exist*" (28:1027); or that, upon perceiving purposiveness in creation, we are "compelled" to believe that behind creation stands an intelligent supreme cause (27:716). In "The Only Possible Ground of Proof for a Demonstration of God's Existence," Kant makes the striking claim that failure to believe in a wise author of nature when confronted with the functional complexity of living organisms is not the result of a lapse in reasoning but rather of a malformed disposition (2:125). In the same essay, he speaks of a common sense that "leads us directly" to a belief in God "without the sophistry of subtle inferences" (2:65). Such language suggests that when Kant claims in the second *Critique* that belief in God "has itself arisen from the moral disposition" (5:146), the "arising" he has in mind is not one of inference from premise to conclusion, but the rather the immediate production of belief from an underlying doxastic propensity.

Kant's Populism

The idea that basic religious beliefs are generated by the native moral dispositions of the human mind, and not the art of reasoning, sits well with what I call Kant's populism: the notion that the beliefs required for a good human life are the currency of common sense and not restricted to or dependent upon the accomplishments of an intellectual elite. True religion, Kant says in the *Religion*, must be accessible to all, not just the wise: "the whole human race should be capable of this faith…even the ignorant or those most limited conceptually, must be able to lay claim to such instruction and inner conviction" (6:181). As it turns out, this cosmic fairness requirement is satisfied by the fact that true religion is "inscribed in the heart of all human beings" (6:159). So "if one wanted to make an experiment, he would find that this faith can be elicited from every human being, upon questioning, in its entirety, without it ever having been taught to him" (6:181-2).

The same sentiment is expressed in the first *Critique*. The line from the previous section about what common human understanding can accomplish apart from the advice of philosophers is intended, rhetorically, as an expression of incredulity that such an august power as pure reason can do little more than clear the ground for religious convictions. Kant immediately responds in his own voice: "But do you demand then that a cognition that pertains to all human beings should surpass common understanding [*den gemeinen Verstand*] and be revealed to you only by philosophers?" (A831/B859). That so little hangs on the inferential labors of reason goes to show that

> in what concerns all human beings without exception nature is not to be blamed for any partiality in the distribution of its gifts, and in regard to the essential ends of human nature even the highest philosophy cannot advance further than the guidance that nature has also conferred on the most common understanding [*dem gemeinstem Verstande*]. (A831/B859)

I suggest that we give a dispositional reading to the phrase "guidance of nature" [*die Leitung der Natur*]. The subjective basis for religious belief is, Kant notes earlier in the Canon, causal, not logical (A820/B848, A828/B856).

The picture of common religious belief formation I have been developing follows these basic contours: prior to and independently of the moral argument for God's existence, common human understanding operates not logically but dispositionally. It takes us from certain experiences to belief in God and in a future life. It does not do so by way of explicit inference. Rather, upon having certain kinds of experience, one finds oneself, under the direction of this disposition, having a certain kind of belief. Later, one can spell out the logic of that transition, but the transition itself is not originally an operation based on explicit awareness of the evidential relations between propositions. This, of course, is the main point of reformed epistemology of religious belief. Alvin Plantinga, in "Reason and Belief in God," describes how a such disposition might operate in various settings:

> When life is sweet and satisfying, a spontaneous sense of gratitude may well up within the soul; someone in this condition may thank and praise the Lord for his goodness…Upon reading the Bible, one may be impressed with a deep sense that God is speaking to him. Upon having done what I know is cheap, or wrong, or wicked, I may feel guilty in God's sight and form the belief *God disapproves of what I have done.* (Plantinga 1990, p. 80; order of examples altered)

Now turn to Kant's own description of the doxastic work of the common moral disposition in the third *Critique*. The parallels with the phenomenology of religious belief offered by Plantinga should be obvious:

> Consider a person at those moments in which his mind is disposed to moral sensation. If, surrounded by a beautiful nature, he finds himself in peaceful and cheerful enjoyment of his existence, he feels a need to be thankful to someone for it. Or if, on another occasion, he finds himself in the same state of mind under the press of duties which he can and will satisfy only through voluntary sacrifice, he feels a need to have done something that was commanded and to have obeyed an overlord. Or if he has in some heedless way acted contrary to his duty, although without having become answerable to other people, nevertheless a strong self-reproach will speak to him as if it were the voice of a judge to whom he must give account for his action. (5:446)

These feelings, and the beliefs embedded within them, are connected to a moral disposition and take place, Kant claims, "without any regard to a theoretical proof" (5:446); here the "inner moral vocation" of the mind is "directing us to conceive of the supreme cause" (5:448). A natural reading of this passage would lead us to believe that, for Kant, belief in God is a product of a moral disposition triggered by certain circumstances—here the experience of natural beauty, of duty, and of guilt. This reading is supported by Kant's claim in the *Lectures on Metaphysics* that cognition of the existence of God and a future life is available to every human being on the basis of "common sense" simply by "considering nature and one's state." No speculative inquiry, he says, is required (29:938), just an experience of the starry heavens above and the moral law within.

Critical Philosophy as Explication and Defense

Up to this point I have been working with a sharp distinction between the dispositional and evidential basis for religious belief. The distinction has been of some service in laying out the issues. But it is now time to blur it. Although the two poles of the distinction still hold, a gradient needs to be introduced to accommodate the way Kant thinks about the relation between the two. With this move, the binary distinction between dispositional and evidential grounds for religious belief morphs into a continuum between the implicit and explicit rationality of religious belief. At the extreme ends of the continuum the dispositional and evidential labels still apply; but the intervening gradient highlights an underlying continuity between the two along with the intermediate degrees of consciousness or explicitness attending the grounds of belief. On the side of common understanding, one finds oneself compelled, led, or guided to a belief by some native disposition; on the side of philosophical reflection and analysis, one begins to apprehend reasons for that belief, reasons that were implicit in the dispositional arrangements of common sense, but are now articulated to the point where their evidential relations can be appreciated. Between the two, there is a continuity of content, which is why the philosophical arguments developed from the *Beweisgründe* of common sense remain in principle accessible to common sense, and why, as Kant claims in the logic lectures, the content of common sense remains the touchstone for good philosophy, however much philosophy may add from its own resources (9:57, 9:79; see also 7:139-40 and 20:301). It is also why, in the transition from the wholly pre-reflective beliefs of the common understanding to the explicit philosophical account of their rationality, it is hard to draw a firm line of demarcation. As Kant notes, "There is some difficulty in determining the limits where the *common* use of the understanding ends and the *speculative* begins" (9:27).

The relation between common sense and philosophy can be understood in terms of the biological metaphor Kant employs in describing the structure and development of our cognitive capacities and the analytic task of critical philosophy. The metaphor is drawn from the embryological debates circulating through the German academy during the eighteenth century. The two sides of this debate were the "preformationists" and the "epigeneticists." Preformation theories, already advanced by Malebranche in 1674, held that organisms were constituted in miniature in the act of creation and encased in either the ovaries or spermatozoa. Future generations lie embedded in prior generations like a series of Russian dolls, waiting their appointed times of growth and discrete viability. Epigenetic theories held that organisms are not preformed, but formed afresh in each round of generation from organic matter under the influence of certain "vital powers," or, as Buffon had it (1749), micro-forces similar to those at work in the formation of crystals.[5] In the 1760s, an intermediate theory was developed by Albrecht van Haller and Charles Bonnet. From the preformationists they took the idea of a pre-existing seed (*Keim*) which provides the basic structure of the organism according to its species; from the epigeneticists, the notion that the activation and development of the seed is influenced by forces that mediate between the seed and its environment, giving rise to variation within a species. This mediating factor was most often called an *Anlage* (usually translated as "predisposition"). One might think of *Anlagen* as principles of adaptation, a set of dynamic propensities to respond to the environment. The *Keim* accounts for the relative stability

---

5   Here I follow Phillip R. Sloan in Sloan 2002.

of the species; the *Anlagen* for variation within a species. In "The Only Possible Ground of Proof for a Demonstration of God's Existence" (1763), Kant attributes adaptive variations within a species to a "single predisposition [*Anlagen*]" (2:126, my translation), emphasizing the unity of the cause for a variety of organic effects.

Kant's reference to embryological theory in the announcement for his lectures in physical geography in 1775 (2:429-43) clearly indicates that he subscribed to the middle account developed by Haller and Bonnet. There he states that the basis for the structured unfolding of the parts of an organism lies in seeds [*Keime*]; while the size and relations of the parts of the organism are governed by certain natural predispositions [*Anlagen*] together with variable environmental conditions. In birds of the same species, for example, seeds for an additional layer of feathers will be activated by a natural predisposition in cold climates, and suppressed in hot climates (2:434-5).[6]

It is also clear that Kant used this account of organic structure and variation as a chief metaphor in characterizing our cognitive capacities. The Transcendental Analytic of the first *Critique* should not be understood as an analysis of concepts and their content, but rather, Kant insists, as an analysis of the faculty of understanding itself.[7] It traces *a priori* concepts back "into their first seeds [*Keime*] and predispositions [*Anlagen*] in the human understanding, where they lie ready, until with the opportunity of experience, they are finally developed and exhibited in their clarity by the very same understanding" (A66/B91). The analytic exercise Kant proposes here is carried out in the interest of responding to Hume's skepticism regarding the objective validity of such common-sense concepts as substance and causality. In tracing the origin of such concepts back to the seeds and predispositions of the human mind, rather than experience, he shows that their origin is *a priori*; in providing a defense of their claims to objective validity in the transcendental deduction—whereby he establishes these concepts as conditions of experience—he shows that their claims are necessarily valid for all objects of experience. All this he accomplishes by making the implicit

---

6   In Kant's essay on race (*Die Bestimmung des Begriffs einer Menschenrasse*, 1785), the following picture emerges: both *Keime* and *Anlagen* are built into a *Stamm*, an original generative stock; which seeds are activated, and the degree to which they are activated depends on environmental factors, giving rise to morphological variety within a species or, indeed, within a phylum. Again, organic stability and structural limits are accounted for by the original organization of the *Stamm*; variety by the range of *Keime* embedded in the *Stamm*, and the *Anlagen* by which they are activated. See Lenoir 1980.

7   For a discussion of the significance of the transcendental analytic as the self-analysis of reason, see Smit 1999.

structure and operations of the mind explicit in his particular brand of philosophical analysis.

In recommending this line of response to "Hume's problem," Kant at the same time famously condemns the solution proposed by the Scottish common-sense philosophers. It is important to see here, however, that Kant does not object to common sense itself; he objects only to the appeal to common sense as the final arbiter in philosophical matters. Kant too wishes to defend common sense and its doxastic produce, rooted as it is in the seeds and native predispositions of our cognitive capacities. But the philosophical defense of common sense cannot consist in an appeal to the fact of common sense, nor in an appeal to the utility of common sense, nor in an appeal to the veracity of the Creator of common sense. Rather, it must provide a convincing argument in support of common sense. This requires deep inquiries into the nature of our cognitive faculties. The direct appeal to common sense in the face of skepticism amounts to nothing more, Kant maintains in the *Prolegomena to Any Future Metaphysics*, than defiance without insight (4:269; see also A784-5/B811-2 and A855/B883). What is called for is a philosophical justification of common sense based on insight into the tacit structure and obscure operations of the human mind. Kant takes himself to have provided just such a justification in the Transcendental Analytic of the first *Critique*. Common-sense philosophers, on the other hand, provide no such analysis and argument, a sure sign that they have given up on philosophy—and on an adequate defense of the very faculties they claim to honor.

Common Sense, Skepticism, Critical Philosophy

In his first *Critique*, Kant establishes the pattern of his general conception of the relation between philosophy and common sense. That pattern has a tripartite dialectical structure: Default Position/Potential Defeater/Critical Defeater-Defeater. The default position is grounded in the dispositional arrangements of common sense and its doxastic output. This position is on occasion confronted by potential speculative defeaters (for example, Humean skepticism). In defense of the default position, critical philosophy provides speculative defeaters for those defeaters, which common sense is incapable of providing on its own.[8]

---

8   See Guyer 2003 for a similar representation of the relation between common sense and philosophy. Guyer, however, claims that in Kant's view common sense is subject to a "natural dialectic" and is thus inherently dependent on critical philosophy for its coherence. I think common sense is not dependent upon critical philosophy for the truth of

The philosophical defense of common sense, however, is not imported from the outside; rather, philosophy defends common sense by making explicit its implicit rationality. Between common sense and philosophy, then, one should expect a commonality of content, even if there is a difference in the degree of awareness of that content.[9]

This basic dialectical pattern is also exemplified in Kant's critical work in moral philosophy, and again in his philosophy of religion. The relation between common sense and critical moral philosophy is already foreshadowed in the Transcendental Aesthetic of the first *Critique*, where Kant says that "the concept of right that is used by the healthy understanding contains the very same things that the most subtle speculation can evolve out of it, only in common and practical use one is not conscious of these same manifold representations in these thoughts" (A43/B61). Later, in the Preface to the *Groundwork*, Kant again characterizes moral philosophy as an explication, or analysis, of common human understanding. In moral matters, Kant claims, the common understanding is largely correct (4:391); it stands in need of no enlightenment from the moral philosopher. Thus in the *Groundwork* he proposes only to "proceed analytically from common cognition" to the determination of its supreme principle (4:392). The task is to "explicate the concept of a will that is to be esteemed in itself and that is good apart from any further purpose, as it already dwells in natural sound understanding and needs not so much to be taught as only to be clarified" (4:397). What is good is done solely out of respect for the moral law—this is in fact the principle of "the moral cognition of common human reason" (4:403). In firm possession of this principle, common human reason has no need of philosophy in order to know what counts as a moral action (4:404). In fact, philosophical reflection on this point is often counter-productive, muddying the antecedent clarity of common moral judgment. Kant notes in his logic lectures that "the common understanding often judges more correctly concerning matters of morality and duty than does the speculative" (9:79). If philosophy is to provide any assistance to common moral understanding, it

---

its claims; but it may be dependent upon critical philosophy for the correct ontological interpretation of its claims, thus sparing it from various antinomies. For Kant's reservations about the philosophical competence of common sense, see B167-8, A473/B501, and A528/B556.

9   I am not arguing that the doctrines of Transcendental Idealism are implicit in common sense. Philosophy brings something of its own construction to the debate with the skeptics. But it is important to realize that, in the elaboration of his theoretical philosophy, Kant is attempting to preserve and defend the content of common-sense against its detractors. In his practical philosophy, on the other hand, I think it is entirely plausible to hold that Kant is elevating the content of common sense to the level of theory; see A43-4/B61.

can do so only by defending what such understanding already knows against various errant moral theories motivated by our natural propensity to subordinate duty to inclination. Otherwise common moral understanding has no need of philosophy.

Although here we do not have an example of philosophy analytically deriving belief in God from common moral understanding, we do have a case of philosophy standing in relation to common understanding as *explicans* to *explicatum*. Can we take the moral argument for God's existence to be a continuation of this line of philosophical explication: from our native grasp of the moral law to the end envisioned by that law, then to the condition of the possibility of realizing that end? This is how Kant represents the situation toward the end of the third *Critique*. Having spelled out once again the moral proof for God's existence, Kant points out that "This moral proof is not any newly invented argument, but at most only a newly articulated one; for it lay in the human faculty of reason even before its earliest germination, and with the progressive cultivation of that faculty has merely become more developed" (5:458).

When we move from the domain of practical philosophy to religious belief, the general settings for Kant's approach still hold. Core religious beliefs—belief in God and in an afterlife—are generated by native moral predispositions operating upon certain kinds of experience, as the descriptive passage from the third Critique above suggests. Such beliefs do not require proofs either for their production or for their justification. To hold otherwise would be to limit justified religious belief to a small subset of humanity, violating Kant's deeply held populism. At the outset of his pre-critical essay on the design argument, Kant freely admits that what is essential in religious belief has been delivered to us through the agency of common sense, apart from the argument he is about to expound:

> I do not esteem the use of an endeavor, such as the present one, so highly as to suppose that the most important of all our cognitions, *there is a God*, would waver or be imperiled if it were not supported by deep metaphysical investigations. It was not the will of Providence that the insights so necessary to our happiness should depend upon the sophistry of subtle inferences. On the contrary, Providence has directly transmitted these insights to our natural common sense [*natürlichen gemeinen Verstande*]. And, provided that it is not confused by false art, it does not fail to lead us directly to what is true and useful, for we are in extreme need of these two things. (2:65)

The equanimity of common-sense belief in God is disturbed, however, once the false art of religious skepticism makes its appearance. At that point, a simple appeal to common sense will do little good. Philosophy must come to the rescue. But here the dialectical situation differs markedly from the one created by Humean skepticism, as the issues under contest—the existence of God and the reality of an afterlife—go far beyond speculative reason's sphere of cognitive jurisdiction. Critical philosophy is not in a position to directly rebut arguments for atheism by way of positive arguments for God's existence, for it has already decided that the arguments for God's existence represent the illegitimate extension of pure reason in its speculative employment. The only response left is to undercut potential defeaters on the same grounds. Granted, the existence of God cannot be proved—but, Kant insists, neither can it be disproved: "...the same grounds for human reason incapable of asserting the existence of such a being [God], when laid before our eyes, also suffice to prove the unsuitability of all counter-assertions (A640-1/B668-9; see also A742/B770, A753/B781, and 27:531). Thus, "criticism puts an end for all future time to objections against morality and religion in a *Socratic* way, namely by the clearest proof of the ignorance of the opponent" (Bxxxi). This is Kant's version of negative apologetics: "By defense [of the faith]...I understand not the augmentation of grounds of proof for its assertion, but rather the mere frustration of the opponent's illusory insights, which would demolish our own asserted propositions" (A776/B804; see also A740/B768). This kind of critical metaphysics "serves more to prevent errors than to amplify cognition" (A851/B879).

While critique undercuts speculative arguments against God's existence, the moral argument for God's existence does not meet the speculative argument for atheism head on—for the latter claims to be a matter of knowledge, while the moral argument justifies belief on subjective grounds. In matters beyond the bounds of sense, reason has no objective grounds for its pronouncements. Here it must allow itself to be guided by the "subjective causes" and requirements embedded in the noetic structure of the mind. That is to say, reason must orient itself with respect to the issues of the supersensible by reference to its own needs:

> ...so I shall consult, not speculative grounds, but my own needs, and can satisfy myself no otherwise than by accepting it. Thus ratiocination in religious matters is dangerous. Were our religion to rest on speculative grounds, it would be but weakly assured if one wanted to demand proof for everything, for reason may go astray. (27:313)

The need Kant has in mind here is the need to postulate the existence of God and the reality of an afterlife in order to make sense of our moral experience. This is far less than a demonstrative proof of these two points, for it is possible that we live in a morally tragic universe. But if we are to honor the integrity of moral experience, we must believe in God and an afterlife as conditions of the possibility of realizing the end to which we are directed by the moral law. Once the decks are cleared of speculative arguments both for and against the existence of God, the felt needs of the morally disposed life take command—and require moral faith.

The tripartite pattern of Default Position/Potential Defeater/Critical Defeater-Defeater thus repeats itself in the domain of religious belief. In the *Lectures on Metaphysics*, Kant states that, "the existence of God and the hope of a future life can be cognized by any human being by common sense by considering nature and one's state, and thus one has no need of speculative inquiry, which in any event can occur with only very few human beings." This is the default position. "But," he goes on,

> this is merely a practical faith, with which a human being can be puzzled by every speculative doubt. In order to dissolve these speculative doubts and investigations, which cannot be refuted by practical faith and yet [are] indispensable to our reason, speculative principles must also be opposed, and metaphysics does this. Its main use is thus to purify our cognition from errors and to guard it from them. (29:938)

Once a potential speculative defeater makes itself known, a speculative response is required. Fire must be fought with fire. Simply holding on to the doxastic products of common sense will no longer do. This is why Kant rejects common-sense philosophy.

In these and related passages, Kant is silent on the justificatory issues this scenario brings up: do all those who believe by way of practical faith lose their warrant once a philosopher expresses a speculative doubt? Or does the loss affect only those who become aware of such a doubt? If so, does mere awareness that there is a doubt suffice to deprive one of one's warrant? Or does one have to understand this doubt and see it as a genuine threat? What if one is too dull to understand the logical force of the doubt? Are all those who are aware of it and understand it obliged to respond by way of speculative counter-arguments, however philosophically inept they may be? Or are only those skilled at responding in kind obliged to carry out the critical task? If so, does the justification by which others, less theoretically inclined, continue to believe depend on the success of the efforts of their speculative representatives? Do the counter-arguments offered on their behalf only have to be objectively successful if justification for all is to be regained? Or do these efforts not only have to be successful, but also be known to be successful? Does Kant envision a division of labor here? And if so, how does the work of the speculation specialists come to benefit those who remain on the level of practical faith? Here, as far as I can tell, the textual trail grows cold. Given Kant's populism, however, it is likely that he holds that only the philosophical justification of religious belief, in some abstract sense, depends on the success of critical philosophy, and that this a matter whose significance is largely confined to the schools. In the B Preface to the first *Critique*, Kant admits that the transcendental critique will "never become popular"; but he also maintains that it "has little need of being so." For "just as little as the people want to fill their heads with fine-spun arguments for useful truths, so just as little do the equally subtle objections against these truths even enter their minds" (Bxxxiv).

In his pre-critical essay, *Dreams of a Spirit-seer Elucidated by the Dreams of Metaphysics* (1766), Kant claims that "sound common sense often apprehends a truth before it understands the reasons by means of which it can prove or explain that truth" (2:325). I have argued that, for Kant, the apprehension of the truth concerning God's existence is produced by a disposition embedded in sound common sense—specifically, by a moral disposition. This disposition produces the metaphysical and religious beliefs required to sustain the commitments the moral law requires of us. It also lends an appropriate level of warrant to the beliefs it produces, apart from any arguments that may be marshaled in their favor. This warrant is only confirmed, not created, by the arguments that render the latent rationality of the disposition manifest when the beliefs produced by that disposition come under attack by philosophical skeptics. And it is only in the event of such an attack that the arguments become necessary. In a telling metaphor at the very end of the first *Critique*, Kant claims that the kind of metaphysics he favors can only serve as the "*bulwark* [*Schutzwehr*] of religion" against the raids of a lawless speculative reason; it "cannot be the *foundation* [*Grundfeste*] of religion" (A849/B877, my emphasis). That foundation, I have argued, lies in the widely distributed dispositional arrangements of common sense. If I am right, and if reformed epistemology of religious belief is built around the idea that belief in God is initially warranted by virtue of having been properly produced by relevant dispositions, apart from any arguments, then Kant—more than Reid—is to be numbered among its predecessors.

CHAPTER 10

Kant on the Hiddenness of God[1]

Eric Watkins

Kant's sustained reflections on God have received considerable scholarly attention over the years and rightly so.[2] His provocative criticisms
of the three traditional theoretical proofs of the existence of God and
his own positive proof for belief in God's existence on moral grounds
have fully deserved the clarification and analysis that has occurred in
these discussions. What I want to focus on, however, is the extent to
which Kant's position contains resources sufficient to answer a line of
questioning about the existence of God that has recently been called the
problem of the "hiddenness of God" in contemporary discussions in
philosophy of religion. If God exists roughly as the Judeo-Christian
philosophical tradition conceives of him, it is puzzling, at least prima
facie, as to why he does not make his existence overwhelmingly obvious to one and all, but rather is hidden from us. For if God is omnipotent, as the tradition maintains, it seems that he would have the power
to reveal himself to us and, for that matter, with sufficient clarity that
we would be left with no doubt about the matter. And if, as the tradition
maintains further, it is important to God that we accept his existence
and reject false idols who would pretend to divine status, it would seem
that he has a significant reason to reveal himself to us. In short, given
that God can make his existence obvious to all, and that doing so would
fulfill an important purpose, why does he remain hidden from us?[3]

---

1   This essay first appeared in *Kantian Review* 14:1 (2009) pp. 81-122. I am grateful to the
    editors of that journal for permission to re-publish it here.
2   Notable examples of discussions on these topics include Adams 1995, pp. 75-95, Plan-
    tinga 1974, and Wood 1970.
3   There are many dimensions to the issue that goes under the name "the hiddenness of
    God." Howard-Snyder and Moser 2002 distinguish, for example, between an existential
    and an evidential problem. Van Inwagen 2002, pp. 24-32, distinguishes between moral
    and epistemological problems, and restricts the moral problem to the problem of evil.
    As we see below, Kant is interested in both the moral problem (though not restricted to
    the problem of evil) and the evidential or epistemological problem.

One line of argument that responds to this question is based on the *practical* consequences that would ensue if we were to encounter God in our immediate experience. If, for example, God revealed himself to us in a booming voice that resounded throughout the earth and that was accompanied by supporting displays of seemingly unlimited power, and if he then announced what we were to do and what the consequences of disobedience would be, it is certainly plausible, at least prima facie, to think that this experience would lead us to alter our behavior and be much more inclined to act as God commanded. Kant draws on this kind of case (and the intuitions that support it) near the end of the *Critique of Practical Reason* and argues that if we had knowledge of God's existence in this way, our actions would no longer have moral worth, since they would be based on hope (for eternal bliss) and fear (of eternal damnation) rather than on the sole morally worthy motive of duty. Only if God is hidden, therefore, could our actions have moral worth, and insofar as giving us the possibility of acting morally is one of God's central purposes in creation, God would have a reason to remain hidden from us that might outweigh his reasons to the contrary. This line of argument can also be developed, however, along slightly different lines. Instead of emphasizing the conditions of moral worth directly, one could argue that knowledge of God's existence and of the severe punishment that he would mete out for any misdeed would in effect serve as a coercive threat such that one could not act freely, or at least not with the kind of freedom that would be morally significant (which might or might not then entail via some further step that our actions have no moral worth). On this version of the practical argument, God would need to remain hidden so that knowledge of his existence would not preclude our ability to act freely.

A second line of argument stems from *theoretical* considerations that Kant develops in the *Critique of Pure Reason* and the *Critique of Practical Reason*, as well as in his lectures on religion.[4] The main idea one can find in these works is that God could decide whether or not to make his existence obvious to us on the basis of the practical grounds just mentioned, only if he is *able* to do so, but God, despite being omnipotent, may be said, in a certain sense, to lack this ability. For while God has the ability to do anything logically (or metaphysically) possible, he cannot make his existence known to us *if* what prevents him from doing so is an essential limitation in *us* rather than in him, and in

---

4   In this paper I largely abstract from the complicated issue of the relation between theoretical and practical reason as well as from Kant's acceptance of rational "*Glaube*" and his adherence to the so-called "moral argument" for God's existence. For a provocative discussion of the "unity of reason" see Neiman 1994, esp. chapters 3 and 4.

fact Kant repeatedly argues for this position. In the first *Critique*, e.g.,
he explicitly denies that we can have theoretical knowledge of God (a
denial that is intended to make room for the possibility of a practically
based *belief* in God), arguing that God cannot be known to us either by
theoretical reason alone—by means of one of the traditional theistic
proofs—or by being an object of experience for us—an object that
could be given to us in sensible intuition just as all other objects of
experience must be. While Kant's criticisms of the traditional theistic
proofs have been discussed in the literature at length and are thought by
many to pose significant obstacles to a priori lines of argument, his
other, lesser-known reasons for asserting the hiddenness of God have
received little attention.[5] This is unfortunate, since on further investigation, these considerations turn out to be both rich and pertinent to understanding more fully the relevant options concerning the hiddenness
of God.

In this paper, I first argue (A) that despite the considerable initial
intuitive plausibility it has, the practical line of argument is not compelling.[6] For one, at least in one of its versions, it makes commitments that
are more controversial than they are convincing. For another, even
when a revised version of that argument is developed, one can worry
both about its consistency with other systematically important features
of Kant's position and about its basic cogency. I then argue (B) that
despite the unexpected failure of the practical argument, Kant's theoretical line of argument can be articulated in four different ways and
that two of them are quite plausible. What's more, although a Humean
might find this general kind of argument congenial, Kant has special
resources to offer in support of it, which Hume is not in as good of a
position to provide. As a result, Kant's most plausible explanation of
the hiddenness of God advances powerful considerations that non-
Kantians could accept as well. This is not to say that Kant's position is
the only possible account of the hiddenness of God.[7] It can lay claim,

---

5 For one now classic discussion of Kant's criticism of the ontological argument, see
   Plantinga 1974.
6 See, e.g., Neiman 1994, pp. 162-163, for an apparent endorsement of Kant's argument.
   Indeed, Neiman thinks that the argument contains "a critique of all forms of positive
   theology far more devastating than the theoretical incoherence of which they were accused in the first *Critique*" (p. 163.).
7 The range of accounts here is quite broad. At the one extreme is the belief that God
   remains hidden for the simple reason that he does not exist. This view has been defended by Schellenberg 1993. At the other extreme is either the voluntarist claim that God
   needs no reason to act as he does or the view, defended by Kvanvig 2002, pp. 149-63,
   that there is no problem of the hiddenness of God. There are of course a host of other
   possibilities between these extremes.

however, to being a serious and sophisticated possibility that has not received the attention it deserves.

A. Practical Arguments

I begin consideration of the practical line of argument for the hidden-ness of God by reconstructing (1) Kant's most explicit argument in the second *Critique*—which one might call the argument from moral worth—refining it further so as to avoid certain immediately obvious difficulties, but ultimately rejecting it on the basis of two fundamental objections. I then turn to reconstructing (2) a related argument for the hiddenness of God—which one might call the argument from divine coercion—before finding it unconvincing as well, albeit for different reasons.

A.1 Hope, Fear, and Moral Worth

In the final section of the Doctrine of Elements in the second *Critique*, titled "On the Wise Adaptation of the Human Being's Cognitive Facul-ties to His Practical Vocation," Kant describes what would be the case if we somehow had all of the theoretical knowledge that we desired. He suggests that with all of our theoretical aspirations fulfilled, our practi-cal inclinations would first demand that they be satisfied and the moral law would then express both the limits that we should not transgress in the pursuit of our inclinations, and the higher end to which they should be subject. However, instead of a conflict arising in us between our inclinations and our moral disposition—as one might expect and as is actually the case, on Kant's view, where the moral strength of our soul would, it is to be hoped, ultimately (*allmählig*) win out— Kant offers the following description of what our situation would be:

> *God and eternity with their awful majesty* would stand unceasingly *before our eyes*.... Transgression of the law would, no doubt, be avoided: what is com-manded would be done; but because the *disposition* from which actions ought to be done cannot be instilled by any command, and because the spur to activ-ity in this case would be promptly at hand and *external*, reason would have no need to work itself up so as to gather strength to resist the inclinations by a lively representation of the dignity of the law; hence most actions conforming to the law would be done from fear, only a few from hope, and none at all from duty, and the moral worth of actions, on which alone in the eyes of su-preme wisdom the worth of a person and even that of the world depends, would not exist at all. As long as human nature remains as it is, human con-duct would thus be changed into mere mechanism in which, as in a puppet

show, everything would *gesticulate* well but there would be no *life* in the figures. (5:147)

Kant's explicit line of argument in this passage is that if we had knowledge of God's existence, then i) we would not transgress the moral law, ii) we would act out of fear and hope (which are to be understood in this case as particular kinds of inclinations) rather than out of respect for the moral law, iii) because knowledge of the external presence of God would cause inclinations in us that would conform to the moral law with such great strength that iv) there would be no need for reason to develop so as to combat any remaining wayward inclinations (since, in this case, there would be none), v) our actions would have no moral worth, vi) the entire world would, at least viewed from a divine perspective, be worthless as well, and vii) human beings would be mechanical puppets rather than genuine, living agents. Since states of affairs v)-vii) are to be rejected, we can infer (via extended *modus tollens*) that we do not have the kind of complete knowledge that we seem to desire. As a result, in this context Kant concludes that our cognitive faculties, *including* their limitations, are well-suited to our practical, or moral, vocation, since they allow for the possibility of actions possessing moral worth that make the world valuable by allowing what would otherwise be mere mechanistic puppets be full-fledged agents.

To be sure, Kant's articulation of this argument involves more points than are minimally necessary for the formulation of an argument establishing the conclusion that God has reason to remain hidden from us. For example, such an argument does not require Kant's claim (in vi)) that the world would be worthless if human beings did not perform actions that have moral worth. For one can acknowledge that the world might have valuable features beyond morally worthy actions and still hold that, all else being equal, a world with morally worthy actions is more valuable overall than one without. And it is also not necessary to assume that one would be unable to transgress the moral law (in i)). For one, Lucifer seems to have done precisely that in the face of God's existence.[8] For another, the remaining steps of the argument (ii) through vii)) follow even if this point is not explicitly assumed.[9] As a result, in the spirit of charity, one can pare down Kant's argument to the following:

---

8 Interpretation of the case of Lucifer is complicated. It is generally agreed, however, that if the account derived from Christian mythology is an accurate report, as opposed to a purely metaphorical or symbolic story, Lucifer was cast out of heaven for rebelling against God. What motivated him to rebel (pride) and what form his rebellion took are less clear.

9 In fact, i) seems to follow from iii), rather than be an assumption that entails it.

P1   If we had knowledge of everything, then we would have knowledge of God's existence and of his promise of eternal reward and his threat of eternal punishment for our good and bad actions (respectively).

P2   If we had knowledge of God's existence and of his promise of eternal reward and his threat of eternal punishment for our good and bad actions (respectively), then (a) we would have to act out of hope or fear (or a combination thereof) and (b) we could not act out of respect for the moral law.[10]

P3   If (a) we would have to act out of hope or fear (or a combination thereof) and (b) we could not act out of respect for the moral law, none of our actions could have moral worth.

P4   At least some of our actions could have moral worth.

C1   We do not have knowledge of everything, specifically, of God's existence and of his promise of eternal reward and his threat of eternal punishment for our good and bad actions.

This argument, while certainly an improvement in several respects over the more detailed formulation, still encounters two fundamental difficulties. First, Kant's explicit justification for P2 seems problematic. In the passage quoted above, Kant argues that reason would have no need to develop since our inclinations would already dictate that we act in accord with the moral law. However, there is a noticeable gap between the claim that there is *no need* for reason to develop and the further claim that reason *would not* in fact develop and thus would not be capable of leading us to act out of respect for the moral law rather than from inclination. Kant's idea seems to be that our inclinations come first and *only* if our inclinations do not motivate the proper actions would reason be called on to do so.[11] However, one can imagine a number of alternative scenarios here. For example, one view, advanced by Lessing, is that we act out of hope and fear in our early childhood, but increasingly come to act on the basis of reason as we mature, not because inclinations lead us astray and thus force the development of reason, but rather because reason develops on its own and takes over naturally.[12] Put in slightly different terms, this argument presupposes

---

10   While this premise may not hold for Lucifer, Kant explicitly restricts this line of argument to human beings in the phrase "as long as human nature remains as it is." As a result, the relevance of Kant's arguments to devils or angels will not be considered in the rest of this paper.

11   See, for example, Kant's narrative in the *Conjectural Beginning of Human History*, esp. at 8:111.

12   Lessing's view, as expressed, e.g., in Lessing 1780, is of course directed at the development of reason in the species rather than in the individual, but the plausibility of his claim in the case of the species derives from features of individual members of the species. It is a separate question as to why reason should take over what inclination is

that we would act on the basis of hope and fear when these are present in sufficient strength, but it is simply not clear why inclinations should be accorded such absolute priority and why reason could not come to have a supporting, or, for that matter, even decisive role.

Second, Kant's argument relies on his distinctive and highly controversial claim about the moral worth of actions in P3, namely that they have moral worth only if they are done out of duty, or respect for the moral law, and not on the basis of inclinations. While part of the controversy about this claim concerns the exegetical question of how to understand the role that inclinations might still play for Kant in morally worthy actions (in cases of mixed motives), the part that calls this argument into question is the more fundamental connection that it requires between moral worth and the motive of duty. For one can maintain that what makes an action morally worthy is either the nature of the action or its consequences (or some combination thereof), in which case our actions would have moral worth even if they were motivated entirely by an intense fear of God's wrath, as long as they were the right kinds of actions or had the best consequences. As a result, both P2 and P3, the central assumptions in Kant's argument, face fundamental objections, and the argument from moral worth must be rejected.[13]

A.2   God, Coercion, and Freedom

One can, however, abstract from the issue of moral worth and identify a second version of the practical line of argument that is prima facie plausible. This version shares a similar starting point with the first, namely that if we had knowledge of everything, including God's existence and his promise of eternal reward and threat of eternal punishment, then we would act out of hope and fear (P1 and P2 (a) above). In short, our knowledge of God's presence would have consequences for how we act. However, it diverges from the first version of the argument by not being committed to the claim that it would prevent our acting out of respect for the moral law (P2 (b)) and thus preclude the possibility of the moral worth of our actions (P3). That is, this version of the argu-

---

doing satisfactorily. One possibility is that reason generates the right action necessarily, whereas inclinations get it right only contingently.

13   Kant might not be particularly bothered by these objections, since he thinks that he has adequately defended his views on the role of inclinations in our actions and moral worth. However, the third objection to the argument from divine coercion discussed below would apply to this argument as well and represents a problem for Kant that is not external to his larger position.

ment does not try to prove that our knowledge of God affects the moral worth of our actions as such.

Instead, this version maintains that knowledge of God's existence would have consequences for the prior, or more basic question of whether we could act freely at all. It attempts to do so by exploiting the intuition that if we knew of God's existence and his promises and threats, we would be coerced into doing what he commands, since our knowledge of the magnitude of God's rewards and punishments would leave us with no genuine choice in the matter. After all, the benefits of any finite good that we might desire clearly pale in comparison with the infinite suffering we would have to endure as divine punishment for choosing it against his will.[14]

While Kant's primary intent in the passage from which we extracted the first version of the practical argument was to emphasize the (alleged, but not substantiated) connection between our knowledge of God and (the impossibility of) the moral worth of our actions, the passage also contained hints of this second version. For Kant does make the claim—which turned out to be irrelevant to the first reconstruction—that we would in fact always do what God commanded, and he does also state that what would cause us to do so is primarily the fear stemming from the "awful majesty" of God and eternity, which suggests that it is the magnitude of God's threat of eternal punishment that would be the relevant factor in our actions. While Kant seems to allow us some freedom in our actions by conceding that God, by means of his commands, cannot directly cause a disposition in us to act as we do, the entire second half of the quotation is devoted to showing that knowledge of God would achieve this result indirectly instead. In fact, the passage concludes rather dramatically by suggesting that in such a scenario we would be mere puppets, where the implicit contrast is with beings that are endowed with freedom and autonomy.

If, therefore, there is a sufficient textual basis for attributing this line of reasoning to Kant, we can proceed to reconstruct the argument in more detail and with greater precision as follows.

> P1   Assume we know that God exists and threatens us with eternal and infinite punishment for non-compliance with his commands.[15]

---

14   For discussion of this particular argument, see Murray 1993, pp. 27-35.

15   I focus here exclusively on punishment and whether it amounts to coercive threat. There is a question as to whether rewards could be coercive as well, since they display a structure similar to that of threats, the primary difference being that the one traffics in negative consequences of transgressions, whereas the other involves positive consequences of obedience. Since our intuitions are less clear about rewards and whether they could be coercive, I do not consider them further here.

P2 If we know that God exists and threatens us with eternal and infinite punishment for non-compliance with his commands, we are subject to a coercive threat.

P3 If we are subject to a coercive threat, then we cannot exercise morally significant freedom.

C1 We cannot exercise morally significant freedom. (from P1-P3)

P4 But we can exercise morally significant freedom.

C2 P1 is false; it is not the case that we know that God exists and threatens us
with eternal and infinite punishment for non-compliance with his commands.

Before turning to an evaluation of this argument, it is helpful to be clear
about two points. First, the phrase "morally significant freedom" in P3
requires some clarification, for we have, it seems, conflicting intuitions
about the exact nature and consequences of coercion. Sometimes we
think that coercion forces one to perform a certain action such that one
could not have acted freely, or done otherwise, at all. On this view,
coercion precludes (even libertarian) freedom. However, sometimes we
think that coercion does not literally *force* one to perform a certain action, since it is still possible, at least metaphysically speaking, that the
person instead accept whatever the threatened consequences are, even if
the person would have been absolved of any moral responsibility for
the action had it been performed. The classic case of the bank robber
holding a gun to my head may illustrate the view that I still *could* in
some sense decide not to hand over the money, though I am not morally
responsible for handing over the money should I do so. In the latter
case, my action, though free in some thin metaphysical sense, is not
morally significant. To say that coercion rules out that we can act with
"morally significant freedom" is therefore meant to say either that we
cannot act freely at all or that we cannot act freely such that we must
also be held morally responsible for our actions.

Second, P2 is a central, and extremely complex, assumption in the
argument, since it focuses on the notion of coercion (rather than on the
consequences thereof for moral worth) and subsumes the divine case
under it. Even in the absence of a formal definition of a coercive threat,
one can identify two factors that form a core part of its content, which
can help us to see why one might think that God's threat of punishment
would be an instance of it.[16] First, one person, A, threatens another, B,
only if B believes that A is in a position to bring about or withhold significant negative consequences for B, and that whether A will bring

---

16 For contemporary discussion of the notion of coercion, see Nozick 1969, pp. 440-72,
Yaffe 2003, pp. 335-56, and Ripstein 2004, pp. 2-35.

about or withhold such consequences depends on whether B performs an action, C, that (B believes) A wants B to perform.[17] Second, such a threat is coercive only if the consequences in question are perceived by B to be overwhelmingly negative, where "overwhelmingly" indicates not any absolute magnitude, but rather a magnitude that is relative to the threshold at which B is no longer thought to have a morally significant free choice about whether to do C.

Given this analysis, it can seem that knowledge of God's existence and the threat of eternal and infinite punishment for transgressions of his commands would be coercive for us (or at least satisfies two central conditions thereof). For if we know that God exists and is omnipotent, then we believe that he is in a position to bring about or withhold significant negative consequences for us, and whether he will do so depends on whether we obey his commands. We also know that the magnitude of the consequences of disobeying God's commands—infinite and eternal punishment—would be maximal and thus as overwhelming for us as anything could possibly be.[18] Thus, both of the conditions that are required for a coercive threat are satisfied and it can therefore seem that knowledge of God's existence serves as a coercive threat to our acting freely.

Despite the prima facie plausibility of this argument, however, it suffers from two significant problems, one specific to Kant's broader project, the other for the cogency of the argument on its own terms. The first problem is that if the argument were successful, it would make Kant's overall position inconsistent. For if successful, it would show that God must remain completely hidden from us (insofar as we are to be able to act with morally significant freedom), but elsewhere in the second *Critique* Kant also presents an argument for the existence of God that he takes to be convincing. Granted, it is not a theoretical argument, the possibility of which he rejects in the first *Critique*, but rather is based on practical considerations concerning the possibility of our acting morally and is therefore called a "postulate".[19] However, regardless of the subject matter on which it is based, if successful, it establishes that we must accept God's existence, which directly conflicts with God's hiddenness.

---

17 This premise would need to be made much more precise, since as stated, it is open to various counter-examples. Stating this premise such that it avoids these problems would, if at all possible, require more time and space than is warranted by current purposes.

18 One might think that punishment should be proportioned according to the magnitude of the misdeed such that one might spend only a finite amount of time in purgatory for a minor transgression. Even so, the punishments could still be overwhelming.

19 See Wood 1970, for detailed reconstruction and discussion of this argument.

One might object that the conclusion of Kant's practical argument is not *knowledge* of God's existence, but rather something weaker, namely *belief* (*Glaube*), and maintain that this distinction removes the inconsistency. For belief, as Kant characterizes it, is an assent (literally, "*für wahr halten*," or "holding-for-true") whose justification is only subjectively sufficient and not objectively sufficient, by which he means that we do not have empirical evidence in support of the proposition, but have, none the less, other reasons in its favor that are sufficient for us to accept it.[20] However, if we do not know, but rather merely believe that God exists and will punish us for transgressing against his commands, it might seem that God's threat has lost some of its force, perhaps enough for it to no longer be coercive. If I have some doubts about whether the person making the threatening remarks will actually bring about the negative consequences and thus suspect that this person might rather be bluffing, I might well be reasonably tempted to call the bluff.

However, this objection is based on a misunderstanding of the notion of belief with which Kant's moral argument operates. Despite the objective insufficiency of the justification with which we assent to God's existence according to the moral argument, the justification is still subjectively sufficient, and the assent it supports is completely genuine and not a fictionalist acting *as if* God were to exist (though in reality he does not). That is, the difference between knowledge and belief does not concern the *degree* either of justification or of assent (strong versus weak), but rather the *kind* of justification (objective versus subjective). As a result, belief in God's threat of eternal and infinite punishment could be just as coercive as knowledge would be and if the belief is based on practical reason and nothing else (as it is in the argument Kant presents), our assent will be at least as strong as most of our empirical knowledge. Thus, the argument from divine coercion arises even if we believe rather than know God's existence. So this argument still encounters a problem of internal inconsistency with Kant's own argument for the existence of God.[21]

---

20   For a helpful detailed discussion of this distinction and of the broader taxonomy of attitudes that we might have toward a proposition, such as conviction, opinion, and persuasion, see Chignell 2007a, pp. 323-60.

21   One might argue that this inconsistency is not necessarily problematic. For the way in which we come to have knowledge of God's existence may still be compatible with God's threat not having what Murray calls sufficient "epistemic imminence" (Murray 1993, p. 32). The idea is that people may still smoke even though they know that smoking will kill them, so the threat of death, even though known by them, does not have sufficient epistemic imminence for them. However, in addition to the purely philosophical objection that the cases are not exactly analogous, given that smokers know not that smoking will kill them, but rather only that it makes this more likely, which is

Second, the argument itself (as opposed to its relations to other Kantian doctrines) seems subject to question on three fronts. For one, the picture suggestive of the charge that divine coercion results from knowledge of God's commands and of the punishment that would accompany disobeying his commands, might be thought to be incomplete in important respects. In particular, belief in divine grace can give rise to a somewhat different picture, one that could avoid this charge. For the possibility of divine grace calls into question our putative knowledge that divine punishment will be of infinite magnitude, because God can forgive us for our seemingly inevitable trespasses such that we need not resign ourselves to eternal damnation, even if it is fully deserved.[22] Coming to a proper understanding of the extent of divine grace and of the conditions under which it might be granted are a matter of debate, but the mere possibility of divine grace affects the cogency of the argument from divine coercion by calling into question whether God's apparent threats must be viewed, all things considered, as genuine.[23]

For another, the argument simply assumes without justification that human actions are motivated by their consequences rather than their intrinsic rightness and wrongness. That is, it assumes that it is the magnitude of the divinely enforced consequences of our not doing A that can coerce us into doing A. However, one can certainly imagine rejecting such a view in favor of a position according to which one acts on the basis of the rightness or wrongness of one's action. Indeed, a similar point was made with respect to the argument from moral worth, since that argument assumed that our actions had to be motivated by inclinations rather than anything else (whether it be by reason or the intrinsic nature of the action in question).

Moreover, this point becomes particularly important if one considers whether God's commands coincide with or diverge from our own independent moral intuitions of what is right and wrong. If they coincide, then God's "threat" of eternal punishment could well be completely idle if I am motivated entirely by the rightness of the action. Perhaps, for instance, God threatens to punish acts of pedophilia severely, but my refraining from committing such acts is in no way based

---

unlike the case of divine punishment, the exegetical question of how to understand how Kant might attempt to avoid the inconsistency still remains. Unfortunately, this extremely important topic would require detailed discussion not possible in the context of this paper.

22   If divine grace were contingent on one believing that God exists and has issued the relevant promises and threats, then this objection would be moot, but one would need to provide an argument for this claim about divine grace.

23   For discussion of the difficult issue of how God's forgiveness might be understood, see Hare 1996, esp. chapters 2, 9, and 10.

on, or motivated by, that threat, esp. if I have no inclination to perform such acts (e.g., if there is no possible description under which such acts can seem attractive or good to me). God's "threat" is thus completely irrelevant to me; I act freely in refraining from such actions—even if it is true that I would not act freely, were I to have strong inclinations toward such actions that I was able to resist successfully only due to God's threats. So, if the external commands coincide with what we think is right on independent grounds, then it is far from clear that we are truly being coerced.[24] If, by contrast, the actions God commands were to diverge from our own independent moral intuitions, the situation would admittedly be more complicated. Two scenarios, however, are clearly relevant. One is that God might want to test one's faith by issuing counter-intuitive commands (and correlative threats), but one's faith can be tested only if we exercise our free choice, so the threat cannot be so great as to remove the possibility of free action. Another is that one might think of God's "promises" and "threats" as opportunities for us to show that we are primarily concerned about doing the right thing and thus being morally upstanding persons of integrity rather than bowing to arbitrary external pressure.[25] On either alternative, it is possible to view God's threats not as coercive and as precluding freedom, but rather as occasions for us to demonstrate our autonomy and integrity.

Finally, even if one were to grant the connection between God's threats and the denial of morally significant freedom, the hiddenness of God still does not necessarily follow. For it seems possible, at least prima facie, that God reveal himself and yet not issue any promises or threats regarding our behavior. That is, one could split P1 apart into two separate premises—with one concerning God's existence and the other concerning his threats—and grant the former, while denying the latter. Alternately, one could grant that God exists and that he makes threats, but deny his threats have the specific content that would be required to destroy our freedom. (One can imagine, for example, that his threat is: "Act freely or else!") The question then is whether it is really possible that God could make his existence known and not make the precise kinds of promises and threats that are required. Since Kant distin-

---

24 One might claim that divine external commands take precedence over other motivations and that the presence of such an external command thus amounts to coercion. However, even if examples of external commands overpowering other (e.g., straightforwardly moral) motivations can be produced, one would have to argue that such precedence was necessarily the case for divine commands.

25 There are naturally other alternatives that one might consider here. Perhaps, for example, self-assertion is a basic value and overwhelming threats are the severest test of this value.

guishes quite explicitly between God's ontological and psychological predicates (e.g., at 28:1020-1), it is clear that he accepts the conceptual space for this possibility.[26] Further, while it is plausible to think that given his goodness, God could not actively deceive us (e.g., by feigning indifference toward our actions on the grounds that the trivial undertakings of finite creatures such as ourselves have no importance for a being of his magnitude), it is far from clear that God could not withhold information and simply be silent on this particular issue or act in ways that were even conducive for our acting with morally significant freedom.[27]

Thus, while the argument from divine coercion can seem intuitively plausible, especially when one thinks of a direct confrontation with a divine threat, it turns out that the argument is not compelling when one considers either its consistency with Kant's other commitments or its intrinsic cogency. For it is inconsistent with Kant's practical argument for the existence of God, which is a systematically indispensable component of his larger project, and it is open to three further objections. For one, the possibility of divine grace could lead one to reject the idea that God's pronouncements should really be taken as threats. For another, even if God intends to punish those who disobey his commands, it is not necessarily the case that people must be motivated to act on the basis of these threats, especially if they have no inclination to act contrary to actions that they know, on independent grounds, to be morally required. Third, it seems that God could reveal his existence, while refraining from making any promises or threats at all, much less ones that might preclude morally significant freedom. As a result, the argument from divine coercion is not convincing.

---

26 Kant sometimes (e.g. at 28:999-1000) draws the distinction in terms of transcendental and natural predicates. Pat Kain has rightly pointed out that Kant might try to close the gap between the ontological and psychological (or transcendental and natural) predicates such that P1 could not be split into two separate premises in this way. The most promising line to pursue here would be to bring in Kant's moral argument. As noted above, these issues cannot be discussed here.

27 One might argue that God would have to reveal not only his existence to us, but also whatever else was necessary for our flourishing and thus his commands as part of what is necessary for our salvation. However, the general principle that God would have to reveal to us whatever is necessary for our flourishing can cut both ways. For if the divine commands were coercive and morally significant free actions are a highest value, then it would follow that God could not issue any commands (if he revealed his existence to us).

B. Theoretical Arguments

If the practical line of argument for divine hiddenness is thus not successful in either of its versions, the theoretical line of argument still remains, that is, the possibility that God cannot decide to reveal himself to us, because he is unable to do so, given that he is not the kind of being that we are capable of knowing, due to our cognitive limitations. Kant states the main point succinctly: "if God should really speak to a human being, the latter could still never *know* that it was God speaking. It is quite impossible for a human being to apprehend the infinite by his senses, distinguish it from sensible beings, and *be acquainted with* it as such [*ihn woran kenne solle*]" (7:63).

After first briefly articulating (1) the basic framework that Kant establishes for considering the possibility that we might have knowledge of God, I consider four different arguments for the hiddenness of God that are based on Kant's explicit claims about God not being an object of experience—though there are significant differences between how direct or indirect the experience might be in each case.[28] The first two arguments, which are based on understanding God either as an object that could not be given to us in space and time (2) or as an unconditioned object (3), are not, I suggest, fully convincing. The second two arguments, which are based on conceiving of God either as a perfect being (4) or as infinite (5), are, by contrast, considerably more plausible. While other thinkers, such as Hume, might agree wholeheartedly with the thrust of these arguments, Kant is in a unique position to support them more fully, given his reflections on the nature and limits of our cognitive abilities, yet *without* thereby relying on the more controversial features of his analysis of cognition that others might find objectionable (6). As a result, Kant's explanation of the hiddenness of God advances considerations that non-Kantians could accept as well.

B.1 On the Conditions of Knowledge and their Application to God

According to Kant, two conditions must be met for an object to be experienced, or known: 1. The object must be *given* to us in intuition (either directly or indirectly, e.g., via inference from immediate experience), where intuition for us must be spatial and temporal; and 2. The object must be *thought* through concepts, or grasped by means of cer-

---

28 In some cases, the experience in question would be directly of God. In other cases, the experience would involve inferences from features of the actual world to God's existence, while yet others depend on comparisons with possible worlds.

tain forms of thought, which, when stripped of all empirical content, are called categories. Thus, to take an ordinary empirical case, I can know, or experience, the book in front of me (that it is heavy, or at rest) because (1) it is given to me through my senses (that of sight or touch) and (2) I have the concept of "book", which I am justified in applying to that object whenever it is given to me in the appropriate way, e.g. when the object is given to me in intuition such that it displays in some manner the various features or "marks" that are contained in the concept. The position Kant develops in detail in the first *Critique* is naturally much more complex, involving numerous controversial features, but these two very basic conditions, which are intuitively plausible in their own right, represent the core of his account.[29]

If we apply these two conditions to the case of God, we obtain the following two questions: 1. Could God be given to us in intuition? 2. Do we have a concept of God? We can immediately see that the second question is, in one rather trivial sense, unproblematic. We must have at least a rudimentary concept of God (e.g., as, minimally, a perfect creator of the world) insofar as we are able to ask what it is that is supposed to be hidden in the first place. That is, the fact that we have a concept of God is presupposed by our very questions concerning his existence and hiddenness. As a result, difficulties concerning our ability to know God's existence must involve, at least in part, the first question pertaining to how God could be given to us through our senses. As we shall see, however, Kant's arguments end up depending on answers to both questions, albeit in different ways.

B.2 God's Existence in Space and Time

In what could appear to be the most straightforward Kantian line of argument for divine hiddenness, one might suggest that God cannot be known because he would have to be given to us in space and time, but this cannot happen since God's essence or features are incompatible with his being spatio-temporal. There are numerous ways in which one might develop the details of this line of argument. For example, in his General Remarks on the Transcendental Aesthetic added to the second edition of the first *Critique*, Kant objects that if space and time were not forms of intuition, but rather forms of things-in-themselves (which is how he understands Newton's position), then i) God would have to exist in space and time and ii) space and time would also condition

---

29   See Watkins, 2008, pp. 512-531, for a discussion of some of the complexities of Kant's
      position.

God's existence, but this latter claim contradicts the orthodox conception of God as a completely unconditioned being (B71-2). Alternately,
one might think that if God existed in space and time and space and
time were, as Kant maintains, forms of intuition and, according to the
strictures of transcendental idealism, ideal, or subject-dependent, then
God would have to be, at least in part, ideal, or subject-dependent,
which might seem to be counterintuitive.[30]

Though these arguments are worth pursuing in greater detail, rather
than engaging in long-standing discussions of whether or not space and
time are forms of intuition and what follows from such an assertion for
God's existence, I propose to focus on the following line(s) of thought.
God cannot be given to us in *space*, because anything spatial, such as
matter, must be, Kant thinks, infinitely divisible, whereas God is traditionally thought to be simple and thus completely indivisible.[31] In his
lectures on the Philosophical Doctrine of Religion, Kant explicitly argues that God is also not in *time* on the following grounds: "if God
were in time, he would have to be limited. But now he is a *realissimus*,
and consequently he is not in time" (28:1039). As a result, one might
argue that since God cannot be given to us in either space or time, God
cannot be an object of knowledge for us.[32]

The most immediately puzzling feature of this argument is Kant's
claim that anything that exists in time is necessarily limited, since it
hardly sounds as if it is analytic and yet no support is provided on its

---

30 One might also argue that God could not be given in space and time on the grounds that
    God would then stand in reciprocal causal relations with his creation, which contrasts
    with the traditional conception of God according to which God is not acted on by the fi-
    nite substances he creates. This argument could be supported by the argument of the
    Third Analogy of Experience and passages from the transcripts of Kant's metaphysics
    lectures (28:42, 28:205, and esp. 29:926). I thank Karl Ameriks for reminding me of
    these further dimensions of Kant's position.

31 Leibniz (1989) expressly develops this line of argument in the third letter of his cor-
    respondence with Clarke. Also, one need not be committed to the *infinite* divisibility of
    space to support this claim. It is enough if whatever God is supposed to be is divisible
    even to some extent. So unless God is a sub-atomic particle, "string", or other such
    smallest spatial entity, God will be divisible (even if not infinitely).

32 Kant's argument can be reconstructed as follows:
    P1 Objects of experience must be given in space or time.
    P2 Anything spatial is limited and divisible.
    P3 God is omnipresent and indivisible.
    C1 God is not spatial (and thus cannot be given in space). (from P2 and P3)
    P4 Anything temporal is limited and changeable.
    P4' Anything temporal requires continuous appearing and disappearing.
    P5 God is eternal and immutable (and does not continuously appear and disappear).
    C2 God is not temporal (and thus cannot be given in time). (from P4/P4' and P5)
    C3 God is not an object of experience. (from C1 and C2)

behalf. The claim is clarified to a certain extent by Kant's discussion of the eternity of God later in his lectures on religion. There he asserts:

> the existence of a thing in time is always a succession of parts in time, one after the other. Duration in time is, so to speak, a continuous disappearing and a continuous beginning. We can never live through a certain year without already having lived through the previous one. But none of this can be said of God, since he is unalterable. Hence, since it is a continuous limitation, time must be opposed in quality to an *ens realissimum*. (28:1043-4)

Again, we encounter the claim that existing in time is to be viewed as a limitation and thus as something that is incompatible with God as a most real being, but now we can see Kant hinting at why he thinks that this must be the case: An object existing in time is thought to involve a continuous appearing and disappearing as its states come into and go out of existence at each moment of time. Since God is immutable, it is clear that his state could not come into and go out of existence continuously and that God therefore cannot exist in time. And since objects must be given to us in time to be known, God cannot be known by us.

However, as soon as the argument is spelled out further in this way, it is clear that its force is limited. For it depends on a very specific understanding of how objects exist in time, namely as a series of continuous appearings and disappearings of an object's states. If one were to conceive of God's existence in time differently, the argument would no longer hold. Whether rightly or wrongly, Kant explicitly rejects as contradictory the idea that "all the consecutiveness of time be thought as simultaneous in God" (28:1044), i.e. that God is *simultaneously* aware of states that we know to occur *successively*. However, even if we grant Kant this controversial point, it does still seem that one could represent God as existing in time in the minimal sense that he exists at every moment in time without thereby being committed to the further claim that God's states come into and go out of existence at each moment of time. Since God's state never changes, there is no reason to think that his state comes into, only in order to go out of existence. Instead, it seems possible that he is eternal in the sense that he always exists in one and the same, unchanging state.[33]

If one could know God as temporal in this very restricted sense, one might still object that he could not be given to us in *space* and that he must for that reason be hidden (if one also concedes that inner sense must get its objects from outer sense). Granted, if God were related to space by having a particular organic body enclosed in a limited region of space as human beings do, then one would be forced into the diffi-

---

33   On the basis of this kind of consideration Descartes grants that God has no modes, since modes are for him features of objects that necessarily involve change.

cult, but perhaps not impossible position of attributing a kind of fini-
tude to an infinite being. However, just as attempting to attribute tem-
porality to God required careful articulation of God's immutability and
eternity, so too trying to ascribe spatiality to God might simply call for
a more nuanced understanding of God's omnipresence.

Specifically, one could claim that God is not present in space in virtue of the same factors that finite bodies are, namely by means of the
exercise of attractive and repulsive forces.[34] Instead, God could be present throughout space (and thus in all spaces) in some other way.[35] For
example, one might think that God *concurs* in the activity of all finite
bodies such that they are jointly able to fill determinate regions of
space.[36] That is, if finite substances cannot be the ultimate source of
their own existence and activities, but instead require divine concourse,
as is commonly (though not universally) held among philosophical
theologians in the early modern period, then God might be said to be
present in every region of space that bodies occupy by means of his
concourse.[37] In this way, God could be omnipresent without being limited, since he exists at every point in space and yet is not acted on by
other bodies that occupy other regions of space by means of their own
finite activities. Therefore, there is, it seems, an acceptable sense in
which God could be viewed as omnipresent in space without being
limited, just as there was for God's eternal existence in time. Accordingly, it does seem possible, at least in principle, that God could exist in
space and time in these ways.[38]

---

34 For a comprehensive account of Kant's views on causality (which includes discussion
of attractive and repulsive forces and how they are specific instances of his more general model of causality), see Watkins 2005.

35 Newton (in the Appendix to 1730) and Clarke (in his correspondence with Leibniz)
famously argue that God is immediately present to all things and that space is, as it were, the *sensorium* of God, which suggests that God is not present in space in the same
sense in which bodies are.

36 In a passage from the lectures on religion, Kant is reported to have said: "Of the concept
of matter, after I remove everything negative and sensible inhering in it I retain nothing
but the concept of an externally active power, and of the concept of spatial presence if I
leave out the condition of sense (i.e. space) nothing but the pure reality of presence. I
will be able to apply to God, therefore, only the real itself, power and presence"
(28:1022). So if one says that God is present in space, Kant seems to be open to understanding this claim such that God is present in space not by being extended in the
way in which bodies are, but rather by being the power through which bodies exist.

37 In fact, Kant seems to suggest just such a view in his pre-Critical period in the *Nova
Dilucidatio* (1:415) and in the Inaugural Dissertation (2:396, 2:410, and 2:414).

38 One might develop this line of argument for the hiddenness of God further as follows. If
God were to exist in space and time, then God would be ideal, on the grounds that everything in space and time is, according to Kant, ideal. However, God is the most real of
beings and is thus not ideal. Therefore, God cannot exist in space and time.

However, it is one thing for God to exist in space and time, another to be given to us therein. Put slightly differently, even if it were granted that God exists in space and time in the manner described above, could we *experience* God as such? If it is possible for us to experience finite substances as finite and as standing in need of God's concourse at all times, then we could, it seems, also (at least indirectly) experience God as existing in space and time. Accordingly, for this argument for the hiddenness of God to be convincing, one would have to argue that we could not experience finite substances in this way, but it is unclear how this requirement could be met. In fact, given that Kant identifies space and time as forms of intuition, one might think (though incorrectly, in my view) that every object given in space and time is thereby knowable, which suggests that no argument against the possibility of experiencing God in this way could be developed (since it would violate this principle). As a result, this particular argument for the hiddenness of God, while not obviously false, also does not appear to be capable of carrying much independent weight.

B.3   God as an Unconditioned Object

Since it is not impossible that God could exist in space and time and on that account be an object of experience, it is natural to turn to other features contained in the concept of God that Kant emphasizes to see whether they are inconsistent with God being an object of experience. One of the most fundamental ways that Kant has of conceiving of God is as the unconditioned, more specifically, as an unconditioned object that contains conditions for the conditioned objects that we experience in the world (e.g., A559/B587). This way of describing God follows directly from his more systematic interests in two ways. First, Kant characterizes reason as the faculty that starts with our judgments about conditioned objects and then searches for their conditions until it attains completeness (or absolute totality) in the series of conditions (e.g., A408ff./B435ff.). Pursued along one dimension, one naturally arrives at

---

However, this argument is not, I think, particularly compelling for two reasons. First, it is not clear that being real is incompatible with being ideal. For it seems possible that God could have two "aspects" just as human beings might, one noumenal and real while the other is phenomenal and ideal. Second, even if the first objection did not hold, this argument would be of little use outside of the context of Kant scholarship, since the assumption that space and time are merely subjective and hence idealistic forms of intuition is a distinctively Kantian claim that finds little resonance elsewhere. So while the argument might be acceptable in a certain context, it would not be appropriate in a broader setting.

the idea of God as the unconditioned condition of the world. Second, Kant's interest in the possibility of metaphysics proper (as consisting of synthetic a priori claims) makes it important for him to find a way to characterize God in terms that can also be used to describe the other objects of traditional metaphysics, such as the immortality of the soul, the world as a totality, and our freedom (Bxxx). Given this broader philosophical interest, it is important for Kant to think of God as an unconditioned condition of the world.

While Kant seems to treat both the notion of a condition and the correlative notion of the unconditioned as primitives—at least to the extent that he does not provide any explicit definition of either one— one can form a first intuitive grasp of them by considering the examples he gives of unconditioned objects.[39] Kant repeatedly asserts that our free or spontaneous actions are unconditioned and what he has in mind is that such actions are first causes, i.e. causes that are not caused by any prior event to bring about the effects that they do. Kant also describes the world as a totality as an unconditioned object. In this case, his idea is not that the world as a totality is uncaused—since it may well be caused by God or some other being—but rather at least that its primary features are not determined by anything else. Specifically, certain spatio-temporal features of those objects that constitute the world are not determined by anything without, for there is no reference point external to them with respect to which they could be understood properly as far as, e.g., their spatio-temporal locations are concerned. God, I take it, is unconditioned in both of these senses. God is obviously not caused by anything else, so he is metaphysically independent and self-sufficient. Nor must one appeal to anything else to understand God's nature, so his nature is explanatorily independent as well.

Now given that Kant not only characterizes God as an unconditioned object, but also attaches systematic weight to this characterization, one might naturally think that this characterization immediately points to his reason for thinking that God cannot be given to us in intuition. For if no unconditioned object can be given to us in intuition, that is, if all objects that are given to us must be conditioned, then God cannot be given to us in intuition and Kant will have given us a principled account of the hiddenness of God. Moreover, there is clear textual evidence that Kant is committed to the claim that no unconditioned object can be given to us in intuition. In his resolution to the Antinomy of Pure

---

39 This notion is primitive not only in the sense that Kant leaves it undefined, but also in the sense that it is a notion that is prior even to the categories. For at least the categories of substance, causality, and mutual interaction employ it.

Reason he explicitly remarks: "For the absolutely unconditioned is not encountered in experience at all" (A510/B538).

Unfortunately, however, Kant never provides any explicit argument for this claim in its most general form. That is, nowhere does he explain why the unconditioned could not be given to us in intuition. The mere fact that something is an object of knowledge does not analytically entail that it must be conditioned in the relevant sense. Even if it is true that objects must satisfy the conditions of the possibility of experience, it does not follow that these objects are thereby conditioned in the relevant sense, because the notion of an epistemic condition that is intended in the phrase "conditions of the possibility of experience" is distinct from the various notions of condition that Kant has in mind in calling God an unconditioned object.

Moreover, the claim is not obviously true. It seems possible, at least prima facie, that one could encounter an object that was not conditioned by anything else and that did not depend on anything else for its primary features. For in saying that an object is unconditioned, one is making only a negative assertion, namely that it is not conditioned by anything else, but it could turn out, it seems, that after investigating a particular object exhaustively (or as exhaustively as is reasonable to establish knowledge) one might find no respect in which it depends on anything else, in which case the conclusion that it is unconditioned would seem warranted.[40]

That Kant does not present such support is particularly unfortunate insofar as it would represent a significant systematic advantage for him to have a general argument that would also immediately rule out the possibility that we could experience the other objects that he characterizes as unconditioned. For then Kant would have a justification that went a long way toward establishing that all of these objects of traditional metaphysics must be viewed not as knowable appearances, but rather as things-in-themselves that lie beyond the purview of our cognitive abilities, and he would thus have demonstrated central aspects of transcendental idealism. As it is, this kind of argument to the hiddenness of God (and to transcendental idealism) is not possible.

---

40   Elsewhere, I consider various arguments Kant develops both for any unconditioned object in general and for unconditioned, that is free and spontaneous, actions in particular.

B.4 God's Perfection

In his discussion of rational theology in his lectures on religion, Kant distinguishes between transcendental, natural, and moral theology and articulates different concepts of God that would be proper to each. In transcendental theology, God is represented as the *cause* of the world, in natural theology as the *author* of the world, and in moral theology as the *ruler* of the world. Kant repeatedly claims that the concept of God that is most indispensable throughout rational theology is that of transcendental theology, since its use of purely ontological predicates allows for a determinate concept of God, unlike, for example, the concept of God employed in physicotheology, which "can never give a determinate concept of God without transcendental theology" (28:1008). The most prominent predicates employed in transcendental theology are those of reality, with the result, as we have seen earlier, that God is to be thought of as an *ens realissimum*, or most real being, possessing no limitations in his reality (5:100 and 8:400n.). As a result, "the precise concept of God is the concept of a most perfect thing" (28:1008).

Not only is perfection an essential feature of the determinate concept underlying the rest of rational theology, but it also provides Kant with a powerful argument for the hiddenness of God. For immediately after marking the contrast between precise and imprecise concepts of God, he objects to the possibility that we might have experience commensurate with this precise concept: "But I can never derive such a concept from experience, for the highest perfection can never be given to me in any *possible* experience" (28:1008, my emphasis).[41] Shortly thereafter, he makes a point one could easily be familiar with from Hume, namely that our experience is, in effect, too small for such a concept: "Our experience of the world is too limited to permit us to infer a highest reality from it. Before we could argue that the present world is the most perfect of all possible ones and prove from this that its author is the highest perfection, we would have to know the whole

---

41   Kant's argument can be reconstructed formally as follows:
  P1   God is a perfect being.
  ["The precise concept of God is the concept of a most perfect thing" (28:1008).]
  P2   If knowledge of the perfection of the actual world cannot be justified (by any possible experience), then knowledge that there is a perfect being, namely God, cannot be justified (by any possible experience).
  P3   Knowledge of the perfection of the actual world cannot be justified (by any possible experience).
  ["But I can never derive such a concept from experience, for the highest perfection can never be given me in any possible experience" (28:1008).]
  C1   Insofar as God is perfect, God's existence cannot be known (by any possible experience).

totality of the world, every means and every end which is reached by it" (28:1009). Kant's argument here might seem to be the simple empiricist point that our experience of the world happens to be too restricted in scope to allow for experience of God; since we do not know what is happening outside of a very small part of the universe, we are not justified in assuming that a perfect being must be responsible for it.

However, in both of these quotations, Kant goes beyond what we happen to experience of this world, citing *possible* experience and *possible* worlds. And in the second *Critique* Kant uses the precision of the concept of God to express the stronger argument explicitly.

> Since we can be acquainted with this world only with respect to a small part, *and can even less compare it with all possible worlds*, we can infer from its order, purposiveness, and magnitude a wise, good, powerful, and so forth author, but not his omniscience, omnibenevolence, omnipotence and so forth. One can also even grant: that one is authorized to supplement this unavoidable deficiency by means of a permitted, entirely reasonable hypothesis, namely that if wisdom, beneficence, and so forth are all displayed in all the parts that offer themselves to our closer cognition, it will be exactly the same in all the rest and that it is therefore reasonable to attribute all possible perfection to the author of the world; but these are not inferences through which we think something to ourselves based on our insight, but rather only rationales that one can attribute to us and yet still require a recommendation from elsewhere to make use of it. The concept of God therefore always remains, on an empirical path (of physics), a not precisely determined concept of the perfection of the first being, in order to view it as appropriate for the concept of a divinity (but nothing at all is to be accomplished with metaphysics, in its transcendental part). (5:139, my emphasis)

Part of what Kant is saying here is not merely that the experience that we in fact have of this world is too limited to justify the ascription of perfections to God as the cause of the world, but also that even if we were justified, as we are not, in assuming that the rest of this world is like the part of the world that we have experienced, one would still not be warranted in attributing perfection to the cause of this world.[42] For as Kant points out, to determine that this world is perfect (so as to draw the further inference from the perfection of the world to the perfection of God, which, though potentially problematic, can be granted for the sake of argument), one would have to have knowledge not only of the entirety of this world, but also of all other possible worlds such that the

---

42 This line of argument is not entirely distinct from the physico-theological argument Kant considers and rejects in the first *Critique*, since it does depend on an inference from the perfection of the world to the perfection of the cause of the world. While the current discussion is supposed to be distinct from the traditional theistic proofs, the physico-theological argument shades into the current considerations in a way that makes reference to that argument unavoidable.

ascription of perfection to this world could be justified.[43] For we would have to know that no other possible world is better than this one and it seems impossible to determine that without significant knowledge of all other possible worlds.

However, on what kind of grounds could we justify such knowledge? Straightforwardly empirical grounds seem inadequate insofar as they speak merely to how things happen to be in this world and thus do not provide any information about other possible worlds. Now, unlike some, Kant is open to the possibility of a priori knowledge, but even Kant's comparatively robust account of a priori knowledge seems insufficient in this case. For one, synthetic (or substantive) a priori claims will hold only for a limited set of possible worlds, namely those that can be considered by beings having space and time as forms of intuition. On Kant's account, space and time are not absolutely necessary features of any possible world, but rather features that are necessary only for those worlds in which we could have "experience" in Kant's technical sense. For another, even if we could somehow have (very general) a priori knowledge of all other possible worlds, what would be required is to have knowledge of every possible world's degree of perfection (so as to make the comparison possible). If one grants that each world's degree of perfection would depend on a wide range of specific (and highly empirical) events that occur in it, then it follows that we could not have a priori knowledge of it.[44] In short, since we do not have appropriate knowledge of the relevant features of other possible worlds, we cannot know that this world is the most perfect of all possible worlds, nor that God must be the perfect being who is the cause of it.[45]

It is worth remarking that Kant is implicitly criticizing the potential misuse of a characteristically Leibnizian idea. Leibniz inferred— whether rightly or wrongly, can remain undecided—that since God is

---

43 This argument presupposes, as Kant seems to grant, that perfection is, least in part, a relative concept. Otherwise, the comparison to other possible worlds that Kant makes would be irrelevant. Kant acknowledges this point implicitly in his discussion of the perfection of the world in his metaphysics lectures. See, e.g., 29:936.

44 I am grateful to Dana Nelkin for helping me to be much clearer about the issues raised in this section in general and this paragraph in particular.

45 Kant's argument in support of P3 can be formulated as follows:

   P1' To know that the actual world is perfect, I would have to know that no other possible world is better.

   P2' Empirical grounds are insufficient to establish that no other possible world is better than the actual world.

   P3' A priori grounds are insufficient to establish that no other possible world is better than the actual world.

   P4' All grounds of knowledge would have to be either empirical or a priori.

   C1' Knowledge of the perfection of the actual world cannot be justified.

perfect, the world he creates must be the best of all possible worlds.[46] Anything less would entail a lack of perfection, a defect in God's knowledge, power, or goodness. According to Leibniz, our knowledge of the perfection of the world depends entirely on our *prior* knowledge of God's perfection, and not on our knowledge that all other possible worlds are less perfect than this one. Kant is pointing out that it would be a mistake to turn the entailment relation around and attempt to use our experience of the world to establish the existence of a perfect cause of it. As long as we have no substantial access to the relevant features of other possible worlds that is independent of our knowledge of God, we have no grounds for asserting that we can experience either a perfect world or a perfect being that would be the cause of it. So even if ours is a perfect world, created by a perfect God, our cognitive limitations—in this case our lack of sufficient knowledge of other possible worlds—would keep us from knowing it as such.

B.5   The Infinity of God

A final line of argument for the hiddenness of God is based on the conception of God as an infinite being, that is, as having the infinite attributes of omnipotence, omniscience, and omnibenevolence. As we saw above in the course of his discussion of the postulate of God's existence in the second *Critique*, Kant distinguishes between being very powerful, knowledgeable, and good, which are attributes that can be ascribed to finite creatures, and being omnipotent, omniscient and omnibenevolent, which alone can be attributed to God.[47] In light of this conception of God, one can argue for the conclusion that no being possessing such attributes could be given to us in sensibility, or, to put it more precisely, we could not know that we were encountering a being that had precisely those attributes rather than lesser versions thereof.[48] In short, since God's infinite attributes extend beyond what could be given to us, one can assert that God must be hidden from us.

The central question that arises for this line of argument concerns why the infinite attributes of God could not be given to us. Rather than investigating the nature of our empirical evidence to see what it supports—a task Kant undertakes in the first *Critique*, where he ends up with a conclusion that supports this line of thought—what turns out to

---

46   See Adams 1972, pp. 317-32.
47   See 5:131.
48   That is, one could experience a being that happened to be infinite, but one could not experience that it was an infinite being.

be crucial is seeing precisely how Kant understands God's infinite attributes. In his lectures on religion Kant attempts to determine how to ascribe only realities to God as an *ens realissimum*, and his primary concern is to make sure that none of the limitations that attach to the realities that we experience end up being attributed to God. If we remove all of the limitations from the realities we want to ascribe to God, we are then left with an understanding of God as an unlimited, or infinite, being, a being that is omnipotent, omniscient, and omnibenevolent.

But precisely how is the infinitude of God's attributes to be understood? Certain ways of understanding God's infinitude are, Kant thinks, unacceptable. His main target in this context is the notion of mathematical infinity. For it is, he claims, a concept that can represent not an absolute magnitude, but rather only one that is relative to us. As he puts it: "infinity never determines *how* great something is; for it does not determine the measure (or unit)" (28:1017).[49] He illustrates this claim with the example of representing, or measuring, infinite space. Whether one chooses miles or diameters of the earth as one's unit, one will represent space as being larger than any number of the units chosen, and thus as infinite. At the same time, although both magnitudes are infinite, the one infinity will be greater than the other. Kant infers from this that

> the concept of infinity expresses only a relationship to our incapacity to determine the concept of magnitude, because the magnitude in question is greater than every number I can think of, and hence gives me no determinate concept of the magnitude itself. Fundamentally, therefore, when I call an object infinite, the only advantage this gives me is that I gain an insight into my inability to express the magnitude of this object in numbers ... but in this way I can never learn to recognize its absolute magnitude. (28:1017)

That is, the notion of mathematical infinity represents not an intrinsic property of God—the absolute magnitude of his existence or properties—but rather a limitation of us—our inability to represent God's absolute magnitude. Unlike the argument based on God's perfection, where the problem was that our *evidence* is insufficient to amount to a proper justification, the crucial point here lies with the *concept* of God not being determinate enough to deliver the kind of content that might allow for knowledge of God. Kant explicitly draws this conclusion as follows:

> Thus we see that I cannot come a single step further in my cognition of God by applying the concept of mathematical infinity to him. For through this con-

---

49   I read Kant's claim about the infinity of space at A32 as invoking this kind of mathematical notion.

cept I learn only that I can never express the concept of God's greatness in
numbers. But this gives me no insight into God's absolute greatness. (28:1018)

If the mistake Kant is warning against is that of attempting to understand infinity in mathematical terms, then one could presumably avoid
this mistake simply by rejecting the analogy with mathematics and
employing concepts that are more appropriate. Kant explicitly endorses
this idea when he notes:

> I cannot see why I ought to express an ontological concept … in terms of
> mathematical infinity. Should I not rather use a term congruent with the con-
> cepts of this science, instead of permitting an ambiguity by usurping an ex-
> pression from another science, thus running the risk of letting an alien concept
> creep in as well? (28:1018)

But then the question is: What is the appropriate concept? Kant considers the following option: "Might we perhaps succeed in finding this
measure [of God's absolute greatness] by means of the concept of
metaphysical infinity? But what is the meaning of 'metaphysical infinity'?" (28:1018). In the course of answering these questions, Kant repeats the familiar claim that one can attribute to God only realities. The
crucial issue here is how we can represent these realities properly, i.e.,
as expressing "God's absolute greatness."

Kant explains that such realities can be represented in two ways, either by being given through pure reason, independently of experience,
or by being encountered in the world of sense. Kant endorses this first
way, but notes that it suffers from serious limitations:

> I may ascribe the first kind of reality to God without hesitation, for realities of
> this kind apply to things in general and determine them through pure under-
> standing. Here no experience is involved and the realities are not even affected
> by sensibility. Hence if I predicate them of God I need not fear that I am con-
> fusing him with an object of sense. (28:1020)

If we represent God as having infinite attributes, where the infinitude of
his attributes is understood in terms of pure realities that are represented
solely by the pure understanding (or reason), then there is no problem
about ascribing these attributes to a proper concept of God. However, in
that case one has conceded that the object of this concept of God cannot
be given through sensibility, which, in light of Kant's requirement that
objects must be given to us to be known, is simply to concede that God
must be hidden from us.

What is the case, however, if we attempt to understand God's attributes by considering those predicates that could also be ascribed to
objects that we experience through our own senses? Kant describes the
results in this case as follows:

> What kind of predicates shall we take from experience and be able to unite
> with the concept of God?—Nothing but pure realities! But in the whole world

there is no thing that has *pure* reality, but rather all things which can be given through experience are *partim realia, partim negativa.* … Hence I must first proceed *via negativa*; that is, I must carefully separate out everything sensible inhering in my representation of this or that reality, and leave out everything imperfect and negative, and ascribe to God the pure reality which is left over. But this is extremely difficult, for often very little or nothing is left over after I reject the limitations; or at least I can never think of the pure positive without the sensible element which is woven into my representation of it…. But if the negative element cannot be separated without canceling the concept at the same time, then in this case I will not be able to predicate of God the concept at all [*so werde ich im letztern Falle den Begriff gar nicht von Gott prädiciren können*]. (28:1021)

If I consider the predicates that I attribute to typical sensible objects (including predicates expressing power, knowledge, and goodness), then these predicates will be a mixture of a reality and a negation of that reality such that the relevant object has a specific, limited degree of that kind of predicate. However, since God is an *ens realissimus* endowed with omnipotence, omniscience, and omnibenevolence, no such limitations can be ascribed to him. As a result, to have any chance of representing God one must separate off the limitations that attach to the sensible predicates under consideration, in which case two outcomes are possible. A) If one can separate the limitations from these predicates, then there are two possibilities. 1) Either nothing is left, in which case one is not in fact ascribing any content to God in ascribing the predicate to God and there would be no way for us to know that we were experiencing such a being, given that the concept would supply us with no features that we could look for in our experience. 2) Or "very little" is left, in which case the concept contains insufficient content to represent God in a way that would allow us to distinguish experience of God from that of other beings.[50] B) If, by contrast, the limitations cannot be fully separated from the predicate, then it is immediately clear that one cannot ascribe the predicate to God, since doing so would be to ascribe limitations to a being that exists without limitations. As a result, no knowledge of God as an *ens realissimus* is forthcoming via the "way of negation" and the concept of God that contains the infinite attributes of omnipotence, omniscience, and omnibenevolence, is not one whose object we could know.

Kant's focus on the concept of infinity and on the limitations that affect its content thus puts him in a position to develop a sophisticated and plausible argument for the hiddenness of God. While it is uncontroversial to note that God is an unlimited, or infinite, being, Kant astutely points out that the content of this concept is highly problematic

---

50   Unfortunately, Kant offers surprisingly little justification for this claim.

with respect to how we might experience its object. For regardless of whether one focuses on a mathematical sense of infinity or different ways of understanding it in a metaphysical sense, insight into and experience of God's absolute or infinite intrinsic magnitude remains elusive.[51]

B.6 Hume and Kant on our Cognitive Limitations

If one reflects at this point on Kant's overall goal and his strategy for attaining it by means of the arguments articulated above, one might suspect that he is following Hume's lead on this issue. Both deny that God is an object we could experience, and there are some striking analogies between several of his arguments and the well-known reflections that Hume presents on this topic in the *Enquiry Concerning Human Understanding* (1966) and *Dialogues Concerning Natural Religion* (1977).[52] In fact, at a very general level, both thinkers hold that our cognitive abilities are so limited that the evidence we could obtain by means of them is insufficient for us to justify knowledge of the existence of God as traditionally conceived and that God, if he exists, must therefore be hidden.[53]

However, it would be a mistake to make too much of these similarities and to infer that Kant's best arguments do not go beyond Hume's considerations in any significant way. Two points of contrast are instructive in the present context. First, Kant's account of our cognitive abilities allows the argument based on God's perfection to depend on a less robust assumption about what evidence we have and to support a more persuasive argument. To this end, recall Hume's and Kant's ap-

---

51 One might object that there could be ways in which one could come to experience God other than via his perfection or infinity, and thus that even if one grants the arguments reconstructed in B.4 and B.5, the conclusion that we cannot experience God does not follow. However, for this objection to be plausible, one would have to explain what other features of God we could experience that would enable us to experience God as distinct from other kinds of beings, and the challenge that the argument of B5 presents is that the paucity of the content of our concept of God could well exclude any plausible alternative to the ones considered. I thank James Messina for pointing out this objection clearly.

52 Determining Kant's reception of Hume and its influence on his thought is not entirely straightforward, even if it is safe to conjecture that Kant must have read the first *Enquiry* by the early 1760s and the *Dialogues* shortly after its posthumous publication. While certain arguments regarding the theistic proofs in the first *Critique* sound extremely similar to lines of thought found especially in the *Dialogues*, Kant had been developing and expressing fundamental criticisms of these proofs as early as the early 1760s.

53 By "cognitive abilities" I have in mind only those abilities that pertain to knowledge as such (and not belief).

peals to experience when they argue that one could not acquire knowledge of God as a perfect being. Hume's claim was that we could not infer to God's existence on the basis of the empirical evidence actually available to us, because we have experienced only a small corner of the universe for only a very short period of time. Actual experience does not warrant, Hume thinks, an inference to an architect of the world, much less to an omnipotent creator.[54] Kant, by contrast, claimed that we could not infer God's existence even if we prescinded from these contingent limitations and assumed that our experience were much more complete than it in fact is, because we cannot in principle have the kind of experience that would be required to establish God's perfection. In short, on Kant's account, regardless of what our actual experience happens to be, no possible experience could warrant knowledge of God's existence.

To bring out more clearly the relative strengths of these two strategies, imagine that someone claimed to have an impression of the perfection of the world (and was also inclined to infer on that basis to the existence of God as its perfect cause).[55] Now Hume's first response to such a case would surely be to note that he himself lacks such an impression. However, if this were all Hume had to say, he would be in a weak position, since he would have to concede that such an impression is possible in principle, given that he places no principled restrictions on what impressions we can have. As a result, Hume would be forced to appeal to the particular contents of other impressions he has in the hopes that they conflict with and thus somehow disqualify the impression of the perfection of the world in question. Although the various apparent evils in the world might seem to put Hume on somewhat stronger ground, the strength of his response is still limited, since others may well have experienced more (or different parts) of the world and may have come to see how what appear at first glance to be imperfections in the world are merely apparent. This argument thus ends up being decided by what kind of interpretation one can impose on the complex and variable impressions that we have of the world and how plausible each interpretation is, but, unlike the case of the self, there is little reason to expect widespread agreement and a high degree of certainty about the results here. In short, the complexity, contingency, and flexibility that Hume associates with our actual experiences renders him unable to articulate an especially robust response to such a claim.

---

54 Of course, Hume develops further criticisms in the *Dialogues*.

55 One can imagine further that when questioned, this person reported that this impression includes the information that this world is better than any other, i.e., the impression is not one of merely apparent perfection.

Kant, by contrast, is in a position to exclude such a claim on principled grounds. For his notion of possible experience and the account of
our cognitive faculties that supports it rules out that we could have an
impression of the perfection of the world. For on Kant's account, whatever impressions we have, they must be of objects that are given to us,
and objects can be given to us only if they exist and act on us. As a
result, we can have impressions only of the actual world, not of other
possible worlds, since all merely possible worlds do not stand in causal
relations with us. However, if an impression of the perfection of this
world entails that we also have an impression of all other possible
worlds (an entailment established by the argument from perfection described above), it follows from the fact that we cannot have impressions
of these other possible worlds that we also cannot have an impression
of the perfection of this world.

Now it is true that Kant's account is more complicated and robust
than Hume's insofar as it allows that we can have knowledge that is not
based on sensory impressions, and thus that we can have some knowledge of other possible worlds, but he also wants to insist that even so,
there are strict limits to our knowledge of other possible worlds. Specifically, any object of knowledge, whether actual or not, must be an
object of possible experience, e.g., must be able to be given to us
through our forms of intuition. Because some possible worlds would
presumably not satisfy those conditions (e.g., those that are merely
metaphysically possible and not also epistemically possible for us),
Kant will hold that we cannot have substantive (i.e., non-analytic)
knowledge about them (which would presumably include their relative
degree of perfection). While Kant goes on to make further claims about
the conditions of the possibility of experience (e.g., that space and time
are our forms of intuition and, in fact, nothing more than that), these
more controversial claims are not required for present purposes.[56]
Rather, all that is needed to establish the conclusion more firmly than
Hume's argument does is that we cannot have knowledge of *all* other
possible worlds, and that is both much less controversial and much less
complicated than what is required by the strategy that Hume is forced
to pursue, though the latter does call forth an impressive display of
rhetorical skill. In sum, Kant's focus on the forms through which objects are given to us rather than on the content that we happen to receive through them allows him to see more clearly how possible rather
than actual experience places limits on the empirical evidence that we

---

56   For example, Hume might reject the requirement that impressions must be of spatio-
     temporal objects. That is, he might grant that all of his impressions happen to be of spa-
     tio-temporal objects, but reject the claim that they must necessarily be of such objects.

could have, limits that preclude the possibility that we could have knowledge of God's existence.

The second relevant point of contrast between Kant's and Hume's accounts of our cognitive limitations concerns not the nature of the evidence that would be needed to justify knowledge of God, but rather the requirements that derive from the concepts involved in such knowledge. On Hume's account, the main limitation that pertains to what he calls ideas is that they must be derived from sense impressions. Ideas are for him merely fainter copies of original impressions and he rejects both innate ideas and any process of abstraction by means of which ideas could be formed that might be so different in kind that they could not in principle match up with our impressions. Now according to Hume, our idea of God is not derived directly from an impression of God, but rather is formed indirectly by taking finite exemplars of certain properties (e.g., the strength of an athlete, the intelligence of a scholar), extending them as far as we can in our imagination (to what he calls omnipotence and omniscience) and then conjoining them into a single entity (a perfect, infinite being). The question then is just whether our empirical evidence or the causal reasoning based on it can validate an idea our imagination has created from sensory materials in this way. Hume presents a sustained argument that it cannot do so in the case of God, but it is crucial to note that his argument is based, as we saw, on the content of the impressions that he happens to have rather than on his account of ideas. For the limitations that attach to our idea of God, according to Hume, derive simply from our imagination and thus do not suggest that there must be a fundamental or principled mismatch between our idea of God and the relevant evidence.[57] Instead, we lack knowledge of God's existence because of the (limited) nature of the evidence that we happen to have.

Kant, by contrast, acknowledges a difference in kind between the sensory impressions by means of which empirical objects are immediately given to us, and the concepts that our understanding uses to think and cognize objects. In fact, some of the most central philosophical and systematic passages in Kant's corpus (e.g., the Transcendental Deduction and the Schematism) are devoted precisely to the task of showing the conditions under which the gap between sensory impressions and a

---

57 In other words, since, on Hume's account, we represent God's infinite magnitude by means of the imagination merely as much, much bigger than the size of anything we have experienced so far, it is not impossible that our very next impression couldn't be exactly as big as our imagination had thought God is. Now a Humean could respond by stipulating that our idea of God will be formed by having the imagination take our biggest impression and extend that impression in some direction, but that would lead to an implausible instability in our idea of God.

priori concepts can be closed. The interesting point in the current context, however, is that limitations unique to our concept of God are what drive Kant's argument concerning the infinity of God. One might think, for example, that the notion of mathematical infinity can be understood clearly and precisely, which would be advantageous to us in representing God (since these features might seem to help us to attain the determinate concept of God characteristic of transcendental theology). However, Kant shows quite effectively that this concept is not in fact in a position to capture the absolute magnitude of God, since it is based on our selection of a unit that establishes nothing more than an indeterminate relation between God's magnitude and that of other things, which means that we are representing only an arbitrary and relative rather than an absolute and intrinsic concept of God's magnitude. Thus it is the very structure of the concept of mathematical infinity that precludes it from being used for knowledge of God's nature, rather than the evidence we might accumulate.

The concept of metaphysical infinity, to which Kant turns as the sole remaining possible concept with which to understand God's magnitude, suffers from a different set of limitations. If the properties (or realities) that a metaphysically infinite being would have to have to an unlimited degree, are identified through pure reason and devoid of sensory content, then the corresponding concept of God cannot by definition be fully satisfied by any object given to us in experience.[58] In this case, the concept has been formed by means of a process that builds epistemic limits right into its content and rules of application.[59] If the properties (or realities) that such a being would have are identified through encounters with objects in the world of sense, the situation is more complicated. Given Kant's view that all instances of sensory content involve negations that are inconsistent with God's nature, they must be separated off, but the content that remains is, at best, extremely limited. In fact, the limitations are so severe that the most pressing question is whether any content remains at all or rather whether the concept is altogether devoid of content. Kant ultimately holds that the concept of God does have some meaningful content, but due to the limitations in the content of our concepts, the very content of the concept of God keeps us from applying it in experience. In sum, because Kant's account of our cognitive powers allows him to articulate both a

---

58   That is, we might be able to experience an object that happened to have the properties contained in the concept of God, but we could not experience the object *as* having those properties.

59   While Kant thus disagrees with Hume about the existence of fully a priori concepts, he agrees with Hume that rationalists wrongly attribute too much content to them.

plausible distinction between concepts and sensory impressions and, as a result, limitations to the content of certain concepts, he is in a position to explain more clearly and powerfully than is Hume why our concept of God is such that finding evidence that might support it turns out to be impossible.

We can thus see how two of Kant's arguments for the hiddenness of God arise from basic features of his account of our cognitive abilities and the limitations therein. The argument based on God's perfection depends on Kant's analysis of the conditions under which objects can be given to us (or, to put it in more contemporary terms, on the limits to the kind of evidence we could have), while his argument concerning God's infinite magnitude turns on limitations that adhere to the concept of infinity. We can also see how these arguments rely on premises that are more fundamental than Hume's, but without relying on distinctively Kantian assumptions.[60] Instead, Kant emphasizes the conditions that hold for objects to be given to us and the independent content of the concept of God for which we might try to find appropriate evidence. The contrasts between the foundational features of Hume's and Kant's accounts of our cognitive abilities thus turn out to illuminate the nature of the assumptions of Kant's arguments, showing them to be plausible in their own right, even if they are often overshadowed by other, more controversial claims Kant makes in conjunction with them.

Conclusion

In this paper I have argued that Kant presents two different kinds of arguments for the hiddenness of God, one practical, the other theoretical. The practical argument is based on the idea that if we had knowledge of God's existence, we would be unable to act in ways that God would want us to. On one version of the argument, our actions could have no moral worth, on the other, we could not act with morally significant freedom. Unfortunately, neither of these arguments is successful, since both assume, controversially, that fear of divine punishment and hope for divine reward would trump any other motives that we might have and that God could not reveal himself without also issuing threats and promises. The theoretical line of argument, by contrast, appears more promising. While two versions of this line of argument

---

60   Nor do they rely on other assumptions that might be controversial. For example, one
     might claim that human beings' cognitive limitations are a consequence of original sin.
     However, any further claim about the cause of our limitations is not required as a foun-
     dation for Kant's arguments.

are not fully convincing, two others are much more plausible. For the evidence available to us is insufficient to support the claim that God is perfect, and our concept of God's infinite magnitude is too thin to represent God adequately or to give us content robust enough to identify God on that basis. One striking feature of both of these arguments is that they follow straightforwardly from basic features of Kant's account of our cognitive faculties and their limitations, features that differ from Hume's, but without being so distinctively Kantian to be unacceptable outside the context of Kant's Critical project. As a result, Kant's critical philosophy provides an especially helpful framework for articulating one significant account of why God must be hidden from us.[61]

61 I thank Karl Ameriks, Michael Hardimon, Kristen Irwin, Monte Johnson, Pat Kain, James Messina, Dana Nelkin, Sam Rickless, Clinton Tolley, Merold Westphal and audience members at the Society of Christian Philosophers Eastern Meeting, held at Houghton College (May 2006), for helpful comments on an earlier version of this paper. I owe special thanks to Graham Bird, Andrew Chignell, Pat Kain, and Mike Murray for extensive discussion and myriad helpful critical remarks on earlier versions of this paper. Two anonymous reviewers of *Kantian Review* also provided extremely helpful comments, for which I am grateful. Needless to say any errors are entirely mine.

CHAPTER 11

Kant's Account of Practical Fanaticism

Rachel Zuckert

Many seventeenth- and eighteenth-century philosophers argue that political legitimacy, morality, and knowledge are not to be grounded on divine right, religiosity, or revealed doctrine, but rather on reason and rational knowledge of human nature alone. These philosophers are both inspired by scientific advances and also attempting to limit the power of religion in response to centuries of religiously inspired political violence in Europe. Hobbes, Spinoza, Locke, Shaftesbury, Hume, Voltaire, and Diderot, for example, criticize religious doctrines not only because (or when) such doctrines comprise unfounded claims to knowledge, but also because they inspire religious fanaticism, ensuing in sectarian violence, persecution, torture, and war. These thinkers by and large argue that fanaticism is the expression of irrational, emotional aspects of human psychology, exploited by some forms of religion: political ambitions of religious leaders, hopes and fears of the population, overweening conceit, or a diseased melancholy. Thus, religious fanaticism or "enthusiasm" could, they argue, be curbed by reducing the political power of religious institutions, by rational polemics against the claims to superior knowledge and morality of religious leaders, by rational politics that could address people's earthly hopes and fears, and by education, the inculcation of instrumental and/or moral rationality in the population at large.

Kant is recognizably a participant in this tradition. Kant too argues that politics ought to be governed by a rational principle of right and take the form of republican government; that freedom of religion (and the independence of political governance from religious institutions) ought to be instituted in such a state; that morality derives from principles of pure practical reason; and that human beings may legitimately claim to know scientific laws concerning objects of sensible experience, but not to have knowledge of God or other spiritual, supersensible matters. And Kant too repeatedly and pejoratively characterizes various forms of belief in or behavior guided by religious (or other) conceptions of the supersensible as "fanaticism" (*Schwärmerei*).

In comparison to many Enlightenment figures (particularly those of the French Enlightenment), however, Kant's understanding of the relation between the human presumption to knowledge of the supersensible and the deliverances of reason is more sympathetic to the claims of religious belief and more qualified in advocating the corrective power of reason against it. For Kant famously claims that his Critical philosophy "makes room for faith": though we cannot know that God exists or that we have free wills or immortal souls, we may have faith and hope concerning these beliefs; they cannot be shown to be irrational, incoherent, false, etc. More strongly, Kant argues that these central ideas of religion are necessarily formed by pure reason itself and can be rationally justified as subjects of legitimate belief on practical grounds.

Thus Kant holds that our claims to know the supersensible can be limited only through critique, a *self*-critical investigation of reason by reason itself. As I shall suggest, Kant's conception of fanaticism—his account of its origins, motivations, and the nature of its error—also reflects this more qualified endorsement of reason. I shall suggest that by contrast to many of his predecessors and contemporaries, Kant does not treat fanaticism as expressing or originating wholly from sensible emotions or interests, opposed to and "overpowering" reason. Rather, though sensibility (including emotional sensibility) is central to his account of fanaticism, Kant holds that the fanatical stance incorporates and depends on rational projections or aspirations. Moreover, Kant's distinction between theoretical and practical reason generates an interesting, dual account of fanaticism, or (in the terms of the theme of this volume) of how human beings may stand in the wrong relation to the supersensible: he identifies both a theoretical fanaticism, a kind of cognitive error, and a practical fanaticism, a specifically *practical* error in our relation to the supersensible.

The aims of this paper are, then, primarily expository: to reconstruct from Kant's scattered pejorative remarks an account of fanaticism—particularly practical fanaticism, as it is the most pressing, worrying form of fanaticism, both for Enlightenment figures and for us, and possibly the more difficult case for a Kantian analysis. I shall begin by presenting Kant's account of theoretical fanaticism, before turning to its relation to practical reason and to his account of practical fanaticism. First, however, I shall make several clarificatory remarks concerning Kant's terminology.

Some Remarks concerning Terminology

As I have indicated, I will be concerned with Kant's conception of *Schwärmerei*, and will argue that this may be analyzed as comprising two sorts of errors: "theoretical fanaticism" and "practical fanaticism." As these neologisms suggest, Kant's conception of *Schwärmerei* does not map neatly onto current English usage of "fanaticism" (which does not have a "theoretical"/epistemic cast or subcategory). Perhaps for this reason, the Cambridge translations of Kant's works tend to render *Schwärmerei* as "enthusiasm," thus also bringing it into contact with eighteenth-century British discussions concerning problematic types of religious belief and action. Before embarking on my interpretation of Kant's account, therefore, several remarks concerning my terminological choices—and the eighteenth-century context—are in order.

There are good reasons for translating *Schwärmerei* as "enthusiasm," for the usage of these two terms in the eighteenth century is roughly coincident, and considerably broader and less defined than the already somewhat fuzzy "fanaticism" in current English usage (to which I shall turn in a moment). "Enthusiasm" was used, sometimes in association with "zeal," "bigotry" and (more infrequently) "fanaticism," to characterize religious sectarianism, extremism, and violence (see, for example, Locke 1700, IV.xix.11-2, Shaftesbury 2001b, pp. 183, 216[1], and Hume 1985, p. 77). But it was also used to refer to a wider range of beliefs and behaviors, to "groups and individuals who claimed to have direct divine inspiration, who prophesied about future events…, who claimed to perform miracles…whose activities…involved physical manifestations such as convulsions," or who were characterized by "exaggerat[ed]…religious spirituality" or endorsed an "emotional, personal, and…experiential type of religion" (Kors 2003, pp. 1 and 6; see also Passmore 2003 and Tucker 1972). Thus "enthusiasm" need not refer to any sort of practical attitude, much less a tendency to violent action—as "fanaticism" connotes today—but may refer more broadly to emotional excess or mistaken belief held on the grounds of questionable evidence. Specifically, such questionable evidence—as is suggested in the etymology of "enthusiasm"—often comprises putative direct personal revelation or inspiration.[2]

---

1   Shaftesbury also uses this term to refer to non-religious states of mind—for example, philosophical inspiration or excitement—and not necessarily to criticize them (see, e.g., Shaftesbury 2001b, pp. 119, 123ff., 139). Shaftesbury 2001a likewise contains both pejorative and positive usages.

2   There also appears to be a relatively pervasive, largely positive British (and French) usage of "enthusiasm" to refer to artistic inspiration; see, for example, Reynolds 1997, pp. 27, 142. I leave this positive meaning of "enthusiasm" out of account, however, as it

In eighteenth-century German usage, *Schwärmerei* has similarly broad connotations; in Duden 1999-2004, for example, the sixteenth-century usage of this term is glossed as *wirklichkeitsfern denken, sich begeistern* (thinking in a way distant from reality, being excited or in heightened "spirits"). This term had been introduced (largely by Martin Luther) as a pejorative characterization of religious sects outside of established churches that valued personal, emotional relationships to God, mystical revelations, and practices like speaking in tongues (Brecht 1990, pp. 137-95; s.v. Duden 1999-2004, Grimm 1899, Kors 2003). "*Schwärmerei*" like "enthusiasm" thus was used to identify groups or persons as politically problematic: because of their emotionally charged character and their oppositional stances toward established religion, such sects threatened social order.[3] Indeed, by contrast to "enthusiasm," the etymological origins of "*Schwärmerei*" connote dangerous, disorderly group phenomena: "*Schwarm*" or "*schwärmen*" were (and are) used literally of bees. But "*Schwärmerei*" was used too to refer to a broad range of behaviors and beliefs and to convey a range of corresponding criticisms—e.g., over-emotionality, errant belief in perception of ideal reality or in personal revelation—and, most generally, to refer to craziness of belief or behavior, perhaps by extending "swarm" to refer to disorderly "movement" of thoughts and emotions (as suggested in Campe 1810). Thus a *Schwärmer* is also called a *Fanatiker* (a less frequently used Fremdwort), but also a *Visionär, Fantast*, or *Verrückter* (visionary, fantasist, or crazy person) (s.v. Campe 1810, Sanders 1865, Grimm, 1899).

---

seems to be a relatively independent usage (though of course connected through the concept of "divine inspiration," often attributed to artists), and one that is not reflected in Kant's usage concerning fanaticism or artistic genius. (Kant *may* understand poetic *Schwärmerei* to be an exceptional, unproblematic case, perhaps because the poet makes no truth claims, though I have discovered only one passage (8:393) that possibly—*not* unambiguously—contains such a usage).

3   Some, indeed, have proposed that one should understand fanaticism as a political, group phenomenon, not as a state of mind or attitude of individuals. For example, Spinoza's discussion of "superstition" suggests that fanaticism characterizes groups comprising on the one hand unscrupulous leaders attempting to gain power, and on the other hand followers whose fears and hopes are manipulated by such leaders (Spinoza 2007, pp. 3-12). Shaftesbury suggests, alternatively, that enthusiasm comprises a group infection of melancholy, and thus is a manifestation of (what we would call) mob psychology (Shaftesbury 2001a). In the twentieth century, Gabriel Marcel argues not only that fanaticism is characteristic of groups but also that the *content* of fanatical belief ought to be understood as the endorsement of a group ("us") versus other groups ("them") (see Crosson 2003). I shall, however, leave the question raised by such accounts—whether fanaticism ought to be understood as a fundamentally political, group phenomenon—aside. For though these accounts capture an element of fanatical behavior and its political relevance, Kant (like many others, including Hume and Locke) conceives of fanaticism as characterizing individuals.

"*Schwärmerei*" in Kant's usage tends to have this broader extension, for Kant often uses it to characterize epistemic failings, thereby
deemphasizing the political connotations of the term. (Here, as I shall
discuss, Kant is not too distant from Locke's account of enthusiasm in
the *Essay Concerning Human Understanding*.) Kant frequently uses
this term to refer to those who make mistaken claims to knowledge
superior to that of ordinary human beings, usually of supersensible
reality. Like some British critics of enthusiasm, Kant often associates
Schwärmerei with mysticism, but also criticizes as *Schwärmer* neo-
Platonists who claim to have immediate, intuitive knowledge of the
Forms (8:392n, 398), Spinoza and Spinozists (8:143n), and even Locke,
for claiming to garner *a priori* concepts (including that of God) from
empirical evidence, thereby "opening the gates" to *Schwärmerei*
(A95/B127). Kant's most extensive discussion of *Schwärmerei* is in the
early work, *Dreams of a Spirit Seer Elucidated by Dreams of Metaphysics*, his mocking engagement with Emmanuel Swedenborg's
claims of extrasensory perception of another world of spirits. Here and
elsewhere, Kant classes *Schwärmerei* as a form of madness.

Despite these commonalities between "*Schwärmerei*" and "enthusiasm," I translate the former as "fanaticism"—and emend the Cambridge translations quoted here, correspondingly—for several reasons.
First, Kant himself employs two distinct terms, *Schwärmerei* and *Enthusiasm* (or *Enthusiasmus*). Though he often links the two, he also
distinguishes them, and treats the latter (but never the former) on occasion in a guardedly positive way. In the *Critique of the Power of Judgment*, Kant distinguishes between *Schwärmerei* and *Enthusiasm* as
Wahnwitz and *Wahnsinn*—madness of "wit" or reason and of sense—
respectively (5:274-5; cf. 7:202-3). In *Observations on the Feeling of
the Beautiful and Sublime*, Kant distinguishes fanaticism from enthusiasm on the grounds that the former "believes itself to feel an immediate
and extraordinary communion with a higher nature," whereas enthusiasm is being "inflamed by any principle above the proper degree,
whether...maxims of patriotic virtue, or of friendship, or of religion,
without the illusion of a supernatural communion having anything to do
with it" (2:251n)[4]. Here as elsewhere, Kant criticizes enthusiasm for
comprising an excess of feeling—or, in his later technical terms, an
Affekt—but, by contrast to fanaticism (in this passage, *Fanaticism*), this
state is not delusory per se, but rather is problematic only because of its
degree (of feeling). Similarly, in his "Essay on Mental Illnesses," Kant
suggests that Rousseau—whom Kant of course admires—might be
deemed an "enthusiast" for the morally good, and claims that "nothing

---

4   The translation quoted here is from Kant 1960.

great can be accomplished without enthusiasm," a frequently repeated slogan in the eighteenth century (2:267, my translation; cf. 5:272 and 5:274). And in *Conflict of the Faculties*, Kant argues that the sympathetic enthusiasm of spectators for the French Revolution, though not entirely praiseworthy (because, again, it is an "affect"), is a sign of the moral progress of humankind (7:85-6).

Thus Kant appears to have a concept of "enthusiasm" not too dissimilar from that in contemporary English usage, though more pejoratively tinged (perhaps corresponding to our "over-enthusiastic"): as a state of high emotionality about, or passionate commitment to, some principle or idea or value. Kant's contrasting usage of *Schwärmerei* is reflected better, I suggest, by "fanaticism" in its contemporary English usage. Like "fanaticism," this term has unambiguously pejorative meaning for Kant.[5] "Fanaticism" like *Schwärmerei* evokes a religious context, viz., claims to religious knowledge, as well as religious extremism or emotionalism, though both may be extended to refer to other, not explicitly religious, phenomena—whether (say) extremism inspired by political ideology (in contemporary English usage), or (in one of Kant's other usages) problematic moral self-satisfaction. For Kant, as indicated in the quotation from *Observations*, the crucial element of the core, religiously oriented sense of this term is the connection of *Schwärmerei* to the supersensible: as noted, he uses this term most frequently to refer to forms of pretended knowledge of or value derived from the supersensible (including God).

As I have also noted, the extension of "*Schwärmerei*" in Kant's usage is broader than the extension of "fanaticism" in current English usage;[6] I shall refer to his epistemically oriented conception as "theo-

---

5   See Tucker 1972 on changes in English usage. The Grimms identify a "milder" usage of *Schwärmerei* and cognates in the latter half of the eighteenth century (which also appears to be the primary twenty-first-century usage; see *Duden* 1999-2004): as *Begeisterung*, excitement, passionate commitment, with weaker pejorative connotations of (excessive) emotionality and fantasy. I disregard this "mild" conception of *Schwärmerei* because it is not characteristic of Kant; Kant appears rather (if rarely) to use "*Enthusiasm*" in this sense. Arnulf Zweig claims that Kant does not always use "*Schwärmerei*" (and cognates) "abusively," but his evidence for this claim—that Kant refers to an unstable female admirer (Maria von Herbert), in the context of presenting her letters to another woman as an example of mental sickness, as *die kleine Schwärmerin*—is unpersuasive (Zweig 1967, p. 14). Such affectionate descriptions tinged with contempt (often directed toward women) are not a sign that the terms used are not pejorative; compare: "little idiot."

6   Notably, it is eighteenth-century *French* usage—at least as presented in the *Encyclopédie*—that is closest to twenty-first-century English usage: though the *Encyclopédie* entries on *enthousiasme* and *fanatisme* do include some pejorative conceptions of the former, and associate the latter with mysticism, they largely treat the former positively (as

retical fanaticism" to mark this difference. But, finally, I use "fanaticism" because I wish to argue that Kant provides an account of fanaticism—as I shall term it, "practical fanaticism"—that addresses (something like) what we currently mean by this term. That is, in current English usage, "fanaticism" is usually understood to refer to a problematic practical stance or attitude, an extremely strong, overriding adherence to some principle, idea, or aim—often religious—that may lead to equally extreme, violent, destructive action. Thus, for example, R.M. Hare defines a fanatic as an idealist who endorses his ideal in such a way as to "override all considerations of people's interests, even the holder's own in actual or hypothetical cases" (Hare 1965, p. 176), and A.P. Martinich defines a fanatic as "a person who purports to place all...value in things of some transcendent realm [and attaches]...no or only derivative value...to this world" (Martinich 2000, p. 419).[7] It is this sort of practical attitude which is, I submit, most of interest, most pressing in its claims to be understood (and combated), for us and for eighteenth-century thinkers.

The distinction I draw between theoretical and practical fanaticism is not explicitly Kant's own, but does reflect Kant's distinction between the theoretical and practical uses of reason: *Schwärmerei* may be understood as a wrong relation to the supersensible, either theoretically or practically. Because it figures most prominently in Kant's discussions, I shall first consider his conception of theoretical fanaticism. As I shall suggest, this account can serve both as a contrast case and as a model for Kant's conception of practical fanaticism.

Kant's Account of Theoretical Fanaticism

Kant refers pejoratively to a wide range of beliefs, attitudes, states of mind, etc. as *Schwärmerei*. This may therefore appear to be a multipurpose term of Kantian insult, but the various beliefs and states of mind do (mostly) fit Kant's general characterization of fanaticism in the third *Critique*: the "delusion of being able to see something beyond all bounds of sensibility" (5:275)—that is, to know the supersensible through some sort of intuition. Swedenborg's claims to experience ghosts and the neo-Platonists' putative direct apprehension of non-

---

a state of artistic or other inspiration), and strongly associate the latter with religiously inspired violence.

7　The colloquial, extended meaning of this term, as in "sports fanatic," also tends to have practical connotations, i.e., to refer to stances or attitudes closely associated with action or values.

sensible Ideas both constitute claims to "see"—intuit, directly perceive—ideas or entities that are beyond the reach of ordinary, natural
sensibility.[8] This conception also informs Kant's claim that Locke
"opens the door" to fanaticism: Locke claims to have direct, sensible
experience of causes, and to be able to prove God's existence from
experiential premises. Against Locke, Hume is right, Kant claims, to
hold that sensible experience by itself cannot provide grounds for either
of these *a priori* concepts or claims; Locke purports to "sense" objects
or states of affairs that are in fact beyond sensibility. This definition too
explains Kant's association of theoretical fanatics with visionaries and
mystics: such persons claim directly to intuit events or entities that tran-
scend ordinary sensible experience.[9]

Such claims to knowledge are, on Kant's view, mistaken. Famously, Kant denies that human beings are capable of any knowledge
concerning the supersensible, or of things-in-themselves, viz., of things
not as they appear to (natural) sensibility; the Dialectic in the *Critique
of Pure Reason* aims precisely to establish this claim. Kant's criticism
of theoretical fanaticism is, however, more specific than this global
denial of human knowledge concerning the supersensible. For, as suggested in the quotation above, such beliefs are delusional not simply
because they make claims to knowledge of the supersensible, but (on
Kant's polemical redescription) because these claims are nearly self-
contradictory—viz., to have (had) *sensible* experience of the super- or
non-sensible.[10] The fanatical claim to knowledge is thus mistaken, on
Kant's view, because it confuses sensible and intelligible objects and/or

---

8 This understanding of fanaticism informs Kant's attack on the neo-Platonists throughout "On a Recently Prominent Tone of Superiority in Philosophy" and "What Does it
Mean to Orient Oneself in Thinking?"; see especially 8:398. It is less clearly present in
Dreams, but it is implicitly (I believe) employed in Kant's analysis of the "delusion"
encapsulated in the concept of spirit beings (2:347-8) and in Kant's description of Swedenborg at 2:364-5.

9 Kant's claim that Spinoza and Spinozists are *Schwärmer* (8:143n) seems to fit less well
with his definition, but it may be so read. Kant attacks Spinoza for adumbrating a rationally incomprehensible concept of God. Though Kant does not explicitly so argue, insofar as Spinoza claims to cognize such a God, such cognition cannot be rational cognition and therefore must be a form of intuition. Thus on Kant's view Spinoza and
Spinozists are in essence pretending to sense (intuit) the supersensible (God).

10 Though the claim to sense the non-sensible is (as so-stated) self-contradictory, I qualify
that description because Kant holds that God is or would be an intuitive intellect (one
that intuits the supersensible, or non-sensible) (see, e.g., B145-6). The intuition of the
non-sensible is, therefore, not absolutely impossible or contradictory on Kant's view,
but merely unavailable to human beings, given the discursive character of our intellects
(see, e.g., 8:389, 401n).

corresponding types of knowledge.[11] Hence Kant's criticism of fanaticism even in his pre-Critical period, when he claims that human beings *can* attain knowledge of things-in-themselves or noumena: the fanatical error is to fail to recognize that such knowledge may be obtained only through pure reason, not through sense experience or intuition (then, in the Critical period: if we *were* to know about things-in-themselves, this knowledge *would be* pure rational knowledge).[12]

I shall not attempt to reconstruct Kant's arguments for this position. Such arguments rely, as should be clear, on Kant's foundational, sharp, and contestable distinction between sensibility and understanding (and/or reason), and his corresponding denial of the possibility of (human) intellectual intuition.[13] But I do wish to emphasize the distinctiveness of Kant's account. To do so, I shall compare it to Locke's better-known treatment of enthusiasm in the *Essay Concerning Human Understanding*.

Like theoretical fanaticism on Kant's view, enthusiasm, according to Locke, is primarily a cognitive mistake, an ill-founded claim to knowledge based on putative direct experience of objects or events beyond the reach of natural human cognitive abilities—or, more briefly, on personal, "inner" revelation. Like Kant, Locke suggests that enthusiasm arises from over-heated imagination or unrestrained "fancies" (Locke 1700, IV.xix.3; cf. 2:341-7, 7:172). Nonetheless, we may note two significant differences between Locke and Kant, concerning a) the character of fanatical/enthusiastic cognitive error; b) the psychological sources of such belief, particularly the roles of reason and of the emotions, passions, or interests therein. (In the next section, I will discuss a

---

11 Here I follow the analysis in Grier 2001. My interest in the topic of this paper, and my approach to it are inspired by this book, as well by Grier's (unpublished) paper, "Illusion, Subreption, and the Kantian Sublime," an early version of which was presented at the Pacific Division meeting of the American Society for Aesthetics, at Asilomar, Cal., in March 2001.

12 Many of the rational errors that Kant identifies in the Dialectic of the first *Critique* are apparently similar, viz., are fallacies of ambiguity that result from the illicit replacement of a pure logical concept (e.g., of substance) with the schematized version of that concept (e.g., a persisting entity) that may be legitimately, meaningfully applied only to objects of sensible experience. (This is particularly apparent in Kant's treatment of the Paralogisms.) Though this error—which, following Grier 2001, I call "dialectical error"—might be traced, broadly speaking, to a failure to distinguish properly between sensibility and understanding, as a conceptual mistake it is nonetheless not identical to the fanatical error of pretending directly to *intuit* supersensible entities.

13 Alison Laywine argues, indeed, that Kant's pre-Critical attack on fanaticism in *Dreams* constituted a significant step toward the formulation of his Critical distinction between understanding and sensibility, and the limitation of human knowledge to the realm of sensible experience (Laywine 1993).

third, crucial difference, concerning c) the connection between this epistemic error and practical fanaticism.)

Predictably, because Locke does not endorse Kant's strict distinction between sensibility and understanding (or reason), he understands the enthusiast's error differently. Locke does not deny the possibility of direct personal revelation[14]: it is possible to receive direct illumination from God, and thereby acquire knowledge not possible through the operation of natural human faculties (*Ibid.*, IV.xviii.3, IV.xix.5). Moreover, because God is the ultimate, absolute source of truth, such illumination would be a determinative source of knowledge (*Ibid.*, IV.xviii.10). (For Locke—by contrast to Kant—the immediacy and passivity of such revelation would not count against its epistemic status: direct sensible apprehension of simple ideas is, after all, Locke's gold standard for knowledge, in contrast to Kant's conception of human cognition as discursive.) Locke argues, however, that one may never have sufficient grounds for belief *that* this illumination *was* from God—instead of one's own imagination or the intervention of "some other spirit" (*Ibid.*, IV.xix.10). Thus one ought never to take such (possible, pretended) revelation to be determinative, particularly if it contravenes the (also God-given) findings of natural cognition (*Ibid.*, IV.xviii.5).

The enthusiast overlooks the fact that he has no rational grounds for claiming that his ideas come from God, Locke argues, because of passions or interests—Locke mentions conceit, melancholy, vanity, laziness—that override his "love of truth" (*Ibid.*, IV.xix.1-8). These passions might, moreover, provide an illusion of justification for the enthusiast's belief: he might claim, Locke suggests, that his strong feelings concerning his belief are evidence that it is the result of divine revelation (*Ibid.*, IV.xix.10). Locke counters that this argument begs the question: "*It is a Revelation because they firmly believe it*, and *they believe it, because it is a Revelation*" (*Ibid.*).

As suggested above, Kant's account of theoretical fanatical error differs from Locke's in ways reflecting their differing epistemologies. Kant purports to rule out fanatical claims *in principle*—it is *impossible*

---

14 I gloss enthusiasm on the Lockean conception as "private" or "personal" revelation because Locke distinguishes such revelation both from miracles and from traditional, public revelation in texts, both of which (he wishes to argue) provide "outer" and therefore grounds for belief that can be rationally scrutinized and even rationally approved (Locke, 1700, IV.xviii.6, IV.xix.15). Kant would likely disagree on this point, but for my purposes here, this disagreement is not crucial: theoretical fanaticism, on Kant's view, is like Lockean enthusiasm an "inner" state, a claim to direct personal experience.

for us to sense the non-sensible, so claims to do so are *always* false[15]—while Locke more modestly attempts to establish that such claims are insufficiently justified (though they might be true). Their analyses thus have differing burdens of proof: Locke's is to establish how (pretended) direct cognition of God's revelation can be distinguished from direct sensible cognition of existing things (also not ultimately justified rationally on Locke's view),[16] Kant's is to establish the distinction between the objects of (human) sensibility and understanding/reason in terms stark enough to justify his claims concerning the impossibility of intuiting the non-sensible.

More important here, however, is the contrast between the roles of reason and passion on their analyses: for Kant (and not for Locke), fanaticism crucially involves reason, and is not necessarily to be traced to (or identified with) emotion, passion, or interest.[17] On Locke's view, enthusiasts, under the influence of passion, simply fail to employ reason, in the sense that they fail properly to consider the justificatory grounds (or lack thereof) for their beliefs. By contrast, Kant suggests that fanaticism is "to dream in accord with principles, [or] to rave with reason [*mit Vernunft rasen*]" (5:275, translation modified; cf. 7:203). A role for reason is suggested in Kant's general characterization of fanaticism as well: in order to believe that one senses the supersensible, one must conceive of the supersensible. Such a conception is not derived from sensibility, on Kant's view, or even from imagination (as the faculty that assembles and associates the sensibly given), but rather from understanding or reason.[18] Thus the theoretical fanatical mistake is not

---

15 Thus, for example, in "On a Recently Prominent Tone of Superiority in Philosophy," Kant denies that we could even make "probable" claims, or have opinions, about supersensible entities because about these "no theoretical knowledge is possible" at all (8:396-7n). Kant here also puts forth a Lockean argument concerning the unprovability of claims to have received testimony (revelation) from supersensible entities.

16 Something like this objection is raised against Locke's account of enthusiasm in Mavrodes 1989.

17 These two points together are arguably the core of Kant's distinction between fanaticism and enthusiasm: enthusiasm *is*, on Kant's view, an excessive emotional state—an *Affekt*—which may, but need not, involve reason (i.e., it may, but need not, have as its object a rational idea, e.g., of the moral good or of God).

18 This is a core Kantian doctrine; for its articulation in relation both to dogmatism and to fanaticism, see 8:142-3. In *Dreams*, however, Kant appears to consider Swedenborg's fanaticism as a "delusion of sense" (rather than of reason) (see 2:361). Though I cannot argue for this claim here, I believe that Kant's later conception of fanaticism is a better characterization even of his view in that early work.
   Kant's full view concerning the origin of our concepts/ideas of supersensible entities is more nuanced than suggested here. In *Religion within the Boundaries of Mere Reason,* Kant suggests—in a way similar to Hume in his *Natural History of Religion*—that "veneration" of invisible beings arises originally out of fear at human powerlessness and desire to influence the world in our favor; later in human history, religious concepts are

to fail to employ reason, but to employ reason wrongly, to confuse its ideas with the sensible, to take their objects to be revealed sensibly.

Correspondingly, Kant does not (only) invoke extra-rational emotions to explain fanatical error. Kant does—more strongly than Locke—associate theoretical fanaticism with pride: fanatics believe that they are superior to the common run of human beings (who do not intuit the supersensible), and that they do not need to (in fact cannot) explain their beliefs to others (see 2:251 and 8:389-90, 394-5). But in many of these passages, Kant seems to identify pride as a consequence of, rather than a motivation for, fanatical belief.[19] Kant suggests, rather, that the source of such pride, the *schwärmerisch* claim to sense the supersensible, arises from the (uncriticized) aspirations of theoretical reason itself. Reason, Kant writes in "On a Recently Prominent Tone of Superiority in Philosophy," "irresistibly drives us to [make] the transition to the supersensible" even if, when properly employed, it comes to recognize its own limitations (8:404).[20]

On Kant's view, reason is therefore responsible for at least two crucial elements in the fanatical mistake: the conception of the objects of putative extra-sensory sensible experience, and the "desire" for knowledge of those objects. Driven by this aspiration of reason, the fanatic might attempt to "exhibit" the rational ideas—i.e., to present the objects of such ideas by generating imaginative projections and putative sensible representations of supersensible entities (as Kant suggests that we try and fail to do for the idea of infinity, in his account of the mathematical sublime (5:251ff.)). Indeed, Kant suggests in "What does it Mean to Orient Oneself in Thinking?", putative fanatical intuition may

---

rationally (re)formulated or purified (6:175-6). This fuller account is, however, not crucial here since Kant's primary examples of fanaticism are historically late, and thus are positions that incorporate (though not appropriately) the rational idea of God or of the supersensible more broadly.

19 Indeed, in his account of the passions in the *Anthropology from a Pragmatic Point of View*, Kant understands pride (as one of the "passions" [*Leidenschaften*]) to be itself dependent on, to involve, reason (in this case, comparative and pragmatic reasoning concerning one's relations to others), albeit a perverted reason that not only fails to identify the proper (viz., moral) relations to others, but also is mistaken in its chosen means to a pragmatic end (to manipulate others, which is, Kant argues, bound to fail if done in a prideful way) (see 7:266, 272-3). In this conception of pride (and reason), Kant is likely following Rousseau.

20 This claim is also central to Kant's dissection of the Mendelssohn/Jacobi debate in "What Does it Mean to Orient Oneself in Thinking?" and to his analyses of metaphysical error in the first *Critique*; on these, see Grier 2001 and Wood 1978. In Johnson 2006, Gregory Johnson also emphasizes the connections between the metaphysical aspirations of reason and *Schwärmerei*, but focuses more on biographical and psychological connections.

be (a misinterpretation of) "reason's feeling of its own need" for know-ledge of the supersensible (8:136-7, 139-40n).

These two roles for reason in theoretical fanatical error, as well as the character of such error (the conflation of the rational and the sensi-ble) are, I shall argue, also central to Kant's account of practical fanati-cism. But, as I shall now argue, again via comparison with Locke, Kant's understanding of practical fanaticism cannot follow directly from his understanding of theoretical fanatical error.

Theoretical Fanaticism and Practical Reason

In his treatment of enthusiasm, Locke does not explicitly discuss practi-cal fanaticism, but he refers there in passing to "action" or "conduct," suggesting that practical fanaticism may be understood as either a spe-cies or a consequence of the cognitive error of enthusiasm (Locke 1700, IV.xix.3-6).[21] Specifically, practical fanaticism might, on Locke's view, be understood as enthusiasm concerning moral or practical beliefs. The enthusiast might believe that "One ought to kill all non-believers," a practical truth, has been revealed to him by God and therefore act upon this belief. Or Locke might understand fanatical action to be a result of (cognitive) enthusiasm: the fanatic is one who makes mistaken claims to knowledge, specifically to knowledge concerning the highest things (God) with the most absolute warrant (as from God). Therefore, the fanatic will take himself to be justified in acting to promote those be-liefs by whatever means necessary, to the exclusion or violation of other interests, common moral beliefs, etc. So Locke suggests (with a nice twist) when he writes that the enthusiast "tyrannizes over his own mind" (in coming to believe something without adequate evidence) and therefore will be inclined to impose upon others (Locke 1700, IV.xix.2).

These Lockean analyses of practical fanaticism are, I believe, both plausible and familiar.[22] They would explain why Locke (along with many other philosophers) takes the primary philosophical response to (practical) fanaticism—analysis (and, one hopes, thereby defusion) of it as error—to be epistemological, viz., to establish that there are no good

---

21 Locke does discuss practical fanaticism in his *Letters on Toleration*, in which he argues (among other things) that sectarian fanaticism—which he, like his contemporaries, sees as a great political danger—may be defused by political toleration. Such arguments are not inconsistent with the *Essay* account, but as noted above, I shall not attend here to specifically political treatments of fanaticism.

22 A similar view is endorsed in Passmore 2003; he rightly takes it to be (derivable from) the view propounded by the British empiricists, particularly Locke.

epistemic grounds for fanatical belief and therefore that such beliefs cannot justify action, much less extreme, violent action.

Kant cannot, however, endorse an analysis of this sort. Despite the role of reason in theoretical fanaticism on his view, Kant like Locke holds that self-critical theoretical reason can identify the error in theoretical fanaticism. This analysis does allow Kant to dismiss some beliefs and (therefore) consequent actions as fanciful imaginings—for example, perhaps, Swedenborg's claims to "see dead people." [23] But this theoretical limitation on human cognition is not, Kant famously holds, determinative for *practical* reason, nor for a practical orientation toward the supersensible: the Critical limitation on theoretical reason "makes room for faith," for belief justified on practical grounds. And of course Kant argues in the *Critique of Practical Reason* that belief in the supersensible—notably in the existence of God—*is* justified on moral grounds. Because of this distinction between theoretical and practical reason, Kant may not simply treat practical fanaticism—a practically wrong relation to the supersensible—as a species or consequence of theoretical fanatical error.

Indeed, Kant appears to hold an almost inverse position: *practical* reason (and its legitimate connections to the supersensible) is the most potent source of *theoretical* fanaticism. This temptation to theoretical fanaticism from practical reason is perhaps most clearly seen in *Dreams*. In the "dogmatic" first part of this work, Kant constructs a "fragment of occult philosophy" or of "metaphysics" that might support (theoretical-fanatical) claims to know about a spirit world (2:329). The strongest piece of evidence for such a belief, Kant suggests, is morality, the "strong law of obligation and the weaker law of benevolence," or the "rule of a general will," which often require that we act against our self-interest. We feel ourselves constrained by these "purely spiritual" laws, which "never fail to assert their reality in human nature" (2:335). These laws, Kant claims, might constitute a "world of all thinking beings" under a systematic constitution, in which virtue and vice would have their appropriate consequences, as they do not in the order of nature, where "clandestine motives" and "secret malice" may be rewarded by "physical success" (2:336). Thus, Kant suggests, our awareness of moral obligation and our conception of a moral order distinct from the

---

23 See "What Does it Mean to Orient Oneself in Thinking?," 8:137: concerning some
    beliefs or ideas, it is mere "impertinent inquisitiveness straying into empty dreaming to
    investigate them—or play with such figments of the brain" but this does not apply to the
    concept of God, even for theoretical reason. That concept (Kant argues) is necessary
    both for theoretical and practical reason; in the first case, our claims concerning it are
    restricted by the self-critique of reason, but this critique does not restrict the practical
    use of that concept.

physical order of nature seem to ground claims to knowledge of a spirit world.[24]

On this presentation, the pretended knowledge of a spirit world fits Kant's definition of fanaticism: it is a claim to sensible representation of the supersensible. For Kant suggests that we are aware of moral laws as felt impulses, or even "sensation," resultant from the active "force" of spiritual wills upon one another (2:334-5). The spirit world is thus understood as parallel to the physical, sensible world, viz., as comprising individual objects (spirits) related by reciprocal influence—and the dogmatist claims to know this through "feeling."

This conception of a moral spirit world and of our cognizance of it is distant from Kant's Critical moral philosophy in a number of ways, most obviously in that Kant later argues emphatically that morality is known by and derived from pure practical reason, rather than feeling. But it is important to note the continuities between Kant's pre-Critical and Critical claims. In his Critical moral philosophy, Kant continues to hold that morality consists in a "law of obligation" distinct from the laws of nature. This law likewise constitutes a systematic world order different from that of nature: the realm of ends, or, ultimately, that in which the highest good is realized, in which happiness is alllocated in proportion to virtue. And pure rational morality grounds claims concerning the supersensible. As Kant emphasizes in the second *Critique*, pure practical reason "furnishes objective reality" to the supersensible concepts of God, the immortality of the soul, and freedom (5:6). More strongly, Kant argues that pure practical reason requires that we *must* understand ourselves to be free, and that we may legitimately—indeed ought to—"postulate" the existence of God and the immortality of our souls (5:122-34).[25] And Kant even holds that it is legitimate to have sensible feelings of or in response to these rational ideas, in the form of

---

24 Laywine argues that this part of *Dreams* is meant by Kant as a parody of his earlier metaphysical pretensions (Laywine 1993, chapter five). Though *Dreams* is a strange, ambiguous work, I think that this suggestion cannot be quite right. As I discuss in the text, the similarities between the discussion in *Dreams* and Kant's mature moral philosophy suggest that Kant takes *something* about that view seriously, as do Kant's expressions of his attraction to the idea of the spirit world throughout the work. Though Kant appears to conclude that beliefs in the spirit world are unfounded, this conclusion seems to follow not from definitive argument, but rather from something like an ancient skeptical argument form (of equipollence), which leads us to suspend judgment, and to concentrate on "cultivating our garden," i.e., on the important matters of practical life. Moreover, he never quite returns, in the later skeptical arguments against knowledge of the spirit world, to discuss (or dismiss) the status of morality suggested in the first "dogmatic" part.

25 See Wood 1970 for the canonical treatment of these views.

respect for the moral law (5:71ff.), though such feelings are not the grounds of (our recognition of) the bindingness of the moral law.

Likewise, though less prominently than in *Dreams*, Kant continues to argue that such practical commitments might lead to theoretical fanaticism (or something akin to it). One ought, Kant argues, to "guard against a *mysticism* of practical reason, which…puts under the application of moral concepts real but not sensible intuitions (of an invisible kingdom of God) and strays into the transcendent" (5:70-1). Such "mysticism" is similar to the view proposed in *Dreams*: one comes to hold this mystical view, Kant argues, by mistaking a "symbol" of moral lawfulness—the lawfulness of nature—that may aid us in determining whether an action accords with moral requirements, for a "schema" that actually determines parallel relations (e.g., of "active force") among spiritual objects.

Against this temptation to theoretical fanaticism from practical reason, Kant employs his theoretical analysis and criticism of fanatical (and dialectical) error. Kant argues that morality is grounded not on intuition, but on a "*rationalism* of judgment" (5:71) and thus licenses no claims to "see" (sense, feel) the supersensible (moral world). More specifically, Kant suggests that the mystic errs not only in claiming sensibly to represent the purely rational, but also and thereby in misrepresenting the character of her (erroneous) cognitive claims. In claiming to "see" the moral world, that is, the mystic elides the conceptually mediated character of her claims: she (mis)uses the *concept* of physical relations as a "schema" in her representation of moral relations.[26] This usage is illegitimate because, as Kant argues in the first *Critique*, the concepts and laws of nature do not legitimately apply to non-sensible, purely rational objects beyond experience; the attempt so to apply them is the source of dialectical error.[27]

Thus practically based claims to intuitive knowledge of the supersensible fall, on Kant's view, to the same criticisms to which he subjects theoretical fanaticism in general. With respect to such practical claims, however, Kant adds a further proviso, namely that moral claims (including those that refer to the supersensible) do not license *any* theoretical knowledge claim. Moral claims concerning the supersensible *are* justified, Kant emphasizes, but are so justified *only* for the "practical use" of reason (5:5); they are relevant only to the rationality of action. The realm of ends is not a world of which we are aware, but rather, as

---

26   Kant aptly describes this position in "On a Recently Prominent Tone of Superiority in Philosophy" as the promulgation of a "hyperphysics" (8:400n).

27   Here I rely again on (a simplified version of) Grier's analysis of dialectical error (Grier 2001).

one formulation of the moral law, is a requirement concerning what we ought to do. Faith in God and belief in the immortality of the soul are, likewise, necessary "postulates" required for moral agents consistently and rationally *to will*, i.e., pursue and strive after, the highest good—articles of faith rather than knowledge. Even our own freedom, which is demonstrated by the "fact of reason," the fact that we are obligated by the moral law, remains nonetheless unknown; for this idea, despite its necessity from a practical point of view, is "inscrutable" (5:275). We can establish, theoretically, that such freedom is possible, but—as Kant writes in the *Groundwork of the Metaphysics of Morals*—we cannot comprehend it, can "comprehend [only] its incomprehensibility" (4:463).[28]

Hence Kant's frequently repeated claims concerning the compatibility of theoretical and practical reason on the Critical view. Theoretical reason can establish no truths whatsoever about the realm of the supersensible; such ignorance "makes room" for faith concerning that realm. Practical reason thus is permitted to refer to the supersensible. As suggested in *Dreams*, then, practical reason may provide our strongest ground for—or strongest temptation to—both metaphysical dogmatism and theoretical fanaticism.[29] But, properly understood, its claims do not violate the Kantian prohibition on knowledge beyond experience because they concern such entities "only in a practical respect" (8:401n) or are not knowledge claims proper.[30]

This Critical move brings us to the conclusion of this section: precisely because Kant endorses the strictly *practical* significance and legitimacy of belief in supersensibles, he cannot use his criticism of theoretical fanaticism, straightforwardly, to ground an account of (all) practical fanatical error. In practical belief, on Kant's view, one may employ concepts and make claims that are *not* grounded from a theo-

---

28 In the second *Critique*, Kant claims that we *do* know we are free, though we do not have "insight" into such freedom (5:4). I cannot see how Kant could defend this stronger claim, however.

29 This view is expressed as well in "On a Recently Prominent Tone of Superiority in Philosophy" (8:405), "What Does it Mean to Orient Oneself in Thinking?" (8:138-9), and "Treaty of Perpetual Peace in Philosophy" (Kant's essay that follows up on "On a Recently Prominent Tone"), 8:419. Though he does not state it outright, Kant's discussion of metaphysical dogmatism (which is not identical to theoretical fanaticism, but akin to it in its pretensions to know the supersensible) in the first *Critique* suggests that it is motivated by practical considerations; see, particularly, A462-476/B490-504.

30 See 8:397n, for both prongs of this Kantian view (in the context of a discussion of fanaticism): that practical reference to the supersensible is not ruled out because of our theoretical ignorance, and that such references do not constitute knowledge, but are related to action alone. See also A808/B836 for a somewhat ambiguous presentation of this position.

retical point of view; the analysis of a theoretical error cannot, *ipso facto*, establish a practical one. As I shall now suggest, however, Kant also provides an account of specifically *practical* fanatical error.

Practical Fanaticism

Kant's practical philosophy provides some obvious materials for criticism of fanaticism as a practical error. Extreme forms of fanaticism—those that involve immoral action, including action that harms the fanatical agent herself—may be condemned as violations of the moral law. The claim that God "told me" to do such things cannot, moreover, justify the abrogation of the moral law. For, Kant argues, the only legitimate, practically rational conception of God is derived from morality itself (e.g., as a "holy will" that acts in accord with the moral law infallibly, or as the guarantor of the possibility of the highest good). Thus God cannot consistently be understood to command that which is immoral. More broadly, insofar as the fanatic invokes God's command as a guide to action—as opposed to or simply independently of the moral law as the law of pure practical reason itself—the fanatic acts heteronomously.

In a footnote to "On a Recently Prominent Tone of Superiority in Philosophy," (8:395-6n), moreover, Kant suggests that his analysis of theoretical fanaticism may be extended (*mutatis mutandis*) to the practical sphere. Practical reason provides us with legitimate concepts of the supersensible—of God and of the morally good—and these ideas are also legitimate objects of feeling (moral feeling). Nonetheless, Kant argues, such feeling does not identify the good or ground moral claims (that would be a mistaken "eudaimonism"). Rather, moral feeling is an *effect* of one's recognition of the validity of the moral law. Thus, Kant argues again, one may not legitimately claim to cognize the supersensible (in this case, the practical ideas of morality, God, and freedom) *through* sensibility, or on the basis of feeling.

This analysis suggests that the practical fanatic, like the theoretical fanatic, conflates the deliverances of sensibility and those of pure reason, or (more specifically) takes sensibility itself to provide, or to give access to, the ideas or objects of pure reason. From this analysis, however, it is not clear if practical fanaticism is a specifically *practical* error: the fanatic may (on a "meta-level") misunderstand the sources of her practical ideas, but how will this misunderstanding manifest itself in her will or action? Perhaps the practical fanatic would act on principles drawn from sensibility (feeling), unsubordinated to and unconstrained by moral rationality. Thus her failure would be like that of the egoist or hedonist (or even the moral-sense theorist who acts in accord with his theory). But fanaticism seems to be a distinctive practical stance, involving distinctive principles or motives for action. And as I shall now suggest, Kant does provide an account of a distinctive practical fanatical error, as indeed comprising a fundamental confusion concerning the relationship between the sensible and the rationally conceived supersensible—though of a more specific form than that suggested in "On a Recently Prominent Tone of Superiority in Philosophy."

To do so, I turn to Kant's most explicit discussions of religious fanaticism, in *Religion within the Boundaries of Mere Reason*. Here Kant again associates fanaticism with mysticism, visions, or the delusion of receiving "illuminations" (6:83). The fanatic believes that he can "*perceive* [God's] heavenly influences" (6:174).[31] This description of religious fanaticism is reminiscent of Kant's analysis of theoretical fanaticism, and he appears to criticize it as delusory for the same reasons: "nowhere in experience," Kant asserts, "can we recognize a supersensible object" (6:174). Or again: "this feeling of the immediate presence of the highest being...would constitute the receptivity of an intuition for which there is no sense in human nature" (6:175).

But Kant implies that such fanaticism is not solely a theoretical error. Rather, it is also and more importantly a *practical* attitude or desire: the fanatic "*want[s]*" to have such experience, desires "even to *produce* these effects [of grace] in" herself; she "*striv[es]*" for a supposed contact with God" (6:174, my emphasis). Thus religious fanaticism is a form of desire—of striving, of aiming to produce objects or attain ends.[32] Kant's most urgent criticism of it, correspondingly, concerns its status as a desire dangerous to morality: fanaticism is the "*moral* death of the reason without which there can be no religion, because like all morality in general, religion must be founded on principles" (6:175).

This "moral death" of reason is not simply (as Kant's language here might suggest) the subordination of reason to sensible inclinations (or delusory feelings), but the death of reason *as* action-guiding or *as* practical. The fanatical desire is dangerous precisely because it is a desire for passivity. As Kant puts it, on the fanatical view one becomes pleas-

---

31 Kant's discussions of fanaticism in the *Religion* tend to occur in the context of discussions of grace and its antinomial status (i.e., as both a necessary and a problematic, incomprehensible, and morally dangerous concept in rational religion). Thus a full account of such delusion would require an investigation of grace, which, unfortunately, I cannot provide here.

32 Kant defines desire as the faculty by which we "cause the actuality of the object" of our representation (see, e.g., 20:206).

ing to God not through moral action, but rather through "(*merely passive*) inner illuminations" (6:83, my emphasis). In aiming to have feelings—passively received representations, states of being affected—the fanatic aims not to act (morally or otherwise), but to be in a state of non-activity, of pure receptivity. Thus, Kant concludes, the fanatic "is kept ever distant from the good based on *self-activity*" (*Ibid.*, my emphasis).[33] So Kant suggests too in his late essay, "The End of All Things," in describing mysticism—perhaps the most extreme, self-conscious version of practical fanaticism. According to the "monstrous system of Lao-kiun [i.e., Buddhism]," Kant writes, "the highest good consists in nothing, i.e., in the consciousness of feeling oneself swallowed up in the abyss of the Godhead by flowing together with it, and hence the annihilation of one's own personality" (8:335). In order to attain union with God, that is, the mystic detaches himself from his own rational personality, aims precisely at the abdication of agency, even the "annihilation of [his] own personality," in favor of a state of feeling, of passivity or being affected—the "moral death" of practical reason.[34]

Thus—unlike the egoist or the moral sense theorist, but perhaps like the hedonist—the fanatic privileges sensibility (feeling) precisely as passive, as opposed not only to the laws of practical rationality (or morality), but also, more broadly, to agency as such. But practical fanaticism is also distinguished from all of these stances because it consists in an illicit combination of sensibility *with* reason or rational ideas. The fanatic privileges sensibility (feeling) precisely as (putative) feeling *of* rationally conceived objects—most prominently God and God's grace—and thereby as having the *status* of rational ideas or rational laws.[35] As Kant suggests, the fanatic takes having such feelings to be the "*highest* good," to have unconditional value. This notion is derived from and formulated by reason alone on Kant's view: it is reason that not only formulates the idea of God, but also seeks the unconditioned,

---

33 The concerns Kant raises about grace are similar, though they do not explicitly concern putative feeling of the supersensible: belief in the doctrine of grace (and that of Christ's atonement for our sins) might, if wrongly understood, lead human beings to take up a passive stance, simply waiting for divine grace, rather than understanding themselves to be obliged to act morally.

34 In "On a Recently Prominent Tone of Superiority in Philosophy," Kant suggests that this passivity might itself be interpreted as a ground for pride in one's superiority over others: the fanatic holds that he, unlike others, does not have to "work" to attain truths, but rather receives them directly and without effort, through revelatory intuition (8:390, 393-5).

35 In the *Religion*, Kant suggests briefly that fanaticism involves reason (6:174), though he does not explicitly draw this suggestion out as I have done here.

the necessary source or basis of the conditioned—in this case, the unconditioned (highest and complete) good.[36]

Like theoretical fanaticism, then, practical fanaticism arises from a
conflation of sensibility with rational ideas, and arises in concert with
the aspirations of reason (to identify the unconditioned). Here, however, this conflation takes practical form: it is not (primarily) a claim
that one *cognizes* the supersensible through sensibility, but rather that
the highest good (a rational idea, to be *brought about* through rational
action) is instantiated *in* sensibility, in a feeling to which the fanatic
attributes the status of a rationally articulated end. Practical fanaticism
is, then, as nearly self-contradictory as "sensing the supersensible": it
identifies receptive, sensible passivity as the aim of self-directing rational agency; it is the view that one becomes a better agent by eliminating one's agency.[37]

By contrast to theoretical fanaticism, however, practical fanaticism
may not be dismissed by Kant as erroneous because we can have *no*
legitimate practical sensible response (feeling) to the supersensible
(rational ends and postulates). For Kant argues not only that we have
moral feeling, but also that we have quite legitimate feelings of religious inspiration or awe for God as the holy will. Such feelings are,
when properly understood, means to moral edification: prayer and religious address inspire exaltation and emotion, which strengthen one's
commitment to moral self-improvement (6:198n; cf. 6:113-4, 8:402-
3).[38]

The practical fanatical error comprises, therefore, two more specific
errors. First, the practical fanatic confuses emotional sensibility and
sensation: he misinterprets a feeling of his own state (pleasure, or being
moved by religious or moral ideas) for a sense experience of or received from the *object* of those ideas (i.e., has "delusory heavenly feelings"). Second, and consequently, the fanatic understands an effect of
the moral, religious articulation of ends (to be brought about by him)
itself as an end, indeed as the ultimate accomplishment of his highest
aims. Thus such practical fanaticism is "practical delusion

---

36   The search for the unconditioned is the central activity Kant attributes to reason in the
     first *Critique*; it also is meant to explain how and why reason formulates its ideas of su-
     persensible realities.

37   Insofar as this passivity is identified with a state of grace, moreover, this aim for human
     agency might be said to be delusory or contradictory in a somewhat different way as
     well: one is aiming to bring about that which (by definition) one cannot bring about,
     that which can only be bestowed by God. So Kant may suggest at 6:174.

38   In concert with his criticisms of religious fanaticism, Kant warns, however, that such
     emotion does not itself constitute moral edification—alone, it is merely the "music of
     sighs and of ardent wishes"—but must be supplemented and "built upon" by principles
     and the self-inculcation of dispositions to perform duties (6:198n).

[*Wahnglaube*],'' as Kant characterizes it, namely, satisfaction with the "consciousness of possessing a means to a certain end (before we have availed ourselves of it)" which is the "possession of this end in representation only"—in brief, the presumption that one has achieved an end that one has not (6:168n). And, importantly, through its relation to rationally articulated ideas, laws, and objects, practical fanaticism (mis)construes its mere "means" as unconditionally, absolutely valuable ends.

Thus, I suggest, Kant provides an analysis of practical fanatical error that is (*mutatis mutandis*) parallel to his analysis of theoretical fanaticism. The role for reason in practical fanaticism allows Kant to distinguish fanaticism from egoism or hedonism as a specific form of practical error. For neither of these non-moral stances takes its end(s) to have the unconditional status of rational, moral laws or ends—my own personal desires or pleasures are more likely to be taken as conditional and contingent—nor to be validated by their (putative) connection to supersensible reality.

Fanatical Action

We may ask, however, whether this account of a distinctive fanatical error can account for anything like what we understand by fanaticism: an absolute endorsement of an ideology (often religious), taken to justify violent, immoral action. Can Kant's analysis of a problematically passive attitude shed any light on the excessively *active* phenomena that Hare or Martinich or the *Encylopédie* authors aim to understand? Are Buddhists really the most dangerous, morally problematic fanatics?

Given his historical context, it is surprising that Kant hardly attends to extreme, religiously inspired violence.[39] Nonetheless, his account of fanaticism may, I suggest, provide grounds for an analysis and criticism of such fanatical action as well.

I would argue, first, that Kant's account of fanaticism is meant to characterize the ultimate principles, motives, attitudes, or grounds of fanaticism, which may underlie fanatical action. That is, just as Kant focuses in *Groundwork* I on the shopkeeper's motives and action in order to make clear the difference between moral and prudential rea-

---

39   The only instance of which I am aware is Kant's somewhat cursory treatment in the *Religion* of an inquisitor, who believes that "a supernaturally revealed divine will...permitted him, if not even made a duty for him" to condemn a "so-called heretic" to death (6:186). Kant's concerns here are more with the state of the inquisitor's conscience than with understanding the inquisitor's action as an example of religious delusion, though his discussion suggests (unsurprisingly) that he takes it to be such.

sons for the same, externally legal action, so too in his treatment of fanaticism, Kant articulates underlying motives and attitudes, even for apparently unproblematic actions (or, in this case, paradigmatically the absence of action). In other words, as noted at the opening of the previous section, obviously *immoral* fanatical action may be condemned by Kant as contrary to the moral law. By focusing on more externally benign forms of fanaticism, Kant calls attention to the problematic grounds or motives of such action (or non-action) that might be confused with proper religious devotion.

Moreover, we can discern how the purposeful passivity of the fanatical attitude can nonetheless ensue in action (ultimately, immoral action) by attending to Kant's account of superstition (*Aberglaube*), another form of religious delusion. As with fanaticism, Kant analyzes superstition in the *Religion* as a practically, rather than theoretically, problematic attitude: the superstitious agent is one who takes actions that are morally indifferent to be justified, indeed to be of supreme worth, because they render the agent pleasing to God, or are decreed by God (e.g., 6:174).[40] Kant identifies these actions largely with the practices of church communities (e.g., praying, church attendance) or with practices recommended by scriptural or religious tradition (e.g., pilgrimage to Mecca, practicing kosher).

This religious delusion is, Kant claims, distinct from that of fanaticism. While the fanatic takes herself to be in union with God, to have immediate experience (feeling) of God and thereby to be immediately blessed, the superstitious agent understands God to be a separate being, to be placated, pleased or flattered. This delusion arises, correspondingly, not because of the agent's experience of "heavenly feelings," but because the superstitious agent wrongly conceives of God anthropomorphically, in accord with the analogy of a human ruler (6:168-9). Human rulers, Kant suggests cynically, are most pleased by actions that unambiguously testify to one's obedience and recognition of their power; thus actions commanded by the ruler, for which there is no other reason than to show obedience, will best please him. The superstitious delusional applies this image to God, concluding that God will be best pleased not by moral actions, which are independently good, but rather by non-moral actions performed solely to please Him (6:103).[41]

---

40 Kant's usage of his technical terminology wavers, however: at 6:52-3, Kant characterizes superstition not as the attempt to influence God—which here he calls "thaumaturgy"—but as belief in miracles (cf. 8:145). As with fanaticism, it is quite open to Kant to identify theoretical as well as practical errors in superstition, but I concentrate only on the latter.

41 The Kantian distinction between fanaticism and superstition is close to Hume's between enthusiasm and superstition (Hume 1985), though Hume analyzes the difference bet-

Despite these differences between fanaticism and superstition, they have broadly similar structures. Like the fanatic, the superstitious agent eschews moral agency, aiming to influence God, to gain God's grace or merit in His eyes, without striving for virtue. Also like fanaticism, superstition involves a mistake concerning the relationship between supersensible (moral, practically rational) ends and sensibility, though of a somewhat different kind. For, Kant argues, the superstitious agent believes that his actions, which are "merely natural," rather than morally grounded, might influence the supersensible, whether God or "something which is not nature (i.e., the ethical good)" (6:104-5).[42] The error of superstitious agents, like that of fanatics, thus consists in misattributing practically rational, moral status—i.e., here, that which is pleasing to God—not to moral agency, but to something else (here, something "merely natural," or morally indifferent).[43]

Superstition may include, then, some of the attitudes and actions that were of most concern to Enlightenment figures, and to which we might refer as "fanatical." The superstitious belief that particular, non-moral, scripturally based and/or traditional practices of a sect are commanded by God, or could alone render human beings worthy, might lead, for example, to sectarian persecution or conflict, and corresponding transgression of moral norms. For the putatively commanded actions may include conversion or persecution of others, but may also more indirectly lead to sectarian conflict due to differences of opinion on these (in fact inessential, non-universal) religious matters.

Though Kant does not explicitly so argue, moreover, superstition may be both facilitated and heightened by fanaticism; indeed, I would argue that something like superstitious action is the active expression of the fanatical attitude.[44] The fanatical "moral death" of practical rational-

---

ween them as lying in different emotional sources (arrogance/hope vs. fear), not in different forms of practical rational error.

42 This characterization suggests that superstition is not only a perversion of moral rationality, but is also a failure of technical rationality—in identifying inappropriate means to an end. Thus too superstition, like fanaticism, may be understood as a practical delusion in accord with Kant's characterization at 6:168n: it does not identify having certain means to an end as having already accomplished that end, but instead identifies faulty means to an end—or, perhaps better, it takes it that there are fully separate means to moral ends, whereas in morality, each action is partially constitutive of the end (achieving morality, achieving moral character), though of course never fully accomplishing that end.

43 This claim is based on Kant's larger argument in the *Religion* that church practices and Scriptural revelation are mere "vehicles" for true (pure rational, moral) religion.

44 Kant himself suggests two other connections between fanaticism and superstition. On the one hand, Kant briefly suggests an inverse relationship between these delusions: "*False devotion (bigotterie, devotio spuria)* is the habit of placing the exercise of piety, not in actions well-pleasing to God (in the fulfillment of human duties) but in direct

ity facilitates superstition, first, because in aiming to be purely passive, to annihilate one's personality, one can come to see oneself as an "instrument of God," one's actions not subject to individual choice, responsibility, or critical reflection.[45] Thus a fanatic may light upon sectarian practices as (purported) expressions or instantiations of God's will or commands, and expressly refuse to exert any critical reflection or individual responsibility concerning these practices.

More strongly, the fanatical belief that one is unified with God, thereby somehow gaining absolute worth through thoroughgoing passivity, is likely to express itself in superstitious action in a broader sense, namely in "merely natural" action (including not only communal religious practices, but any action based in sensible inclination or feeling) to which one attributes unconditional worth. For one cannot avoid action altogether, even if one aims at thoroughgoing passivity. And, as we have seen, the fanatic attributes unconditional worth to her passive states, her feelings, as immediately instantiating God's presence; thus she may attribute such status indiscriminately to any of her passively received inclinations, to any or all of her sensibly-motivated actions.

So Kant suggests in his discussions of moral fanaticism in the second *Critique*. Unlike the religious fanatic, the moral fanatic does not claim to have "heavenly feelings" (of God's presence), but rather takes pleasure in, is inspired by sublime feeling in response to, her own supersensible moral capacity. Like the religious fanatic, however, the moral fanatic takes the pleasurability, the passivity, of such self-appreciation to be itself the highest good, invested with unconditional value.[46] This self-appreciation, Kant claims, leads the moral fanatic to understand her *every* action as worthy, for (she believes) her sublime *capacity* for morality (as opposed to the actual exercise of such a capac-

commerce with God through manifestations of awe; this exercise...adds to superstition the delusion of allegedly supersensible (heavenly) feelings." (5:185n, translation modified) This passage suggests that the fanatical state proper (and mystical, devotional practices aimed to produce it) may be understood as a way to influence God (viz., as a form of superstition). On the other hand, in "On a Recently Prominent Tone of Superiority in Philosophy" (8: 400-2n), Kant suggests that *theoretical* fanaticism may give rise to superstition: if one believes that one sensibly intuits God, then one will form an anthropomorphic conception of God, which therefore entails a superstitious relationship to this purported agent. These are also possible and (I believe) consistent accounts of the relation between fanaticism and superstition, which might lead to similar motivational and active stances to that I discuss in the text.

45 It might also, by undermining the rational autonomy of the believer, facilitate manipulation by church leaders ("priestcraft"); on Kant's criticism of priestcraft as inconsistent with enlightenment and rational autonomy (and his correlative defense of rational religion as promoting them), see Wood 1991.

46 Hence Kant's strong identification of moral fanaticism with aestheticized conceptions of morality or "nobility."

ity) can itself ground merit (5:84-5; cf. 5:155-7); she does not need, she takes it, to engage in rational reflection or to submit to the moral law in order to be worthy. So too, I suggest, might the religious fanatic interpret her own passive states and consequent actions: as invested with ultimate value, due to her (purported) connection to the supersensible, in this case God rather than moral capacity.

Thus, though superstitious action may be made more obviously immoral when it is attached to immoral religious doctrines or exemplars (Kant briefly adverts to the Abraham and Isaac story at 6:187 as an example), the fanatical attitude furnishes a more radical ground, a heightening or intensification, for the immorality of such action: the presumption that one's feelings are themselves imbued, one is oneself passively imbued, with moral, unconditional worth. Superstition alone, on Kant's account, is a somewhat craven attitude (wishing to please God, understood as an alien, demanding tyrant) or one, as Kant also claims, motivated by laziness: the superstitious agent avoids the difficulties of moral striving by performing instead the more easily fulfilled requirements of ritual practice (6:200). Such an attitude may not ensue in extreme, violent action, or a presumption to trump moral claims, but only a calcified ritualism. By contrast, the fanatical construal of one's own feelings, inclinations, and passive states as themselves of the highest value, as testifying to a connection to the highest, supersensible reality, can provide the apparent justification required for extreme fanatical action. Indeed, as Kant writes,

> If the delusion of this supposed favorite of heaven reaches heights of fanaticism, to the point of imagining [bis zur schwärmischen Einbildung...steigt] that he feels the special effects of faith within him (or even has the impertinence of trusting in a supposed hidden familiarity with God), virtue finally becomes loathsome to him and an object of contempt. (6:201)

Concluding Remarks

This complex Kantian account (of the fanatical-superstitious agent) provides, I suggest, a persuasive and non-reductive characterization of fanaticism in comparison to the suggestions proffered by his predecessors. And it allows Kant to incorporate that which is persuasive in Hare's and Martinich's proposed definitions of fanaticism, without the difficulties attendant upon these proposals.

By contrast to the proposals of his Enlightenment predecessors, Kant's suggestion that the fanatical attitude is not simply the result of extreme emotion opposed to the claims of reason, but rather incorporates rational ideas, is better able to characterize a distinctive fanatical character. Violent fanatics are, one might note first, not necessarily agents who act without thinking, overcome by emotion, but often plan their actions with cool precision. More importantly, by identifying a pure rational "component" to fanatical attitudes, Kant can explain the trumping, unconditional status claimed by religious fanatics for their feelings and actions: these are not simply powerful feelings—or simply mistaken, self-interested beliefs—but ones that are taken to override other emotions, interests, or projects because of their connection to supersensible entities (God) and the rationally conceived unconditionality of moral value. Moreover, the fanatical identification of passivity, of the annihilation of agency, as the highest good can explain not only the suppression of ordinary moral reflection in the fanatic, but also the striking preponderance of self-sacrifice in fanatical action, the way in which such self-sacrifice is taken to endow ultimate justification on the fanatic's projects.[47] And finally, more broadly, the Kantian account captures, it seems to me, the peculiarly tragic character of violent fanaticism, of atrocities committed out of moral righteousness, out of openness to claims of unconditional value.

Both Hare and Martinich attempt, in their definitions of fanaticism, to capture the trumping character of fanatical claims: whether by the precedence of an ideal over all interests, including the agent's own (Hare), or by the privileging of the transcendent over all worldly matters, including the agent's life or happiness (Martinich). These accounts suffer, however, from weaknesses as well. As David Norton argues, Hare's conception of fanaticism does not distinguish it from moral idealism; the moral idealist too (arguably, and certainly on a Kantian view) takes moral value to trump all other interests, including the agent's own (Norton 1977). On Martinich's view, too, a moral idealist might well be counted a fanatic, for the moral idealist (on a Kantian view) might be understood to be guided by an idea of the transcendent—e.g., of pure virtue, not fully attainable by this-worldly finite human agents—as of supreme value, above merely worldly interests. Martinich's view seems, moreover, unable to account for fanatical action or engagement *in* the world: if the fanatic cares exclusively about the transcendent, it is unclear why he would engage in action to transform this world (though its destruction might testify to the superiority of the transcendent).

Kant's account of fanaticism also calls for an argument shoring up his sharp distinction between moral idealism and/or rationally grounded

---

47 This is an aspect of fanatical behavior that is inexplicable on Locke's account, and even on Hume's: Hume suggests that enthusiasts are characterized by excessive pride and exuberance of hopeful feeling, which would not seem to lead to any form of self-sacrifice.

religious (i.e., moral) faith and fanaticism, which I have not provided.[48] But the role of sensibility in fanaticism may help here. On the one hand, the fanatic's identification of feeling—passivity, abnegation of agency and responsibility—as her ultimate good serves to distinguish this attitude from moral idealism, a full embrace of responsible agency. And, on the other hand, the fanatic's assimilation of sensibility and the supersensible, her endowment of actual feeling and consequent action with transcendent or unconditional value, allows one to explain fanatical engagement in the world. On the Kantian view, that is, the fanatic does not simply oppose the given world to transcendent values or entities, but believes that in her own states and actions (and not in others or their actions), the transcendent is made real.

Thus too, and more broadly, Kant's account suggests—in a way anticipatory of the ideologically inspired horrors of the twentieth century—the double-edged character of our pure rational aspirations, of our ability, through pure reason, to formulate and strive after transcendent, supersensible objects or ideals corrective of the given natural world. This capacity, as Kant influentially and movingly argues, is the source of human dignity, but, as in fanaticism, it may also be the source of inhumanity.[49]

---

48 The required argument would need to address the well-known "empty formalism" charges against Kantian morality, for Kant's criticisms of superstition turn on the (contrasting) identification of purely, rationally grounded action. One might, then, come to understand two of Hegel's objections to Kantian morality to be deeply connected: the empty formalism objection is, of course, powerfully formulated by Hegel, but Hegel also suggests that he takes Kantian morality ultimately to comprise (or to ensue in) a form of fanaticism.

49 I owe thanks to Kyla Ebels-Duggan, Jon Garthoff, Les Harris, and the participants in a workshop at Notre Dame (Karl Ameriks, Andrew Chignell, Patrick Frierson, John Hare, Patrick Kain, James Krueger, Benjamin Lipscomb, Houston Smit, and Angela Smith) for comments on drafts of this essay, and to Allen Wood for helpful comments about Kant's philosophy of religion.

References

Adams, Robert, 1972, "Must God Create the Best?" in: *The Philosophical Review*, 81, pp. 317-32.

--, 1979, "Moral Arguments for Theistic Belief," in: C. F. Delaney (Ed.), *Rationality and Religious Belief*, Notre Dame: University of Notre Dame Press, pp. 116-40.

--, 1995, "Moral Faith," in: *Journal of Philosophy*, 92, pp. 75-95.

--, 1997, "Things in Themselves," in: *Philosophy and Phenomenological Research*, 57, 801-25.

--, 1999, *Finite and Infinite Goods: A Framework for Ethics*, Oxford: Oxford University Press.

Allison, Henry (Trans. and Ed.), 1973, *The Kant-Eberhard Controversy*, Baltimore: Johns Hopkins University Press.

--, 1983, *Kant's Transcendental Idealism: An Interpretation and Defense,* New Haven, CT: Yale University Press.

--, 1990, *Kant's Theory of Freedom*, Cambridge: Cambridge University Press.

--, 2001, *Kant's Theory of Taste*, New York: Cambridge University Press.

--, 2002, "Editor's Introduction to 'What Real Progress has metaphysics made in Germany since the time of Leibniz and Wolff?'," in: Henry E. Allison and Peter Heath (Eds.), *Immanuel Kant: Theoretical Philosophy after 1781*, Cambridge: Cambridge University Press.

--, 2006, "Kant on Freedom of the Will," in: Paul Guyer (Ed.), *Cambridge Companion to Kant and Modern Philosophy*, New York: Cambridge University Press, pp. 381-415.

Ameriks, Karl, 1982, "Recent Work on Kant's Theoretical Philosophy," in: *American Philosophical Quarterly*, 19, pp. 1-24.

--, 2000a, *Kant and the Fate of Autonomy*, New York: Cambridge University Press.

--, 2000b, *Kant's Theory of Mind*, Oxford: Clarendon Press (second edition).

--, 2003, *Interpreting Kant's Critiques*, Oxford: Clarendon Press.

--, 2005, "A Commonsense Kant?" in: *Proceedings and Addresses of the American Philosophical Association*, 79, pp. 19-45.

--, 2006, *Kant and the Historical Turn: Philosophy as Critical Interpretation*, Oxford: Clarendon Press.

Anderson-Gold, Sharon, 1986, "Kant's Ethical Commonwealth: The Highest Good as a Social Goal," in: *International Philosophical Quarterly*, 26, pp. 23-35.

--, 2001, *Unnecessary Evil*, Albany, NY: SUNY Press.

Aquila, Richard, 1979, "Things in Themselves and Appearances: Intentionality and Reality in Kant," in: *Archiv für Geschichte der Philosophie*, 61, pp. 293-307.

Audi, Robert, 2001, "A Kantian Intuitionism," in: *Mind*, 110, pp. 601-35.

Baier, Annette, 1980, "Secular Faith," in: *Canadian Journal of Philosophy*, 10, pp. 131-48.

Beck, Lewis White, 1960, *A Commentary on Kant's Critique of Practical Reason*, Chicago: University of Chicago Press.

Beiser, Frederick, 2006, "Moral Faith and the Highest Good," in: Paul Guyer (Ed.), *The Cambridge Companion to Kant and Modern Philosophy*, Cambridge: Cambridge University Press, pp. 588-629.

Bennett, Jonathan, 1966, *Kant's Analytic*, Cambridge: Cambridge University Press.

--, 1974, *Kant's Dialectic*, Cambridge: Cambridge University Press.

Bielefeldt, Heiner, 2001, *Kants Symbolik: Ein Schlüssel zur kritischen Freiheitsphilosophie,* Freiburg and Munich, Karl Alber. [English trans., 2003, New York: Cambridge University Press, 2003.]

Bird, Graham, 1998, "Kantian Themes in Contemporary Philosophy," in: *Proceedings of the Aristotelian Society*, 72, pp. 131-51.

Brecht, Martin, 1990, *Martin Luther: Shaping and Defining the Reformation 1521-1532*, James Schaaf (Trans.), Minneapolis: Fortress Press.

Campe, Joachim Henrich, 1810, *Wörterbuch der deutschen Sprache*, Bd. 4, Braunschweig: Schulbuchhandlung.

Caswell, Matthew, 2003, *Kant's Conception of the Highest Good* (Dissertation), Philosophy, Boston University.

Caswell, Matthew, 2006, "Kant's Conception of the Highest Good, the *Gesinnung*, and the Theory of Radical Evil," in: *Kant-Studien*, 97, 184-209.

Caygill, Howard, 2003, "Kant's Apology for Sensibility," in: Brian Jacobs and Patrick Kain (Eds.), *Essays on Kant's Anthropology*, Cambridge: Cambridge University Press, pp. 164-93.

Chalmers, David, 2002, "Does Conceivability Entail Possibility?" in: T. Gendler and J. Hawthorne (Eds.), *Conceivability and Possibility*, New York, Oxford University Press.

Chignell, Andrew, 2006, "Beauty as a Symbol of Natural Systematicity," in: *British Journal of Aesthetics*, 46, 4, pp. 406-15.

--, 2007a, "Belief in Kant," in: *Philosophical Review*, 116, 3, pp. 323-60.

--, 2007b, "Kant's Concepts of Justification," in: *Nous*, 41, 1, pp. 33-63.

--, 2007c, "Kant on the Normativity of Taste: the Role of Aesthetic Ideas," in: *Australasian Journal of Philosophy*, 85(3), pp. 415-33.

--, 2008, "Are Supersensibles Really Possible? Kant on the Evidential Role of Symbolization", in: V. Rhoden, T. Terra, G. Almeida (Eds.), *Recht und Frieden in der Philosophie Kants*, Berlin, DeGruyter.

--, 2009, "Kant, Modality, and the Most Real Being," in: *Archiv für Geschichte der Philosophie*, 91(2), pp. 157-92.

--, 2010, "Real Repugnance and our Ignorance of Things-in-Themselves: A Lockean Problem in Kant and Hegel," in: F. Rush, K. Ameriks, J. Stolzenberg (Eds.), *Internationales Jahrbuch des Deutschen Idealismus*, 7, Berlin, DeGruyter.

Chignell, Andrew and Nicholas Stang, 2010, "Postulate des empirischen Denkens," in: G. Mohr, J. Stolzenberg, M. Willaschek (Eds.), *Kant-Lexikon*, Berlin, Walter de Gruyter.

Cohen, Hermann, 1978, *Kommentar zu Immanuel Kants Kritik der reinen Vernunft*, New York: G. Olms.

--, 1987, *Kant's theorie der erfahrung*, New York: G. Olms.

--, 2001, *Kant's Begründung der Ethik*, New York: G. Olms.

Crawford, Donald, 1974, *Kant's Aesthetic Theory*, Madison: University of Wisconsin Press.

Crosson, Frederick J., 2003, "Fanaticism, Politics, and Religion," in: *Philosophy Today*, 47, pp. 441-7.

Darwall, Stephen, 2004, "Respect and the Second-Person Standpoint," in: *Proceedings and Addresses of the American Philosophical Association*, 78, pp. 43-59.

Descartes, René, 1985, *Principles of Philosophy* (first edition 1644), in: John Cottingham, Robert Stoothoff, and Dugald Murdoch (Eds.), *The Philosophical Writings of René Descartes: Volume I*, Cambridge: Cambridge University Press, pp. 179-291.

Duden: Das große Wörterbuch der deutschen Sprache in 10 Bänden, 1999-2004, Online-Ausgabe, Mannheim, Leipzig, Wien, Zürich: Dudenverlag.

Engstrom, Stephen, 1992, "The Concept of the Highest Good in Kant's Moral Theory," in: *Philosophy and Phenomenological Research*, 52, pp.747-80.

--, 2002, "Introduction," in: Werner Pluhar (Ed.), *Critique of Practical Reason*, Indianapolis: Hackett, xv-liv.

Ferreira, M. Jamie, 1983, "Kant's Postulate: The Possibility *or* the Existence of God?" in: *Kant-Studien*, 74, 75-80.

Firestone, Chris, and Stephen Palmquist (Eds.), 2006, *Kant and the New Philosophy of Religion*, Bloomington: Indiana University Press.

Franks, Paul, 1997, "Freedom, *Tatsache* and *Tathandlung* in the Development of Fichte's Jena *Wissenschaftslehre*," in: *Archiv fuer Geschichte der Philosophie*, 79, 310-23.

Frierson, Patrick, 2003, *Freedom and Anthropology in Kant's Moral Philosophy*, Cambridge: Cambridge University Press.

--, 2006, "Kant's Empirical Account of Human Cognition," in: *Philosopher's Imprint*, 5.7, pp. 1-36, http://hdl.handle.net/2027/spo.3521354.0005.007

Gendler, T.S. and J. Hawthorne (Eds.), 2002, *Conceivability and Possibility*, New York, Oxford University Press.

Grenberg, Jeanine, 2005, *Kant and the Ethics of Humility*, Cambridge: Cambridge University Press.

Grier, Michelle, 2001, *Kant's Doctrine of Transcendental Illusion*, Cambridge: Cambridge University Press.

Grimm, Jacob and Wilhelm Grimm, 1899, *Deutsches Wörterbuch*, Bd. 9, Leipzig: Hizel Verlag.

Guevara, Daniel, 2000, *Kant's Theory of Moral Motivation*, Boulder: Westview Press.

Guyer, Paul, 1979, *Kant and the Claims of Taste*, Cambridge: Cambridge University Press.

--, 1987, *Kant and the Claims of Knowledge*, Cambridge: Cambridge University Press.

--, 1998, "Symbols of Freedom in Kant's Aesthetics," in: Herman Paret (Ed.,) *Kant's Ästhetik/ Kant's Aesthetics/ L'esthéthique de Kant*, Berlin: DeGruyter.

--, 2000a, *Kant on Freedom, Law, and Happiness*, Cambridge: Cambridge University Press.

--, 2000b, "The Unity of Nature and Freedom: Kant's Conception of the System of Philosophy," in: Sally Sedgwick (Ed.), *The Reception of Kant's Critical Philosophy: Fichte, Schelling and Hegel*, Cambridge: Cambridge University Press, pp. 19-53.

--, 2003, "Kant on Common Sense and Scepticism," in: *Kantian Review*, 7, pp. 1-37.

--, 2005, *Values of Beauty*, New York: Cambridge University Press.

Hanna, Robert, 2004/2009, "Kant's Theory of Judgment," *Stanford Encyclopedia of Philosophy (Summer 2009 Edition)*, <http://plato.stanford.edu/archives/sum2009/entries/kant-judgment/>.

Hare, John E., 1996, *The Moral Gap: Kantian Ethics, Human Limits, and God's Assistance*, Oxford: Clarendon Press.

--, 2001, *God's Call: Moral Realism, God's Commands, and Human Autonomy*, Grand Rapids: William B. Eerdmans.

Hare, R.M., 1965, *Freedom and Reason*, Oxford: Oxford University Press.

Helm, Paul, 2004, "Reid and 'Reformed' Epistemology," in: Joseph Houston (Ed.), *Thomas Reid: Context, Influence, and Significance*, Edinburgh: Dunedin Academic Press, pp. 103-22.

Henrichs, Jürgen, 1968, *Das Problem der Zeit in der praktischen Philosophie Kants*, Bonn: Bouvier.

Henrich, Dieter, 1966, "Über Kants Entwicklungsgeschichte," in: *Philosophische Rundschau*, 13, pp. 252-63.

--, 1994, "Ethics of Autonomy," in: Richard Velkley (Ed.), *The Unity of Reason: Essays on Kant's Philosophy*, Cambridge, MA: Harvard University Press, pp. 89-121.

--, 2009, "Hutcheson and Kant," in: Karl Ameriks and Otfried Höffe (Eds.), *Kant's Moral and Legal Philosophy: The German Philosophical Tradition*, Cambridge: Cambridge University Press, pp. 29-57.

Hobbes, Thomas, 1642, *Elementorum philosophiae sectio tertia, de cive (De Cive)*, Paris.

--, 1650, *Humane Nature: Or the Fundamental Elements of Policie (Part of Elements of Law)*, London.

Hochstrasser, T.J., 2000, *Natural Law Theories in the Early Enlightenment*, Cambridge: Cambridge University Press.

Höffe, Otfried, 1992, *Immanuel Kant*, Munich: C.H. Beck.

Howard-Snyder, Daniel and Paul Moser (Eds.), 2002, *Divine Hiddenness: New Essays*, Cambridge: Cambridge University Press.

Hudson, Hud, 1994, *Kant's Compatibilism*, Ithaca: Cornell University Press.

Hume, David, 1966, *An Enquiry Concerning Human Understanding*, L. A. Selby-Bigge (Ed.), New York: Oxford University Press.

--, 1985, "Of Superstition and Enthusiasm," in: *Essays Moral, Political, and Literary*, Eugene F. Miller (Ed.), Indianapolis: Liberty Fund: Indianapolis, pp. 73-86.

Jacobi, F.H., 1787, *David Hume über den Glauben oder Idealismus und Realismus*, Breslau.

Johnson, Gregory, 2006, "The Tree of Melancholy: Kant on Philosophy and Enthusiasm," in: *Kant and the New Philosophy of Religion*, Chris L. Firestone and Stephen R. Pamquist (Eds.), Bloomington and Indianapolis: Indiana University Press, pp. 43-61.

Kain, Patrick, 2003, "Prudential Reason in Kant's Anthropology," in: Brian Jacobs and Patrick Kain (Eds.), *Essays on Kant's Anthropology*, Cambridge: Cambridge University Press, pp. 230-65.

--, 2004, "Self Legislation in Kant's Moral Philosophy," in *Archiv für Geschichte der Philosophie*, 79, pp. 257-306.

--, 2005, "Interpreting Kant's Theory of Divine Commands," in: *Kantian Review*, 9, pp. 128-49.

--, 2006, "Realism and Anti-Realism in Kant's Second *Critique*," in: *Philosophy Compass*, 1, pp. 1-17.

--, 2009, "Kant's Defense of Human Moral Status," in: *Journal of the History of Philosophy*, 47, pp. 59-102.

Kang, Y.A., 1985, *Schema and Symbol: A Study of Kant's Doctrine of Schematism*, Amsterdam: Free University Press.

Kant, Immanuel, 1902-, *Kants gesammelte Schriften,* Königlich Preussischen Akademie der Wissenschaften (Eds.), Berlin, Walter de Gruyter.

--, 1930, *Lectures on Ethics*, Louis Infield (Ed.), London: Methuen.

--, 1956, *Critique of Practical Reason,* Lewis White Beck (Trans.), Indianapolis: Bobbs-Merrill.

--, 1960, *Observations on the Feeling of the Beautiful and Sublime*, John T. Goldthwait (Trans.), Berkeley: University of California Press.

--, 1978a, *Anthropology from a Pragmatic Point of View*, Victor L. Dowdell (Trans.), Carbondale: Southern Illinois University Press.

--, 1978b, *Foundation of the Metaphysics of Morals*, Lewis White Beck (Trans.), New York: Prentice Hall.

--, 1991, *Bemerkungen in den "Beobachtungen über das Gefühl des Schönen und Erhabenen,"* Marie Rischmüller (Ed.), Hamburg: Felix Meiner.

--, 1993, *Grounding for the Metaphysics of Morals*, James Ellington (Trans.), Indianapolis: Hackett.

--, 2004, *Immanuel Kant: Vorlesung zur Moralphilosophie*, Werner Stark (Ed.), Berlin: de Gruyter.

Kierkegaard, Søren, 1954, *Fear and Trembling*, Walter Lowrie (Trans.), New York: Doubleday.

Kors, Alan Charles (Ed.), 2003, *Encyclopedia of the Enlightenment*, vol. 2, Oxford: Oxford University Press.

Korsgaard, Christine, 1996a, *Creating the Kingdom of Ends*, Cambridge: Cambridge University Press.

--, 1996b, *The Sources of Normativity*, Cambridge: Cambridge University Press.

--, 1996c, "From Duty and for the Sake of the Noble: Kant and Aristotle on Morally Good Action," in: Stephen Engstrom and Jennifer Whiting (Eds.), *Aristotle, Kant, and the Stoics: Rethinking Happiness and Duty*, Cambridge: Cambridge University Press, pp. 203-36.

--, 2009, *Self-Constitution: Agency, Identity and Integrity*, New York: Oxford University Press.

Krasnoff, Larry, 1999, "How Kantian is Constructivism?" in: *Kant-Studien*, 90, pp. 385-409.

Kuehn, Manfred, 1985, "Kant's Transcendental Deduction of God's Existence as a Postulate of Pure Practical Reason," in: *Kant-Studien*, 76, 152-69.

--, 1987, *Scottish Common Sense in Germany: A Contribution to the History of Critical Philosophy, 1768-1800*, Kingston and Montreal: McGill-Queen's University Press.

--, 1995, "The Moral Dimension of Kant's Inaugural Dissertation: A New Perspective on the 'Great Light' of 1769?'," in: Hoke Robinson (Ed.), *Proceedings of the Eighth International Kant Congress 1995*, 1, Milwaukee: Marquette University Press, pp., 373-92.

--, 2001, *Kant: A Biography*, Cambridge: Cambridge University Press.

--, 2004, "Einleitung," in: Werner Stark (Ed.), *Immanuel Kant: Vorlesung zur Moralphilosophie*, Berlin: de Gruyter, pp. vii-xxxv.

Kvanvig Jonathan, 2002, "Divine Hiddenness: What is the Problem?" in: Daniel Howard-Snyder, and Paul Moser (Eds.), *Divine Hiddenness: New Essays*, Cambridge: Cambridge University Press, pp. 149-63.

Langton, Rae, 1998, *Kantian Humility*, New York: Oxford University Press.

Laywine, Allison, 1993, *Kant's Early Metaphysics and the Origins of the Critical Philosophy*, Atascadero, CA: Ridgeview.

Lenoir, Timothy, 1980, "Kant, Blumenbach, and Vital Materialism in German Biology," in: *Isis*, 71(1), pp. 77-108.

Leibniz, Gottfried, 1988, "Méditation sur la notion commune de la justice (Meditations on the Common Concept of Justice)" (1702-1703), in: Patrick Riley (Ed.), *Leibniz: Political Writings*, Cambridge: Cambridge University Press.

--, 1989, *Philosophical Essays*, Roger Ariew and Daniel Garber (Eds.), Indianapolis: Hackett Publishing Company.

Lessing, Gotthold Ephraim, 1780, *Die Erziehung des Menschengeschlechts*, Voß: Berlin.

Lipscomb, Benjamin J. B., 2005, "Power and Authority in Pufendorf," in: *History of Philosophy Quarterly*, 22, pp. 201-19.

Locke, John, 1689, *Two Treatises of Government*, London.

--, 1700, *Essay Concerning Human Understanding* (4th edition), London.

Louden, Robert, 2000, *Kant's Impure Ethics: From Rational Ethics to Human Beings*, Oxford: Oxford University Press.

--, 2007, "Editorial Notes," in: Günther Zöller and Robert B. Louden (Eds.), *Anthropology, History, and Education*, Cambridge: Cambridge University Press.

Łuków, Pawel, 1993, "The Fact of Reason: Kant's Passage to Ordinary Moral Knowledge," in: *Kant-Studien*, 84, pp. 204-21.

MacIntyre, Alasdair, 1984, *After Virtue*, South Bend: University of Notre Dame Press.

Mariña, Jacqueline, 2000, "Making Sense of the Highest Good," in: *Kant-Studien*, 91, pp. 329-55.

Martinich, A.P., 2000, "Religion, Fanaticism, and Liberalism," in: *Pacific Philosophical Quarterly*, 81, pp. 409-25.

Mavrodes, George, 1989, "Enthusiasm," in: *International Journal for Philosophy of Religion*, 25, pp. 171-86.

Meerbote, Ralf, 1984, "Kant on the 'Non-Determinate Character of Human Actions'," in *Kant on Causality, Freedom and Objectivity*, William A Harper and Ralf Meerbote (Eds.), Minneapolis: University of Minnesota Press, pp. 138-63.

Moore, A. W., 2003, *Noble in Reason, Infinite in Faculty: Themes and Variations in Kant's Moral and Religious Philosophy*, New York: Routledge.

Murdoch, Iris, 1970, "On God and Good," in: Iris Murdoch, *The Sovereignty of Good*, New York: Routledge.

Murphy, Jeffrie G., 1965, "The Highest Good as Content For Kant's Ethical Formalism," in: *Kant-Studien*, 56, pp. 102-10.

Murray, Michael, 1993, "Coercion and the Hiddenness of God," in: *American Philosophical Quarterly*, 30, pp. 27-35.

Neiman, Susan, 1994, *The Unity of Reason: Rereading Kant*, New York: Oxford University Press.

Nelkin, Dana, 2000, "Two Standpoints and the Belief in Freedom," in: *The Journal of Philosophy*, 157, pp. 564-76.

Newton, Isaac, 1730, *Opticks, or Treatise of the Reflections, Refractions, Inflections & Colours of Light*, London.

Nietzsche, Friedrich, 2002 (1885), *Jenseits von Gut und Böse. Zur Genealogie der Moral*, Giorgio Colli and Mazzino Montinari (Eds.), Munich: Deutscher Taschenbuch Verlag.

Norton, David L., 1977, "Can Fanaticism be Distinguished from Moral Idealism?" in: *Review of Metaphysics*, 30, pp. 497-507.

Nozick, Robert, 1969, "Coercion," in: Sidney Morgenbesser, Patrick Suppes, and Morton White (Eds.), *Philosophy, Science, and Method: Essays in Honor of Ernest Nagel*, New York: St. Martin's Press, pp. 440-72.

O'Neill, Onora, 1989, *Constructions of Reason*, Cambridge: Cambridge University Press.

--, 1997, "Kant on Reason and Religion," in: Grethe B. Peterson (Ed.), *The Tanner Lectures on Human Values* 18, Salt Lake City: University of Utah Press, pp. 267-308.

--, 2003, "Constructivism in Rawls and Kant," in: Samuel Freeman (Ed.), *The Cambridge Companion to Rawls*, Cambridge: Cambridge University Press, pp. 347-67.

--, 2004, "Self-Legislation, Autonomy and the Form of Law," in: Herta Nagl-Docekal and Rudolf Langthaler (ed.), *Recht-Geschichte-Religion. Die Bedeutung Kants für die Gegenwart*, Berlin: Akademie, pp. 3-26.

Passmore, John, 2003, "Fanaticism, Toleration and Philosophy," in: *The Journal of Political Philosophy*, 11, pp. 211-22.

Paton, H. J., 1936, *Kant's Metaphysic of Experience*, London: G. Allen & Unwin, ltd.

--, 1947, *The Categorical Imperative: A Study in Kant's Moral Philosophy*, London: Hutchinson.

Pistorius, Hermann Andreas, 1786, "Rezension: Grundlegung zur Metaphysik der Sitten von Immanuel Kant," in: *Allgemeine deutsche Bibliothek*, 66, pp. 447-63.

--, 1794, "Rezension: Kritik der praktischen Vernunft, von Immanuel Kant," in: *Allgemeine deutsche Bibliothek*, 117, pp. 78-105.

Plantinga, Alvin, 1974, *God, Freedom and Evil*, New York: Harper and Row.

--, 1990, *The Twin Pillars of Christian Scholarship*, Grand Rapids: Calvin College and Seminary.

Pogge, Thomas W., 1997, "Kant on Ends and the Meaning of Life," in: Andrews Reath, Barbara Herman and Christine Korsgaard (Eds.), *Reclaiming the History of Ethics: Essays for John Rawls*, Cambridge: Cambridge University Press, pp. 361-87.

Post, Gaines, 1972, "Vincentius Hispanus, 'Pro Ratione Voluntas,' and Medieval and Early Modern Theories of Sovereignty," in: *Traditio*, 28, pp. 159-84.

Postema, Gerald J., 2001, "Law as Command: The Model of Command in Modern Jurisprudence," in: *Philosophical Issues*, 11, pp. 470-501.

Prauss, Gerold, 1983, *Kant über Freiheit als Autonomie*, Frankfurt am Main: Vittorio Klosterman.

Proops, Ian, 2003, "Kant's Legal Metaphor and the Nature of a Deduction," in: *Journal of the History of Philosophy*, 41, pp. 209-29.

Pufendorf, Samuel Freiherr von, 1672, *De Jure Naturae et Gentium, Libri Octo (Of the Laws of Nature and of Nations)*, Lund.

Rauscher, Frederick, 2002, "Kant's Moral Anti-Realism," in: *Journal of the History of Philosophy*, 40, pp. 477-99.

Rawls, John, 1977, *A Theory of Justice*, Cambridge, Mass.: Belknap Press.

--, 1980, "Kantian Constructivism in Moral Theory," in: *Journal of Philosophy*, 77, pp. 515-72.

--, 2000, *Lectures on the History of Moral Philosophy*, Barbara Herman (Ed.), Cambridge, MA: Harvard University Press.

--, 2009, *A Brief Inquiry into the Meaning of Sin and Faith*, Thomas Nagel (Ed.), Cambridge, MA: Harvard University Press.

Raz, Joseph, 1975, *Practical Reason and Norms*, Oxford: Oxford University Press.

Reath, Andrews, 1988, "Two Conceptions of the Highest Good In Kant," in: *Journal of the History of Philosophy*, 27, pp. 593-619.

--, 1989, "Kant's Theory of Moral Sensibility," in: *Kant-Studien*, 80, pp. 284-303.

--, 2006, *Agency and Autonomy in Kant's Moral Theory*, Oxford: Oxford University Press.

Reinhold, Karl Leonhard, 2005, *Letters on the Kantian Philosophy*, Karl Ameriks (Ed.), James Hebbeler (Trans.), Cambridge: Cambridge University Press.

Reynolds, Sir Joshua, 1997, *Discourses on Art*, Robert R. Wark (Ed.), New Haven and London: Yale University Press.

Riley, Patrick, 1988, *Leibniz: Political Writings*, Cambridge: Cambridge University Press.

Ripstein, Arthur, 2004, "Authority and Coercion," in: *Philosophy and Public Affairs*, 32, pp. 2-35.

Sanders, Daniel, 1865, *Wörterbuch der deutschen Sprache*, Bd. 2, Leipzig: Otto Wigand Verlag.

Savile, Anthony, 1993, *Kantian Aesthetics Pursued*, Edinburgh: Edinburgh University Press.

Schellenberg, J. L., 1993, *Divine Hiddenness and Human Reason*, Ithaca: Cornell University Press.

Schicker, Rudolph, 1991, "'Sic volo sic iubeo stet pro ratione voluntas': Kant als Rezipient Juvenals und das Problem einer transzendental begründeten Ethik," in: Gerhard Funke (Ed.), *Akten des Siebenten Internationalen Kant-Kongresses*, II(1), Bonn: Bouvier, pp. 397-404.

Schmucker, Josef, 1961, *Die Ursprünge der Ethik Kants in seinen vorkritischen Schriften und Reflectionen*, Meisenheim am Glan: Anton Hain.

Schneewind, J. B., 1984, "The Divine Corporation and the History of Ethics," in: Richard Rorty, J. B. Schneewind and Quentin Skinner (Eds.), *Philosophy in History*, Cambridge: Cambridge University Press, pp.173-91.

--, 1998, *The Invention of Autonomy*, Cambridge: Cambridge University Press.

Schwaiger, Clemens, 2004, "Denken des 'Uebersinnlichen' bei Kant: Zu Herkunft und Verwendung einer Schlüsselkategorie seiner praktischen Metaphysik," in: Norbert Fischer (Ed.), *Kants Metaphysik und Religionsphilosophie*, Hamburg: Meiner, pp. 331-45.

--, 2009, "The Theory of Obligation in Wolff, Baumgarten, and the Early Kant," in: Karl Ameriks and Otfried Höffe (Ed.), *Kant's Moral and Legal Philosophy: The German Philosophical Tradition*, Cambridge: Cambridge University Press, pp. 58-73.

Shaftesbury, Second Earl of (Anthony Ashley Cooper), 2001a, "Letter Concerning Enthusiasm to My Lord Sommers," in: *Characteristicks of Men, Manners, Opinions, Times*, vol. I, Indianapolis: Liberty Fund, pp. 1-36.

Shaftesbury, Second Earl of (Anthony Ashley Cooper), 2001b, "The Moralists; A Philosophical Rhapsody," in: *Characteristicks of Men, Manners, Opinions, Times*, vol. II, Indianapolis: Liberty Fund, pp. 101-247.

Shell, Susan Meld, 2009, *Kant and the Limits of Autonomy*, Cambridge, MA: Harvard University Press.

Siep, Ludwig, 2009, "What is the Purpose of a Metaphysics of Morals? Some Observations on the Preface to the *Groundwork of the Metaphysics of Morals*," in: Karl Ameriks and Otfried Höffe (Ed.), *Kant's Moral and Legal Philosophy: The German Philosophical Tradition*, Cambridge: Cambridge University Press, pp. 77-92.

Sloan, Phillip, 2002, "Preforming the Categories: Eighteenth-Century Generation Theory and the Biological Roots of Kant's A Priori," in: *Journal of the History of Philosophy*, 40(2), pp. 229-53.

Smit, Houston, 1999, "The Role of Reflection in Kant's Critique of Pure Reason," in:
Pacific Philosophical Quarterly, 80(2), pp. 203-23.

--, 2000, "Kant on Marks and the Immediacy of Intuition," in: *Philosophical Review*,
109, pp. 235-66.

--, n.d., "What Can We Know about Things in Themselves?" (unpublished).

Smith, Norman Kemp, 1923, *A Commentary on Kant's 'Critique of Pure Reason'*,
London: Macmillan and Co.

Spinoza, Benedict de, 2007, *Theological-Political Treatise*, Jonathan Israel (Ed.), Michael Silverthorne and Jonathan Israel (Trans.), Cambridge: Cambridge University
Press.

Strawson, Peter, 1966, *The Bounds of Sense*, London: Methuen.

Sussman, David, 2001, *The Idea of Humanity: Anthropology and Anthroponomy in
Kant's Ethics*, New York: Routledge.

Timmermann, Jens, 2007, "Das Creditiv des moralischen Gesetzes," in: *Studi Kantiani*,
20, pp.111-5.

Tucker, Susie I., 1972, *Enthusiasm: A Study in Semantic Change*, Cambridge: Cambridge University Press.

Tuggy, Dale, 2004, "Reid's Philosophy of Religion," in: Terence Cuneo and René van
Woudenberg (Eds.), *The Cambridge Companion to Thomas Reid*, Cambridge:
Cambridge University Press, pp. 289-312.

Van Inwagen, Peter, 2002, "What is the Problem of the Hiddenness of God?" in: Daniel
Howard-Snyder and Paul Moser (Eds.), *Divine Hiddenness: New Essays*, Cambridge: Cambridge University Press, pp. 24-32.

Voltaire, 1765, *Dictionnaire Philosophique, Portatif (Philosophical Dictionary)*, Ge-
neva: Gabriel Gasset.

Watkins, Eric, 2005, *Kant and the Metaphysics of Causality*, Cambridge: Cambridge
University Press.

--, 2008, "Kant and the Myth of the Given," in: *Inquiry*, 51, pp. 512-31.

Willaschek, Marcus, 1991, "Die Tat der Vernunft: Zur Bedeutung der Kantischen
These vom 'Factum der Vernunft'," in: Gerhard Funke (Ed.), *Akten des Siebenten
Internationalen Kant-Kongresses*, II(1), Bonn: Bouvier, pp. 455-66.

Williams, Bernard, 1981, "Persons, Character, and Morality," in: *Moral Luck*, New
York: Cambridge University Press, pp. 1-19.

Wizenmann, Thomas, 1787, "An den Herrn Professor Kant von dem Verfasser der Resultate Jacobi'schen und Mendelssohn'schen Philosophie kritisch untersucht von einem Freywilligen," in: *Deutsches Museum*.

Wolterstorff, Nicholas, 1996, *John Locke and the Ethics of Belief*, Cambridge: Cambridge University Press.

Wood, Allen, 1970, *Kant's Moral Religion*, Ithaca: Cornell University Press.

--, 1978, *Kant's Rational Theology*, Ithaca: Cornell University Press.

--, 1984, "Kant's Compatibilism," in: Allen Wood (Ed.), *Self and Nature in Kant's Philosophy*, Ithaca: Cornell University Press, pp. 73-101.

--, 1991, "Kant's Deism," in: *Kant's Philosophy of Religion Reconsidered*, Philip J. Rossi and Michael Wreen (Eds.), Bloomington and Indianapolis: Indiana University Press, pp. 1-21.

--, 1992, "Rational Theology, Moral Faith, and Religion," in: Paul Guyer (Ed.), *Cambridge Companion to Kant*, Cambridge: Cambridge University Press, pp. 394-416.

--, 1999, *Kant's Ethical Thought*, Cambridge: Cambridge University Press.

Yaffe, Gideon, 2003, "Indoctrination, Coercion, and Freedom of Will," in *Philosophy and Phenomenological Research*, 67, pp. 335-56.

Yovel, Yirmiahu, 1980, *Kant and the Philosophy of History*, Princeton: Princeton University Press.

Zammito, John, 2002, *Kant, Herder, and the Birth of Anthropology*, Chicago: University of Chicago Press.

Zuckert, Rachel, 2004, "Review of *Interpreting Kant's Critiques* by Karl Ameriks," in: *Notre Dame Philosophical Reviews*, http://ndpr.nd.edu/review.cfm?id=1431.

--, Rachel, 2007, "Kant's Sublime Rhetoric," in: Uwe Steiner and Günther Lottes (Eds.), *Immanuel Kant: German Professor and World Philosopher*, Hannover: Wehrhohn, pp. 107-24.

Zweig, Arnulf, 1967, "Introduction," in *Immanuel Kant: Philosophical Correspondence, 1759-99*, Arnulf Zweig (Ed. and Trans.), Chicago: University of Chicago Press, pp. 3-32.

Index

"n" after page number indicates a footnote on that page.

Allison, Henry 72, 95 , 111–112 , 113n, 114, 116, 118, 120, 125–126n, 182n, 219n, 222n, 225n

Ameriks, Karl 1–2, 5–7, 14, 16n, 18, 34n, 188n

Anscombe, G. E. M. 33–34

Aristotle 74–75

Baier, Annette 151, 153, 154n, 156–157, 159n, 160–167, 169

Baumgarten, Alexander G. 29, 42, 44

Beck, Lewis White 10, 164n, 230

Beiser, Fredrick 2–3, 26–27

Bennett, Jonathan 1

Bonnet, Charles 247–248

Brecht, Martin 294

Campe, Joachim H. 294

Caswell, Matthew 226n

Caygill, Howard 213

Chalmers, David 194

Chignell, Andrew 8, 15, 18, 177n, 178, 211n, 212n, 215, 216n, 265n

Clarke, Samuel 271n, 273n

Cohen, Hermann 1

Descartes, René 234

Diderot, Denis 291

Eberhard, Johann 198

Ellington, James 52–53n, 57n

Engstrom, Stephen 155–156, 166–167

Feuerbach, Ludwig 194

Franks, Paul 220–221

Freud, Sigmund 49–50

Frierson, Patrick 8–9, 109n

Grenberg, Jeanine 8–9, 109

Grier, Michelle 299n

Grimm, Jacob and Wilhelm 294, 296n

Guevara, Daniel 62n

Guyer, Paul 25n, 144n, 199n, 226, 249n

Gregor, Mary 53n, 68n

Haller, Albrecht 247–248

Hardy, Lee 16, 75n

Hare, John 26, 139n

Hare, R.M 50, 297, 312, 316–317

Hegel, G. W. F. 115, 129–130

Helm, Paul 233

Henrich, Dieter 30

Hobbes, Thomas 222n, 291

Hudson, Hud 111

Howard-Snyder, Daniel 255n

Hume, David 27, 89n, 90, 137, 239, 248–249, 252, 257, 269, 277, 284–287, 288n, 289–291, 293, 298, 301n, 317n

Hutcheson, Francis 37

Jacobi, F. H. 198

James, William 90–91, 194

Johnson, Gregory 302n

Juvenal 220–221

Kain, Patrick 13, 15–16, 18, 223, 228n, 268n

Kierkegaard, Søren 33–34, 49

Kors, Alan 293–294

Korsgaard, Christine 4, 8, 56n, 84–87, 89, 92–93, 95–102, 108, 151–152, 159–160

Krueger, James   12
Kuehn, Manfred   6, 23, 24, 27, 29–31,
    33, 37–40, 44, 74n
Laywine, Alison   299n, 305n
Lehmann, Gerhard   28
Leibniz, Gottfried   180n, 195, 198,
    271n, 273n, 279–280
Lessing, Gotthold   30, 260
Lipscomb, Benjamin   5–7, 18
Locke, John   18, 185–187, 207, 234,
    291, 293, 295, 298–304
Łuków, Pawel   222n
Luther, Martin   294
MacIntyre, Alasdair   105
Malebranche, Nicolas   247
Martinich, A. P.   297, 312, 316–317
Meerbote, Ralf   111
Mendelssohn, Moses   38
Menzer, Paul   28
Moser, Paul   255n
Murdoch, Iris   49–51, 70
Murphy, Jeffrie   10–11
Murray, Michael   265n
Neiman, Susan   257n
Nelkin, Dana   9, 85–92, 96n, 106
Newton, Isaac   270, 273n
Nietzsche, Friedrich   208
Norton, David   317
O'Neill, Onora   84–86, 93, 101, 108n
Paley, William   200
Parfit, Derek   182
Pascal, Blaise   90–91
Passmore, John   293, 296n
Paton, H.J.   1
Pistorius, H. A.   221, 222n
Plantinga, Alvin   233, 245–246
Plato   205–206
Post, Gaines   221

Postema, Gerald   221
Proops, Ian   219n, 222
Pufendorf, Samuel   66, 221
Rawls, John   3–6, 8, 11–12, 24, 26–
    27, 33n, 84, 161, 222
Reath, Andrews   53n, 63n, 151, 153,
    154n, 158, 162–163, 167–172
Reid, Thomas   233–234, 238, 254
Rischmüller, Marie   31n, 35
Rosseau, Jean-Jacques   31n, 33n, 38n,
    295
Sanders, Daniel   294
Schiller, Friedrich   30
Schneewind, J.B.   149–151, 158, 166,
    169, 173
Shaftesbury, Second Earl of   291, 293,
    294n
Smith, Norman Kemp   1
Spinoza, Benedict   144n, 291, 294n,
    295, 298n
Stark, Werner   28
Strawson, P.F.   1
Sussman, David   10–12, 226n
Swedenborg, Emmanuel   295, 297,
    301n, 304
Tucker, Susie   293
Tuggy, Dale   233
Van Inwagen, Peter   255n
Voltaire   291
Watkins, Eric   9, 16–17, 84, 86, 93n,
    95, 98–100, 103
Willaschek, Marcus   219n, 220
Williams, Bernard   148n
Wizenmann, Thomas   194n, 198
Wolff, Christian   36n, 38, 41, 198
Wood, Allen   50n, 75, 83, 111–112,
    116, 142n, 159
Zuckert, Rachel   10, 18
Zweig, Arnulf   296n